Mac OS® X Snow Leopard™ Server FOR DUMMIES®

by John Rizzo

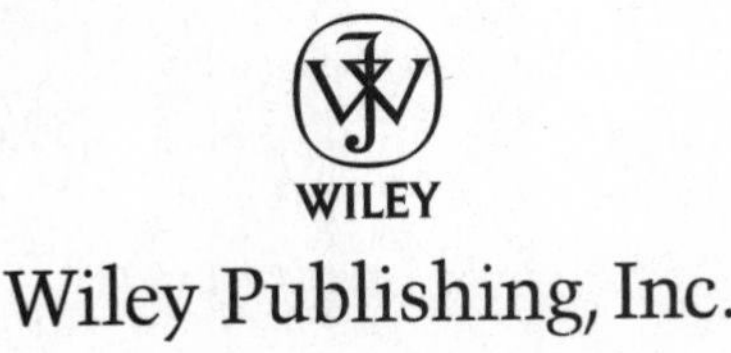

Wiley Publishing, Inc.

Mac OS® X Snow Leopard™ Server For Dummies®

Published by
Wiley Publishing, Inc.
111 River Street
Hoboken, NJ 07030-5774
www.wiley.com

Published by Wiley Publishing, Inc., Indianapolis, Indiana

Published simultaneously in Canada

For general information on our other products and services, please contact our Customer Care Department within the U.S. at 877-762-2974, outside the U.S. at 317-572-3993, or fax 317-572-4002.

For technical support, please visit www.wiley.com/techsupport.

Wiley also publishes its books in a variety of electronic formats. Some content that appears in print may not be available in electronic books.

Library of Congress Control Number: 2009937831

ISBN: 978-0-470-45036-9

Manufactured in the United States of America

10 9 8 7 6 5 4 3 2 1

About the Author

John Rizzo has been writing about computers for over 20 years. His work has appeared in CNET, *Macworld, PC Magazine,* eWeek.com, the *San Francisco Chronicle,* and other publications. He's a former columnist for *MacUser, MacWeek,* and *Computer Currents.*

John is the author of a dozen books, including *Mac Mini Hacks & Mods For Dummies* (Wiley), *Moving to Windows Vista* (PeachPit), and *Mac Annoyances* (O'Reilly). He's also written several books on Mac-and-Windows cross-platform networking, and other topics on Mac and Windows hardware and software.

John publishes the web site MacWindows.com, which since 1997, has been the Web's largest news and information resource devoted to helping Macs users get along in a Windows world.

John is also a member of the Board of Trustees at the San Francisco Community College District, where he chairs the Facilities and Technology Committee.

Dedication

To the educators who use technology to provide their students the skills to live creatively and think critically.

Author's Acknowledgments

I'd like to thank the *Snow Leopard Server For Dummies* team for coming through.

Phil Burk wrote Chapter 7 on Active Directory, and did a great job, doing justice to the phrase "magic triangle."

Kyle Looper arranged to make a real, live Active Directory network available for testing with the Snow Leopard Server beta. This was no small feat, as he was on the front lines battling bureaucrats and juggling scheduling issues. Kyle also was a great help with the planning for this project.

Nicole Sholly, as the lead editor, kept track of the numerous pieces of the pie.

Publisher's Acknowledgments

We're proud of this book; please send us your comments at `http://dummies.custhelp.com`. For other comments, please contact our Customer Care Department within the U.S. at 877-762-2974, outside the U.S. at 317-572-3993, or fax 317-572-4002.

Some of the people who helped bring this book to market include the following:

Acquisitions, Editorial

Project Editor: Nicole Sholly

Acquisitions Editor: Kyle Looper

Copy Editor: Jennifer Riggs

Technical Editor: Dennis Cohen, Daniel Eran

Editorial Manager: Kevin Kirschner

Editorial Assistant: Amanda Graham

Sr. Editorial Assistant: Cherie Case

Cartoons: Rich Tennant (`www.the5thwave.com`)

Composition Services

Project Coordinator: Kristie Rees

Layout and Graphics: Joyce Haughey, Julie Trippetti, Christine Williams

Proofreader: Laura L. Bowman

Indexer: Sharon Shock

Publishing and Editorial for Technology Dummies

Richard Swadley, Vice President and Executive Group Publisher

Andy Cummings, Vice President and Publisher

Mary Bednarek, Executive Acquisitions Director

Mary C. Corder, Editorial Director

Publishing for Consumer Dummies

Diane Graves Steele, Vice President and Publisher

Composition Services

Debbie Stailey, Director of Composition Services

Contents at a Glance

Table of Contents

Introduction

Shakespeare almost said, "Servers are such stuff as dreams are made on." If he had said it, he would've meant that the computer user's illusion of direct access to the world is built upon servers. (Pretty deep for a book about computers, isn't it?) The reality is that every connection, communication, and bit of information that the user sees goes through servers — ubiquitous, imperceptible, indefatigable.

But only if you make it so. You're going to set up Apple's Snow Leopard Server for your users, configure the wonderful services it offers, and keep it running. This book will help you do it.

About This Book

Mac OS X Snow Leopard Server For Dummies takes you through the steps required to get your users doing amazing and productive things. I provide step-by-step procedures to accomplish specific tasks, such as configuring an e-mail server and setting up user accounts. In some instances, I also describe how to set up your user's Mac or Windows PC to work with the server.

This book also introduces you to the tools that Apple provides with the server and the best ways to use them. With some of Snow Leopard Server's features, there are just too many options and network configurations to take you through every possible scenario. The book considers the most common scenarios and describes the best practices you should adopt. I also describe the new features in Snow Leopard Server that you'll want to know about (trust me on this). I've peppered the chapters with plenty of tips and tricks that will help you become proficient. I'm a fan of the English language, so I favor it over the techno-babble found in much of computing. (Although the term *Uniform Resource Locator* may mean something specific to software engineers, *Web address* works just fine.) Where the techno-babble is unavoidable, I provide explanations. You will not, however, find the word *empower* in this book. A writer can be pushed only so far.

Conventions Used in This Book

Flip through this book and you'll find different uses of type to point out different things. Here's what I do:

- In the step-by-step directions, the actions you perform are in bold type, **like this.** The description of what happens after the action is in normal type.
- To point out a Web address, the book uses a font that looks like this: `www.apple.com`. You'll see the same font in the rare instances that I show you something that you need to type in a command line (in the Mac's Terminal application), such as `fsck -fy`, and for text that a command line returns to you in response.
- In other rare cases that you need to use a menu at the top of the screen, this book uses a convention that looks like this: File⇨Get Info, which means you need to choose Get Info from the File menu. For menus that aren't at the top of the screen, such as pop-up menus, I don't use this convention. Don't worry, I almost never ask you to use menus at the top of the screen in this book, so you rarely see this.
- To indicate folders, I use Apple's standard notation. For instance, to indicate the Utilities folder, which is inside the Applications folder, I will say /Applications/Utilities/ in normal type.

What You're Not to Read

When it comes down to it, you really don't have to read any of this book. Look at the pictures, hide a copy of a good mystery novel inside it to read on the subway, or use it to prop up a kitchen table leg. As long as you buy it, I'm okay with it. (It makes a great gift, by the way.)

If you're going to read this book, you don't need to read the whole thing or to read it in any particular order. The book is organized in a logical manner from beginning to end, but it's not a narrative. Rather, it's *modular.* You only need to read the portion that applies to a specific project or technique.

If you already have Snow Leopard Server installed, you can skip Part I. And you don't have to read Part VI to accomplish any server project. Consider it the chocolate center of a Good Humor bar.

Within most of the parts, the chapters are arranged from more general to more specific. For instance, if you're a Windows administrator with experience with Active Directory, you can go right to Chapter 7, which deals specifically with Macs and Microsoft networks.

If you want, you can skip the text next to the Technical Stuff icons. I won't be insulted (well, not much), but I think you'll enjoy them.

Did I mention that *Mac OX X Snow Leopard Server For Dummies* makes a great gift? If so, you don't have to read this sentence.

Foolish Assumptions

Unlike some other computer books, you won't find a lot of filler here — no dissertations that have no bearing on the task at hand. I assume that you bought this book to accomplish specific tasks using Snow Leopard Server.

You also won't find lectures on what's in the Print dialog or how to search for a file. That's because I assume that you're already a computer user. But I don't assume that you're an Apple-Certified System Administrator. I explain the alphabet soup of acronyms that you find in some of the Server's techno-speak.

Don't worry if you're new to the Mac. I explain any Apple-specific knowledge that you need to know. Experienced Mac users can skip bits of Mac-specific material. There won't be a test on your Mac savvy at the end of the book.

Similarly, you don't need any experience with Windows if you want to support Windows clients with your Mac server. I show you what you need to know.

I don't make any assumptions about what hardware you're running. For the purposes of this book, it doesn't matter — Snow Leopard Server is scalable to any Intel-powered Mac, from mini to Xserve. I provide some guidance as to what Mac is right for you in Chapter 2.

How This Book Is Organized

*Mac OS X Snow Leopard Server For Dummie*s is organized into six parts, each with several related chapters inside. The parts are arranged in order of how you might go about using the server. But you don't have to read the book sequentially, as each part can stand alone as a sort of minibook on a topic. You don't even have to read all the sections in any particular chapter. You can use the table of contents and the index to find the information you need and quickly get your answer. I recommend taking, at least, a glance at Part I. You'll find some information about installing Snow Leopard Server that you won't find in Apple's documentation.

Part I: Getting Snow Leopard Server Up and Running

I start this section with a description of Snow Leopard Server — what it comes with, what you can do with it, and what you need to get it running. If you need some advice on which Mac model to use as your server and what should be in it, look in this section. I also describe some hardware needs in the server and on the network. If you haven't already installed Snow Leopard Server, you'll find step-by-step directions in Part I.

This part of the book ends with a description of server virtualization. I take you through the how's and why's of setting up a server in a virtual machine, which most people will find useful for one reason or another. If you don't know what a virtual machine is, go to Chapter 4 right now.

Part II: Creating and Maintaining User Accounts and Directories

For networks with more than a handful of users, setting up user directories can help automate security and simplify maintenance. This part describes what you can do with a directory, including setting up user authentication and connecting your server to a bigger network.

The section also covers the options you have for directory services, including Open Directory, which comes with Snow Leopard Server. I devote Chapter 7 to the issue of using Snow Leopard Server to connect your Macs to Microsoft Active Directory, which is common on Windows networks.

Part III: Serving Up Files and Printers

Part III covers the meat and potatoes of servers: sharing files and printers with multiple users. File and print sharing were the first tasks for servers when personal computers came on the scene in the 1980s. Sharing is still the most common task, though other services are often wrapped around it.

Your users can be running Macs or Windows. I'm agnostic here, and Snow Leopard Server supports both. But there are differences in how you set up the server for the different users. If you haven't had experience with one or the other, I'll cover for you.

Part IV: Facilitating User Collaboration

This is one of the longer parts of this book. Snow Leopard Server offers an array of services that help users work with each other. Some of these are new to Snow Leopard Server. Part IV covers e-mail, calendar sharing, meeting scheduling, and the sharing of contacts. There are also Web-based services, from your basic Web site to wikis and blogs.

I describe how to set up these services and point out some of the more interesting and perhaps less obvious things you can do with them.

Part V: Managing Clients

Client computers, the Macs and PCs on the network, can be a chore to maintain all by yourself. Fortunately, you can use your server to automate some of this for you. This part describes how to use the tools for doing this. You can even manage the notebook computers that float in and out of the building.

Viruses, data spies, identity thieves, and other threats are all commonplace in the electronic world that computers live in. Chapter 18 describes how to keep the nasties out and how to enable users to access the server remotely without letting in the malware.

Part VI: The Part of Tens

I show you ten nifty things you can add to Snow Leopard Server that can make it even more useful, or at least more interesting. Part VI also delivers ten quick tips for doing even more with Snow Leopard Server.

Icons Used in This Book

To make this book easier to use, you'll find five icons to the left of the text. These are here to help find information as you flip through the pages. Think of them as signposts, each pointing to a different way to think about what's being said.

Here are the icons you'll find:

Tips are the best bits of the description that make the job easiest or better. They aren't always the only way to get something done, but they do point out the best way to accomplish a task. Sometimes you can reuse a tip for other tasks.

When you see this icon, I'm flagging something that you don't want to forget to do, unless you want to mess up what you're doing. Or, it could mean that I've mentioned this item before, but I'm repeating it for emphasis.

The Warning icon highlights lurking danger. With this icon, I'm telling you to pay attention to what you're doing or to what you shouldn't do.

This icon marks a general interesting fact that's a technical explanation of what's going on or why you need to do something. I didn't want to turn this book into one of my old college engineering textbooks, so I kept the tech stuff short.

Readers who have extensive backgrounds with Windows but who may be new to Macs can be on the lookout for these icons. This icon points out terminology or features that have equivalents in the Windows world.

Where to Go from Here

The section, "How This Book Is Organized" gives you a good idea as to where to begin with this book. Where you start is up to you — begin with Chapter 1, dive right into file servers in Chapter 9, or check out the tips in Chapter 19. Be sure to check out Chapter 4 to see if you want to install Snow Leopard Server in a virtual machine. Use this book as a reference (a *For Dummies* technical encyclopedia) or read it from start to finish for the complete picture. However you use it, I won't be offended. I wrote this book so that you can find all sorts of useful information however you choose to approach it.

Part I
Getting Snow Leopard Server Up and Running

"Oddly enough, this has been the least disruptive part of our move to Client/Server computing."

In this part . . .

Snow Leopard Server is an amazingly versatile and scalable solution, serving a small workgroup or acting as part of an integrated network of thousands of users. So it may not be surprising that the process of getting it up and running can involve vastly different software and hardware configurations.

This part describes the many different services available to your users and the hardware the server runs on, from the little Mac mini to the beefy Xserve, and how to pick the best Mac model for your use of the server.

Snow Leopard Server offers several possibilities of installation, depending on your use. The part shows you how to get ready for your installation and how to install it in different scenarios, including how to set up Snow Leopard on a Mac without a monitor.

This part also gives you another installation option: virtualization. This technique lets you set up a test server without needing to dedicate a Mac to the purpose. Virtualization also enables you to run multiple instances of Snow Leopard Server on one Mac. You can even run Snow Leopard Server and Windows Server on the same Mac.

Chapter 1

Snow Leopard Server: An Overview

In This Chapter

- Answering the burning question: Why do I need a server?
- Exploring the services and tools in Snow Leopard Server
- Discovering what's new in Snow Leopard Server
- Keeping out of trouble with Apple

It comes with a wide array of user services: file and print sharing, calendar, contacts, Web, e-mail, instant messaging, media streaming, and more. It's versatile enough to support Macs and PCs running Windows, Unix, and Linux. It even supports iPhones.

It's reliable; built on the solid foundation of Unix. At the same time, it has the ease of use of a Macintosh. Anyone can set it up, get it running, and manage it, and you won't need an IT department. Seriously technical professionals will find tools for the kind of configuration customization that they're accustomed to.

It is Mac OS X Server.

Snow Leopard Server (also known as Mac OS X Server 10.6) is the seventh major version from Apple. Unlike Microsoft, which releases the Windows user version before the server version, Apple develops user and server versions at the same time. Snow Leopard Server looks like the copy of Snow Leopard running on users' Macs. And Mac OS X Server runs on Apple hardware, of course — it runs on any Mac that Apple makes today, as well as some older models. Snow Leopard Server can be used at home, in a small business, or by a department in a large business.

In this chapter, I describe what you can do with Snow Leopard Server, providing an overview of all the services in one place. I also point out what's new and improved in this version. But first, see what a server can do for you.

Why You Need a Server

You've probably discovered that you can have a small network without a server. Macs and PCs can talk to each other. They can share files and printers, and you may be able to use a router to share an Internet connection.

But a server enables users to collaborate in ways that aren't possible without it. A server gives you control; it centralizes data, making it easier to manage. A server provides fast access to information and collaborative tools and provides network security.

So what's a server that does all this great stuff? *Server* refers to software, hardware, or both. Server software can be the whole package, such as Mac OS X Server, or one of its features, such as the e-mail server. The Mac that Mac OS X Server runs on is also referred to as a server. *Client* can refer to the Mac or PC sitting on a user's desk, or to a piece of user software, such as an e-mail client, that talks to server software.

Top ten reasons you know it's time to buy a server

At some point, you'll *need* to add a server. Here are the top ten reasons you know it's time to buy a server:

10. **You have too many computers to go around futzing with them all.** With centralized management of client computers, you can set users' passwords and settings for network access and install software on the client computers from the server. A server doesn't eliminate messing with individual clients but can cut it down quite a bit.

9. **Users keep running out of hard drive space.** Instead of replacing or adding hard drives on multiple users' computers, put one or more hunking, huge hard drives in a server that everyone can use.

8. **Users need special software that everyone can access.** Database software, accounting software, or software specific to your line of business needs a central location.

7. **You have critical data that would cause big problems if you lost it.** Storing mission-critical files in one central location makes them easier to back up than when the files sit on user machines.

6. **Your Mac slows when other users are trying to get files off it.** Your Mac or PC should work for you, not for other users. A server frees up your computer for your work. Servers can also handle multiple users faster than a client computer, so users get faster access to files.

5. **You have two or more dialup accounts to the Internet.** With a server, you can share high-speed Internet access for a number of Macs and PCs. Yes, you can share an Internet account with a user's Mac, but not nearly as securely as with a server.

4. **People in your group need to connect to your network from home or while traveling.** Your server can provide secure, encrypted access to your organization's network, even while the user sits across the ocean sipping a cappuccino in a Wi-Fi cafe in Piazza Navona.

3. **You're sharing printers for two or more computers.** You can share a printer that's connected to a user's Mac with other users, but it can bog down that user's machine. And if he happens to shut down the Mac, the printer goes with it. The print server in Mac OS X Server has lots of goodies, both for users and for you, the administrator.

2. **You want to share files but you don't want everybody on the network to have access to the same files.** When users log in to a server, the server *authenticates* them, which tells the server who they are. Servers can dole out access rights *(permissions)* that determine which user can see or access which files. Network administrators often consider this the number one reason to get a server, but I have one more.

1. **The number one reason that you know it's time to get a server:** You want to do *all* these things and maybe more.

Why you need a Snow Leopard Server

Any server platform does the great things described in the preceding section. Your PC-savvy friends may be telling you to get a Windows server. You'll need it, they say, to support your PCs. Not so — Mac OS X Server supports Windows clients better than Windows servers support Mac clients.

Your computer geek friend will roll his eyes and tell you that a Linux server is the only logical choice. He'll tell you Linux is inexpensive and reliable, and that many of the servers powering the Internet are running Linux. All true, but it takes an expert to configure and maintain a Linux server. And it still doesn't support Mac clients as well as Snow Leopard Server does.

Still not convinced? Well, you probably are because you're reading this book. But maybe your boss isn't convinced. Here are some reasons why your server should be Snow Leopard Server.

The price is right, or which version is for me

I have nothing against Windows and Linux servers — they can scale up to some very large networks, which Mac OS X Server isn't designed to do. But Windows servers can cost thousands of dollars more than Snow Leopard Server, and Linux costs you in terms of expertise.

Windows server versus Snow Leopard Server

Mac OS X Server is inexpensive compared to Windows servers. Microsoft has a complicated pricing model with multiple different configurations with multiple options. Snow Leopard Server comes in one version, with no restrictions on the number of clients. And it's half the price of the unlimited, previous version, Mac OS X Server 10.5.

Microsoft Windows servers not only start out at higher price points, but there's a charge for the number of clients you have on the network. If you want to add more computers to your network, you have to write another check to Microsoft. With Mac OS X Server, there's no per-client fee. Add as many Macs, PCs, or Linux machines as the server hardware can handle.

Linux versus Snow Leopard Server

A third popular option is a Linux server, which can be less expensive than Snow Leopard Server, depending on which company you get it from. But it may or may not come with the full suite of services found in Mac OS X Server. Add to that the cost of the time spent adding all the services to a Linux server and configuring it, assuming you have sufficient Linux expertise, or paying someone else to do it, and you'll find that Snow Leopard Server is still a bargain.

Better service for Mac clients and iPhones

Snow Leopard Server supports Mac clients better than any other server. For instance, Snow Leopard Server offers services specifically for the Apple software on your users' Macs, including Address Book and iCal (see Chapters 11 and 12, respectively). Snow Leopard Server turns these into groupware apps, and works more smoothly for the user and the administrator than other servers and Mac clients. There's a server version of the Mac's Spotlight, which makes searching the server quick and easy.

But even for generic services, such as file sharing, Mac OS X Server serves Mac clients better than other servers. The Mac OS X Server supports any filename that the Mac supports, and it doesn't split files into two parts or leave small, empty files on the server, which are problems that can occur when Mac clients access Windows and Linux servers.

If iPhones are part of your network, Snow Leopard Server supports them. The Server includes optimizing wikis and blogs for viewing on iPhone and can "push" calendar invitations and events to them.

What Comes with Snow Leopard Server

Snow Leopard Server isn't one server, but more than two dozen servers and tools for managing the Mac clients. I first look at the servers that you get with Snow Leopard Server.

Servers in Snow Leopard Server

Most services can be administered with one piece of software — the Server Admin tool — which displays a list of services, as shown in Figure 1-1. Most of these services are set up automatically when you install Mac OS X Server. You turn many of them on and off with a few mouse clicks.

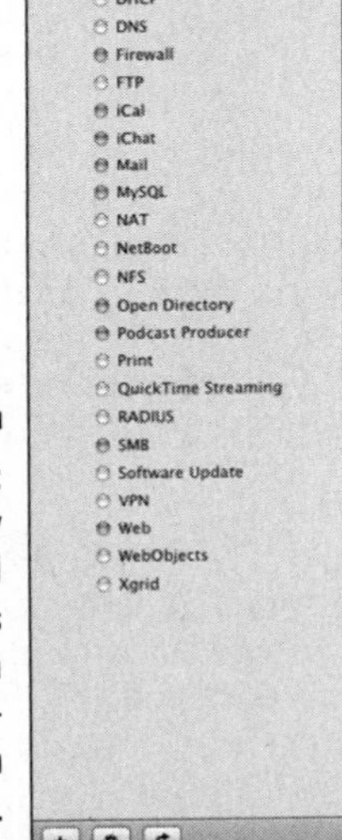

Figure 1-1: Snow Leopard Server is actually a set of several dozen servers.

On smaller networks, you can run all your servers on one sufficiently powered Mac. On larger networks, you may want to put some of these services on another server.

File server

The bread and butter of a server, the file server may be the only reason that some people use Snow Leopard Server. File servers provide folders that everyone on the network can see. You can also limit access so that some people can't get into certain folders. Mac OS X Server comes with several different ways to share files. The main two are the Mac-native Apple Filing Protocol (AFP), which is Mac only, and Microsoft's Server Message Block (SMB), both listed in Figure 1-1. Flip to Chapter 9 for more on file servers.

Print server

Share printers between Mac and Windows users. You can manage the print queues and give certain users or print jobs priority. You can also keep certain users from using certain printers.

Spotlight Server

For Mac users, Spotlight is an indispensable search feature that lets you find a file almost instantaneously. Spotlight Server does the same for files on the server without bogging down server performance. Spotlight Server does this by indexing the content of the files. This server also provides advanced search features, including Boolean logic and the use of quoted phrases, and stores search criteria in the form of Smart Folders.

Directory services

Mac OS X Server uses the standards-based Open Directory to store and manage the user account info and other user data that's used for all the services. You can connect the server to other directory services on the network, including Microsoft Active Directory. To keep the network secure, directory services authenticates clients that log in with the LDAP, Kerberos, and SASL standards. Chapter 5 describes what all these standards are.

Address Book Server

New to Snow Leopard Server, Address Book Server enables users to share both personal and group contacts with the Mac Address Book or a CardDAV-compatible client. See Chapter 11 for the scoop on Address Book Server.

iCal Server

Users on the network can schedule meetings and events, book conference rooms, and view each others' calendars. People can send an invitation to a meeting that includes an agenda and then can accept the invitation. The iCal Server keeps track of who is inviting whom and what the group schedules are at any point in time. iCal server works with the iCal calendar on Mac OS X 10.5 and later as well as with some other open source projects supporting the CalDAV standard. Chapter 12 describes setting up and running iCal server.

iChat Server

Instant messaging isn't just for mobile phones. Users of Mac OS X, Windows, and Linux (as well as iPhones and other handhelds) can have a virtual meeting by using iChat instant messaging. The server supports audio and video also well. iChat can be used without a server, but the server adds encryption security. The server also stores each user's account info so that a user can iChat from any computer.

Internet gateway services

Mac OS X Server can act as an *Internet gateway,* providing the computers on the network with access to the Internet while protecting the network from intruders. You can get these services in other ways, such as in a wireless router or from other servers on a larger network, but Mac OS X Server has them if you need them. These services are

- **Network address translation (NAT):** A gateway between your private network and the public Internet. NAT allows you to have a single IP address from your Internet service provider but have all your computers connected to the Internet. This is cheaper than paying for IP addresses for each computer. With NAT, the individual IP addresses of your computers aren't visible to the outside world, but your computers can still receive e-mail and visit Web sites.
- **Dynamic Host Configuration Protocol (DHCP) server:** Assigns the local (private) IP addresses to your computers when you're using a NAT gateway.
- **Domain name server (DNS):** It translates a domain name, such as `mycomany.com`, from an IP address. DNS service is required for just about all network services, including Web, mail, directory services, and calendaring.
- **Firewall:** Mac OS X Server comes with a firewall to protect your server from intruders. Chapter 18 describes Snow Leopard Server's firewall.
- **Virtual private network (VPN) service:** A secure method of enabling people to access your network and server via the Internet from home or on the road. The VPN service in Mac OS X Server supports several different standard methods of access.

E-mail server

The Snow Leopard Server e-mail server is faster than those in earlier versions of Mac OS X Server. Also new are e-mail rules on the server and automatic "I'm on vacation messages" for the users. Snow Leopard Server blocks spam and e-mail that contain viruses from reaching users' desktops, and can make e-mail available from a Web browser. You can read more about the e-mail server in Chapter 14.

Web server

Snow Leopard Server's Web server is really a package of technology, starting with the Apache Web server — the most popular Web server on the Internet. The Web server also includes some sophisticated tools, such as the MySQL database and a Perl plug-in that's loaded with the Web server. The Perl programming language is used for Common Gateway Interface (CGI) scripts for creating dynamic Web pages and for functions, such as taking data that a user enters in a Web-based form and moving it to the database. Along the programming lines are also Ruby on Rails, Capistrano, and Mongrel.

But you don't need to be a programmer to take advantage of these features, as a lot of this technology is under the hood. For instance, enabling users to access their e-mail from a Web browser requires only a single mouse click in the Web pane of Server Preferences (see Figure 1-2).

Figure 1-2: The Web pane of Server Preferences makes it easy to enable server features.

Wiki Server and blogs

Part of the Web server functionality is the automatic creation of a full-featured *wiki* — a Web site that users can edit from their Web browser. In your organization, you can use wikis as a group collaboration tool for projects or brainstorming. Users can edit text, add hyperlinks to Web pages, and upload photos and documents to share, and then review the history of the changes that have been made and revert to earlier versions. Wikis automatically update to tell readers what changes other users have made.

The Wiki Server is also blogging software. Blogs in your organization are great for posting status updates and reports. Like blogs on the Internet, the Snow Leopard Server blog feature has a space at the bottom for users to post comments. You can also create group calendars as part of the wiki.

QuickTime Streaming Server and QuickTime Broadcaster

Great for doing Web broadcasting of live events and on-demand Webinars, the QuickTime Streaming Server puts out high-quality audio and video. You use QuickTime Broadcaster to capture and encode the sound and video to send to the streaming server.

Podcast Producer

Podcast Producer is actually a set of software that automates the capture, creation, and distribution of video and audio. You and your users can record a lecture, training video, or student project, and Podcast Producer automatically adds, encodes, renders, and compresses titles and other elements based on your criteria, and it automatically publishes it on a Web site or via iTunes. Snow Leopard Server added new capabilities to Podcast Producer, including the ability for Windows users to get into the action, which is described in Chapter 15.

Software update server

You can restrict what software updates get installed on client Macs as well as when they get installed. This gives you a chance to test updates first. The client Macs get the updates from the server instead of downloading them individually.

NetInstall

This lets you install Mac OS X upgrades on users' Macs, requiring that their updates come from Mac OS X Server and not directly from the Internet. Because Mac OS X updates can sometimes cause incompatibilities with older software, you can test an upgrade first before rolling it out on all the client Macs at the same time. NetInstall also lets you restore, from the server, a customized Mac OS X configuration to Macs that need it.

NetBoot

NetBoot is great for a group of Macs that are available to multiple users, such as in a school computer lab or a classroom. This service enables Mac clients to boot up from the server instead of from their own hard drives. The NetBoot server can use a single disk image to boot multiple Macs. This prevents the boot system from being altered or tampered with, and makes sure that every system boots in exactly the same configuration. NetBoot also lets you update the system software of all the Macs at one time, simply by updating the disk image on the server.

Management tools

In addition to providing services to client computers, Snow Leopard Server comes with a set of software for managing these servers. You can install several of the tools on any system running Mac OS X 10.6 on the network, allowing you to keep the server Mac out of sight in a secure location.

Flipping through this book, you see that I mostly describe two tools — Server Preferences and Server Admin. Workgroup Manager is the third most mentioned tool. The other tools play smaller, more specialized roles.

One major change from earlier versions of Mac OS X Server is that you can now use Server Preferences and Server Admin at the same time, instead of choosing one or the other. This means that you can do some basic configuring with Server Preferences, where it's easier, and go to Server Admin or Workgroup Manager when you need to get deeper.

You can find these tools in the /Applications/Server/ folder in Snow Leopard Server. If you want to install the server administration tools on another Mac on the network but don't happen to have your server installation disc with you, you can always download them from Apple's Web site for free. Point your browser at `www.apple.com/downloads` and then search for *server admin tools* in the Web page's Search box.

Server Assistant

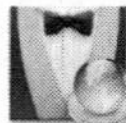

When you finish installing Snow Leopard Server, Server Assistant opens and sets up basic network connectivity as well as several of the services, such as Internet sharing and file sharing. Most of this setup is automated, as Server Assistant detects the condition of the network and checks for an Internet connection.

Server Preferences

For simpler networks, you can spend most of your server management time in Server Preferences. Similar in look and feel to System Preferences on Mac OS X clients, Server Preferences (see Figure 1-3) gives you quick access to setting windows for users and the services they're allowed to access. Click one of the icons, such as iCal or Mail, to configure that service.

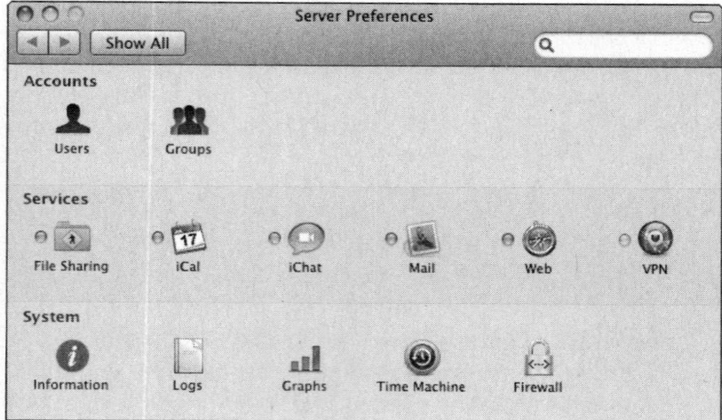

Figure 1-3: Server Preferences gives you easy access to configuring services.

You can assign user passwords and manage mail, calendar, and iChat servers. Turning on file sharing and sharing folders in Server Preferences (see Figure 1-4) is a lot like it is on Mac clients. You can also change firewall settings and turn on remote access via a virtual private network. The Time Machine icon lets you set automated backups of server data.

Figure 1-4: The File Sharing pane of System Preferences.

Server Status Dashboard widget

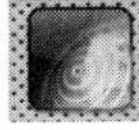

If you're a Mac user, you're familiar with Dashboard widgets. Hit the F4 key and up pops a Calculator, the weather, and other small applets. They disappear when you click something else. Mac OS X Server has a Server Status Dashboard widget, shown in Figure 1-5, that you can use on the server or on any Mac on the network.

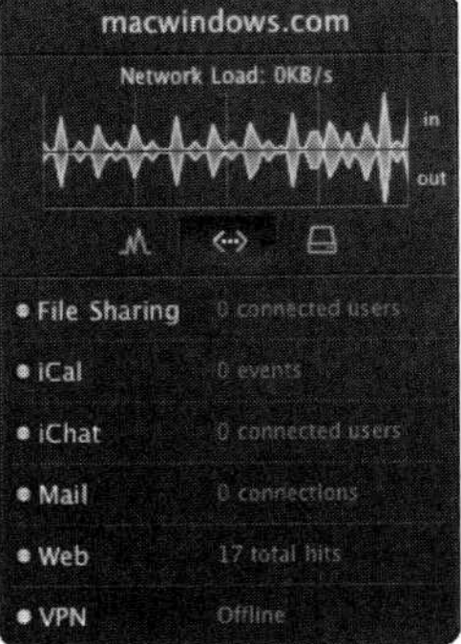

Figure 1-5: The Server Status Dashboard widget lets you keep an eye on several server parameters.

Server Admin

You can use Server Admin to do everything that you can do in Server Preferences, but Server Admin gives more options and much more fine-grained control over the setup. Server Admin also gives you access to services that aren't available in Server Preferences, such as the MySQL database server, QuickTime Streaming Server, and software update server. In Figure 1-6, the services that are deselected aren't configurable from Server Preferences. Server Admin also can keep track of multiple servers and the services they're running.

Select the services to configure on this server:

- [x] AFP
- [ ] DHCP
- [ ] DNS
- [ ] Firewall
- [ ] FTP
- [x] iCal
- [x] iChat
- [x] Mail
- [ ] MySQL
- [ ] NAT
- [ ] NetBoot
- [ ] NFS
- [x] Open Directory
- [ ] Podcast Producer
- [ ] Print
- [ ] QuickTime Streaming
- [ ] RADIUS
- [x] SMB
- [ ] Software Update
- [x] VPN
- [x] Web
- [ ] WebObjects
- [ ] Xgrid

Figure 1-6: Server Admin lets you turn on the more advanced services that don't appear in Server Preferences.

Workgroup Manager

Workgroup Manager is a more advanced tool for setting and managing user accounts than Server Preferences. You can use Workgroup Manager to control aspects of users' computers. For instance, you can require users to change passwords at regular intervals, create standardized preference settings for client Macs, or allow only certain applications to run. If you're concerned about security, you can block certain computers from seeing external hard drives or from burning CDs and DVDs. You can create groups to manage settings for sets of computers at once.

System Image Utility

You can use System Image Utility to create Mac OS X disk images to be used to boot Macs from the server with NetBoot or to install on multiple Macs with NetInstall. (See the "NetBoot" and "NetInstall" sections earlier in this chapter.)

You can create a NetInstall or NetBoot disk image in two steps, or you can customize settings to include your own items in the disk image. You can also include a Boot Camp partition in a disk image if you want a client Mac to boot with Microsoft Windows.

RAID Admin

RAID Admin is a tool for managing and monitoring a RAID array. A *RAID* is a group of hard drives that act together to provide redundancy so that if one drive fails, no data is lost. RAID Admin displays the status of a RAID(s), the hard drives in it, and the network connections. RAID Admin can send you an e-mail if it detects a problem with a RAID component.

Server Monitor

Server Monitor lets you keep tabs on server hardware, specifically Apple's Xserve box. Server Monitor can display a graph of the internal temperature of one or more Xserve(s), list warnings and failures, display the power usage, and show how much hard drive space and memory are in the Xserves on your network. You can set Server Monitor to send you an e-mail message if it detects a hardware problem in an Xserve box.

If you have Snow Leopard Sever installed on another type of Mac, you won't have any use for Server Monitor.

Xgrid Admin

Xgrid Admin is designed to monitor arrays of Macs working together as one entity. The most practical use that Apple gives is with Podcast Producer, which can use Xgrid to spread the work of processing video across multiple Macs, automatically. Xgrid Admin enables you to monitor an Xgrid and to manage computing jobs that are going on.

Apple includes Xgrid Admin along with the more everyday server administration tools, almost as a dare to find out what you can do with it. If you tie together enough Macs, you can have ordinary user Macs by day and the combined power of a supercomputer by night. Stanford University uses an Xgrid of several hundred Macs to perform complex calculations related to molecular physiology and pharmacology.

You can find a very thorough description of Xgrid at `www.macresearch.org/the_xgrid_tutorials_part_i_xgrid_basics`.

Command-line administration

If you're a deft Unix coder who likes to really get into it, you can use the Unix command-line tools that come with Mac OS X to configure and manage Snow Leopard Server. You can also use these commands from a non-Apple Unix or Linux computer on the network. But even if you aren't a Unix geek, you may come across a tip that can work around a problem by typing a couple lines of text.

Unix commands are accessible in the Terminal application on every Mac OS X machine. You can use one of the Unix shells that come with Terminal: `sh`, `csh`, `tsh`, `zsh`, and `bash`. If you're managing one or more servers over a network, use `ssh`, or *Secure Shell.* Rest assured though, Unix commands are not required to set up or manage Snow Leopard Server.

What's New in the Snow Leopard Operating System

Aside from the new services and features in the server, the Snow Leopard operating system doesn't seem like the big leap forward that Mac OS X 10.5 Leopard was. Snow Leopard doesn't have a list of dozens of new user features and services the way Mac OS X 10.5 and Leopard Server did. Don't let this fool you. The Snow Leopard operating system was a major upgrade — it's just that the features are under the hood. Snow Leopard is a bigger, faster, more stable version of Leopard.

Snow Leopard is Leopard on steroids.

Apple focused on improving performance and stability by adding some powerful cutting-edge technologies under the hood. Snow Leopard is faster in a number of different ways, in various circumstances and types of uses. As a server, Snow Leopard can do more things at the same time; it can handle more users and run more services without slowing down.

64-bit through and through

Snow Leopard is now completely 64-bit, from the lowest levels of the kernel to the bundled application and server software. The main benefit is faster performance in everything that you do with the operating system, with every piece of software. Snow Leopard is quite a bit faster than Leopard, even when running 32-bit applications.

Tiger and Leopard had some 64-bit components, but the lower levels of the operating system were 32-bit. This includes the kernel, the central controller of the operating system, and the device drivers.

If you're from the Windows world, you may know that Windows Vista has separate 32- and 64-bit versions for 32- and 64-bit PC hardware. The 64-bit Snow Leopard also runs on 32-bit Mac hardware, but it isn't as fast as on 64-bit hardware. Every Mac model that Apple builds is now 64-bit. If the Mac has an Intel Core 2 Duo or later processor, it's 64-bit. The earlier Core Duo processor is 32-bit.

The 64-bit kernel in Snow Leopard also makes better use of large amounts of RAM (random access memory) over 4GB. A 32-bit system can address 2^{32} bits of memory, which is just over 4 billion bits, or 4GB of RAM. Through some programming tricks, Leopard can use up to 32GB, but it's not as efficient as Snow Leopard. A pure 64-bit system can address 2^{64} bits *natively* so that amounts over 4GB are accessed directly.

Using multiple cores: Grand Central

Snow Leopard may be 64-bit to the core, but today's Macs have processors that contain at least two computing cores, which gives you the equivalent of two processors in one chip. Mac Pro has eight processing cores, located in two quad-core processors. Unfortunately, operating systems haven't been too successful at getting the software to use all the cores at the same time. The more cores in a computer, the more difficult it is to use them at the same time.

Snow Leopard includes a technology — *Grand Central* — that makes the operating system aware of all the cores in the Mac. Grand Central abhors idle processing cores and spreads the workload across them all. Grand Central also enables software developers to create applications that can use all the cores. This translates into faster performance for the Mac.

Mac Pro and Xserve hardware, the Macs with the most processing cores, benefit the most from the Grand Central technology in Snow Leopard Server.

OpenCL (Open Computing Language)

Although Snow Leopard now efficiently uses all the processor cores in a Mac, Grand Central isn't the end to parallel processing. Another source of computing muscle often sits idle — the *graphics processor.* This is particularly true in a server, which typically uses only a fraction of the power of a graphics processor.

OpenCL (Open Computing Language) is a technology in Snow Leopard that enables software to use the unused portions of a graphics processor for general-purpose computing.

Running Snow Leopard Server Legally

Since Apple switched to Intel processors in 2006, the lines between Mac and PC have blurred. You can run Windows on your Mac. But you won't see Mac OS X running on Dell PCs or HP laptops. Apple forbids it in the *end-user license agreement* — that long string of legalese that flashes (and that you never read) when you install almost any software. When you click the Agree button, you agree to everything in the license agreement.

The Apple end-user license agreement requires you to run the OS on Apple hardware only. Apple doesn't want Mac OS X running on non-Apple computers. Important to note is that this includes running Mac OS X in virtual machines with software such as VMware Fusion. The bright side is that you *are* allowed to run Mac OS X Server in a virtual machine on a Mac. This could be useful for testing a server configuration before rolling out or running multiple copies of Mac OS X Server on one Mac. But move a Mac OS X Server virtual machine to a PC, and you're in violation of the license agreement.

One more thing to know: Apple does not let you *virtualize* the user version of Mac OS X — only the server. Because of this, throughout this book, I assume you're running Snow Leopard Server on a Mac. Flip to Chapter 4 for more about virtualization.

Chapter 2

Choosing Server Hardware

In This Chapter

- Dissecting hardware requirements
- Selecting the right RAM and hard drives
- Selecting the right Mac for your server
- Considering other network hardware

You've chosen the software — Snow Leopard Server — now you need to pick a Mac to run it on. You can spend anywhere from under $1,000 to over $10,000 (with storage options), and no one Mac model is best for running Snow Leopard Server. It runs on everything from Mac mini to Xserve, with varying amounts of memory and hard drive space. You can't use your old G5 Mac tower because Mac OS X 10.6 Server runs only on Intel processors (a major change from previous versions).

This chapter takes you through criteria for choosing a Mac that best meets your needs as a server. By matching your anticipated uses to the available hardware, you can avoid getting an underpowered Mac server or spending too much for more than you need. If you already have a Mac in mind for use as a server, this chapter helps you decide whether it'll work for what you want to do with it.

Criteria for Selecting Server Hardware

Before you think about processor speeds, do some planning to determine what you'll be doing with the server. Here are the two key issues: how many users access the server and what the users do with it. Neither tells the whole story by itself; both must be considered. When you have this information, your hardware options become clearer.

Number of users

The effect of an increasing number of connected clients on server performance isn't linear. You may not notice slower service as the number of connected clients increase until you get to a *tipping point,* when performance suddenly slows to a crawl.

The lower-end Macs, Mac mini and iMac, can handle a maximum of around 20 to 30 simultaneous client computers doing lightweight tasks. The more hardware-intensive services you run, the lower that number is. With up to ten or so users, the lower-end Macs can handle multiple tasks at once. If you add more users later, you can always add more lower-end Mac servers for other tasks.

The top-of-the-line Xserve can potentially handle hundreds of clients, again, depending on what services you run. With Mac Pro or Xserve, adding more higher-end storage or large amounts of RAM can help enlarge the client load that the server can handle. *Network capacity* (number of Ethernet cards and their speed) is also important on serving large numbers of clients.

Type of use

The number of users doesn't tell the whole story about what Mac to use to run Snow Leopard Server. Five users accessing a database program might require beefier server hardware than ten users accessing a server-based Web site.

In Chapter 1, I describe the services that come with Snow Leopard Server. The following paragraphs describe some typical uses listed in *approximate* order of how much demand they place on your server hardware. I start with a Web server, which places only light demand on hardware, and end with NetBoot, which demands a lot from your server.

Web servers: Lightweight server use

Web servers tend to use low amounts of hardware resources. The server often caches Web pages and doesn't have to access the hard drive to load Web pages. Web serving also doesn't take a lot of RAM or processing power. You can run a Web server on any Mac that Snow Leopard Server runs on, and you can generally run it along with other services without affecting their performances.

E-mail, DNS (domain name service), and Internet gateway functions are similarly lightweight services in terms of server hardware.

File servers: Light on processor, big in storage

File serving is generally not an intensive use of the server hardware and doesn't use a lot of processing power. File servers primarily need a lot of storage. A wide range of Macs can be used as file servers, as long as the Mac has enough hard drive space in one or multiple hard drives. Unless you have a lot of users, file servers can run alongside other services.

File servers also need frequent backups or high levels of redundancy to preserve the data.

The more users and the bigger the users' files, the more total storage you need. Frequent movement of a lot of very large files, such as video, may require a *storage area network (SAN),* which is storage connected directly to a network or *RAID (Redundant Array of Individual Disks)* systems.

If you're backing up users' Macs and PCs to the server with a server-based backup program, consider this in the file-sharing category, a lightweight use of server processing power.

Database server: Moving lots of data

If you install a third-party database server, it can take more resources than file serving, especially if a lot of users are accessing the database. A database server can require more frequent use of the hard drive and processor than file servers, depending on the data being served and how often.

Podcast Producer: Processor-intensive requirements

Podcast Producer or other video-related servers can make heavy use of hardware; it uses a lot of RAM, hard drive space, and processing power for the video encoding. Video encoding is also one of the only Mac OS X Server functions that uses the graphics processor.

Apple encourages Podcast Producer to offload some of the processing to Mac clients with the Xgrid service that comes with Snow Leopard Server. Xgrid uses spare processing power on the clients to avoid bogging down users' Macs. The more client Macs you can take advantage of on the network, the more video you can process.

Directory services: Give it what it needs

Directory services, which is supplied by Open Directory in Mac OS X Server, can be one of the most actively used services on the network. Don't underpower a directory server or you may slow the whole network.

Directory servers store information about users and groups, permissions, and configuration information for client computers; they authenticate clients and store information that determines which clients can access which files. Running directory services on a mid- to large-size network is equivalent to running multiple databases simultaneously. Fast storage is the most important directory services requirement for any size network. A lot of memory is necessary to keep up performance. For large networks, consider dedicating a server for directory services and using one or more other Mac(s) for other services, such as mail.

NetBoot: Heavy-duty server stress

NetBoot probably places more demand on the server's hardware resources than the other services in Mac OS X Server. This is where client Macs boot from the server itself instead of from their local hard drives. Even for a small network, you need a fast Mac server with multiple processors and fast hard drive storage, and lots of it.

You'll also need fast networking. Wireless networking is too slow for NetBoot, which is why it supports only Ethernet connections. A server with multiple Ethernet interfaces can prevent slowdowns.

With a lot of Mac clients, NetBoot may be too much for one server to handle, so the software supports load balancing on multiple Mac servers.

Hardware Requirements for Running Snow Leopard Server

Here are the minimum requirements for running Snow Leopard Server:

- **Computer:** A Mac. Although you can hack non-Apple hardware to run the Mac OS X operating system, it violates the user license agreement.
- **Processor:** Any Intel processor. Mac OS X 10.6 Snow Leopard is the first version of Mac OS X that doesn't support PowerPC processors, which includes the G4 and G5.
- **RAM:** 2GB RAM base. If you're running Podcast Producer, you need an additional 512MB of RAM for each processor core. For example, if your Mac has two dual-core processors, you need 3GB minimum.
- **Hard drive space:** 20GB of free hard drive space.

The processor is, for the most part, determined by the Mac model you use, (see the following sections). Discontinued Mac models may have an Intel Core Duo processor, which is slower than an Intel Core 2 Duo. Quad-core processors are faster yet.

As a rule of thumb, I recommend always more RAM in a computer than the minimum amount of RAM required by the operating system. Some Macs can hold several dozen gigabytes of memory, which is more than most people need. See the section, "Putting enough RAM in your server," later in this chapter for more.

For hard drive storage, you need as big a drive as you have data to store. Hard drive storage is relatively inexpensive.

Selecting Processor, Memory, and Hard Drives

For a server, the amount of RAM that a Mac can hold is almost as important as the processors in it. Select your Mac model for the RAM it holds as well as for the processor. The more expensive Macs hold significantly more RAM than the lower-end models.

With hard drives, you can always replace the hard drive, or in some Mac models, add additional hard drives.

Selecting processors for your Mac servers

With Apple hardware, you can't choose just any processor the way you can with PCs. To get a particular type of processor, you have to select the Mac model. Within each model are some differences in clock speed. Mac Pro and Xserve offer the most options in processors at purchase time, giving you a choice of one or two multi-core processors.

Processors with multiple cores act as multiple processors. So two dual-core processors are equivalent to one quad-core processor. This is why processing power is sometimes described in terms of the number of cores rather than the number of processors.

You don't need a brand-new Mac for Snow Leopard Server. An older Mac is perfectly fine — as long as it has an Intel processor. Any Mac with *Power* in the name, such as Power Mac or PowerBook, has a PowerPC processor. Mac Pro and MacBook use Intel processors. Mac minis and Xserve, however, came in both PowerPC and Intel processor versions. When in doubt, check the About This Mac window (see Figure 2-1), accessible from the Apple menu. This window also tells how much memory you have in the machine.

Figure 2-1: The About This Mac window identifies the processor and amount of RAM.

For most Mac models, you can't upgrade a processor. You can upgrade a processor in Mac Pro, but doing so is difficult and voids the warranty. For a Mac Pro no longer under warranty, check out this Web site:

```
www.everymac.com/systems/apple/mac_pro/faq/
            mac-pro-how-to-upgrade-processors.html
```

Only Xserve has an officially upgradeable processor. Apple even has directions: Go to `www.apple.com/support/manuals` and search for *processor*. You find PDF documents for each Xserve revision, such as *Xserve (Early 2008) DIY Procedure for Processor (Manual)*.

You can't upgrade a PowerPC Mac with an Intel processor. The architecture of the machines is just too different. Don't even try.

Putting enough RAM in your server

RAM is important for speed in the Mac OS X operating system, and this is particularly true for servers. Server applications can often run faster when you add RAM. More RAM also increases the number of simultaneous client connections that the server can handle without bogging down.

For some of the lightweight tasks that I describe in the "Type of use" section earlier in the chapter, or if you have a smaller network, 4GB of RAM may be sufficient. If you're using Mac mini or iMac on larger networks or with multiple services, add as much RAM as the machine will hold, which tends to be 2–4GB, depending on the model and age.

This strategy isn't always practical with Mac Pro and Xserve because filling them to the maximum can run into hundreds or thousands of dollars — a lot of money if you don't need it.

With the previous version, Mac OS X Server 10.5, some people have reported good results with 2GB of RAM serving up to 200 users for light uses. A server with 2GB of RAM may be adequate for a small network of fewer than ten computers for file sharing.

If you've been running the server in normal use for a few hours, you can use Activity Monitor (in the server's Utility folder) to tell whether you have enough memory. At the bottom of the window, click the System Memory tab (shown in Figure 2-2). Look at the Page Ins and Page Outs numbers. If the size of the page outs is more than 5 to 10 percent of the page ins, the operating system is having to write information from RAM to disk because it doesn't have enough RAM. This translates into slower server performance. In this case, add RAM to increase performance.

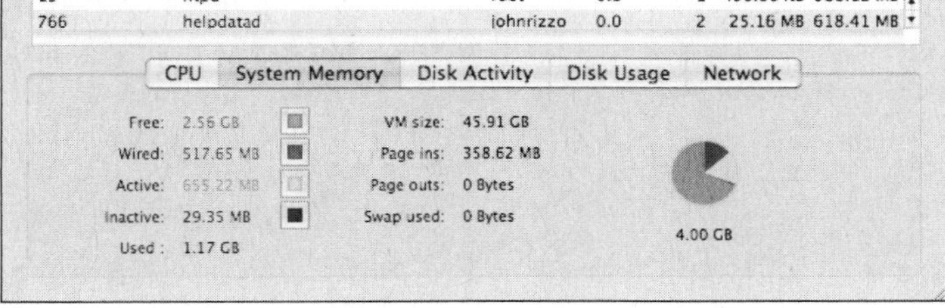

Figure 2-2: Activity Monitor displays the page ins and page outs.

If you do need a lot of RAM, it's cheaper to buy extra RAM and install it yourself rather than buy it from Apple when you order a new Mac. The price difference is under $100 for Mac mini but can be several hundreds of dollars for Mac Pro. To find the best prices, check out Ramseeker (`www.ramseeker.com`), which lets you compare prices from multiple vendors — like Orbitz does with airline tickets. Just select your Mac model from a pop-up menu, and Ramseeker gives you a list of vendors and prices.

Selecting hard drive storage

Apple gives you some hard drive choices when you buy a Mac. The drives vary in capacity, and with some models, you have a choice of rotational speed (see the following section). You can also replace the hard drive in an existing Mac with a bigger or faster drive.

You may also want to look at two other options for expanded capacity, NAS (network attached storage) and SAN (storage area network), which, despite the acronyms, aren't opposites. I discuss both later in this section.

Rotational speed

Rotational speed is a measure of hard drive speed in revolutions per minute (rpm). This is the speed at which the platters inside the drive spin. The faster the rotational speed, the faster the drive performance.

The lowest rotational speed you'll find in a Mac is 4,200 rpm, which Apple used in older Mac mini models. As of 2008, Apple uses 5,400-rpm drives in Mac mini. A speed of 4,200 rpm is very slow for a server and should be replaced.

The next level up is 7,200 rpm, which is the fastest drive you'll see in notebooks and many desktop computers. This is also the standard in high-end Mac Pro and Xserve. Both of these have an option for the next step in rotational speed — 15,000 rpm. (Ten thousand-rpm drives are also available, but Apple doesn't offer them in its lineup.)

You can't replace a drive with a 15,000-rpm drive in most Mac models because 15,000-rpm drives use a different, faster hardware interface — *serially attached SCSI (SAS)* — than slower drives. Drives of the past few years that are 7,200 rpm and slower use the Serial ATA interface. You can't plug an SAS drive into a Serial ATA connector. Mac Pro and Xserve, however, include drive bays that accept either Serial ATA or SAS drives.

The size of a hard drive's cache is also an indication of drive performance: More is better but sometimes isn't noticeable.

Drive form factor

Internal hard drives come in two form factors: 2.5 inches and 3.5 inches (the size of the disc inside the drives). The 2.5-inch drives are traditionally used in notebook computers, but some servers use them as well. Most desktop computers, including iMacs, use the 3.5 inch. The oddball here is Mac mini, which uses a 2.5-inch hard drive.

Server-grade/enterprise-class drives

You'll sometimes see a drive labeled with the interchangeable terms *server-grade* or *enterprise-class.* Apple uses the first term for the drive in its Time Capsule network storage product and in the drives in Xserve server hardware.

The basic feature of a server-grade or enterprise-class hard drive is a high *mean time before failure (MTBF) rating,* which represents the average working life of a drive before it needs repair. The MTBF of some server-grade drives is 1 million hours, which is 114 years! Though not a lifetime guarantee, a high MTBF reduces the chances of hard drive failure during the life of the computer. Manufacturers usually provide longer warranties for server-grade drives, and five-year warranties are common.

A high MTBF rating is not a replacement for backing up. Any hard drive can fail at any time. A high MTBF just lowers the failure probability.

Server-grade/enterprise-class drives also feature high performance. This includes more cache, high rotational speed (such as 15,000 rpm), and faster throughput with an SAS interface. However, you don't need a server-grade drive to get high performance. A server-grade hard drive costs more than an ordinary drive.

Here are two circumstances that might cause you to replace the server Mac's drive with a server-grade model:

- Your network constantly (or frequently) gives the drive a workout, as it might with a large network with dozens or hundreds of users or with a heavily used database on the server.
- You need to keep data safe at all costs, and you can't afford the down-time that restoring data after a failure might give you. Otherwise, you don't need to go out of your way to find a server-grade tag on a drive.

RAID storage

Mac Pro and Xserve contain multiple drive bays that give you the option to set up multiple drives to work together as a RAID (Redundant Array of Individual Disks) to increase performance or protect data, or both. Apple software supports four types of RAIDs:

- **RAID 0** isn't actually redundant, despite the name. RAID 0 uses a *striping* technique to make multiple hard drives work together as a single, fast, large hard drive. Data from a file is fragmented and written on both multiple drives. When reading the file, the system can read the fragments from all the drives simultaneously, greatly increasing performance. RAID 0 also lets you create a very large, single volume for storing giant-sized files, such as video. If one of the drives in a RAID fails, all the data is lost. RAID 0 requires two hard drives minimum.
- **RAID 1** uses a *mirroring* technique to write the same data to two drives simultaneously. If one drive fails, the other drive still contains all the data. RAID 1 requires two hard drives minimum.
- **RAID 5** makes more efficient use of hard drive space than RAID 1 and has better performance. The drawback to RAID 5 is that it requires three hard drives minimum.
- **RAID 0+1** first creates a *RAID 0 striped array* — a very large volume from two hard drives, giving you the fast performance. RAID 0+1 then mirrors the first array with a second striped pair, giving you the redundancy. The drawback is that it requires at least four hard drives.

NAS and SAN

Network attached storage (NAS) is a standalone storage device that plugs directly into the network via Ethernet. Multiple servers or computers can access a NAS device directly. The Apple Time Capsule is an example of a NAS unit, although the Time Machine software isn't well suited toward backing up a server. Other NAS devices often feature multiple drive bays. NAS units are often used for backup.

Whereas a NAS can be a low-end home/office device, a *storage area network* (SAN) is a high-performance, high-cost investment used as primary server storage in large networks. A SAN can be a subnetwork of hard drives connected with a high-speed Fibre Channel switch. Multiple servers can access a SAN, centralizing storage on the network.

Apple offers Xsan software ($999, `www.apple.com/xsan`) that enables multiple desktop and server computers to directly access and share RAID storage. The iCal Server that comes with Snow Leopard Server is optimized to work with Xsan so that multiple iCal Servers can access the same SAN storage. This server *clustering* enables iCal to serve thousands of users. Snow Leopard Server Mail server is similarly optimized for Xsan. Podcast Producer can use Xsan to spread the creation of high-quality video to multiple servers all working on the same video located on the SAN.

If you want to bone up on SANs, try *Storage Area Networks For Dummies,* 2nd Edition, by Christopher Poelker and Alex Nikitin (Wiley).

Choosing the Right Mac for Your Server

There are only four types of Macs to consider using as a server: Mac mini, iMac, Mac Pro, and Xserve. Each is good for some type of network, and no size fits all. The specifications for Mac models change every year, so it's a good idea to check the Apple Web site (`www.apple.com`) from the Tech Specs link on each Mac's Web page.

You don't need a brand-new Mac though because a server is a good use for an older Mac, provided it has enough power for what you plan to do with it and meets the minimum requirements.

You also don't need a monitor connected to the server. After you install Snow Leopard Server, you can run the server *headless,* using the Snow Leopard Server administration tools on another Mac on the network.

This section describes the four Macs, starting with Mac mini for lightweight tasks and ending with Xserve for large networks or heavy-duty tasks. If you haven't read how different server tasks impact the hardware, see the section, "Criteria for Selecting Server Hardware," earlier in this chapter.

Mac mini as a server

Surprisingly, people do use Mac mini as a server. Mac mini can be used for a small group of Macs for basic services or as a general-purpose Web server. You also can use multiple Mac minis to serve larger networks. One commenter at the Apple Discussions forum claimed that his company's data center held 500 Mac minis.

Best uses

Clearly, a Mac mini isn't going to do the work of an Xserve. But a Mac mini might be all the server (or servers) you need. For a network or workgroup of about five client computers, a single Mac mini can handle file sharing, e-mail, Web services, iCal Server, DNS (domain name server), and Open Directory with Kerberos authentication. If you remove some of the weightier tasks, you can increase the size of the network that a Mac mini can serve. Remove file sharing from the list (retaining the Web, e-mail, DNS, and iCal), and the mini is good for a few hundred users.

And you can always spread the load over several Mac minis, as long as you don't tax the hardware. A NetBoot server isn't a good use for Mac mini. You also probably don't want to host user home directories on it.

Pros

Using Mac minis to run Snow Leopard Server has two advantages:

- **Mac minis are cheap.** You can buy four or five for the price of a basic Mac Pro. The cost is low enough that a new mini might be worth springing for rather than using an older and slower Mac that you have around. If you find you're later adding users to your network and outgrowing your Mac mini, you can add more minis for a small investment.
- **Mac minis are small.** At just 2-inches high, a stack of many minis is still smaller than a standard desktop PC. You can easily mount a Mac mini on a wall or under a desk with some of the brackets made for that purpose or of your own design. You can even rack-mount Mac minis as you would with other server hardware. The MX4 Rack Tray (see Figure 2-3) from Macessity ($60, `www.macessity.com`) holds four Mac minis and fits into a standard equipment rack. Mac minis don't generate a lot of heat, so you won't need to use a lot of energy for cooling.

Cons

Mac mini processor speed is the slowest of the four Mac models you'd consider for a server, which limits its uses. Current models have a dual-core processor, which runs Snow Leopard Server better than the single-core processor of earlier Mac mini models.

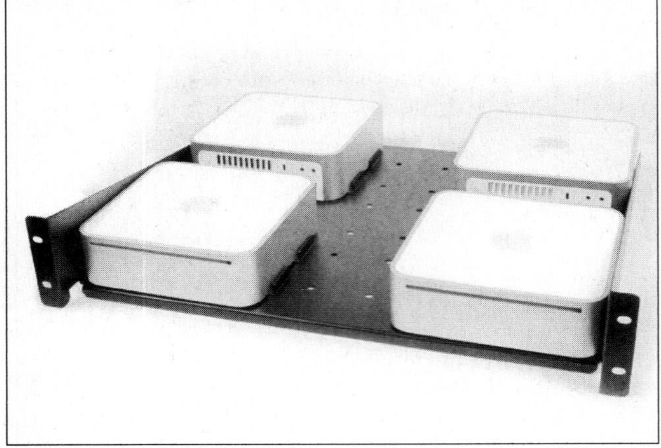

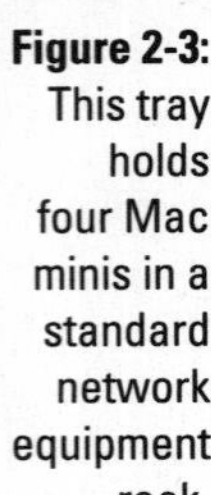

Figure 2-3: This tray holds four Mac minis in a standard network equipment rack.

The main weakness of Mac mini is the hard drive. Mac mini has a relatively slow rotational speed for a server (5,400 rpm) and is of relatively low capacity compared to other 2.5-inch hard drives that are available. You do have some options for upgrading, as described next.

Contrary to popular belief, Mac mini *is* upgradeable. After you get into the box, you can replace the drive with a bigger, faster drive.

Upgrading Mac mini hard drive and RAM

Replacing Mac mini's 5,400-rpm drive with a 7,200-rpm drive not only gives you faster performance, but can triple the amount of storage. Be aware that when you do this, Mac mini runs hotter and the internal fan runs more frequently.

Although Mac mini is officially not user serviceable, you can open it to upgrade RAM and the hard drive. The main thing to figure out is how to open it. The mini is actually quite a bit easier to open than the iMac and takes less than a minute. You need a 1-inch-wide putty knife; it's helpful to bevel one side of the putty knife with some sandpaper first. Then, follow these steps:

1. **Place Mac mini upside down on a towel.**
2. **Position the knife blade where the outer casing meets the inner plastic housing and then press down firmly until the putty knife slips in about half an inch.**
3. **Push the handle of the putty knife outward and down to release the internal plastic tabs. Work your way around the unit until the base is free from the cover.**

   The hard drive is located at the bottom of the internal plastic frame that also holds the DVD drive and the fan.

4. **Remove the frame by removing three small screws that hold it to the base.**
5. **Unplug the small cable for the fan.**
6. **Pull the base straight up, unplugging an interconnect board in the frame from a connector in the base.**
7. **With the frame removed, turn the mini upside down.**

   You find the hard drive attached with four screws.
8. **Upgrade the RAM.**

   You find two slots on the base, connected to the motherboard.

For an illustrated step-by-step guide to taking apart and updating Mac mini, see another book of mine, *Mac mini Hacks & Mods For Dummies* (Wiley). The photos and directions are of the older PowerPC Mac mini, but the basic layout is the same as today's Intel Mac mini.

Replacing a Mac mini DVD drive with a second hard drive

A DVD drive doesn't get a lot of use in a server, but a second internal hard drive would come in handy and would be much faster than an external FireWire drive.

The optical drive is parallel ATA (also known as IDE), while most drives sold today are Serial ATA (SATA). Which means that you need to make sure you buy an IDE drive. They're not as high capacity as SATA, but are still available.

Tom's Hardware (`www.tomshardware.com`) is a good resource for locating hard drives. Look for drives that are internal, 2.5 inch, 7,200 rpm, and have an IDE interface.

Removing the DVD drive is easier than replacing the hard drive:

1. **Remove Mac mini's cover, as I describe in the preceding section.**

   You don't need to remove the internal frame because the DVD drive is right at the top, held in place by four screws, two on each side.
2. **Remove the four screws holding the DVD drive in place. Then remove the two screws that hold the DVD drive to a daughter card that it plugs into.**

   This is where you plug in the new IDE hard drive.

iMac as a server

Running Snow Leopard Server on iMac isn't as common as on Mac mini. Sleek and beautiful, the all-in-one iMac sits in between Mac mini and Mac Pro in terms of power and price. But iMac's bright, clear display and attractive form are wasted when used as a server.

Best uses

A server is a good use of an older iMac (Intel-based) that you might have sitting around. Maybe you're replacing a user's older iMac with the latest and greatest iMac or MacBook. You might buy a new iMac for a server in some situations, such as when you can make use of the display or have some multimedia use in mind.

iMac handles the networks that Mac mini can (which I describe in the preceding section), plus a little more — larger networks, more services, and possibly more internal storage.

Pros

Should you decide to use iMac as a server, you'll enjoy these upsides:

- **Speed:** The performance is surprisingly fast. At any given time, Apple puts faster processors in the iMac than in the Mac mini.
- **Built-in display:** A built-in display is useful if the server is sitting in your office or out in the open, and you want to use it to monitor and administer the server instead of using another Mac. The display can be useful if you're using it for graphical tasks, such as with Podcast Producer.
- **Configuration:** The base configuration has bigger, faster hard drives than the Mac mini. (iMacs use 3.5-inch drives.) You can add a hard drive that's as large as the drive in the Mac Pro and the Xserve.
- **Upgradeable RAM:** You can easily upgrade the RAM by removing two screws that hold a plate on the bottom.
- **Cost:** Cost is quite a bit less than the Mac Pro.

Cons

These downsides can plague you if you use iMac as a server:

- **Hard drive difficult to upgrade:** Except for RAM, the iMac is really not upgradeable, even less so than the Mac mini. Although you can remove the mini's top in a minute when you know how, it's very difficult to disassemble iMac to replace the hard drive. Reassembling it is also difficult. You can find directions if you Google *iMac take apart,* but I don't recommend it.

  If you're buying an iMac for the purpose of using it as a server, consider ordering the largest drive Apple offers.

- **Faster processor requires bigger display:** You have to buy the model with the bigger display to get the faster processors. At this writing, Apple wasn't offering the fastest processors with the smaller display.

Mac Pro as a server

The Apple power workstation also includes features designed for use as a high-powered server. Eight processing cores, expansion slots, multiple internal drives, and multiple Ethernet connections make the Mac Pro (see Figure 2-4) well suited for running Snow Leopard Server in demanding network situations. The Mac Pro doesn't come with a monitor, but the base configuration does include an adequate graphics card.

Figure 2-4: A Mac Pro tower makes a powerful server.

Photo courtesy of Apple

Best uses

A Mac Pro can support file serving for hundreds of active users. For example, Mac Pro works as the file server for an entire school as well as runs third-party server software and NetBoot at the same time. The Mac Pro also works for running directory services and connecting a network of Macs to a Microsoft Active Directory network. If you're only using a server for Web, e-mail, DNS, and light file-sharing tasks, Mac Pro may be more than you need.

Mac Pro is a better choice than Xserve in situations when the server is to be located in a workspace. Mac Pro is quieter than Xserve and has a form factor that fits better in a workspace.

Pros

Mac Pro leaves Mac mini and iMac in the dust as far as performance, and it's just about as fast as Xserve. The high points:

- **Eight processing cores and a fast system architecture.**
- **Four internal hard drive bays, one more than Xserve.** With the optional RAID card, you can use these in a RAID system.
- **The drives are easily accessible and can be replaced without futzing with cables.** Just open the side door and slide them in or out.
- **Room for lots of memory — eight RAM slots.**
- **Two Gigabit Ethernet ports.** This feature is designed for using the Mac Pro as a server. You can use one port to connect to the local network, and another port to connect to the Internet. This enables you to use the Mac server as a gateway, such as running the firewall, virtual private network server, or other gateway services. You can also use the two ports together, for twice the bandwidth.
- **Three extra expansion slots.**
- **Costs less than Xserve, and the starting point has a faster processor than Xserve's base configuration.**

Cons

Mac Pro as a server also has its low points:

- **Processors aren't easily upgradeable.** Apple doesn't support upgrading the processor and doesn't provide directions. You have to pull apart the computer, but the processor does sit in sockets that can be pulled out.

Find a description of how to upgrade the processor here:

```
www.everymac.com/systems/apple/mac_pro/faq/
          mac-pro-how-to-upgrade-processors.html
```

- **Costs more than Mac mini or iMac.** Now you might point out that I also listed cost as a pro, but that's compared to Xserve. Compared to Mac mini or iMac, Mac Pro is a lot of money.

The cost for memory and extra hard drives from Apple is also high. The RAID card is also expensive. You don't have to buy these from Apple, but it's more convenient to have them installed when you buy the Mac.

As I mention earlier, you'll save a lot of money (potentially, many hundreds of dollars in this case) by ordering Mac Pro with the minimum memory, buying your own RAM, and installing it yourself.

Xserve as a server

If you've never seen an Xserve before, you wouldn't know that it's a Mac. The flat, horizontal body, shown in Figure 2-5, is designed to be mounted in a standard 19-inch equipment rack and to be run headless. At 30 inches long, it's a little big for a desk, but if you want to connect a display to it, you can plug in a graphics card.

Figure 2-5: Three Xserves mounted in a rack with a storage array.

Photo courtesy of Apple

Apple's top-of-the-food-chain Mac supports lots of high-powered add-ons, such as internal RAIDs, with multiple, big, high-speed hard drives, including *serially attached SCSI (SAS)* drives, and it sports eight RAM slots. The Mac Pro has all this, but Xserve also has features to keep it running in mission-critical situations. If you need Xserve to run in mission-critical situations, consider getting the AppleCare service plan. Replacement parts aren't cheap, and the tech support lets you minimize or eliminate downtime.

Except for the drastically different shape, Xserve is similar in a lot of ways to Mac Pro. The next three sections help you decide whether you need Xserve or Mac Pro.

Best uses

The Xserve is similarly powered to the Mac Pro, so it can be used for the same uses as Mac Pro, running multiple services for hundreds of users. You may still need additional servers to run some services for very large networks, but the Xserve is better suited than a Mac Pro to a growing network because you can easily upgrade the processors.

The Xserve is also built for mission-critical situations. If you absolutely can't afford to have any server downtime due to hardware failure, the Xserve is better than the Mac Pro. You may never have to shut down an Xserve.

Unlike the Mac Pro, however, Xserve isn't well-suited for sitting in the middle of an office or classroom because of the racket it can make. Xserves are designed to be located in a data center or a ventilated telecom closet.

Pros

The Xserve doesn't give you a significant bump in speed over the Mac Pro, and it has a similar set of expansion slots and high-end hardware options. But the Xserve does have some advantages over the Mac Pro:

- **Features to keep it running and reduce downtime.** Notably:
  - *An option of redundant power supply:* If one power supply fails, the other takes over. Simply pull out a power supply and replace it — without shutting down Xserve.
  - *Hot swappable hard drives:* If a drive fails, you can pull out of Xserve without shutting it down or opening it. However, it has only three drive bays; the Mac Pro has four.
  - *Temperature measurement:* You can read the temperature from Snow Leopard Server's admin tools and set the software to send you an alarm if the Xserve gets too hot.

- **Processors that are officially user-upgradeable.** To get upgrading instructions, go to `http://support.apple.com/manuals` and search for *Xserve processor.* Manuals for the different Xserve model appear in the results.
- **A removable lid that gives you easy access to *everything* inside.**
- **Mountable in a standard 19-inch rack.**

Cons

Disadvantages to using Xserve:

- **Only three hard drive bays:** The Xserve has one less than Mac Pro. This is still a lot of storage but not enough to support an internal RAID 0+1 (as I describe in the "RAID storage" section, earlier in the chapter), as can Mac Pro.
- **Cost:** The Xserve is Apple's most expensive Mac. The base model starts at a few hundred dollars more than Mac Pro, and you spend more for the processors. Xserve's base configuration comes with one quad-core processor; Mac Pro base configuration comes with two. To get equal with Mac Pro base configuration, it costs you another $500 or so.
- **Heat:** Xserve gets very hot and requires adequate ventilation. You'll be fine if you put it in a standard equipment rack, but think twice about stuffing it in a small, unventilated closet.
- **Form factor:** The long, flat shape is good for a rack, but bad for an office or classroom setting.
- **Noise:** Xserve is noisy and distracting sitting in the middle of an office or a classroom. If this is the only place for your server, consider Mac Pro instead.

Considering Other Network Hardware

For most of the book, I assume you have a network. But in case you don't, here's a brief overview of what's needed for a basic network infrastructure. Many different network layouts are possible. In this section, I describe a smaller network, or a *subnetwork,* that you might plug in to a larger network.

It's best if you set up the network (or have a functioning network with DNS in place), connect your clients, and plug in the Mac server before you install Snow Leopard Server. When you run the Snow Leopard Server installer, it gathers data from the network during the setup to automate configuration. (Snow Leopard Server installation is covered in Chapter 3.)

Ethernet switches and cables

Even in today's wireless world, you need some wires for your network infrastructure. The heart of a wired network infrastructure is an *Ethernet switched hub* (or an *Ethernet switch*), a box that everything on a wired network plugs into.

Some Ethernet hubs are without switches, which aren't as fast as Ethernet switched hubs. *Plain* (unswitched) hubs aren't that common, but you don't want one if you find one. Make sure it's a switch.

You can often find Ethernet switches built into other devices, such as wireless access points, Internet routers, firewalls, and virtual private network gateways. Apple's AirPort Extreme and Time Capsule have Gigabit Ethernet switches in them.

Ethernet speeds

Ethernet switches come in different performance levels. You want one that supports *Gigabit Ethernet* (or *1000BASE-T;* a gigabit per second maximum), which is the top bandwidth supported in all Mac models and many PCs. Gigabit Ethernet switches are sometimes referred to as *10/100/1000 switches* because they're backward-compatible with older, slower 100 megabits per second (Mbps) and 10 Mbps Ethernet hardware. If a switch is 10/100, it's only 100 Mbps, one-tenth the bandwidth of Gigabit Ethernet.

Ethernet ports

Ethernet switches have anywhere from 4 to 24 ports (see Figure 2-6, which shows an 8-port gigabit switch). You can also connect (daisy chain) switches together if you outgrow your current switch.

Figure 2-6: An 8-port Gigabit Ethernet switch.

You need one of your switch's ports for your Internet connection (or for a connection to a bigger network). You need another port to plug in the server, another one for a networked printer (if it has an Ethernet port), and another port to plug in to a wireless access point if you're providing Wi-Fi connection to your network. The rest of the ports are for your client computers. Some switches also have USB ports to share a USB printer.

If you're using the server as an Internet gateway, the Internet connection would plug in directly to the server, and the server's second Ethernet port would connect to the switch.

Cables

Ethernet cable comes in several grades. At minimum, you want Category 5e (commonly known as *Cat 5e*) cable for Gigabit Ethernet. Cat 5e cables can be used to a maximum length of about 100 meters from the switch to the computer, though interference can shorten this.

A higher grade of Ethernet cable — Cat 6 — is more immune to noise. Cat 6 can also handle 10 Gigabit Ethernet (10GBASE-T), which some network devices support.

You can also connect a server to a Gigabit Ethernet switch with optical cable known as 1000Base-SX Ethernet. For this, you need a switch with an optical port and Mac Pro or Xserve with a 1000Base-SX Ethernet card in it. The advantages to Optical Ethernet are higher performance and longer distribution due to the near-total absence of electromagnetic interference.

Optional: Wireless equipment

If you decide to go wireless, you shouldn't go *completely* wireless. You should still use an Ethernet cable to connect the server to an Ethernet switch or wireless access point.

Although you can use the wireless AirPort card in Mac server to connect directly to Macs and PCs on a wireless network, I don't recommend it. Doing so makes extra work for the server, and the signal strength and range aren't as good as in a wireless access point, such as Apple AirPort Extreme or many others. The lower the signal strength, the slower network traffic is.

Apple's Airport Extreme and Time Capsule are wireless access points that contain small built-in Ethernet switches. Each supports up to 50 wireless client computers. Time Capsule also contains a hard drive. The clients on a small network can back up to the Time Capsule using the Time Capsule software that comes with Mac OS X 10.5 and later.

You don't need Apple's wireless hardware, however, because plenty available options work. If you get a third-party wireless access point, make sure it supports the 802.11a/b/g/n standard. (The letters signify different revisions to the wireless 802.11 standard, with each successive letter representing a faster standard.) All Macs built today, as well as many PCs, support 802.11n. Older Macs and PCs may only support 802.11g or 802.11b.

UPS for your server

All networks should have an *uninterruptible power supply (UPS)* for the server. This is an external box that keeps the server running in the event of a power failure to the building. Some organizations need to keep the server running through the time of the power failure. A UPS also gives you a chance to shut down the server in an orderly fashion. Simply shutting off the power in the middle of operations can damage the data on the server, and power surges related to the power failure can damage the server hardware.

A basic UPS contains a backup battery and a surge protector. The server's power cable plugs into the UPS and runs off battery power when the building power goes out.

More sophisticated UPS units include *Automatic Voltage Regulation (AVR)*. AVR guarantees a constant level of power to the server in the event of fluctuations in delivered power, including short drops in power levels, or dips or surges that might occur before a total power outage.

One parameter to look at is the electrical load capacity, measured in volt-amps (VA). For Mac mini or iMac, 350VA should do it. For Mac Pro or Xserve, you can start at about 800VA. Extra drives and expansion cards draw more power and require a higher load capacity.

On the lower end, UPS boxes start at about $100 for a single outlet without AVR and can cost several hundred dollars for multiple outlets. Depending on the load capacity, a manufacturer will tell you how long the battery will run the computer, typically an hour or two at these price points, up to eight hours for units costing over $1,000.

A highly respected supplier of solid UPS systems is APC (`www.apcc.com`). APC offers a range of products from home/office to enterprise-class. Tripp Lite (`www.tripplite.com`) and Belkin (`www.belkin.com`) are also known for quality UPS systems.

Chapter 3

Installation and Setup

In This Chapter

- Identifying information you'll need
- Formatting storage
- Installing and configuring locally and remotely
- Setting up an administrator Mac
- Checking DNS and other post-configuration tasks
- Keeping Snow Leopard Server up to date

Snow Leopard Server is the network server for the rest of us. You don't need to be an IT consultant or have multiple certifications in communication technologies. If you do have that expertise under your belt, Mac OS X Server lets you get at the configuration details that you're used to. But you never have to even see these details if you don't need to, and many don't need to.

Before you install, you have to make some choices. Decide whether to do a brand-new installation or upgrade from a previous version of Mac OS X or Mac OS X Server. You also need to decide whether to do the installation right from the Mac or remotely from another Mac. This chapter looks at the options and helps you decide which one is for you.

One more thing: Make sure your server Mac lives up to the hardware requirements and recommendations in Chapter 2 before installing.

A Roadmap to Installation and Setup

Apple has made Snow Leopard Server the easiest professional server to install and configure. But you still have a lot of options to consider before you insert the DVD in the Mac. Which route you take depends on where you want to start from and where you want to go.

Here are the main decision points and tasks for installing and setting up, leaving out some of the details of installing remotely:

1. **Decide whether you want a local install from the Mac server itself or a remote install from another Mac on the network.**

   More steps are involved in a remote installation, but this is the way to install if your Mac doesn't have a display attached.

2. **Collect data about the server and network and then write it down.**

   Apple provides a worksheet for this purpose. I discuss this worksheet in the following section.

3. **Decide whether you want a new installation (commonly known as a *clean install*) or an upgrade.**

   If you configuring a new Xserve, Snow Leopard Server is preinstalled.

4. **Boot from the DVD and install the server software (if not preinstalled).**

5. **If you do a new (clean) installation, decide whether to reformat the hard drive.**

6. **Decide how to manage users and groups: Add them to this server, import them from another server, or use a directory server elsewhere on the network.**

7. **Type in your configuration information.**

   After you finish going through the configuration screens, Snow Leopard Server is ready for action. A remote installation from another Mac on the network has a few more tasks.

8. **Perform any post-installation configuration (such as add users, further configure DNS, or set up relay servers).**

The server should be connected to your network during installation so that it can gather some of the configuration information automatically.

If you've set up Leopard Server, note that the setup procedure is a bit different in Snow Leopard Server. You no longer have choices for Standard, Workgroup, and Advanced configurations. In their place is a simplified choice of where you want the users and groups to reside.

The rest of this chapter looks at the details of this road map. I start with the common point of departure for all installation and configuration routes: collecting network information.

Collecting Info with the Worksheet

Apple provides an Installation and Setup Worksheet file on the Mac OS X Server installation DVD in the Documentation folder. You can print it and use it to record information that you'll need to configure the server.

A good idea is to gather this information before you start installation and configuration. You speed up your setup time by having the info in front of you while you type in the configuration screens. You'll also have a record of how you set up the server all in one place. The Installation and Setup Worksheet is a little like an IRS income tax form; it's over two dozen pages long, including copious instructions. Figure 3-1 shows a small portion of the worksheet. No need to panic though: The sheet encompasses every possible situation, so you won't need to collect all the information listed. The instructions give you a good idea of which section applies to you. The worksheet also tells you what you can skip and when you can skip it. The worksheet is also conveniently arranged in the order that the Server Assistant asks you for the information.

Setup item	Your information
Network services	☐ Ready for Mac OS X Server setup
Welcome—local server *(skip this unless setting up locally)*	
Region:	Select during setup
Automatic setup:	☐ Auto server setup profile saved on an accessible disk
Servers—remote server *(skip this unless setting up remotely)*	
Identify by local hostname or IP address:	
Authenticate with serial number:	
Region—remote server *(skip this unless setting up remotely):*	
Select a region during setup	
Keyboard:	Select an available keyboard layout during setup.
Serial number:	XSVR-106-
Site license information:	Registered to
	Organization:
Transfer an existing server?	☐ Set up a new server ☐ Transfer from:

Figure 3-1: A portion of Apple's Installation and Setup Worksheet.

Locating Hardware ID numbers

There are two hardware identification numbers you need to record: the MAC address and the serial number. If you're going to configure remotely for another Mac on the network, you will need to enter this information to enable the installation software to locate the server.

The *MAC address* doesn't refer to "Mac" as in "Macintosh": it's the acronym for *Media Access Control.* The MAC address is a unique hardware identifier that specifies each Ethernet port or wireless network card, so a Mac can have more than one MAC address. If a Mac has two Ethernet ports, it will have two MAC addresses. The MAC address takes the form of a series of two-digit characters separated by colons, like this: `00:23:32:b5:d0: 43`.

To confuse matters, Apple also refers to the MAC address as the *Ethernet ID.* When you see them, remember that they are both the same.

A different identification number that you may need is the *serial number,* a unique number that identifies every Mac. Unlike the MAC address, a Mac can have only one serial number.

All Macs list the serial number somewhere on the outside case. Many Macs also include the MAC address/Ethernet ID. Here's where you can find them:

- **MacBook and MacBook Pro:** Notebooks aren't great servers, but they do make good testing platforms. Remove the battery and look for the serial and Ethernet ID numbers on a label inside the battery bay.

  For notebooks that don't have removable batteries, the serial number is etched on the back. To find the Ethernet ID on these models, use System Profiler, as described later in this section.
- **Mac mini:** The serial number, along with the Ethernet ID number, is written on the bottom side of the Mac mini, right at the edge, in mini print. You also see a tiny bar code.
- **Mac Pro:** The serial number is written on the backside on a label located under the video ports.
- **Xserve:** In the middle of the rear of the Xserve, you'll find a pullout tab containing the serial number.

If you can't get to the serial number because the Mac is in a difficult-to-reach location, a Mac OS X trick has been around for many years, but even some die-hard Mac fans don't know about it: Choose Apple menu⇨About This Mac. Double-click the Mac OS X version number, and it changes to the hardware serial number (see Figure 3-2).

It's not quite as easy to get the MAC address/Ethernet ID in Mac OS X. You can find it in both System Profiler and System Preferences. Remember that each Ethernet port and AirPort card have a MAC address, so be sure you identify the Ethernet ports that you'll use for your network.

Figure 3-2: Double-click the Mac OS X version number (left) to reveal the hardware serial number (right).

You can use System Profiler to find the Mac address even if you booted up from the Mac OS X Server Install DVD.

1. **If booted from the hard drive, choose Apple menu➪About This Mac and then click the More Info button to launch System Profiler.**

   If booted from the Mac OS X Server Install DVD, click past the initial installation language screen, go to the Utilities menu, and choose System Profiler.

   The System Profiler appears.

2. **In System Profiler's Contents list, click Network (see Figure 3-3).**

3. **On the right side, look for the Ethernet port.**

   Here, the Ethernet ID number is referred to as *MAC Address.*

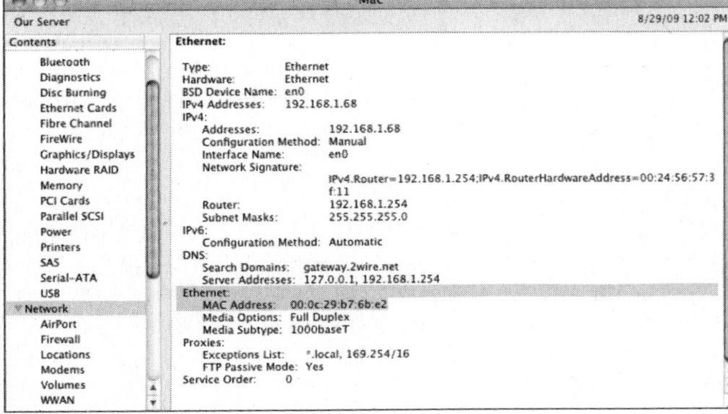

Figure 3-3: System Profiler reveals the MAC address.

System Profiler can also show the serial number; just click Hardware at the top of the Contents list.

If the server Mac is booted from its hard drive, you can also use System Preferences to find the MAC address/Ethernet ID:

1. **Open System Preferences and click the Network icon.**
2. **Click the Ethernet interface that you're interested in.**
3. **Click the Advanced button and then click the Ethernet tab.**

   Here, the MAC number is referred to as *Ethernet ID*.

Although I said that each Ethernet port has a MAC address, the Xserve's built-in Ethernet port actually has *two* MAC addresses: One is used by the server's processor, and the other is used by Xserve's special Lights Out Management processor. This provides hardware remote monitoring and management. For more on Lights Out Management, see this Apple technical article: `http://support.apple.com/kb/TA24506`.

Network ID numbers

When you collect data to enter into your worksheet, a variety of numbers identify your network. You may need this information for each network port you'll use, though some of these numbers may be supplied automatically if your server is connected to the network during installation. The Apple worksheet has some more explanations. Here's a brief description:

- **IP address:** Every computer on the network has an IP address that identifies it to other computers. You record an IP address if you manually assign an IP address to the server, called *static* IP addressing. You can also have the IP address set automatically with DHCP. You assign each Ethernet port an IP address or have it done automatically.

  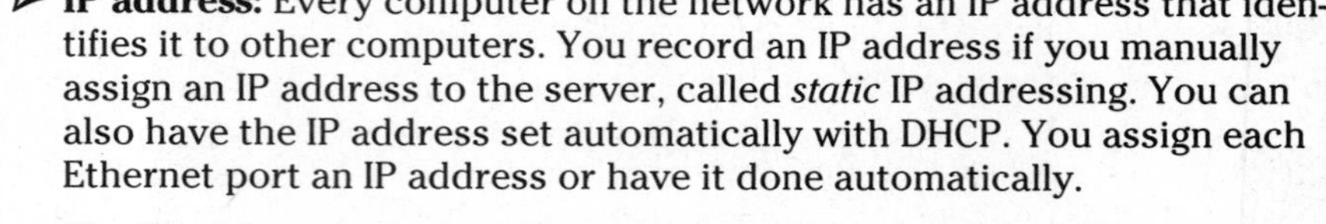

  The IP address is four numbers separated by periods, such as `169.254.13.3`. Each number can be from 0 through 255. See the "Rules for IP addressing" sidebar for more details.

  DHCP refers to *Dynamic Host Configuration Protocol.*

- **Subnet mask:** This is a number in the form of four numbers separated by the dots in which the numbers between the dots are often 255 or 0, such as `255.255.0.0`. Use a different subnet mask for each Ethernet port. The computers connected to a server's Ethernet port are on a subnet. The subnet mask limits the size of the subnet. The subnet mask can also be set automatically via DHCP.

- **Router:** On the Apple worksheet, this refers to the IP address of the hardware that moves data between local subnetworks and the Internet. The router might also have a DHCP server that automatically assigns IP addresses to your server and/or client computers.

  If you have an AirPort Base Station or other Internet router, use its address. Otherwise, get the router address from the same source as your server's IP address.

  If you don't have a router, use the server Mac's IP address.

  If you have your Mac connected to the network during installation, the installer software may detect the router and provide it's IP address.

- **DNS servers:** This refers to the IP address of a domain name services server (DNS). You can have more than one. The domain name comes in the form of `mycompany.com` or `myserver.mycompany.com`. The DNS server translates domain names to IP addresses. If you configure this manually, you'll obtain the IP address of the DNS from your Internet service provider. This is one of the more important settings.
- **PPPoE settings:** These are settings your Internet service provider gives you if the server is getting its IP address and other information via PPPoE, the standard for communications between the server and a DSL connection to the Internet.
- **Primary DNS name:** This is the domain name of a DNS or DHCP server. Use a unique name (such as `ourserver.private`) if you don't have a DNS service. If you do have a DNS server elsewhere on the network, this is set automatically.

  If you're planning to run DNS from this server Mac, be sure that you have the proper domain name for your server. If you get this wrong, it could be difficult to remedy.

- **Computer name:** This is a uniquely Macintosh network name; it identifies Macs that are using the Apple Filing Protocol (AFP) for file and print sharing. When Macs browse for AFP shares or printers, they see the network names of servers or the workstation Macs that have file sharing turned on.

  A Mac computer name can be 63 characters or less. Use Roman characters except for the equal sign (=), the colon (:), or the at sign (@). Spaces are okay. Users find it useful if the name has some significance, such as *Computer Lab Server.*

  If you're using Server Message Block (SMB) file sharing for Windows and Mac SMB clients, Mac OS X Server automatically converts the computer name to an SMB-compatible name.

Rules for IP addressing

When you set an IP address manually (known as *static* addressing), you need to follow some rules. An IP address takes the form of four numbers from 0 through 255, separated by periods, such as `169.254.13.3`.

The total IP address range is `000.000.000.000` through `255.255.255.255`, but within that, there are some ranges that are used for specific purposes, such as public and private IP addresses. A *public* IP address is one that the entire Internet can see. Every computer on the planet that the Internet can see must have a unique public IP address. Usually, your Internet service provider provides a public IP address, either manually or automatically.

A *private* IP address is one that the Internet can't see because the computer is connected to the Internet through an Internet gateway or router. The Internet sees only the IP address of the gateway. The computers on this type of local network use private IP addresses from one of several *private* address ranges. You might give your server a private IP address if another server or hardware box is acting as the Internet gateway. (You can also have a private IP address assigned automatically through DHCP.)

There are several private address ranges. One is the range that starts with `169.254`: `169.254.0.0–169.254.254.255`. ***Note:*** For this range, the last number can be 255, but the one before it can only go as high as 254.

The other two private ranges are `10.0.0.1` through `10.255.255.254` and `192.168.0.1` through `192.168.0.254`.

If you manually configure the IP addresses of your Mac for a local network, you can use IP addresses from any of these ranges as long as all the Macs on the network are in the same range. They also need the same subnet mask, and *no* two computers on your local network or subnetwork can have the same IP address. A subnetwork would consist of all the computers connected to one Ethernet port on the server.

Formatting Storage Drives

If you're upgrading and older version of Mac OS X Server to Snow Leopard Server, you won't format your hard drive, and you can skip this section. You will need to reformat, however, if you are installing on top of a Mac OS X client or if you want a clean installation. If you plan on erasing the boot drive, consider your storage formatting options before installing. Decide whether you will

- Erase the disk you're installing Mac OS X Server on.
- Use a simple erase.
- Divide a drive into multiple partitions.
- Use multiple drives together in a software RAID (redundant array of independent disks).
- Do this before or during the installation process.

Mac OS X Server 10.6 no longer gives you the option of using the Unix File System (UFS). If you upgrade from an older version of Mac OS X Server that has a UFS drive, reformat if you want to use it as a startup drive. Apple doesn't support UFS startup drives for Snow Leopard Server, which means you can run into problems.

In order to reformat a hard drive, you need to boot the Mac from another drive or a DVD drive. The installation process will boot the Mac from the Mac OS X Server Install DVD for you.

If you are installing locally, use Disk Utility to reformat the driver — the installer program won't do it for you. Disk Utility can do a simple erase or do something more complicated, such as create multiple partitions or create a software RAID. You can open Disk Utility when the server Mac is booted from the DVD. Even though the Installer is on the screen, the Utilities menu gives you access to Disk Utility.

For a remote installation, you can't use Disk Utility, but you must use Server Assistant to erase a drive. Unfortunately, Server Assistant can't partition a drive or create a RAID. You will have to use Disk Utility on the server Mac, either before or during the installation.

To open Disk Utility while booted from the DVD, choose it from the Utilities menu.

The simple erase

To erase a startup drive in Disk Utility, select the drive from the column on the left and click the Erase tab. Now choose a format from the Format pop-up menu. Use one of these two formats for a startup disk:

- **Mac OS Extended (Journaled):** The standard format that most people will use.
- **Mac OS Extended (Case-sensitive, Journaled):** Some people who are hosting static Web sites use this format because it improves performance, with a better mapping between URLs and files.

For drives that you won't use as startup disks, you can use the non-journaled versions of these two formats, though there isn't a compelling reason to do so.

To erase a drive with Server Assistant from another Mac on the network, you don't have any choices of format. You can use the standard Mac OS Extended (Journaled) format only.

Partitioning a hard drive

When you *partition* a hard drive, you divide it into multiple volumes. Each volume appears as a separate hard drive to the user. You can use one partition as the startup disk containing Mac OS X Server (the operating system and services), and use another, larger partition to store the user files. If something goes wrong with the user data volume, the server can keep functioning, or at least, it won't have to be re-created. This scheme also prevents the boot partition from running out of disk space because of growing user data.

Having multiple drives is better than multiple partitions, however, because they can increase system performance.

One essential thing to remember about partitioning: You must use the default GUID Partition Table, not the Apple Partition Table. If you use the latter, you won't be able to boot from the drive.

You also need to choose a format. The same guidelines described in the preceding section apply here. Figure 3-4 shows you all the settings you need to configure.

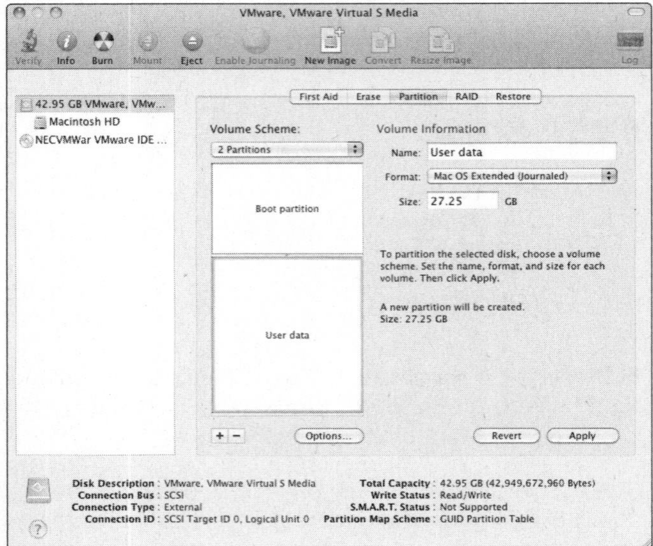

Figure 3-4: Partitioning a drive with Disk Utility.

To partition a drive, either before or during installation, do the following:

1. **Launch Disk Utility.**

   While booted from the Mac OS X Server Install DVD, choose Disk Utility from the Utilities menu.

2. **Click the hard drive you want to partition in the left pane and then click the Partition tab.**

3. **In the Volume Scheme pop-up menu, choose the number of partitions you want to create.**

   The space below the pop-up menu has a number of boxes representing the partition sizes.

4. **Drag the bar that separates the boxes to resize them to the partition size (in gigabytes) that you want for each.**

5. **Click a box to select it and then type a name for it in the Name field for each partition.**

   Figure 3-4 shows that I've used the names Boot Partition and User Data.

6. **In the Format pop-up menu, make sure that Mac OS X Extended (Journaled) is selected.**

7. **At the bottom of the window, check that GUID Partition Table is selected for Partition Map Scheme.**

   If not, click the Options button and select GUID Partition Table.

8. **Click Apply.**

Creating a software RAID

For Macs with multiple hard drives, Disk Utility can set up multiple drives to work together as a software RAID to increase performance, protect data, or both. Software RAID takes some of the computer's processing power, and it isn't as secure as a hardware RAID controller system. For instance, a system crash could affect a software RAID, but would not affect a hardware RAID. However, a software RAID is far less expensive and does provide the benefits of data redundancy. You can also use external FireWire drives in a RAID set.

Here's how to create a software RAID:

1. **Launch Disk Utility.**

   When booted from the Mac OS X Server Install DVD, choose Disk Utility from the Utilities menu. If booted from the hard drive, you'll find Disk Utility in the /Applications/Utilities/ folder.

2. **Click the RAID tab.**

3. **Drag and drop drives from the left pane into the RAID pane.**

   Use drives — *not* volumes — from the left pane. Partitions/volumes are listed under the drive name and are indented.

4. **Type a name for the RAID set in the Name field.**
5. **In the Format pop-up menu, make sure that Mac OS X Extended (Journaled) is selected.**

6. **From the RAID Type pop-up menu, choose Mirrored, Striped, or Concatenated:**

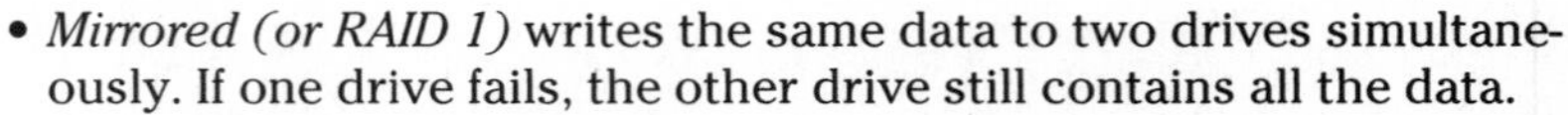

   - *Mirrored (or RAID 1)* writes the same data to two drives simultaneously. If one drive fails, the other drive still contains all the data.

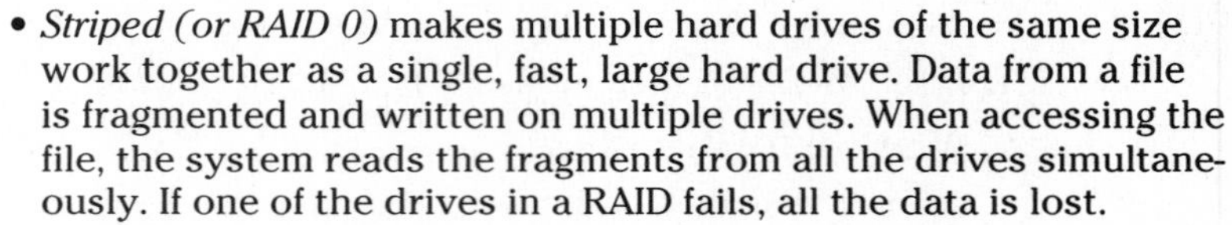

   - *Striped (or RAID 0)* makes multiple hard drives of the same size work together as a single, fast, large hard drive. Data from a file is fragmented and written on multiple drives. When accessing the file, the system reads the fragments from all the drives simultaneously. If one of the drives in a RAID fails, all the data is lost.
   - *Concatenated* combines multiple hard drives into one without the speed benefits of striping, but you can combine drives of different sizes. Concatenating gets really interesting when used with another RAID. For instance, concatenate two FireWire drives that add up to the capacity of the internal drive and then mirror the internal drive with the concatenated FireWire drives. You can also use it to create a RAID 1+0. For example, if you have four drives, concatenate a 2-drive mirror array with a 2-drive striped array. This gives you both the performance of striping with the redundancy or mirroring.

7. **Click the Create button.**

See Chapter 2 for a description of the different RAID types.

Installing and Configuring Locally

This section describes installing Snow Leopard Server *locally* — that is, with you sitting directly in front of the Mac that will be your server. The server Mac should be connected to the network and turned on. It also describes the option of migrating settings and data from another server running Mac OS X Server versions 10.4.11 and later.

If you bought a Mac with Snow Leopard Server preinstalled, skip the "Installing locally" section and go to the "Installing, Part 2: Configuring locally" section. If you want to install Snow Leopard Server remotely from another Mac on the network, skip ahead to the section "Installing and Configuring Remotely."

Installing locally

Installing and configuring probably looks like one seamless process to you. The only thing separating them is an automatic restart of the Mac after the software is installed. This section describes the installation part of the process. This could be a new installation or an upgrade, though the procedure may vary a little.

If you're upgrading an existing server, be sure you back up before installing.

1. **Insert the Mac OS X Server Install DVD into the server Mac.**
2. **Double-click the Install Mac OS X Server icon.**
3. **Click the Restart button in the screen that appears.**

   The Mac reboots from the DVD.
4. **Choose a language (see Figure 3-5) from the dialog and click the round arrow button.**

   The Install Mac OS X Server screen appears. Notice that a menu bar exists with a Utilities menu that gives you access to several utilities (see Figure 3-6). You can use System Profiler to find details of the Mac's hardware. Quitting System Profiler takes you back to the Install Mac OS X Server screen.

Figure 3-5: Choose a language.

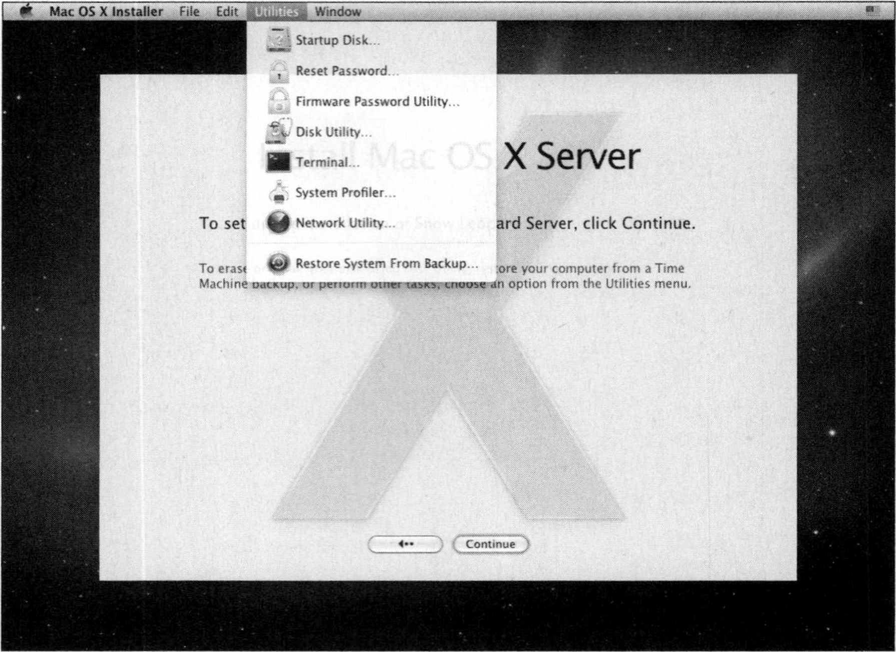

Figure 3-6: A Utilities menu is available while booted from the Mac OS X Server Install DVD.

5. **Choose Disk Utility from the Utilities menu if you want to erase the hard drive, partition the hard drive into multiple volumes, or create a software RAID. If you aren't erasing the hard drive, click Continue at the bottom of the Install Mac OS X Server screen.**

   If you are not erasing the hard drive and the drive contains an older version of Mac OS X Server, the installer program will upgrade the older version of the server.

6. **Click Agree to accept the software license agreement.**
7. **Select a destination drive by clicking it (see Figure 3-7).**

   If you partitioned to multiple partitions, you see icons for them here. (Don't click Install just yet.)

8. **Click Customize to add or remove software from the standard installation.**

   In the dialog that slides down, you can remove languages other than English, and the X11 environment, which are normally installed (see Figure 3-8). You can also add the complete set of printer drivers (12GB worth) that Snow Leopard Server supports.

9. **Click Done when finished.**

10. **Click the Install button.**

    The installer begins installing Mac OS X Server, presenting a progress bar. When finished, the Mac restarts and boots from the hard drive.

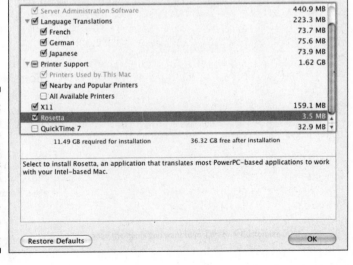

Figure 3-7: Choose a destination drive and customize the installation.

Server Administration Software 440.9 MB
Language Translations 223.3 MB
French 73.7 MB
German 75.6 MB
Japanese 73.9 MB
Printer Support 1.62 GB
Printers Used by This Mac
Nearby and Popular Printers
All Available Printers
X11 159.1 MB
Rosetta 3.5 MB
QuickTime 7 32.9 MB
11.49 GB required for installation 36.32 GB free after installation
Select to install Rosetta, an application that translates most PowerPC-based applications to work with your Intel-based Mac.
Restore Defaults
OK

Figure 3-8: The Customize dialog enables you to add or remove some installation options.

The installation is done, but you can't use the server yet: Server Assistant launches when the Mac reboots. The Snow Leopard server installation process moves to the configuration screens. To continue with your local installation process, read on.

Installing, Part 2: Configuring locally

When the Mac reboots, you'll be looking at the Welcome screen in Figure 3-9. You'll also see this screen if you bought a new Mac with Snow Leopard server preinstalled and turned on the server for the first time. This is the Server Assistant, though the title doesn't appear anywhere.

Before you continue, notice the small question mark button in the lower right of the screen. You can click this in any of the configuration screens to get help. The Help that pops up is specific to the screen, and it's quite, well, helpful.

To save you from an endless procession of steps, I've broken the following process into functional groups.

Welcome

Mac OS X Server is the ideal server solution for small businesses, workgroups, education, and enterprise IT departments.

In just a few steps you can register your Apple product, set up your server and get started deploying standards-based workgroup and Internet services.

Start by selecting your country or region.

United States
Canada
United Kingdom
Australia
New Zealand
Ireland

Show All

Do you need instructions for setting up your server? To learn more click the Help button below.

Go Back
Continue

Figure 3-9: The Welcome screen.

Registration information and migration options

To continue setting up Snow Leopard Server, registering the software with Apple is the first task at hand. This section of the process also gives you the option to migrate configuration information and data from another server. Continue the process by following these steps:

1. **In the Welcome window, select the country in which you're registering and click Continue.**
2. **In the Keyboard screen, select a country for your keyboard and click Continue.**
3. **In the Serial Number Screen (see Figure 3-10), type in the serial number for the Mac OS X Server software and a registration name and click Continue.**

   The next screen asks you if you want to transfer an existing server.
4. **Select one of the following buttons and click Continue:**
   - *Transfer the Information from an Existing Server:* Select this option to move settings and user data from another server or volume or drive installed with Mac OS X Server 10.4.11 or later. A series of screens appears in which you select a server or drive. After Server Assistant moves the settings and data to the new server, proceed to Step 5.

     Server Assistant doesn't migrate all mail server settings. Apple has an article on how to remedy this:

     `http://support.apple.com/kb/HT3768?viewlocale=en_US`
   - *Setup a New Server:* Select this if you aren't migrating from another server.

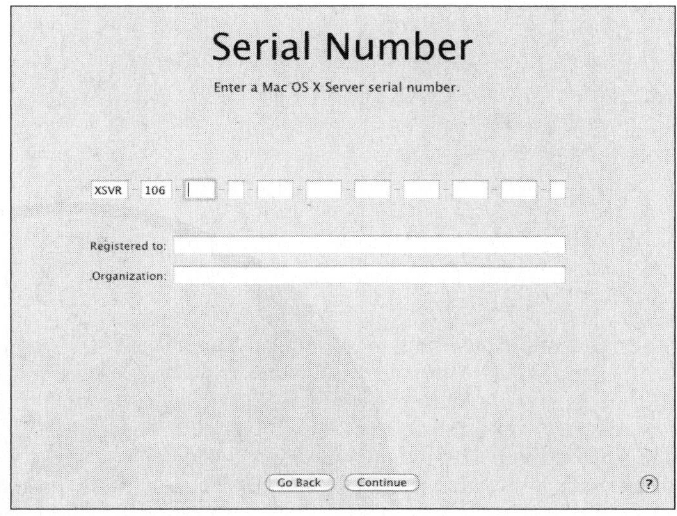

Figure 3-10: The Serial Number screen.

5. **In the Registration screen that appears, type in your name and contact information and click Continue.**

6. **Enter the appropriate information in the A Few More Questions screen and click Continue.**

   This screen asks you nosey questions about how big your network is and what services and clients you'll be running. Don't worry too much about your answers. This isn't configuration information; it is used to help Apple's marketing department keep tabs on how customers are using Snow Leopard Server.

7. **In the Time Zone screen that appears, select your city in the Closest City pop-up menu and click Continue.**

8. **In the Administrator Account screen (shown in Figure 3-11) that appears, enter the name and password for the first administrator account and click Continue.**

Administrator Account

Create a local account that will be used to administer this server. After setup, use Server Preferences to create users and administrators for use with your services.

Name: John Rizzo
Short Name: johnrizzo
This will be used as the name for the administrator's home folder and cannot be changed.
Password: •••••
Verify: •••••
Password Hint: (Recommended)
Enable administrators to log in remotely using SSH
Enable administrators to manage this server remotely
Go Back Continue ?

Figure 3-11: The Administrator Account screen.

This step actually creates two accounts. The first is a primary administrator account with this name and password. The second has the name Local Administrator, with the short name localadmin, with the same password that you entered for the primary admin account. The local admin account can't be used to access the server remotely and is stored locally on the server, not in the network directory. The main purpose is to enable you to log in to the server in case something happens to the primary administrator account.

The Network screen: Setting Network Addresses

Continuing with configuration, Server Assistant asks you for various network addresses and names for network services. This is an important segment of setting up your server, so make sure you get it right. If you don't, you may find yourself in troubleshooting mode once your server is running.

Continuing from the preceding steps, follow these steps:

9. **In the Network Services screen that appears, set the IP address for each of the server Mac's network interface ports displayed on the left.**

   Click an Ethernet port to select it. For each, the default is set to DHCP. For a server, it makes more sense to use static IP addresses and subnet masks. Do this by clicking the Configure IPv4 pop-up menu and selecting Manual, as shown in Figure 3-12. (See the sidebar "Rules for IP addressing," earlier in the chapter, for more information.)

Figure 3-12: The Network Services screen is where you specify the server's IP address.

In order to use the server as an Internet gateway, you need to use at least two Ethernet ports set up differently. The Internet port that's connected to an Internet connection (DSL modem, cable modem, or other) must have a public IP address. Another Ethernet port, going to a wired network or a wireless box like AirPort, can have a private address (such as 10.0.0.1 or 192.168.0.1) either configured manually or automatically.

On Xserve boxes, one or two network ports — *Lights Out Management* — appear in the left pane of the Network Services screen. This refers to Xserve's built-in hardware remote monitoring and management protocol. Lights Out Management gets its own IP address — you must make sure that this IP address is different than any of the other IP addresses on the Mac.

10. **In the Router field, type the IP address of a router on your network, or, if you don't have a router, enter the Mac's IP address.**

    If the server is connected to the network, Server Assistant will detect the router and display the IP address here.

11. **Enter the DNS server and search domain information in the appropriate fields, as shown in Figure 3-12.**

    See the section, "Network ID numbers," earlier in the chapter, for more information.

12. **For advanced settings, such as changing the duplex setting of an Ethernet port, click the Ethernet button and change your settings from the pop-up menus.**

    Don't worry too much about this: You can always go back later to make these changes in the Network pane of System Preferences.

    Check over all these settings in the Network screen for each network interface port you have.

13. **When everything looks good, click Continue.**

Setting Domain Name and Computer Name

Next, the Network Names screen appears (see Figure 3-13). This is an important screen to get right. There are two fields: Primary DNS Name and Computer Name. The first is the more important. Here's what you do next:

14. **In the Primary DNS Name field, verify or type a unique name for your server in the DNS service based on one of these cases:**

    - If you have a DNS server on your network, Server Assistant may fill this in for you. It will be a *fully qualified DNS name,* along the lines of `server10.acme.com`.
    - If you don't have a DNS server on the network, and you don't get DNS service from an ISP, your Mac will be the DNS server for the network. If you want the server to be visible to the Internet, and have a registered domain name, type a fully qualified DNS name similar to this: `myserver.acme.com`.
    - If you don't have a DNS server on the network, and only users on the local network (not Internet users) access the server, then you can make up a name, something like this: `ourserver.private` or `schoolserver.lan`.

The part after the dot can be anything. Just don't use `.local`, or you may interfere with Bonjour service, which is involved with identifying printers and other network resources.

15. **Type a computer name in the Computer Name field of the Network Names screen.**

    The computer name identifies the server to Mac clients with the Apple Filing Protocol (AFP) for file and print services.

16. **If the network names are okay, click Continue.**

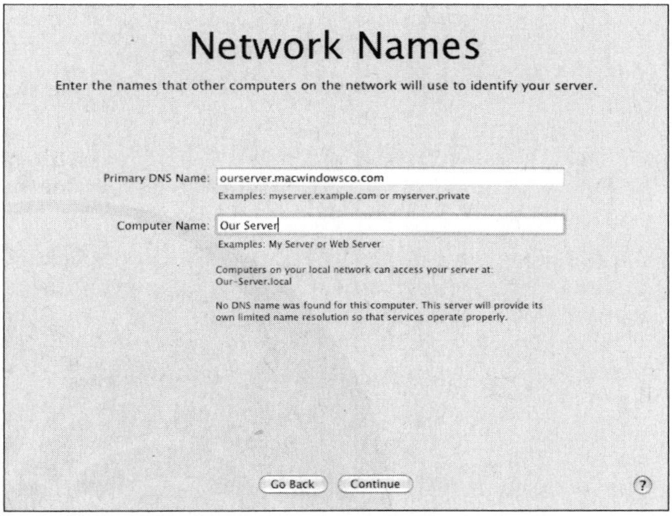

Figure 3-13: The Network Names screen.

Directory services

Now you choose where on the network you will store the directory of users and groups. After you click Continue in the preceding step, the Users and Groups screen appears (see Figure 3-14). Follow these steps:

17. **Select one of three options that determine how the server deals with network directories of users and groups:**

    - *Create Users and Groups:* Select this option if you don't have an existing directory server on the network. This option stores the user and group accounts on your server, making it an Open Directory master. Choose this option if your server is the only server on the network.

      If you choose this option, you'll later type in user accounts manually with Server Preferences.

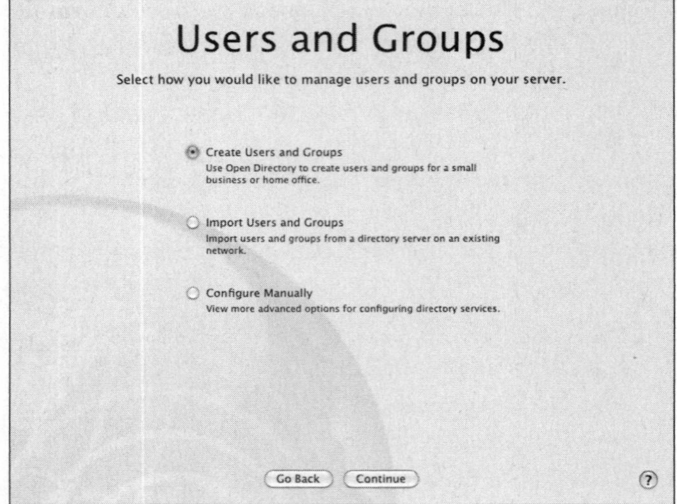

Figure 3-14: The Users and Groups screen presents network directory options.

- *Import Users and Groups:* Select this option to import users from another directory server. This option uses Open Directory on your server Mac to manage users and groups as an Open Directory master. This is a common choice for a Mac acting as a server for a workgroup of clients in a larger organization.

  If you choose this option, you'll later use Server Preferences to import user accounts from the other server.

- *Configure Manually:* This setting gives you two choices. You can set up the server to connect to (or *bind*) to an Open Directory or Microsoft Active Directory running on another server. In this case your server isn't set up as a directory server and won't import users and groups. Alternatively, Configure Manually lets you choose to manually set up your server as an Open Directory master, storing users and groups.

18. **Click Continue.**

    The screen you see next depends on which of the three options you choose in Step 17.

19. **If you selected Create Users and Groups, the Service screen appears, so skip to Step 22.**

20. **If you selected Import Users and Groups, do the following:**

    a. Enter the IP address of a directory server in the Connect to a Directory Server screen or choose it from the pop-up menu.

    b. Click Continue and skip to Step 22.

21. If you selected Configure Manually in Step 17, perform these steps:

a. *(Optional) Select the Connect to a Directory Server check box in the Connect to a Directory Server screen.*

You can also choose to leave this unselected and configure directory services after Mac OS X Server is up and running.

b. *(Optional) Type the address of a directory server on your network or choose it from the pop-up menu.*

This is the directory server that you will bind to.

c. *Click Continue to get to the Directory Services screen (see Figure 3-15).*

d. *(Optional) Select the Set Up an Open Directory Master check box and enter the relevant information.*

If you check this and click Continue, skip to Step 22. If you *don't* check this, the Review screen appears.

e. *If you see the Review screen, click the Details button to review what you've set. Click OK, and then click the Set Up button.*

Server Assistant sets up the server. You skip the rest of the steps here and in the following section, "Final configuration tasks and review." You'll set up services and other details manually.

22. In the Services screen (shown in Figure 3-16), select the check boxes next to the services you want to run (such as Mail, File Sharing, and Calendar), and click Continue.

When you select services here, Server Assistant will set them and turn on the services automatically. You're almost done with installation and configuration of Snow Leopard Server. Proceed to the following section.

Directory Services
Set up an Open Directory master to provide network users and groups, as well as other directory services from your server.
Set up an Open Directory master
Directory Administrator
Name: Directory Administrator
Short Name: diradmin
UID: 1000
Password: <same as local administrator>
Restrict individual user and group access to services
Service access can be changed using Server Admin or Server Preferences.
Users added in Server Preferences will initially be granted access.
Go Back
Continue

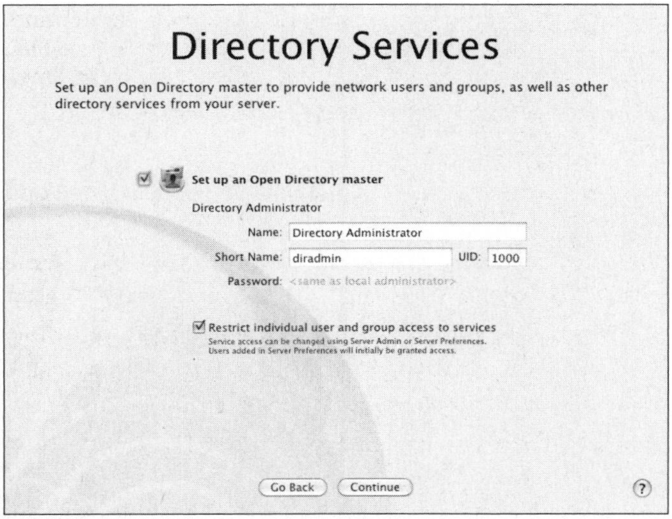

Figure 3-15: You'll see the Directory Services screen if you choose Configure Manually in the Users and Groups screen.

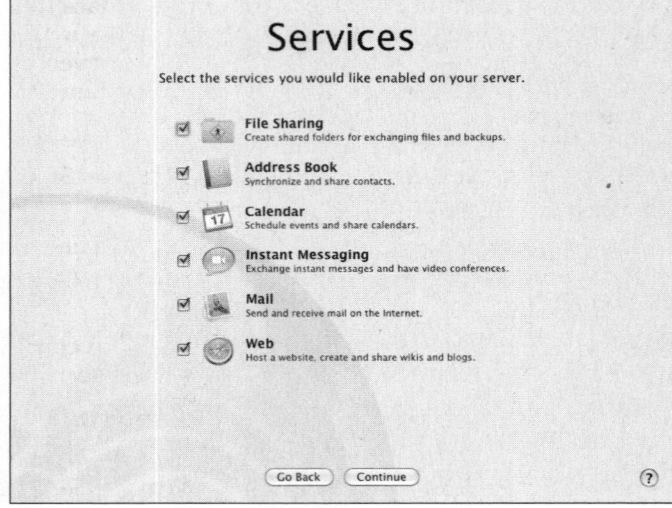

Figure 3-16: The Services screen decides which services will be set up and running.

Final configuration tasks and review

When you get to this point, you're on the homestretch. Choose a few more settings to have Server Assistant automatically configure additional services. You also review what you've done. The first screen you see after clicking Continue at the end of the preceding section is the Client Backup screen, shown in Figure 3-17.

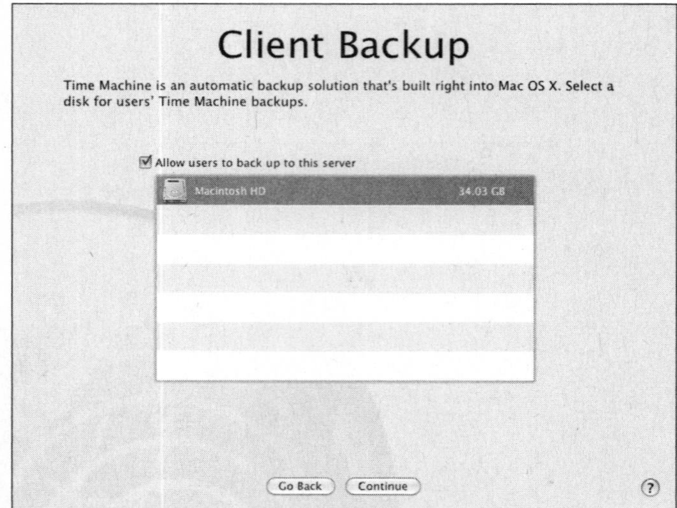

Figure 3-17: The Client Backup screen.

23. **If you want to enable users to back up their client Macs to this server with Apple's Time Machine software, click a drive (or a partition) to select it. If you don't want users to back up to this server, select Do Not Allow Backups to This Server. Click Continue when finished.**

    Time Machine comes with Mac OS X 10.5 clients and later.

24. **In the Mail Options screen that appears (see Figure 3-18), enter information related to running a mail server on this Mac.**

    The Mail Options screen enables you to add the DNS name of a relay server for outgoing mail to the Internet; it also allows you to add a message for new users.

25. **In the Review screen that appears, check through the configuration decisions you've made to ensure everything is in order:**

    a. *Click the Details button to bring up a dialog listing all the settings you've entered (see Figure 3-19).*

    b. *Save the list of settings as a text file by clicking the Save Summary button (visible in Figure 3-19) and then click Save.*

       This can be very useful for troubleshooting later.

    c. *(Optional) To save the settings as a configuration file that you can use to set up another Mac server, click Save Setup Profile and then click Save.*

       This saves the settings as a file called AutoServerSetup.plist.

26. **If something seems amiss, click the Go Back button to make changes to previous setup screens.**

Mail Options

You can use this server to send and receive email on your network and the Internet.
Messages are automatically scanned to protect against viruses and unwanted junk mail.

Relay outgoing mail through:
Some businesses and ISPs require routing all outgoing mail through a relay server. Using a relay server is recommended given your DNS configuration.
Enable SMTP relay authentication
User Name:
Password:
Send a welcome email to new users
Custom Introduction (optional)
The introduction will be included in the mail message when it is sent.
Go Back
Continue
?

Figure 3-18: The Mail Options screen.

27. **Click Set Up when done.**

    The Setting Up screen appears and lists each setup item as it's being configured. The software starts the DNS service, sets up any services, connects to directory servers, or imports data, depending on what settings you made.

When the setup is finished, you're presented with a screen that says the configuration was successful. Press the Go button to restart the server.

Once Mac OS X Server is running, there are likely some more tasks to perform. Go to the section "Post-Configuration Setup," later in this chapter.

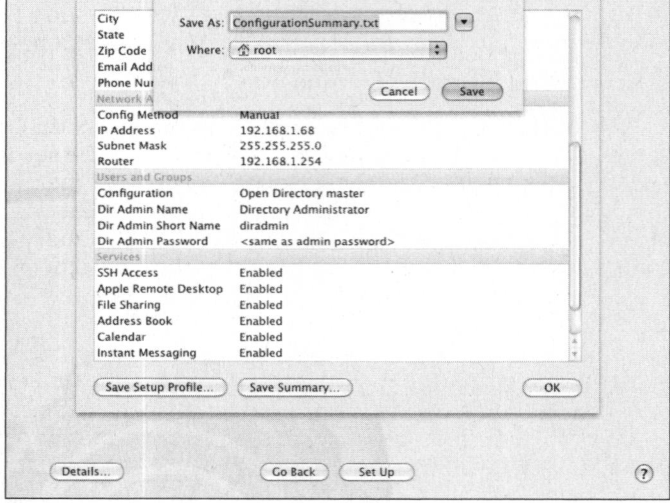

Figure 3-19: The Details dialog in the Review screen lists your settings.

Installing and Configuring Remotely

If your Mac doesn't have a display connected to it, you can install and configure Snow Leopard Server from another Mac on the network. To install remotely, you need to install some software on an administrator Mac running Mac OS X 10.6 or later. You then have to boot the server Mac from the Mac OS X Server Install DVD.

This section covers preparing the administrator Mac, followed by the remote installation procedure, and ending with the remote configuration procedure. If your server Mac has Snow Leopard Server preinstalled, skip to the section, "The remote installation," later in this chapter.

This section describes remote installation and a remote configuration with Server Assistant. You have other ways of installing and configuring remotely. One method is to use screen-sharing software, such as Apple's Apple Remote Desktop, to control the server from the administration Mac. Apple Remote Desktop is sold separately from Mac OS X Server, so I don't cover it in this book. Another way to install and configure remotely is to use Unix commands in Terminal. If you're a Unix guru, go for it. For readers of this book, I'm sticking with Server Assistant.

Connecting the server Mac to the network

Connect the server Mac to the network before you install Snow Leopard Server so that the Server Assistant can gather some information about the network. This is even more important with a remote installation, as you're relying on the network to communicate with the server.

The server Mac needs to be plugged in to the Ethernet ports that you'll use when it is active. If you have only one Ethernet port, plug the server Mac into the Ethernet switch. (Chapter 2 has information about Ethernet switches and cables.) If your Mac has more than one port, decide what you're going to do with them. For instance, you could plug one into a DSL modem or cable modem connection to the Internet and another to your local network. This would enable the server to act as an Internet gateway. (See the "Rules for IP addressing" sidebar, earlier in the chapter.)

If your server has three or more Ethernet ports, you could connect different local subnets to each port. You could also combine two Ethernet ports to work together to improve performance. This, however, might be better to configure after installing the server. See the section, "Post-Configuration Setup," later in the chapter.

Any routers on the network should be tuned in, turned on, and not dropping out. If you have a domain name service (DNS) or automatic IP addressing (DHCP) on your network, make sure they're running. DNS and DHCP can be running on other servers or in an Internet router. Sometimes your Internet service provider supplies DNS service.

Setting up an administrator Mac

The administrator Mac is another Mac on the network that you'll use to install and configure Snow Leopard Server on the server Mac. The administrator Mac can be anything from a MacBook to another Mac with Mac OS X Server already installed on it; it can also be an older PowerPC Mac as well as Intel-based Macs. The administrator Mac must be running Mac OS X 10.6 or later.

To set up an administrator Mac, you need to install Apple's server administration software on it:

1. **Insert the Mac OS X Server Install DVD into the administrator Mac.**

   You can also download the software for free. Go to `www.apple.com/downloads` and search for *server admin tools.*

2. **Open the Other Installs folder on the DVD and then double-click the ServerAdministrationSoftware.mpkg icon.**

3. **Follow directions to install the server administration tools on the hard drive.**

During this process, a folder named Server is installed in the Applications folder. Server Assistant is the software you use to both install and configure the server Mac. You can use the other applications in the Server folder to manage the server remotely.

The remote installation

This section describes how to install Mac OS X Server from another Mac on the network. If Snow Leopard Server is preinstalled on your new Mac, skip to the following section, "Configuring remotely."

You have a few limitations to installing remotely. Unlike a local install (which I describe earlier in the chapter), you can't use Disk Utility during a remote installation; you can erase a disk with Server Assistant only. You also can't use the Customize option to add extra printer drivers to the installation.

The procedure in this section assumes you have an administrator Mac set up on the network. To perform a remote installation of Snow Leopard Server, do the following:

1. **Connect a USB keyboard to the server Mac if you don't already have one connected.**

2. **Boot the server from the Mac OS X Server Install DVD by inserting the disc and turning on the Mac while holding the C key.**

   If the server has a display attached, release the C key when you see the Apple logo. If the server doesn't have a monitor, hold the Option key until you're confident that the server's booted.

Use the internal DVD drive for this procedure. If you use an external FireWire DVD drive, you need a display. In this case, hold down the Option key (not the C key) until you see the icons for the drives. Click the icon for the DVD disc and click the arrow under it.

3. **On an administrator computer, open Server Assistant by opening Server Admin and choosing Installing Remote Server from the Server menu.**
4. **In the Destination window that appears (see Figure 3-20), enter the IP address or DNS name of the Mac you want to install Snow Leopard Server on.**
5. **Enter the first eight digits of the Mac's hardware serial number and then click Continue.**

   See the section, "Locating Hardware ID Numbers," earlier in this chapter.

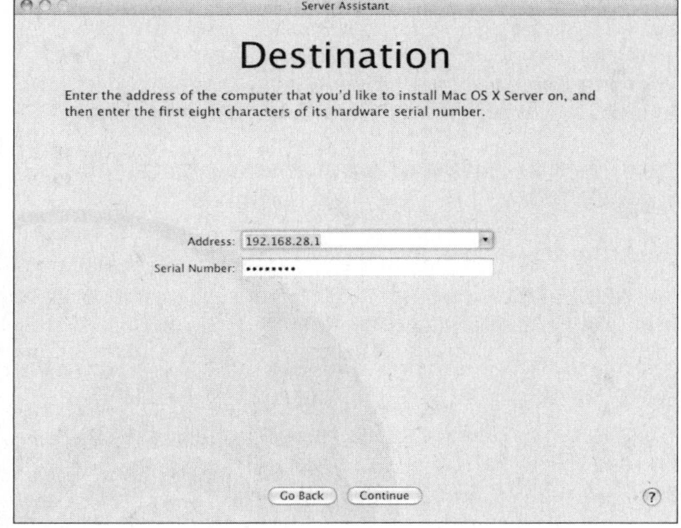

Figure 3-20: A remote install starts with identifying the target Mac with an IP address.

6. **Click through the Language and Software License screens.**

   The Target Disk window appears, displaying the drives or partitions in the Mac.
7. **Click the drive or partition on which you'll install Mac OS X Server and click Install.**

8. **If the location you selected has a version of Mac OS X or Mac OS X Server installed, choose one of these options:**
   - *Erase and Install, Using Mac OS X Extended (Journaled) format.*
   - *Upgrade Mac OS X Server:* This will upgrade the system to Mac OS X Server 10.6. This option is available only if the operating system installed is Mac OS X Server 10.4.11 or later.

Server Assistant checks the installation DVD and then begins installing Mac OS X Server, presenting a progress bar. When the installation is finished, the server Mac restarts and boots from the hard drive. You can now use Server Assistant on your remote Mac to configure the server Mac.

Configuring remotely

If you finished installing Snow Leopard Server remotely, or have a brand-new Mac with Snow Leopard Server preinstalled, you can now configure it remotely. This is similar to setting up locally, except you perform some steps first to connect to the server Mac from the administrator Mac.

You can also configure multiple Macs at the same time if they have the same hardware configuration.

1. **Turn on the server Mac if it isn't already running.**
2. **On an administrator computer, open Server Assistant by opening Server Admin and choosing Installing Remote Server from the Server menu.**

   The Servers window appears, displaying Mac OS X Servers on the local network (the IP subnet).
3. **If your administrator Mac is on the same local network as the server, but it isn't listed, or if it is on a different local network, click the Add button and type in the IP address or the DNS name of the server.**
4. **Use the Add and Remove buttons to create a list of only those servers you want to set up.**
5. **Select a server, click the Authenticate button, and type one of the following in the Password field:**
   - *For a new installation of Snow Leopard Server, type the first eight characters of the server Mac's hardware serial number.*

     (See the section, "Locating Hardware ID Numbers," earlier in this chapter.) If your Mac doesn't have a serial number, type `12345678`.
   - *For an upgraded server, enter the password of the root user account.*

6. **Click Continue.**
7. **Proceed through the configuration screens described in the section "Installing and Configuring Locally," earlier in this chapter.**

Post-Configuration Setup

The installation/configuration process with Server Assistant catches most of the main tasks in getting Snow Leopard Server up and running, but there are still a few things left. Throughout this book, I describe how to set up the various services and how to manage them. But here are a few tasks to tackle before you start serving users, most of which aren't covered elsewhere.

Reviewing the Next Steps PDF file

When Snow Leopard Server starts after installation and setup, you'll find a PDF file called "Mac OS X Next Steps" waiting for you on the desktop. The document is created by Server Assistant, tailored to your specific installation to help you get the server running. This is a handy document to read, because it makes suggestions for changes you need to make to your server and to your network, based on your configuration information.

For instance, if you choose to have the user and group accounts based on your server, the Next Steps document tells you about starting with Server Preferences, Workgroup Manager, and iCal Server Utility, and that a directory administrator has been created with the username "diradmin."

The Next Steps document can tell you if you need to configure port forwarding on a router. Even better, it gives you a list of services that you specified during the configuration, as well as a list of port numbers that are assigned to them.

DNS is an important service to have running correctly. If Server Assistant detects an incomplete DNS setup, the Next Steps document tells what the current setup can and can't do. For instance, it will tell you if the primary DNS name you entered isn't listed in the domain servers that you're using, and what to do about it.

Creating users and group accounts

If you didn't choose to import user and group accounts from another server or bind to another directory server, use Server Preferences to quickly add users and groups. This enables users to log in to the server with passwords and is the basis for e-mail accounts and other services. Here's the quick-and-dirty:

1. **Launch Server Preferences from the Dock and log in.**
2. **Click the Users icon and click the Add (+) button.**
3. **In the dialog that appears, type a username and password, and then click Create Account.**

That's it. Just lather, rinse, repeat, and you'll have a directory of users in a matter of minutes. You can also create groups by clicking the Show All button, clicking the Groups icon, and then by using Steps 2 and 3, though without a password. Click the Members tab, and then click the Edit Membership button to add users to the group.

This is just a brief description to get you up and running. There's much you can do when creating and managing directories and user accounts. Check out the chapters in Part II and Part V of this book.

Introducing DNS

Domain name service (DNS) is the system that *resolves* IP addresses to domain names. For example, when you type `dummies.com` in a Web browser, the DNS system tells your browser the IP address hosting the site at Wiley, allowing your computer to send a request to that host. Without DNS, you'd have to type the IP address of the Dummies Web site in your browser. DNS is not just for the Web, though. It's used for most types of server communications on the Internet and on your local network.

If you correctly entered DNS information during setup, Server Assistant may have done some DNS setup for you. It may be all you need, depending on your network setup and type of Internet connection. If Server Assistant didn't find any DNS server on your network, it configures Local DNS, which enables users on your subnet to access services, but without any Internet connections.

The Mac OS X Server Next Steps document on the desktop will point to some further tasks that you may need to take on with your ISP, your network, or your server. You use Server Admin to configure DNS in Snow Leopard Server.

If you turned on mail service, you'll need to configure DNS on your Mac if you want your e-mail to be used on the Internet. Specifically, you'll need to add a DNS entry called an *MX Record*. Don't worry what that means now — I show you how to do that in Chapter 14.

You don't need to be a domain name guru to run Snow Leopard Server, but DNS is a complicated subject. There are many variables and settings for different situations. In fact, I could write an entire book about DNS service. Fortunately, I don't have to, since Blair Rampling and David Dalan already wrote *DNS For Dummies* (Wiley). It focuses on Windows and Unix servers, but provides the theory and terminology about the DNS system that is common to all servers.

If your server is part of a bigger network that already has DNS servers, check with your network administrators before making changes to DNS on Snow Leopard Server. Otherwise, you could inadvertently cause problems throughout the network. Similarly, if your Internet service provider supplies your DNS service, check with them before making changes.

Understanding DNS concepts: Zones and records

When you configured Snow Leopard Server, Server Assistant may have created a *master zone with reverse lookup* and a machine record for your primary DNS name. A DNS zone is an organization entity that contains different types of records that relate to a domain. You could have a zone that contained IP addresses for servers in the `acmehigh.edu` domain, such as `www.acmehigh.edu` and `mailserver.acmehigh.edu`.

A master (primary) zone contains all of the records for the zone, and it is the Internet's authority on that domain. A secondary, or slave, zone contains copies of master zone information that is stored on another server.

A DNS zone can contain several types of records. Here are the most common:

- **Machine record, also called Address (A):** The basic record that holds the IP address for a domain name for a server or service.
- **Canonical name (CNAME), also called an alias:** You can use CNAMEs to resolve multiple domain names to one IP address (such as abc.com, abc.org, and mail183.abc.com).
- **Mail exchange (MX) record:** This identifies a computer as a mail server. (See Chapter 14 for more on MX records.) MX records are not created by Server Assistant during installation/configuration.
- **Service (SVR) record:** This identifies services that are hosted by one or more servers. It maps requests for the service to an IP address.

To a certain degree, Snow Leopard server automates working with records. Server admin asks you for information about the computer you are adding to the zone, and it creates the zone record that resolves to the computer's IP address. The focus is on the computer rather than the zone records.

Server Admin also automatically creates a reverse lookup zone when you create a master zone. A reverse lookup zone supplies a corresponding domain name when an IP address is presented by another computer.

Using Server Admin to configure DNS zones and records

To get to the DNS settings in Server Admin, select your server in the column at the left, click the triangle next to it, and then click DNS in the list of services. Finally, click the Zones icon in the toolbar. You'll see a window such as the one in Figure 3-21. In this example, there is a master zone with one machine record under it, and a reverse lookup zone. These items were created by Server Assistant during initial server setup.

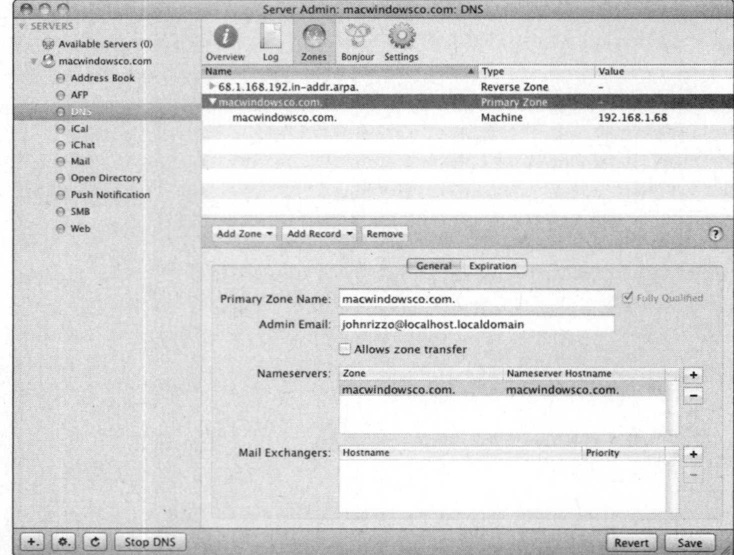

Figure 3-21: DNS configuration in Server Admin.

The top half of the DNS Zones window lists the zones — click the triangle next to a zone to display the records in it. When you click a zone or a record, the bottom half of the window displays fields that are specific to the type of zone or record. These include zone or record names, various domain names, IP addresses, or other information. To edit one of these fields, double-click it and type the new entry.

Some fields give you a choice of using a fully qualified domain name or a relative domain name. If you use the former, include a period at the end for the domain name to signify that it is an FQDN.

Adding a zone

To add a new zone, click the Add Zone button and select Primary Zone or Secondary Zone from the drop-down menu. In the Primary Zone Name field, enter the fully qualified domain name of the primary server. In the Name Servers field, enter the server that is the "authority" for the zone. For a master zone, this is usually the server that is hosting the zone, the server you are configuring. Select the Allows Zone Transfer check box to enable secondary zones to get copies of the master zone. Click the Save button when done.

Adding a record

To add a record to a zone, click a master zone, click the Add Record button (as shown in Figure 3-21), and select a record type. The bottom half of the window changes, depending on the type of record you selected. The Machine Name field is for the hostname of the computer. An SVR record requires that you enter the service type in a special format, which you can choose from a drop-down menu, as well as the port information for the service. Click the Save button when done.

Testing DNS

To check that DNS is properly configured, open Terminal (in /Applications/Utilities/) to access the command line and type `NSLOOKUP` *`hostname`*. If configured properly, the DNS server reports the IP address of the server. To check the reverse, type `NSLOOKUP ipaddress`. If configured correctly, the DNS server reports the hostname for your Mac OS X server. If either of these fails, DNS is not properly configured for your server. (See Chapter 3 for more on DNS.)

Keeping Snow Leopard Server up to date

The Mac's Software Update application automatically checks for updates that Apple recommends you run after you install Snow Leopard Server. Although it's a good idea to check for updates, I don't recommend installing them on your brand-new Snow Leopard Server installation without doing some homework. Apple creates updates to fix problems or make improvements, but despite Apple's best intentions, system updates can also break functionality or cause conflicts with third-party software. You may want to skip an update if it's known to cause problems that would impact what you do with the server.

So instead of blindly installing Apple updates, here's your homework assignment:

- Research what others are seeing.
- Configure Software Update properly.
- Download and test the update on another Mac or in a virtual machine.

Researching the update

Check up on what other people are experiencing with the update. Then, if you decide to go for the update, test it first.

You can check Web sites that cover Apple software updates to see what other users are experiencing with the most recent update. If a lot of people are reporting the same problems with third-party networking or server software, you may want to hold off on the upgrade. Are people reporting that the update fixes any problems that you're seeing? Don't take Apple's word for it.

Here are three Web sites that report problems with Mac updates:

- **MacWindows:** This is my Web site, running since 1997, which focuses on problems and solutions with Macs and PCs working together. When a new version of Mac OS X Server or a client is released, I report problems or bugs that people experience.

  ```
  www.macwindows.com
  ```

- **MacInTouch:** Ric Ford's site specializes in all things Macintosh.

  ```
  www.macintouch.com
  ```

- **Apple Discussions forums:** Click the link for Mac OS X Server 10.6 and check for problem reports.

  ```
  www.apple.com/discussions
  ```

One report of a problem doesn't usually indicate a widespread issue, but if you see the same problem reported on multiple Web sites, beware.

This is true for all your client Macs and Windows PCs. Don't install upgrades for them without researching first and testing the upgrade on one machine before rolling it out on all your clients.

Configure Software Update properly

On every Mac, Software Update is available in the Apple menu. Its preference window, however, is accessible in System Preferences by clicking the Software Update icon. As one of the final touches on your Snow Leopard Server installation, open this preference panel and edit the settings. The default settings aren't exactly dangerous, but they are more appropriate for a client computer than for a server.

By default, Software Update is set to check for updates weekly and to download them. Don't worry, it doesn't install, download, and update; it brings up a dialog asking you if you want to install the update. To prevent this, in the Software Update Preferences window, leave the Download Important Updates Automatically check box turned off.

You might also want to deselect the Check for Updates check box so that the server isn't regularly checking for updates by itself. Best practice is to use the Check Now button to manually check for updates, or simply launch Software Update.

If you want to update your server to a version later than what you have but earlier than the latest, you can. Apple offers older updates at its Web site, which you can download with a Web browser. You can find updates here: `www.apple.com/support/downloads`.

Downloading and testing updates

Test an upgrade on a spare Mac or in a virtual machine before you roll it out on your server. This means downloading the upgrade on your test machine, *not* on your server.

Here's how to safely download an update:

1. **Choose Apple menu⇨Software Update.**

   Software Update automatically checks for new updates. These could be updates to the operating system (a Mac OS X 10.6.x update), updates to components (such as Java), or security updates.

   Security updates are important, but they have also been known to cause compatibility issues.

   Software Update tells you whether it found anything.

2. **If Software Update did find something, click the Show Details button to display the updates.**

   Never install an update without knowing what it is, even on a test machine.

   Software Update shows you a list of the updates it found.

3. **Select the check boxes next to the updates that you want to install.**

4. **Click the Install button.**

You can now test the update. Try replicating the kinds of things your users do. Make sure you test it with both Mac and Windows clients.

Changing Ethernet addressing

After your initial setup, you may need to change the IP addresses of your Ethernet port(s) or change the addressing scheme from automatic (DHCP) to manual (static). You can do this in System Preferences:

1. **Open System Preferences from the Dock or the Apple menu.**
2. **Click the Network icon.**

   The Network window appears.
3. **On the left, you see a list of network ports, including AirPort. Click the Ethernet port you want to configure.**
4. **Click the Configure pop-up menu and choose the type of address you'll use (typically, DHCP or Manually).**
5. **Type in the IP addressing and domain name information in the appropriate fields.**
6. **Click Apply.**

After you change an IP address, you may have to update other settings, such as DNS.

Installation problems

If you're having problems installing or configuring Snow Leopard Server, third-party hardware could be the cause. Generally, it's best to have any internal hardware devices installed in the Mac during Snow Leopard Server installation. But several known conditions may require removing hardware.

For instance, bad RAM (random access memory) can prevent the server Mac from restarting during or after the installation process. *Bad* in this case can either mean defective or not up to Apple's specifications. If you added non-Apple RAM before the installation and are having problems, try removing it.

If you can't start Snow Leopard Server, check to see whether you have a SCSI interface card installed in the server Mac. If so, you may need to attach either a SCSI drive or a SCSI terminator to one of the ports on the card. If that doesn't work, remove the card. Try replacing it after the installation is complete, with the SCSI port terminated or connected to a drive. If Snow Leopard Server still doesn't work, contact the manufacturer to see whether there's an issue with it.

Third-party video cards can also cause problems. If you're having trouble installing, remove the card and try installing Mac OS X Server remotely.

Chapter 4

Running Servers in Virtual Machines

In This Chapter

- Discovering what you can do with virtual machines
- Choosing virtualization software
- Considering hardware requirements
- Installing a guest OS in a virtual machine

Running Snow Leopard Server on a Mac is a powerful addition to a network. Running two Snow Leopard Servers can be even more powerful. Common sense tells you that you need two Macs — but common sense might not know about virtualization.

Maybe you wish you could run a Windows or Linux server on a Mac. While you're wishing, how about running Windows, Linux, and Snow Leopard Server all at the same time, all on the same Mac? You can with *virtualization,* which enables you to run multiple operating systems on one computer. Each operating system is completely separate from the others, running in its own virtual machine.

Virtualization has great benefits, including easy and flexible testing of server setups before rolling them out for your users. For production servers, virtualization can save you money in hardware, add flexibility, and make for quicker disaster recovery. Virtualization has limitations as well, and for production servers, you'll want the higher-end Macs — a Mac Pro or an Xserve — with lots of RAM.

The Reality of Virtualization

Macs are the only computers that allow you to run Mac OS X along with Windows and Linux. Virtual machines on non-Apple PCs can't run Mac OS X.

Apple doesn't permit running Mac OS X on non-Apple hardware in its user license agreement, so the virtualization software makers don't enable it.

Figure 4-1 shows a Mac running two virtual machines — Snow Leopard Server (left) and Windows 7 (right). Both are running on a Mac OS X host, (with the grass desktop). In each virtual machine window, you can control that operating system as you normally would run applications, configure settings, and access the Internet. When the virtual machine is a server, users on the network access it as they would any other server. If multiple virtual machines run on a server Mac, the users see each as a separate server.

For the latest news, tips, and troubleshooting information about running virtual machines on Macs, visit MacWindows (`www.macwindows.com`), a Web site I've been running since 1997.

How virtualization works

With virtualization, there's a host *operating system (OS)* and one or more guest OS's. The host OS boots the real computer (in this book, Mac OS X or Mac OS X Server). On a Mac, a guest OS can be Mac OS X Server, Windows, Linux, and Unix — but not the user version of Mac OS X. Figure 4-2 shows the relationship between the host OS and the guest OS.

Figure 4-1: Snow Leopard Server (left) and Windows 7 (right) running in virtual machines.

Each guest OS runs in a *virtual machine,* which is a kind of a virtual reality for the guest OS. The guest OS thinks it's running on a real computer. Although real hardware's behind the scenes, the guest OS doesn't have direct control over the hard drive, graphics, and other hardware: These pieces of hardware are virtualized in the virtual machine.

For instance, a virtual machine's hard drive (the boot drive) is actually a file on the host Mac. This file can be dozens of gigabytes in size, containing the complete guest operating system and its applications, settings, and documents. The virtual hard drive file is stored on the Mac's real hard drive, but the guest OS doesn't control the entire drive. The virtualization software creates the virtual machine and keeps the guest OS believing that it's living in a real computer. Kind of like *The Matrix,* but without Keanu Reeves.

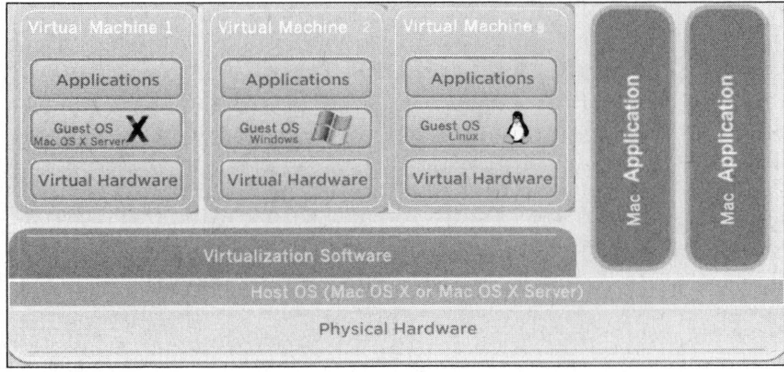

Figure 4-2: A diagram of how virtualization works.

Benefits of virtualization

The ability to run Mac and Windows servers on one Mac is not only useful, but you can also save money by consolidating multiple servers on one machine. Virtualization can also make deployment easier and more flexible. And, it's convenient for testing.

Flexibility in testing servers

Even if you aren't going to run your servers in virtual machines, testing them in virtual machines has benefits. You don't have to dedicate a Mac to the task of testing a server. Test Snow Leopard Server in a virtual machine running on a workstation, or test multiple Mac, Windows, and Linux servers on one Mac.

You can also create multiple server configurations to test different settings, different services turned on, and different third-party applications installed. With virtual machines, you can test new versions of a server alongside the older versions in order to run comparisons. To do this without virtualization, you'd have to use multiple hard drives or erase the hard drive and create multiple partitions. You'd have to reboot the Mac every time you needed to run a different configuration or use multiple Macs.

If you're going to run your production server in a virtual machine, test it in one. After you get your test server configured and tweaked just as you like it, you can easily migrate it to a production server that you want to run in a virtual machine. You don't have to install server software and any extra applications and then configure it all over again. Just move the virtual machine files over to the server Mac.

Server consolidation

Many servers use only a portion of the capabilities of the hardware's processor, RAM, and disk storage performance. Xserve can hold eight processor cores and 32GB of RAM, but few servers would take advantage of all this power. Info-Tech, a research firm, estimates that most servers use 20 percent of their capacity. Putting multiple servers in virtual machines on one computer takes advantage of hardware that'd be wasted. This is known as *server consolidation.*

How many servers you can consolidate with virtualization depends on how heavily they're used and how processor-intensive they are (see Chapter 2 for types of server uses). You can run anywhere from three to a dozen virtual servers on one Mac. One Oregon school district replaced 44 computers running Mac and Windows servers with 7 Xserve computers running Parallels Server virtualization software — thus eliminating 37 computers. This not only saved the district money in terms of hardware, but it saved money from reduced electricity and cooling costs.

Some of this cost savings from server consolidation is offset by the need for server hardware equipped with multiple fast processors and lots of RAM. You may also need multiple Ethernet cards in the server Mac to avoid a bottleneck caused by multiple servers accessing the network.

Faster, easier deployment and disaster recovery

You can easily clone a virtual machine and move it to another computer. This prevents you from having to run the entire server installer to create a second server to take the load off another or to run some different services on the server software. Just create a clone and adjust the settings as needed.

Running a server in a virtual machine also enables you to quickly replace it in case of a failure or data corruption. The strategy is to run the server OS and server software in the virtual machine, but store the user data somewhere else, on another hard drive or other storage medium. When the server goes south, you don't need to troubleshoot, reinstall the OS, or reconfigure it: Just replace the entire virtual machine with a backup copy, and the server is back up and running.

If you want to run an open source OS and server software, you can download preconfigured virtual machines for free, entirely skipping the operating system installation procedure. I describe this in the section, "Virtual appliances," later in this chapter.

Virtualizing Windows clients on Macs

Although this book is about servers, I want to mention that running Windows in virtual machines on users' computers (clients) can give you some of the same benefits of deployment and disaster recovery, which I describe in the preceding section. If you have one or more Windows applications that your Mac users need to run, you have to install and configure Windows and the programs only once, in a virtual machine. You can then copy that virtual machine to all the users.

You can't run a Mac OS X client in a virtual machine, however.

Virtual appliances

A *virtual appliance* is a preconfigured virtual machine, complete with operating system and applications. You don't have to install the OS or the server software on it. Just download the virtual appliance and fire it up with your virtualization software. The major virtualization companies offer free virtual appliances for downloading that contain open source operating systems, such as Ubuntu, Linux, or BSD Unix. They come pre-installed with one or more servers. You'll find virtual appliances preconfigured with DHCP and DNS servers, as well as database, mail, Web, and wiki servers.

Parallels, the maker of Parallels Desktop for Mac and Parallels Server for Mac, offers free virtual appliances at `www.parallels.com/ptn/download/va`. When you download a Parallels virtual machine, choose the Mac download. You get a virtual machine in a standard Mac DMG image file that mounts on the desktop. Inside is an installer that automatically creates a virtual machine in Parallels Desktop or Parallels Server.

VMware, the makers of VMware Fusion for Mac, also offers free open source virtual appliances as well as commercial virtual appliances for sale from commercial developers, such as Red Hat Linux. Check them out at `www.vmware.com/appliances`.

VMware's virtual appliances don't have Mac-specific installers, so you have to install them from within VMware Fusion. Virtual appliances from VMware work on all VMware virtualization software for Mac, Windows, and Linux.

Using Boot Camp versus a virtual machine

Intel-powered Macs running Mac OS X 10.5 and later include Boot Camp software from Apple. After Boot Camp is installed, it turns the Mac into a dual-boot machine, with the ability to start up from either Mac OS X or Windows. The main benefit to Boot Camp over virtualization is that you can get somewhat better performance running Windows with Boot Camp than in a virtual machine. This makes it popular for fans of Windows games.

But for servers, Boot Camp isn't a good option. Boot Camp runs only one operating system at a time, which means your only use would be to repurpose a Mac for use as a Windows server.

Another problem is that at this point, Apple doesn't officially support Windows Server with Boot Camp. Blog posts around the Internet have reported running Windows Server 2008 with Boot Camp, though it isn't a straightforward process due to driver issues. If you're interested in a weekend project, you can find some directions here: `www.harbar.net/articles/mbptb3.aspx`.

To check out Boot Camp, launch the Boot Camp Assistant, which resides in the Macs' Utilities folder inside the Applications folder. You'll also need a Microsoft Windows installation disc handy.

The virtual appliances downloaded from VMware and Parallels don't work on each other's virtualization software. However, both companies supply software that converts the other company's virtual machines into their own formats.

When you start an OS from a downloaded virtual machine, the OS presents you with a login screen. You'll find a login name and password either on the Web site or in a readme file with the download.

Software licensing issues

Cloning and deploying virtual machines can save you money in hardware, but you still need a software license for each instance of Snow Leopard Server or Windows Server (or Windows client) that you run. If you have two copies of Snow Leopard Server running on a Mac, you need to pay for each copy and use separate serial numbers on each.

The same is true for Windows Servers. But, if your organization runs a lot of Windows Server virtual machines, it may own a Microsoft Windows Server Datacenter Edition license, which includes the ability to run an unlimited number of virtual machines running Windows Server — in which case, you can clone away.

Open source operating systems can be replicated without fees, but don't confuse them with some commercial Linux operating systems (such as Novell Open Enterprise Server) that do have license fees.

Choosing Virtualization Software

Three major companies make virtualization software for Macs: Parallels, VMware, and Sun. In a nutshell, here are the choices:

- **Parallels Server:** Costing over $1,200, Parallels Server is meant for serious virtualization of multiple production servers on one Mac. It includes management software for the servers.

  `www.parallels.com`

- **Parallels Desktop:** A user-level, or desktop, application that costs under $100, Parallels Desktop focuses on integration with Mac OS X.
- **VMware Fusion:** Another user-level virtualization package, Fusion is very similar to Parallels Desktop and similarly priced.

  `www.vmware.com`

- **Sun xVM VirtualBox:** Free for personal use and $30 per copy per year.

  `www.sun.com/software/products/virtualbox`

You can use the desktop versions for testing servers or for running services that don't use a lot of system resources. A desktop version won't let you assign as much of the Mac hardware to a virtual machine Parallels Server.

Choosing a desktop virtualization package

Among the three desktop products, VirtualBox has some fans, but it arrived later than Parallels Desktop and VMware Fusion, and it is generally not as advanced. For individuals, the $0 price tag is a plus, but for businesses, the $30 per year license fee will end up costing the same as the others.

Parallels Desktop and VMware Fusion are roughly equivalent. With each new version, one pulls slightly ahead of the other in terms of features, so at any given month, one might be ahead of the other. Both products can import virtual machines from each other, so if you decide to switch, you can move over your virtual machines.

One reason to use VMware Fusion is that it's compatible with its virtual machine formats that run on Windows. Parallels Desktop is compatible with Parallels' Windows products, but VMware is much more widespread. So if you had a Windows server running on the Mac, you could move to a Windows server running VMware's products without having to convert the virtual machine to another format.

On the other hand, Parallels Desktop virtual machines can run in Parallels Server. So if you decided to upgrade, you could easily move a virtual machine, running Snow Leopard Server, Windows, or Linux, to Parallels Server.

When you might use Parallels Server

Parallels Server is the only server-level virtualization software for Macs. Parallels Server costs significantly more than the desktop version but has performance advantages over it. For instance, if your Mac has four or more processor cores, Parallels Server allows you to assign up to four virtual processor cores for each machine, whereas the desktop virtualization applications support up to two cores per virtual machine. You can allocate up to 15 cores total for all virtual machines, more than the 8 possible cores in a server Mac. Parallels Server is also optimized for the Xserve and Mac Pro.

A Parallels Server virtual drive can be larger than the desktop version, up to 2 terabytes (TB — one terabyte equals 1,024 gigabytes). Parallels Server can support up to four 2TB drive channels per virtual machine: two SCSI storage channels and two IDE channels.

Parallels Server for Mac includes a Management Console application that enables you to manage multiple physical servers and applications in virtual machines. Management Console also provides the ability to create a virtual machine template that you can use in multiple virtual machines. The software automatically creates a new IP address for each virtual machine. You can use Management Console on any Mac on the network.

Another feature of Parallels Server is that it runs not as an application, but in a low-level program known as a `deamon`. This means it runs in the background when the Mac boots up, even before the administrator logs in. You don't have an application to launch.

Parallels Server for Mac also includes several tools for creating or importing virtual machines. A migration tool can move setups of physical Mac and Windows servers into virtual machines. You can also import a virtual machine from Parallels Desktop, VMware, and Microsoft formats.

Real and Virtual Hardware Requirements

Like any piece of software, virtualization software requires certain minimum hardware on the Mac. But the software also has *virtual* hardware requirements, which consist of settings in the virtualization software. The most important settings are those for memory and the number of processors. These settings aren't as obvious as they may seem.

To change settings, the virtual machine must be shut down from the guest OS. To get to the configuration window, VMware Fusion and Parallels Desktop both have a Virtual Machine menu. In Parallels, choose Settings from this menu after you select a virtual machine. In VMware, choose Configure. A settings window appears. Figure 4-3 shows the VMware Fusion configuration window, but the other virtualization packages have similar windows.

The following sections describe both real and virtual hardware requirements.

Figure 4-3: The hardware settings window for VMware Fusion.

Memory

For a test machine, have a Mac with at least 4GB of RAM. You can run one or two virtual machines with good results. For a production Mac, have at least 4GB for the host OS (Mac OS X or OS X Server), plus 2GB for each virtual machine that will be running at the same time. If you have a lot going on in the host OS or in the virtual machines, you'll want more. For Mac Pro or Xserve, this isn't a problem. This isn't to say that you should assign 2MB for a virtual machine (which you do in the settings window of the virtualization software). The amount of RAM you specify for the virtual machine doesn't correspond to the amount of RAM the OS usually requires.

Assigning RAM to a virtual machine is tricky. Too little RAM, and the virtual machine runs slowly. But assign too much RAM, and the host Mac OS X might not have enough, which slows down the entire Mac.

What is a bare metal hypervisor?

You may see *bare metal* and *hypervisor* in the documentation and press coverage of virtualization products. *Bare metal* is when guest OS's run on a very small piece of software — a *hypervisor,* which runs on the computer hardware without a host OS.

There are some advantages to the bare metal approach. Unlike a host OS, a hypervisor can't be changed or adjusted, so it's impervious to viruses. Running virtual machines on a simple hypervisor instead of a complex host OS also lessens the chance of glitches in the host OS taking down all the virtual machines.

None of this applies to Macs. As this book was going to press, no virtualization products support running a bare metal hypervisor on Macs. The software developers say that Apple doesn't permit it, again going back to Apple's desire to keep Mac OS X from running on non-Apple hardware. If Apple allowed a virtual machine running Mac OS X Server to run on a bare metal hypervisor, it could easily be moved to a Dell machine and be run there. By requiring Mac OS X as a host OS, Apple keeps Mac virtual machines on its own hardware.

For instance, on a Mac with 4GB of RAM, I find that running Snow Leopard Server in a virtual machine runs the best at VMware's default 1024MB setting — even though Snow Leopard Server requires a minimum of 2GB on a real machine. Increasing the RAM allocation slows it down. On a Mac with more real RAM, increasing the virtual machine's RAM allocation helps.

Processors

The more virtual machines you run and the more you do with them, the more powerful processors you'll need. In addition to speed, faster processors have more processing cores. The processors in modern Macs have either two cores (dual core) or four cores (quad core). In essence, a dual-core processor is two processors in one chip, and a quad core is four processors in one chip. The Mac Pro and Xserve can have two four-core processors, for a total of eight.

With virtualization software, you can assign one or more processing cores to any given virtual machine. Some virtualization software refers to a processing core as a *processor;* others call it a *CPU (central processing unit).* The desktop virtualization programs allow you to assign one or two cores to a virtual machine. Parallels Server allows you to assign up to 4 CPUs per virtual machine, for a total of 15 for all the virtual machines running at one time on a Mac. So if you want to put a processor-intensive service in a virtual machine, you may need Parallels Server and Mac Pro or Xserve.

Like the RAM settings, the processor settings aren't what you might expect. I find that on a Mac with a Core 2 Duo (two processing cores), a Snow Leopard

Server virtual machine runs best by assigning it two processors. You might think that assigning two cores on a two-core Mac leaves nothing for the host OS. You'd be wrong. Assigning only one processor to the Snow Leopard Server virtual machine slows down both the guest OS and the host OS.

Drive storage

You need enough free hard drive space for each virtual machine you run. Snow Leopard Server requires at least 20GB, but it's good to have 30GB of hard drive space available for each virtual machine.

Guest OS's can also access storage outside the virtual machine, where you might keep your user data. This could be an internal partition, a hard drive, a RAID, an external RAID array, or a SAN.

To make use of outside storage, a virtual machine maps the physical drive to a small image file. The operating system thinks the image file is the storage device, but the file points to the physical device. Virtual machines also use drive mapping to access the Mac's DVD drive. You can set the mapping to a DVD disk image, such as a DMG or an ISO file.

Installing an OS in a Virtual Machine

Installing an operating system in a virtual machine is similar to installing an OS on a physical computer but with a few extra steps at the beginning to create the virtual machine into which you'll install the OS.

Virtualization software won't let you use the remote Snow Leopard Server installation procedure I describe in Chapter 3. With Parallels Server, however, you can create a virtual machine on a machine remotely from another computer on the network.

The following sections look at some of the issues with a desktop virtualization application as well as with Parallels Server.

Installing an OS in a desktop version

The procedures for installing an OS in Parallels Desktop, VMware Fusion, and VirtualBox are very similar. Here, I use Parallels Desktop as an example:

1. **Insert the Mac OS X Server Install DVD into the Mac.**

2. **Launch Parallels Desktop.**
3. **In the Welcome to Parallels Desktop window, click Run Windows on Your Mac.**

   If the Welcome window doesn't appear, choose File⇨New Virtual Machine.
4. **Click Continue at the Introduction screen.**
5. **In the Operating System Detection window, select the Real CD/DVD-ROM Drive option (see Figure 4-4).**

   Select the CD/DVD Image option if you have a disk image of the Mac OS X Server Install DVD. (A disk image has a filename ending in `.iso` or `.dmg`.) Click the Choose button to specify the disk image file.

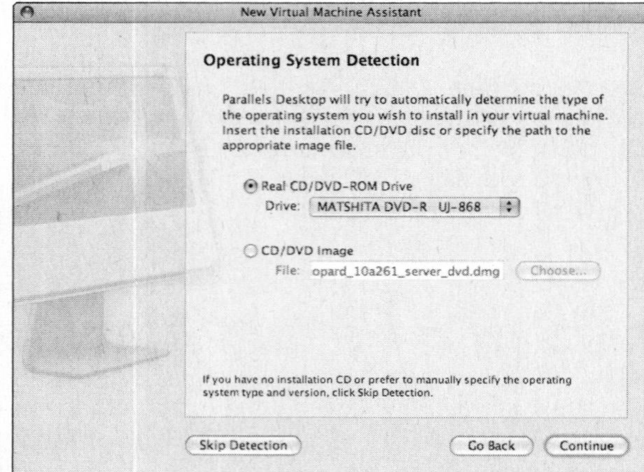

Figure 4-4: Parallels Desktop's Operating System Detection window.

6. **Click Continue.**

   If the software can't detect the operating system you're installing, it presents a window where you choose it from a pop-up menu.

   The Detected System window appears (see Figure 4-5).
7. **(Optional) Change the name of the virtual machine.**
8. **Click the Advanced button (not the Create button).**

   A window in which you can set the number of CPUs and RAM for the virtual machine appears. You can do this later, but the installation process could be very slow if the settings aren't right.
9. **Set the number of CPUs (processor cores) and the amount of RAM you want for the virtual machine (see Figure 4-6).**

New Virtual Machine Assistant
Detected System: Snow Leopard Server
Specify the virtual machine name and location:
Name: Snow Leopard Server 10.6
More Options
Create icon on Desktop
Share virtual machine with other Mac users
Location: nrizzo/Documents/Parallels Choose...
Advanced... Go Back Create

Figure 4-5: The Detected System window in Parallels Desktop.

10. **Click OK and then click the Create button in the Detected System window.**

    A window appears, telling you that a virtual machine has been created. This is true, but it's empty — you still need to install the OS.

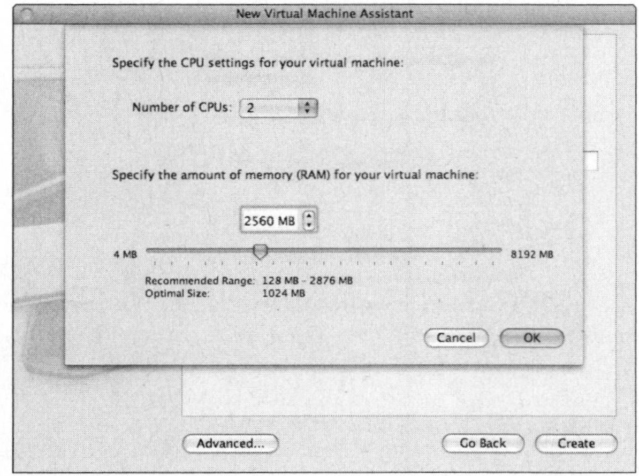

Figure 4-6: Configure RAM and CPU settings.

11. **Click Start.**

    The virtual machine boots from the Mac OS X Server Install DVD — within a window on your Mac. You first see a black screen, followed by the Mac OS X Server Installer starting up in the virtual machine.

12. **Click through the installation screens, which I describe in Chapter 3.**

After the Mac OS X Server is installed in the virtual machine, the virtual machine reboots and presents Apple's Server Assistant and the configuration screens, which I describe in Chapter 3.

Installing an OS in Parallels Server

You create a virtual machine from Parallels Management Console, running either on the server or on another computer on the network. Figure 4-7 shows the Console running on the server with one virtual machine installed on it. The left column lists the servers on the network that have Parallels Server installed. These could be Mac, Windows, or Linux computers. In Figure 4-7, only one computer, `localhost`, is listed. This is the host computer. Under this is a list of virtual machines on that Mac — in this case, one.

To add a new virtual machine with Parallels Management Console, insert the operating system's Mac OS X Server Install DVD in the server Mac and do the following:

1. **In the left column of Parallels Management Console, click the server on which you want to create the new virtual machine.**
2. **Click the New Virtual Machine link below Operations.**

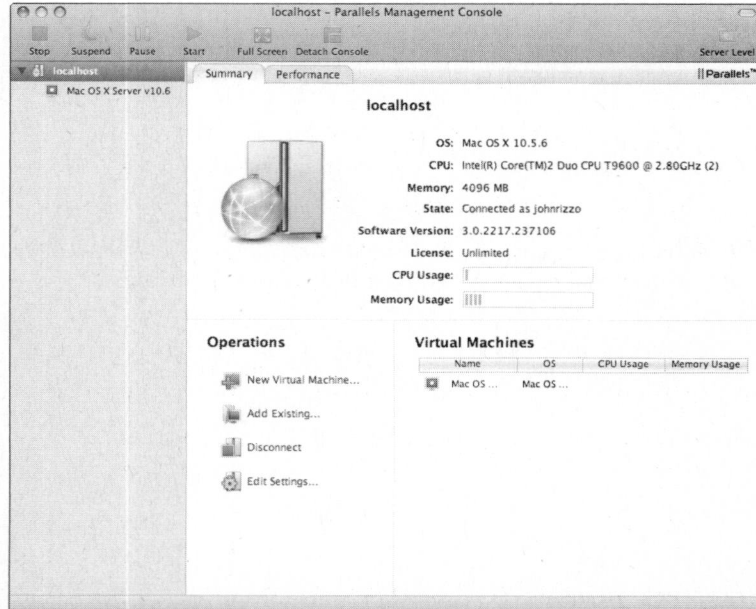

Figure 4-7: Parallels Management Console with one virtual machine installed.

3. **Click through the introduction screens to the Select Operating System screen. Choose an operating system and version from the pop-up menus and click Continue.**

   If you choose Windows, the Virtual Machine Type window appears with the three choices shown in Figure 4-8. If you selected Mac OS X, Linux, or another OS, you see only Typical and Custom options. I recommend selecting Custom to ensure that RAM and processor settings are okay.

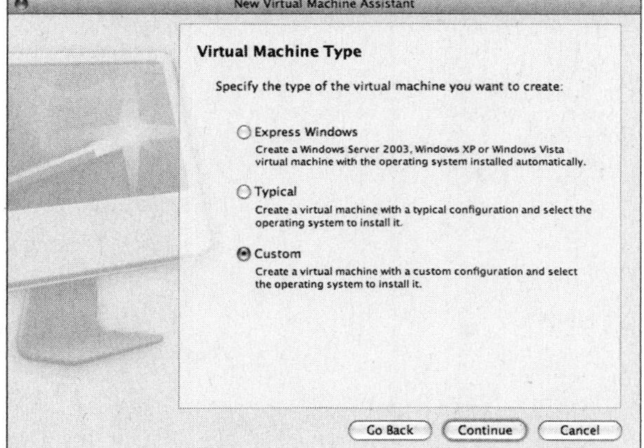

Figure 4-8: Types of installations for Parallels Server virtual machines.

4. **Select a virtual machine type and click Continue.**
5. **Select the number of CPUs (processor cores) and set the RAM for the virtual machine.**
6. **Click New Image File in the Hard Disk Options window.**

   The New Virtual Hard Disk window opens, as shown in Figure 4-9.
7. **Select the Expanding Disk option and choose a maximum size for the virtual hard drive in the Size field. Click Continue.**
8. **Select Bridged Networking in the Networking Type window to give the virtual machine its own IP address. Then click Continue.**
9. **Click through the next few screens, retaining the default selections.**
10. **In the Name and Location window, type a name for the virtual machine. Click the Create button.**

    A virtual machine is now created, and the OS installer launches.

You can create a copy of an existing virtual machine without going through the process of installing a guest OS. In Parallels Management Console, click the virtual machine you want to clone. Under Operations, click the Clone button to create a copy of a virtual machine. Or, if you plan to deploy multiple copies on one or more computers, click Clone to Template.

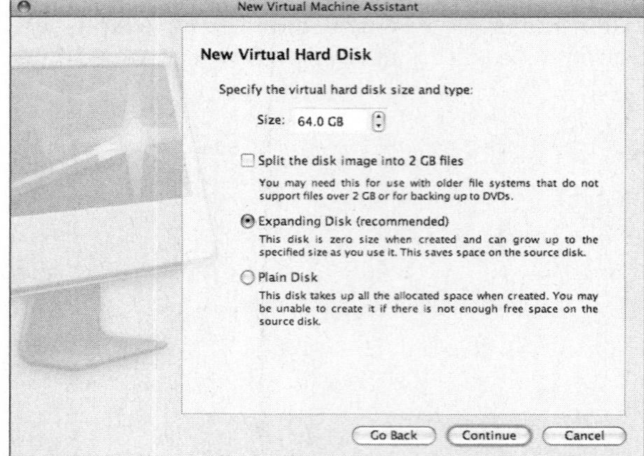

Figure 4-9: Specifying a type of virtual hard drive.

Distributing services in multiple VMs

Parallels Server is designed to run many virtual machines on one high-end Mac server. When given a choice between running a bunch of services in one virtual machine (or real machine) or spreading out the services in multiple virtual machines on the same computer, choose the latter. You get overall better performance and more efficient use of the Mac hardware by cloning the virtual machine and running different services on each clone.

For instance if you run a Windows server in a virtual machine with Exchange Server, it's best to assign four CPUs to this virtual machine and dedicate it for running only Exchange: Run other Windows services in other virtual machines. You can put a Microsoft Active Directory server in another Windows virtual machine. You might be able to pair it up with lightweight services, such as DNS (domain name service). If you run Active Directory in a Windows virtual machine, it might make sense to run Open Directory in a Snow Leopard Server virtual machine on the same Mac.

Other services might be fine in a single virtual machine. Less processor-intensive services, such as Web, e-mail, and file servers that have relatively few simultaneous users, probably wouldn't tax a virtual machine.

Part II

Creating and Maintaining User Accounts and Directories

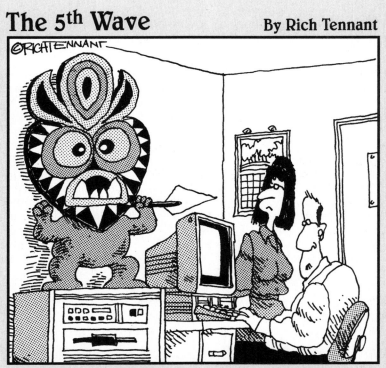

The 5th Wave By Rich Tennant

©RICHTENNANT

"I'm not saying I believe in anything. All I know is since it's been there our server is running 50% faster."

In this part . . .

Users are the reason for servers. Keeping track of the users is the reason for much that's in Snow Leopard Server. This part focuses on managing those users and their computers, covering the range from small networks to large. I begin by describing how to create and maintain user and group accounts. I describe *user authentication,* the process in which a user connects his- or herself to the computer with a name and password. The server also provides *authorization,* the process of controlling access to files and services.

The more users and computers, the bigger the user management task. If you have more than a few users, you may want to set up Directory Services, which let you manage not only user accounts, but the computers themselves. Here, I describe how to use Mac OS X Server's Open Directory to centrally store information about the users and the computers in a single place. A shared directory separates the user from a specific computer so that a user can log in from any computer and access her home directory. This part also describes how you can use Open Directory to set computer policies that determine what software users can install on their computers or what settings the user will experience when he logs in.

On large networks, you may need to access other directory servers hosted on Windows servers. That's no problem for Snow Leopard Server: I describe how to use Mac OS X Server with Microsoft Active Directory.

Chapter 5

Controlling Access with Directories

In This Chapter

- Getting familiar with account types in a directory
- Binding your clients and servers to directories
- Authenticating with LDAP and Kerberos

When your entire network infrastructure entails a computer on a desk in your living room, management of your user accounts and preferences is simple and straightforward. The operating system you prefer makes no difference; your account and data are stored in one physical location. Add a second computer, and maybe a laptop for travel, and you now have two or three sets of user accounts, passwords, and data. You'll spend more time synchronizing your data, but otherwise it's largely the same process.

But multiply the computers by tens, hundreds, or thousands and you see how managing users and data becomes beyond cumbersome in a large network. The solution is to create network directory services to aid managing many computer systems and users. A *network directory* is essentially a shared list of users, accounts, and resources that reside on the network. A directory can reside in one server computer or can be handled by dozens of servers on a large network.

Directory services also handles the job of *authenticating* users, which confirms the identity of users logging in from a client computer. Directory services handles authentication for other services, such as e-mail or file sharing, or to the entire network, or for the entire network at once — known as *single sign-on.*

Snow Leopard Server can host a directory for your network of Mac, Windows, and Linux computers. It can also make use of a directory residing on other servers. And it can help integrate your Mac users into a Windows-based Active Directory network.

Snow Leopard Server supports two directory brands: it can host the open source Open Directory, and connect to Microsoft Active Directory. These are described in Chapters 6 and 7, respectively

This chapter describes the basic concepts about directory services, and how they apply to Snow Leopard Server.

Defining Directories

You're already familiar with a common directory example: the telephone book. Phone books contain a set of information organized in a certain manner: an alphabetical list of people and businesses, their addresses, and their phone numbers. The white and yellow pages are different containers of information (people and businesses, respectively), and phone books are organized and published according to geographic areas.

Electronic directories are similar, containing a hierarchical list of data that describes user accounts, attributes, and preferences, and can contain information about network resources such as printers. The data in a directory may be separated into containers associated with different physical locations, departments, or other conditions.

The structure of a directory's database — the specific types of data it stores and how it's stored — is called a *schema*. Strictly speaking, the directory consists of the schema and the data. *Directory services* is a collection of software that is the framework that shares the information among servers and clients and provides authentication.

Local and shared directories and domains

In most of today's operating systems — both clients and servers — account data and information about the computer is stored in a local database on each system. These databases of users can't be distributed among multiple computers. Regardless of any other choices you make for managing users, you'll always have a local database of user accounts on each computer.

But, if users had to access servers using the server's local directory, the administrator would have to set up accounts on every server machine. And, users might find themselves using different passwords for different file servers.

So, networks use a shared directory instead to enable sharing of the user accounts among multiple servers. Sharing a directory enables users to log on to multiple file servers using the same account and password. Users that are *bound,* or connected with, a directory can access any of the services that reside on servers that are also bound to the same directory. The use of shared directories goes much further, allowing administrators to manage clients and set password policies. It also enables servers to host home folders for computer users. A server-based home folder means that a user can log on to any computer on the network and have access to her data and settings.

Local and shared directories are also sometimes referred to as local and shared *domains;* these terms are used interchangeably. In this context, a domain doesn't refer to registered Internet domains, but is used in the sense of *spheres of influence.* A local domain only has an effect on a computer. A shared domain covers a certain area of the network.

Don't get confused if you see directory domains that end in `.com` or `.net` like Internet domains. Much of this has to do with directory service's heavy reliance on DNS (domain name server) (described in Chapter 2), which you see if you set up a directory in Chapter 6.

Account types in a directory

In network directories, accounts come in many flavors, not just the user account. They include

- **Users:** Usually an individual, but not necessarily unique to a single person. Several individuals who manage a server could access an administrator account; for example. User accounts are the most common you encounter and manage in a directory.
- **Groups:** Combine one or more individual user accounts to form a group account. Common use of a group account provides access to shared data or resources, such as files in a folder.
- **Computers or machines:** Specific computer systems identified in a directory is a computer or machine account.
- **Computer or machine groups:** Yes, as with users, directories can combine several computer accounts into a group. Easily manage multiple computers with a group.

When you're ready to create a directory, the differences and benefits of various accounts become more evident. See Chapter 16 to create and manage these account types in Mac OS X Server.

Binding Clients and Servers to Directories

Any client computer that needs to communicate with the shared directory first needs to know that the directory exists. The computer also must trust the directory and the account data it contains. Servers can also connect to a directory to use the same shared accounts for services such as file sharing and e-mail accounts.

Connecting a client or server to a directory is referred to as *binding.* A client connected to a directory is said to be *bound* to the directory. You'll notice these terms are used frequently in Chapters 6 and 7.

Mac OS X Servers can bind to a variety of directories, including the native Open Directory, Microsoft Active Directory, Novel eDirectory, various OpenLDAP systems running on other Unix and Linux servers, and the legacy Unix formats. Client computers can connect to any or all of these directory services through the Mac OS X Server.

Binding comes in two types:

- **Anonymous bind:** The most common type of bind. Client or server systems connect without first authenticating to the directory. Requests for information from the directory are sent in clear text, although authentication is encrypted by default. Anonymous connections are commonly used with Mac OS X Server's Open Directory.

  You can browse directory information without first binding — most directories are configured this way — from the local network. Using anonymous binding isn't an additional security risk in a default configuration in which anyone can browse the data.

- **Authenticated bind:** Just the opposite of anonymous; a directory administrator account is required to create an authenticated bind, creating a two-way trust between the client and server. Authenticated binding reduces the risk of *man-in-the-middle attacks,* in which an evildoer on your network might attempt to gather information about directory and authentication requests. This would be important in a high-security network environment.

  Many Microsoft Active Directory servers allow authenticated binding only. However, anonymous binding is far simpler and creates less network overhead.

To join a directory in Mac OS X Snow Leopard, you no longer need to open Directory Access and make a number of setting changes. Now the connection process is consolidated in the Accounts pane of System Preferences. See "Binding Clients to the Shared Domain" in Chapter 6 for the steps to connect to an Open Directory server. Figure 5-1 shows a Mac client joining an Active Directory domain; see details on this type of connection in Chapter 7.

Figure 5-1: Join an Active Directory domain from the Accounts pane.

Directory Access is still available for advanced configuration, but it's moved from the Utilities folder to /System/Library/CoreServices.

The Accounts pane in System Preferences shows the status of the directory with the use of a colored dot. Green indicates a good connection to the server. Red indicates an error in the link to the directory. If there is no connection, no dot is displayed.

Another location to look for the status is the login window. Click the gray text indicating the system's name in the login window, just below the Mac OS X logo, to find additional information about the system. This data includes a green or red dot and the status of network accounts. Having this knowledge can help you troubleshoot directory connections right from the login window.

Authenticating with LDAP and Kerberos

Directory services also provide the authentication that allows users to access other services. The common authentication backbone of many prevalent directories is the Lightweight Directory Access Protocol (LDAP) and Kerberos.

These two technologies are built in to Apple Open Directory and Microsoft Active Directory. The descriptions here just scratch the surface of LDAP and Kerberos; for more information on each technology, see `www.openldap.org` and `http://web.mit.edu/kerberos`.

Although directory services facilitate user authentication through passwords, the passwords are not usually stored in directories. That's because anyone with access to the directory can usually browse its information. In Mac OS X Server, passwords can be stored either in the Open Directory Password Server database or in a Kerberos realm, which is a kind of holding place. When authenticating, Open Directory checks with the Kerberos realm first.

In Mac OS X Server, Open Directory never even reads the passwords. Each account password is stored as encrypted value called a *shadow hash* for each user. When the user submits a password for authentication, Open Directory runs it through the hash and compares the values of the hashes. If they match, the user is authenticated. Open Directory doesn't read the actual password.

Open Directory can also serve as a Windows primary domain controller to authenticate Windows clients.

LDAP is the phone book

In most modern network directories, LDAP defines how clients communicate with the directory over TCP/IP networks. The LDAP Data Interchange Format (LDIF) defines how data is stored in the LDAP database. Within directory entries are distinguished names (DN), made up of domain containers (DC), organizational units (OU), and common names (CN).

The LDAP search base, which you see in practice in Chapter 6, tells the client where to start looking for data within the directory — usually account information.

LDAP also has a role to play with the Password Server database, mentioned in the preceding section. When you authenticate against a shared directory in Mac OS X Server, you're telling LDAP who you are, but Password Server checks your password to verify your identity.

Authentication proves who you are with your username and password credentials. *Authorization* is what you can do after authenticated, such as accessing file sharing or viewing your e-mail inbox.

The other directories that Open Directory is compatible with are also LDAP-compatible directories. This includes Active Directory, eDirectory, and others.

Kerberos and single sign-on

One of the problems with standard authentication methods is that a user inevitably needs to connect to many unique services. The user sends a username and password to each one, opening a path for intercepting and cracking your password by an evildoer. Here's an alternative: Kerberos. With Kerberos enabled, the password is never transmitted over the network. Instead, a ticketing system issues encrypted tokens called *tickets*, and authenticates you once, usually from the Mac OS X login window, and subsequent tickets allow access to other shared services.

Think of Kerberos as spending the day visiting a popular amusement park. The first thing you do when you arrive at the park is buy a pass. This is your Kerberos ticket granting ticket (TGT) issued by the Kerberos Key Distribution Center (KDC) when you log in to Mac OS X on a shared directory. At the park, you pay the entry fee and access the grounds all day. This feature, known as *single sign-on*, means that users don't have to keep logging in to various different services all day. Users log in once and get access to the whole park.

However, the pass doesn't automatically mean you can jump on any ride or that you get hot dogs and popcorn. You still need to queue for each ride and pay for your snacks. In Kerberos, your TGT is presented when accessing a service, such as file sharing or e-mail. The KDC creates a new service ticket that your client uses to authenticate to the service. But, the user isn't presented with a login screen after that first login.

When the park closes, your pass is no good for the next day. In Kerberos, when you log out, the TGT and service tickets are destroyed. Should anyone have managed to figure out how to break in to the ticket system, TGTs are good for a set period of time only: ten hours after the login to Mac OS X Server. And, the Kerberos tickets are stored in RAM, not the hard drive.

Mac OS X Server is easy to set up as a KDC — when you (or Server Assistant) set it up as an Open Directory master, a KDC is set up automatically. Open Directory can also make use of another KDC running on another server, such as an Active Directory domain controller. In Mac OS X, you can view, create, and destroy TGTs by using the Ticket Viewer application, as shown in Figure 5-2, found in /System/Library/CoreServices.

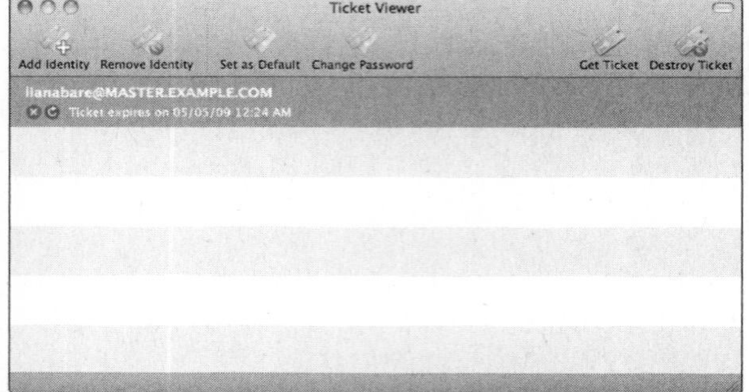

Figure 5-2: Kerberos tickets in Ticket Viewer.

View TGTs and service tickets for the current user, by typing `klist` in Terminal and pressing Return. Here's an example of what you might see:

```
client:~ lianabare$ klist

Default principal: lianabare@MASTER.EXAMPLE.COM

Valid Starting     Expires            Service Principal
06/30/09 14:24:40  06/30/09 00:24:40  krbtgt/MASTER.EXAMPLE.COM@MASTER.EXAMPLE.
              COM
        renew until 06/30/09 14:24:34

06/30/09 14:24:41  06/30/09 00:24:40  afpserver/fileserver.example.com@MASTER.
              EXAMPLE.COM
        renew until 06/30/09 14:24:34

06/30/09 14:24:59  06/30/09 00:24:40  http/ical.example.com@MASTER.EXAMPLE.COM
        renew until 06/30/09 14:24:34

06/30/09 14:26:27  06/30/09 00:24:40  xmpp/ichat.example.com@MASTER.EXAMPLE.COM
        renew until 06/30/09 14:24:34
```

Chapter 6

Setting Up Open Directory

In This Chapter

- Planning for an Open Directory deployment
- Checking DNS and time service
- Creating a master and importing accounts with System Preferences
- Creating Open Directory masters and replicas with Server Admin
- Binding to another directory server
- Creating a Primary Domain Controller for Windows clients
- Archiving Open Directory for backup
- Binding Mac and Windows clients to Open Directory

If you've just set up your server and entered some client accounts, congratulations — you've created an Open Directory master, Snow Leopard Server's shared storehouse for network user and resource information. If you haven't added users, you can easily create a directory using Server Preferences or Workgroup Manager, or both. Use Server Admin to configure the directory services.

You don't have to host your own directory: Snow Leopard Server can connect to other directory servers and use their information. And, you can set up Open Directory and SMB services to serve as a Primary Domain Controller (or a backup domain controller) for Windows clients.

This chapter describes how to set up and manage Open Directory to do these things using Server Preferences for simpler tasks, and Server Admin and Workgroup Manager for more complex tasks.

Introducing Open Directory

Mac OS X Server's Open Directory uses several technologies: Lightweight Directory Access Protocol (LDAP), Apple's Password Server (built on the Simple Authentication and Security Layer, or SASL), Kerberos Key Distribution Center (KDC), and managed clients for Mac OS X (MCX). (Did you get all those acronyms? No? You can read more about LDAP and Kerberos in Chapter 5 and MCX in Chapter 16.)

Briefly, LDAP is a standard communications method for network directories, including Open Directory and Microsoft Active Directory. LDAP is commonly used in mixed networks of Windows, Mac, and Unix computers.

Kerberos is an authentication technology. Integration with Kerberos gives your users the ability to sign in once, usually at the appropriately named login window of their computers. They can then access many different services in an Open Directory domain. In fact, all the commonly used services in Mac OS X Server are *kerberized* — they're compatible with the ticket distribution system used by Kerberos — so users don't have to provide a password when signing in to access Apple Mail, iChat, iCal, and shared folders on your network.

Designating Mac OS X Server as an Open Directory master creates an Open Directory domain. The directory domain can be shared to multiple servers and clients. Creating copies of your Open Directory master on other servers increases speed and reliability of the shared domain.

Open Directory can also access other types of directory domains and the information with them. This includes other LDAP-compatible directories, including Active Directory, as well as Network Information System (NIS), a type of directory service used by some Unix servers. Open Directory can also access the local directory domains of Mac OS X Server 10.6 or later, and in Mac OS X clients. Finally, Open Directory can access BSD Unix flat files, an older but long-used directory service of UNIX systems.

Snow Leopard Server provides a number of tools. You can use Server Admin to manage the Open Directory service. You can use Workgroup Manager to create and manage accounts — users, groups, machine records, and machine groups. For less technical tasks, Server Preferences is also an option for managing Open Directory, creating users and groups, and importing user accounts from another directory. A fourth application, iCal Server Utility, is used to manage resources and locations in iCal. Although iCal is a separate service (which I cover in Chapter 12), the data entered in the iCal Server Utility becomes part of the LDAP database.

Think Before You Jump: Planning for an Open Directory Deployment

You might be tempted, after you read about the benefits of a shared domain in Chapter 5, to jump right in with the instructions you find later in this chapter (in the "Creating an Open Directory Master" section) and create a shared domain. Don't give in to temptation just yet.

First, write something. Your plan is best implemented when it exists in a format that you document and reference. Collaboration is also key when you and your colleagues are simultaneously working toward implementing a shared directory.

Documentation can also save your hide if the worst happens and you're forced to rebuild your directory. And don't forget that you might not be the only administrator of the directory — especially if you finally win the lottery and forget all about your love of Mac OS X Servers. The next guy (or gal) benefits from your documentation too.

Open Directory relies upon other services to run properly. Domain name service and time synchronization are critical to a healthy and happy directory.

Starting an Open Directory checklist

Whether you use a detailed Gantt chart, a whiteboard, a pile of scrap paper, or just a quick sketch on a cocktail napkin, start your Open Directory deployment with a plan. Here are some considerations to ponder prior to your deployment:

- **How many servers do you need?** For a small domain of ten or so users, you could have just one server, but consider a second for larger networks. A minimum of two Open Directory servers provides you with redundancy and failover — the ability to switch automatically to a second server in the event something goes wrong with the first.

  Two Open Directory servers can take you quite far. Apple states that Open Directory's technical limitations are:

  - *LDAP records:* 200,000
  - *Simultaneous client connections:* 1,000

  Each client may open multiple connections to an Open Directory server during the initial login and when requesting additional authentication.

However, a two-server Open Directory deployment handily manages several hundred clients in a local network.

- **Are you accounting for physical security?** The directory servers in your shared domain contain sensitive information, such as user passwords and permissions. Treat your Open Directory servers with the same care and caution as any of the other important data on your network.
- **Who will have responsibility for domain maintenance and backups?** When you specify an administrator to primarily manage your domain, you likely reduce mistakes and complications that result from things like ill-timed software updates and improperly made backups.

Master, replica, and relay servers

Mac servers can play different roles in Open Directory: a master, a replica, or a relay. Another role a Mac server can have is to simply connect, or bind, to a directory. When planning your network, thank about which you'll use.

Open Directory masters

An *Open Directory master* is the primary Open Directory server on the network. If you have a single Mac OS X Server Mac that is hosting a shared list of users and groups, it is an Open Directory master. A master contains a read-write LDAP-compatible database, and hosts the Kerberos Key Distribution Center (KDC) and the Open Directory Password Server database (described in Chapter 5). The Open Directory master is the only server that can make changes to the LDAP-compatible database. (An Open Directory master is analogous to the Primary Domain Controller [PDC] of other shared directory systems — of which Snow Leopard Server can also serve.)

Open Directory replicas

After the Open Directory master, you can add one or more Open Directory *replicas,* which are mirror servers that create a distributed directory environment with redundancy and client failover. Each Open Directory replica has a read-only copy of the LDAP directory, the Password Server database, and the Kerberos KDC that are synchronized periodically with the master and each of the other replicas. Changes to accounts in a domain must be made on the master server. However, password database changes, such as a user changing his password, can be made while connected to any Open Directory server in the domain. (Passwords are not stored in the LDAP database.) Background synchronization among all the Open Directory servers updates the changed data across the domain.

Open Directory relays

You can deploy Open Directory servers in a topology sometimes referred to as a *tree* or a *nested approach*. Each Open Directory master can have up to 32 replica servers. Additionally, each of these replica servers can have up to 32 replicas of its own. Thus, a theoretical limit of 1,057 Open Directory servers exists for a single domain:

1 master + 32 replicas + (32×32) nested replicas

When an Open Directory replica has its own replicas, that server is an *Open Directory relay*. A relay with additional replicas might be useful in a widely distributed network of client systems. An Open Directory master with multiple replicas in Server Admin is shown in Figure 6-1.

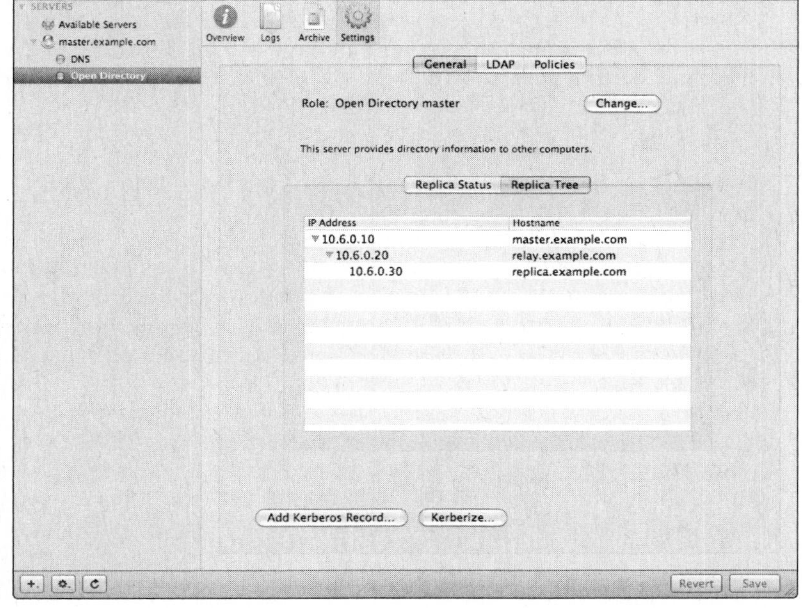

Figure 6-1: Server Admin on an Open Directory master with a relay and a replica.

Open Directory replicas, including relays, that connect directly to the master are first-tier replicas. Replicas that connect to a relay are second-tier replicas.

A good example for the use of an Open Directory relay is a school system with multiple school buildings spread out in a city or a county. You'd install Open Directory relay and additional replicas in each school, while the Open Directory master remains safely installed at the school system's data center away from sticky fingers, which creates a closer, faster connection to the Open Directory domain for clients in each building.

Install the same version of Mac OS X Server on all servers in an Open Directory domain. A deployment of Open Directory servers can't mix older Mac OS X Server releases (Tiger 10.4 or Leopard 10.5, for example) with Snow Leopard. When installing software updates, such as Mac OS X Server 10.6.1, 10.6.2, and so on, start with your replica servers and finish by updating on the master.

Server connected to a directory, but not hosting one

You don't need Open Directory running on every server. Another Open Directory role is to bind to an Open Directory domain instead of hosting one. You avoid the overhead of running directory services on your server, and users still get access to domain resources. You might use this option if your server is running user services, such as file sharing, e-mail, or Snow Leopard Server's wiki collaborative environment. Your services can also make use of Kerberos authentication from the bound server. To connect a server to a directory, you bind it to the domain and add it to the Kerberos realm.

A Mac OS X Server that doesn't host or connect to a shared directory is a *standalone server.* This type of server has only a local database of user and group accounts as in any Mac OS X system and results from selecting Configure Manually in Server Assistant's initial setup and not selecting directory services.

Regardless of the Mac OS X Server Open Directory role, it always has a local database of users. Importantly, don't confuse the local accounts, which can't be shared with other servers and clients with the accounts in the Open Directory domain. In Chapter 16, you see cues in Workgroup Manager that help differentiate which database of accounts you're working with.

After you configure an Open Directory domain, other servers and client systems utilize binding to connect and access the shared directory for authentication and authorization. Clients connect to the fastest responding Open Directory server, based on *ping response times* — the time required for a small packet of data to travel and return to the sender. If the master or any replica servers fail, clients connect automatically to another Open Directory server in the domain without interruption to the user.

Prerequisites

Before running Open Directory, there are two aspects of your network that need to be properly configured first: domain name service (DNS) and time synchronization for Kerberos.

Checking for proper DNS setup

Properly configured DNS is critical to the configuration and normal operation of an Open Directory domain. All Open Directory servers need static IP addresses with two types of records — a fully qualified DNS address (A) and pointer (PTR) records. Verify the server's DNS records prior to promoting a Mac OS X Server to either master or replica status.

In an A record, also called a *machine record,* the system's hostname is resolved to an IP address. That is, when another computer requests the IP address for a given domain name, the machine record supplies it. A pointer (PTR) record, also known as a *reverse lookup*, resolves a domain name for any given IP address. *Reverse resolution* inquires about an IP address and returns the hostname. You'll find more information about hosting your own DNS and creating these records on a Mac OS X Server in Chapter 3.

By default, the domain's LDAP search policy and Kerberos realm are the same as the fully qualified hostname of the Open Directory master and are generated when a server's role is changed to master. Without correct DNS records, promotion to an Open Directory master or replica will likely fail or create only a partially functional domain.

If you don't mind typing a one-line command in the Terminal utility, you can easily verify that DNS forward and reverse lookup is configured correctly. Type this, exactly:

```
sudo changeip -checkhostname
```

If forward and reverse DNS is working correctly, you see this, but with your server information:

```
Primary address      = 192.168.1.69
Current HostName     = ourserver.macwindowsco.com
DNS HostName         = ourserver.macwindowsco.com
The names match. There is nothing to change.
dirserv:success = "success"
```

Synchronizing time for Kerberos reliability

If you plan on using Kerberos as part of your Open Directory deployment (and why wouldn't you?), time synchronization is critical. *Time skew,* or the difference in time between the KDC and clients requesting Kerberos tickets, can be no more than five minutes. Time zones and daylight savings time aren't considered in factoring the time skew as long as the relative time between systems is the same.

In other words, if you have a client in Pacific Time and a KDC in Eastern Time, they both need to be set correctly for their respective time zones. Manually changing the time to match the local time but not changing the time zone causes a time difference of several hours — much more than five minutes. Open Directory compares time based on Universal Decimal Time (UDT).

It's best to set your Mac OS X Server and client systems to use a time synchronization server running the network time protocol (NTP) to avoid problems with Kerberos and single sign-on for users. You probably configured this during initial setup. Apple provides several publicly accessible NTP servers via the Internet, or you can run your own time server on a local network.

A public Internet connection isn't required, but public NTP servers often connect to trusted sources of accurate time data, such as an atomic clock. If you don't use a public server, manually adjust the time of your private time server in the Date & Time pane of System Preferences as the clock skews.

Enabling time server synchronization

Add the NTP server to the Date & Time pane in System Preferences to automatically have the system adjust the clock. These steps set a time server on both Mac OS X clients and Mac OS X Server:

1. **Choose Apple menu⇨System Preferences and then click the Date & Time icon.**
2. **Select the Set Date & Time Automatically check box.**
3. **From the pop-up menu to the right of the check box, choose an Apple public time server or enter another time server in this field.**

   If you're not using Apple's time servers, enter the hostname or IP address of another time server (like those found at `support.ntp.org`) or a private time server on your local network.
4. **Quit System Preferences when you're done.**

Running network time protocol in Mac OS X Server

Many servers can run the NTP service, including Mac OS X Server. If your server has Internet access and you want to trust another NTP server for time updates, follow the steps in the preceding section to set the date and time on your NTP server. Then follow these steps to start the network time protocol:

1. **Open Server Admin and connect to the server.**
2. **Click the server's name in the left column, click the Settings icon, and then click the General tab.**
3. **Select the Network Time Server (NTP) check box and then click Save.**

Follow the steps in the section, “Enabling time server synchronization,” earlier in this chapter, using your NTP server’s hostname or IP address as the time server in the Date & Time pane in System Preferences.

If the time skew is greater than five minutes, Kerberos tickets can’t be generated and single sign-on fails for users.

After you properly configure and verify DNS records and hostnames for your server and set up time synchronization, proceeding with the Open Directory master configuration is a straightforward endeavor with either Server Preferences or Server Admin and its Open Directory Assistant.

Using Server Preferences to Configure Open Directory

Server Preferences is a simplified interface for commonly used services and account management. The application has the look and feel of Mac OS X System Preferences. For a network that requires a simple shared domain, Server Preferences can quite possibly take care of everything you need.

You can do several Open Directory tasks with Server Preferences, depending on how you configured your server during initial installation and setup, including importing users and groups from another directory and creating an Open Directory master.

Server Preferences is also good for adding or removing users and groups and for other user account management tasks. Chapter 16 describes those issues.

Creating an Open Directory master with Server Preferences

If you didn’t choose to create or import during initial installation and setup, you can create an Open Directory master with three mouse clicks in Server Preferences.

Open Server Preferences from the Dock or the /Application/Server folder. If prompted, enter the username and password for the local administrator and click the Connect button. To set up an Open Directory master:

1. **Click the Users icon.**

   You’ll get the window shown in Figure 6-2, which only appears if you haven’t previously chosen to create or import users.

Figure 6-2: Using Server Preferences to set up account management.

2. **Click the Set Up button and then click OK when asked whether you want to host users and groups on the server.**

   An animated gear icon spins, and the status shows Creating Open Directory Master while the server is configured.

   After Server Preferences completes setting up the Open Directory master, the display shows either the Users or Groups management, depending on which option you originally selected in Step 1.

Server Preferences doesn't allow you to change the LDAP search base path or the Kerberos realm name, or to see the confirmation that these settings match the DNS server hostname. If Server Preferences fails to create your Open Directory shared domain, DNS is a likely culprit. An Open Directory master created with Server Preferences also has the default Directory Administrator in the Name box as well as Short Name diradmin and User ID 1000.

Just because you used Server Preferences to create the shared domain doesn't mean you can't also use Server Admin and Workgroup Manager. After the directory is created, you can switch among the applications. However, get in the habit of using Server Admin and Workgroup Manager, or Server Preferences. This helps you avoid confusion about the differences among the many settings for accounts and services.

If you ever need to return a server's Open Directory role to a standalone server or perform other advanced management of Open Directory master, use Server Admin.

Importing directory information with Server Preferences

If, during initial installation and setup, you chose to import information from another directory, you can do it now. When you choose this option in Server Assistant, the server creates an Open Directory master on your server and a connection to the other server.

If you didn't select this option during initial setup you can still import information now. If you don't yet have an Open Directory master, you'll need to first create one, as described in the preceding section.

To make the connection to the other directory server, use *System* Preferences (located in the Dock), not *Server* Preferences. Then use *Server* Preferences to import that account from the other server.

If you don't already have a connection to another directory server, here's how to do it:

1. **Open System Preferences on your server and click the Accounts icon.**
2. **Click Login Options and then click the Edit button.**

   If you see a Join button instead of an Edit button, you haven't created an Open Directory master. Create one as described in the previous section.
3. **Click the Add (+) button, and then select a directory server from the pop-up menu or enter the directory server's fully qualified domain name or IP address.**
4. **Enter the name and password of a user account on the directory server.**

   If the connected directory server allows anonymous binding, the dialog will tell you that you have the option of leaving the name and password fields blank.

Now that you're connected to another directory server, you can import its users and groups. To import individual users, follow these steps:

1. **In Server Preferences, click the Users icon.**
2. **Click the Add (+) button and choose Import User From Directory from the pop-up menu.**
3. **Type the letters of a user's name until you see the full name appear and then select it.**

   You can select Send Imported Users an Email Invitation if you wish.

4. **Click the Import button.**
5. **Repeat Steps 3 and 4 until you're finished importing users.**
6. **Click the Done button.**

To import accounts more quickly, you can import groups from the connected directory server. When you import a group, Server Preferences imports all the user accounts that are members of the group. In fact, Snow Leopard Server will check with the connected directory server for changes that have been made, and will add or remove user accounts on your server if the group membership has changed. (Now that's service!)

To import a group, use the above procedure for importing a user, except in Step 2, select Import Group From Directory from the pop-up menu.

Using Server Admin to Configure Open Directory

Although Server Preferences is easier to use than Server Admin, it can't change the default settings of an Open Directory domain. By using Server Admin to create and connect to domains, you have all the options available to set the LDAP search path (or policy), which defines which directory domains Open Directory can access. You can also set the Kerberos realm, a database containing validation data for users, services, and sometimes servers. You also use Server Admin to set the account options for the directory administrator and to create an Open Directory replica or relay. This following section describes how you can use Server Admin to configure Open Directory.

Working with Server Admin

You can use Server Admin to configure and manage Snow Leopard Server's many services, including Open Directory. To get Server Admin running for the first time, follow these steps:

1. **If not already logged in to the server, log in as the local administrator that you created in Chapter 3 when you installed Snow Leopard Server.**
2. **Open Server Admin from the Dock (or in the /Applications/Server/ folder).**
3. **Select Choose Server⇨Add Server.**

4. **Type the hostname of the server in the Address field and then enter the administrator's username and password.**
5. **Click Connect.**

   For best results, always enter the server's fully qualified hostname. You can also enter the server's name ending in `.local`, if this is what you created in Server Assistant in Chapter 3 when you installed Snow Leopard Server, because DNS wasn't running on your network.

You are now connected to the server and ready to manage its services. Click the triangle next to the server's name to view an expanded list of enabled services. A dot next to each service in the list has a few possible colors:

- *Clear:* Service is enabled but not running.
- *Red:* Service has an error.
- *Light green:* Infrequent, shown sometimes as a service restarts.
- *Dark green:* Service is running normally.

Connecting to an existing directory using Server Admin

Instead of hosting Open Directory on your server, you can have Snow Leopard Server join an existing directory domain that exists on another server. This is called *binding* the server to the directory domain. In addition to using System Preferences to join the server to the domain, you also use Server Admin to properly configure your server and join the Kerberos realm. Follow these steps to bind a server to an Open Directory domain:

1. **In Server Admin, click the triangle next to your server and click Open Directory in the expanded list of services.**
2. **Click the Settings icon and then click the Change button next to the current role to launch Open Directory Assistant.**
3. **Select Connect to Another Directory from the Choose Directory Role screen, as shown in Figure 6-3, and click the Continue button; click the Continue button again to confirm your choice.**

   Open Directory Assistant informs you that the server needs to be bound to the directory.
4. **Click the Open Directory Utility button from Open Directory Assistant, or click the Done button and then click the Open Directory Utility button from Server Admin.**

   Either method opens Directory Utility.

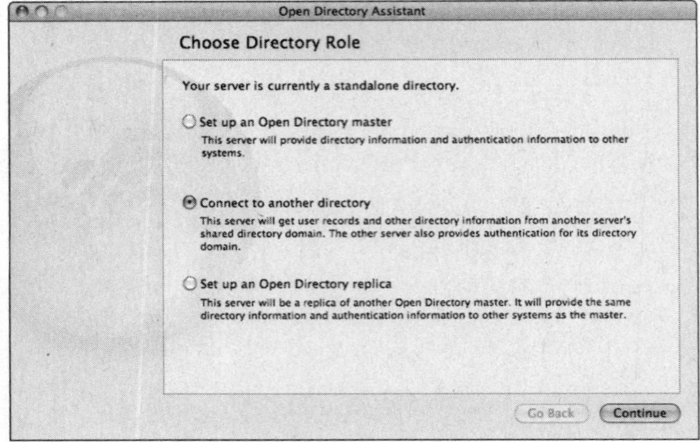
Open Directory Assistant
Choose Directory Role
Your server is currently a standalone directory.
Set up an Open Directory master
This server will provide directory information and authentication information to other systems.
Connect to another directory
This server will get user records and other directory information from another server's shared directory domain. The other server also provides authentication for its directory domain.
Set up an Open Directory replica
This server will be a replica of another Open Directory master. It will provide the same directory information and authentication information to other systems as the master.
Go Back
Continue

Figure 6-3: Changing the Open Directory role to connect to a shared domain.

5. **Click the lock icon and authenticate as the local administrator.**

   The service listings of Directory Utility are shown in Figure 6-4.

6. **Select LDAPv3 from the Services tab and then click the pencil icon.**

Directory Utility
Services
Search Policy
Select a service and click the pencil icon to edit settings.
Enable Name Version
Active Directory 6.0
BSD Flat File and NIS 6.0
LDAPv3 6.0
Local 6.0
Click the lock to prevent further changes.
Apply

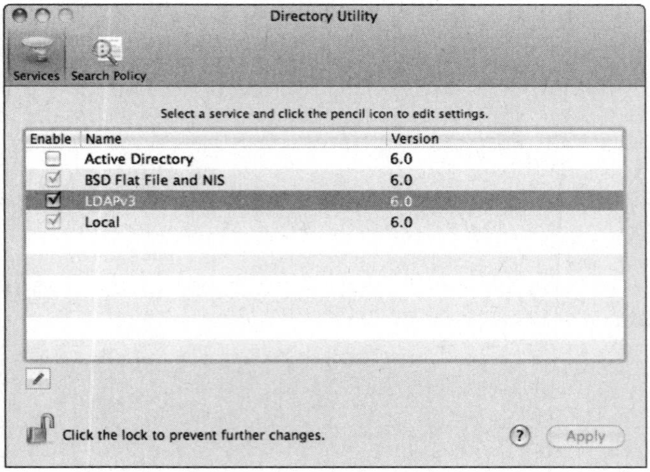

Figure 6-4: Directory Utility's service configuration.

7. **Click the New button and enter the fully qualified hostname of the Open Directory master.**

   By default, Secure Sockets Layer (SSL) is disabled, and the options for authentication and authorization are selected.

8. **Click the Continue button and if prompted, authenticate as the local administrator.**

9. **Configure the binding.**

   See the later section, "Binding Clients to the Shared Domain."

   If desired, you can modify the computer ID and enter the directory administrator username and password to create an authenticated bind. Otherwise, leave those fields blank for an anonymous binding.

10. **Click the Continue button and then click OK. Review the configuration, click OK, and then close Directory Utility.**

    For servers that aren't part of a Kerberos realm, you're finished. Otherwise, for servers in a Kerberos realm, follow Steps 11 and 12.

11. **(Optional) Click the Join Kerberos button in Server Admin if your server is going to be used as part of a Kerberos realm for single sign-on of its services.**

12. **(Optional) Select the shared Kerberos realm (usually named the same as the Open Directory master's fully qualified hostname), enter the directory administrator's username and password, and click OK to continue.**

    Joining the Kerberos realm may take a few seconds. You're finished setting up the directory and Kerberos connection to an Open Directory domain.

After you bind a server to an Open Directory shared domain, you can configure services on the server that are available as options in Workgroup Manager. For example, if file sharing is configured on the connected server, you can now create a share point for home or group folders (see Chapter 9).

Creating an Open Directory master

Follow these steps to create an Open Directory master and a shared directory domain with Server Admin and Open Directory Assistant:

1. **Open Server Admin on the server that will become the Open Directory master and click the server in the left column.**

2. **Click the Settings icon in the toolbar, click the Services tab, select the Open Directory check box, and click the Save button.**

   Skip this step if you previously enabled the service and it's already listed in the server's expanded list of services.

3. **Click Open Directory in the expanded service list and observe the service's current status by clicking the Overview icon.**

   For a server that hasn't yet been configured for a shared Open Directory domain, the status indicates Open Directory Is: Standalone Directory, and LDAP Server, Password Server, and Kerberos all indicate Stopped.

Also notice the clear dot in the expanded server list. No part of the Open Directory service is running.

Figure 6-5 shows the Open Directory service in Server Admin on a standalone server.

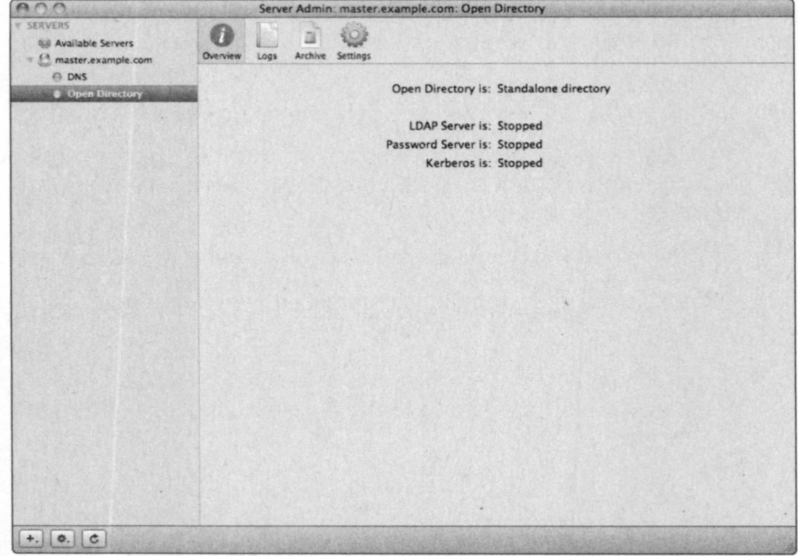

Figure 6-5: The Open Directory service of a standalone server.

4. **Click the Settings icon in the toolbar and then click the General tab.**
5. **Next to the status Role: Standalone Directory, click the Change button.**

   The Open Directory Assistant opens and walks you through changing the server's Open Directory role. You can see the initial screen of Open Directory Assistant in Figure 6-6.
6. **Select Set Up an Open Directory Master from the three options and click the Continue button.**
7. **View and optionally change the directory administrator name, short name, and user ID and then enter a password.**

   The directory administrator user is a critical piece of your shared domain. This user is capable of creating accounts in the directory, modifying the directory, adding and removing replica servers, serving as the Kerberos KDC administrator, and more. This administrator is just as critical to the well-being of your domain as the local administrator is to the server, so the short name and password need to be unique and difficult to guess.

Open Directory Assistant
Choose Directory Role
Your server is currently a standalone directory.
Set up an Open Directory master
This server will provide directory information and authentication information to other systems.
Connect to another directory
This server will get user records and other directory information from another server's shared directory domain. The other server also provides authentication for its directory domain.
Set up an Open Directory replica
This server will be a replica of another Open Directory master. It will provide the same directory information and authentication information to other systems as the master.
Go Back
Continue

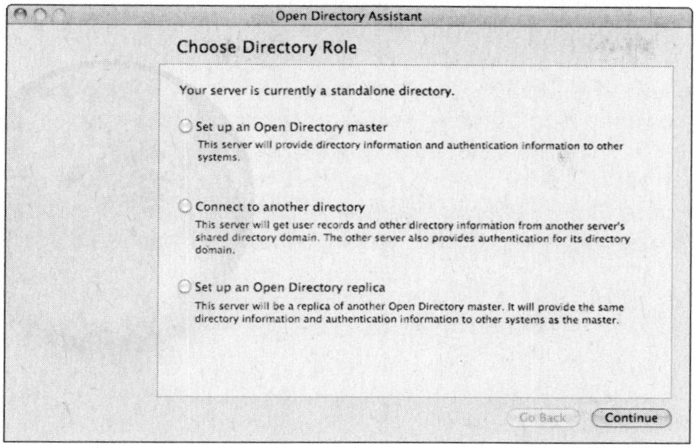

Figure 6-6: The first screen of Open Directory Assistant.

Later, after your domain is configured, you might add more directory administrators if needed. You see this option when you use Workgroup Manager in Chapter 16.

As shown in Figure 6-7, the Name default setting is Directory Administrator, the Short Name is diradmin, and the User ID is 1000. You can modify all these default options; however, keep a record of the directory administrator's short name and User ID — information that's critical if you need to restore the shared domain from a backup archive.

Open Directory Assistant
Directory Administrator
Please enter account information for the new directory administrator account.
This user account will have administrative privileges for the master's domain.
Name: Directory Administrator
Short Name: diradmin
User ID: 1000
Password: •••••••
Verify: •••••••
Go Back
Continue

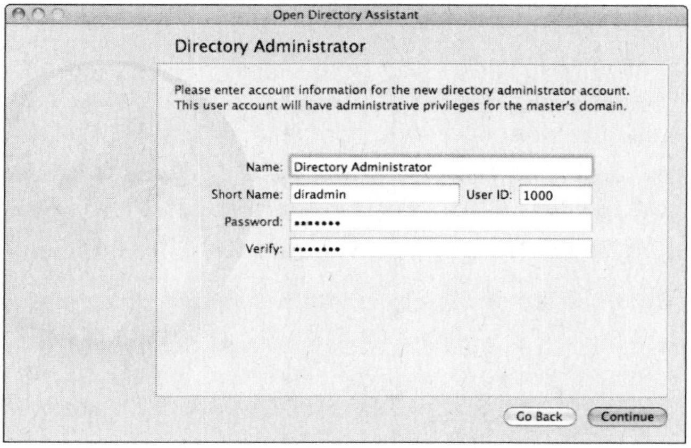

Figure 6-7: The Directory Administrator screen.

TIP

Directory administrator's default name and short name work fine in any Open Directory domain. For stronger security — making it more difficult for someone to guess your administrator's credentials — use a unique name and short name on your server.

8. **Set the Kerberos Realm name and LDAP Search Base path for the shared domain.**

   By default, the Kerberos Realm and LDAP Search Base boxes match the fully qualified hostname of your master server. Advanced users may need to modify these settings, but for most domains, the default options are perfectly acceptable. In Figure 6-8, you can see the correct Kerberos Realm and LDAP Search Base boxes, automatically populated, that match the server's `master.example.com` hostname.

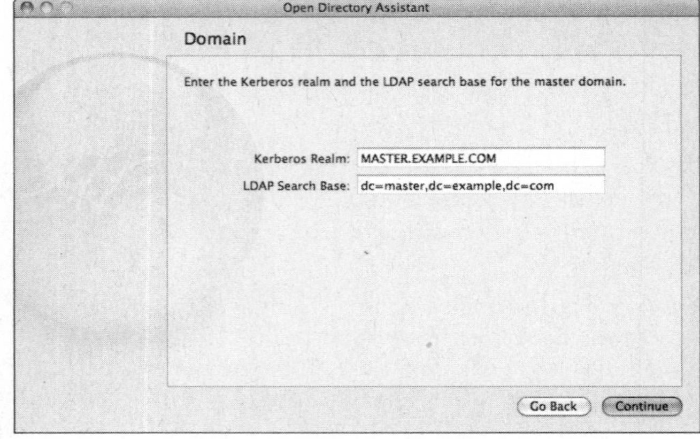

Figure 6-8: The Kerberos Realm name and LDAP Search Base path.

When the realm's name and search base path don't match your server's hostname, it's a good indication that something's gone wrong with your DNS settings. This is your last chance to resolve DNS problems before you continue with your shared domain. Failing to do so likely results in a domain with a broken Kerberos or LDAP, or both.

9. **Confirm your settings so far in the final screen of Open Directory Assistant and then click the Continue button.**

   A list of your settings displays.

10. **Click the Continue button to create the shared directory.**

    The Open Directory Assistant now processes your entries and creates the resources needed on the Open Directory master. The LDAP database, Password Server database, and Kerberos KDC are created and their supporting background processes are started.

11. **Click the Done button after your server's been configured as an Open Directory master.**

    The Open Directory Assistant closes, returning you to Server Admin.

Congratulations, you've successfully created a shared directory. Figure 6-9 illustrates what Server Admin now shows: The Open Directory Is: Open Directory Master, and LDAP server, Password Server, and Kerberos are all Running. Also note the green dot next to Open Directory in the expanded list of services.

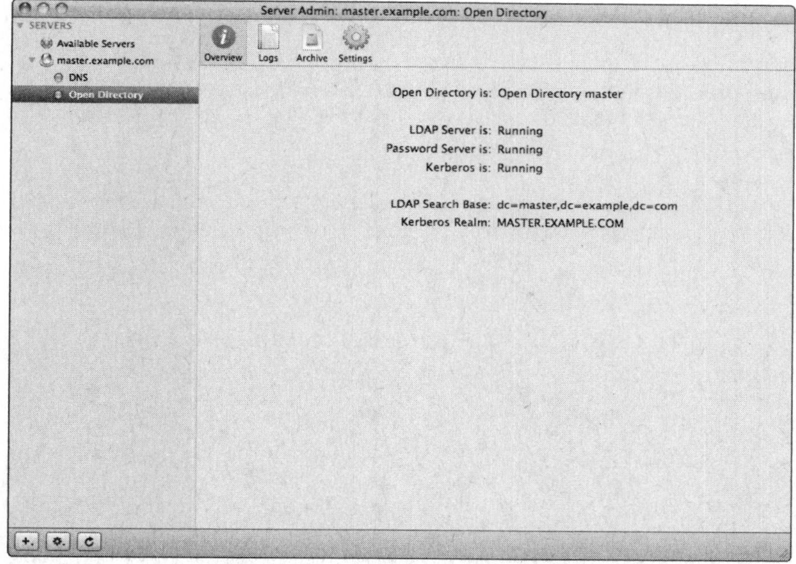

Figure 6-9: Server Admin on an Open Directory master.

Attack of the clones: Creating Open Directory replica servers

An Open Directory replica is essentially a clone of the Open Directory master with copies of the shared domain databases. Having one or more replica on your network greatly helps reduce the load on any one domain server and adds peace of mind in case a server fails.

Unlike creating an Open Directory master in which you could use Server Preferences to change the server's role to a master, you need to use Server Admin to create a replica.

Considerations for DNS records and time synchronization are still valid for replica servers. Use the same DNS and time servers for all Open Directory servers in your shared domain. (See the sections, "Checking for Proper DNS Setup" and "Synchronizing time for Kerberos reliability" earlier in this chapter).

Server Admin is your only choice for changing a server's role to a replica:

1. **Open Server Admin on the server that will become the Open Directory replica and connect to the server.**
2. **Click the Settings icon in the toolbar, click the Services tab, select the Open Directory check box, and click the Save button.**

   Skip this step if you previously enabled the service and it's already listed in the server's expanded list of services.
3. **Click Open Directory in the expanded list of services and observe the current status of the service.**

   The server role should be Standalone.
4. **Click the Settings icon, click the General tab, and then click the Change button next to Open Directory Is: Standalone.**

   Like creating a master server, this action opens Open Directory Assistant, as shown in Figure 6-10.

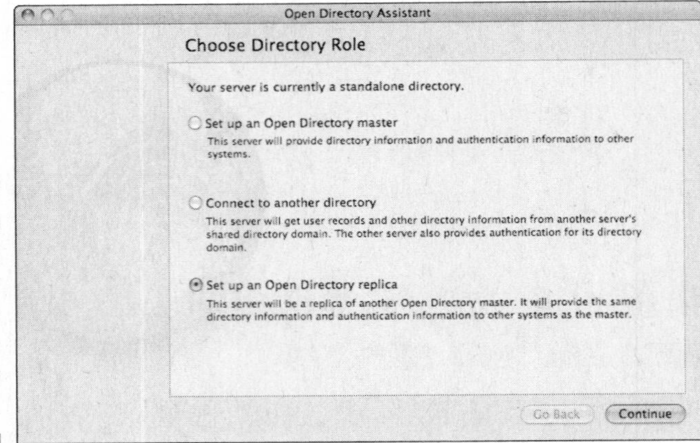
Open Directory Assistant
Choose Directory Role
Your server is currently a standalone directory.
Set up an Open Directory master
This server will provide directory information and authentication information to other systems.
Connect to another directory
This server will get user records and other directory information from another server's shared directory domain. The other server also provides authentication for its directory domain.
Set up an Open Directory replica
This server will be a replica of another Open Directory master. It will provide the same directory information and authentication information to other systems as the master.
Go Back
Continue

Figure 6-10: Creating a replica server with Open Directory Assistant.

5. **Select Set Up an Open Directory Replica and then click the Continue button.**
6. **Enter the IP address or fully qualified hostname of the master server, the master's root password, and the directory administrator's short name and password; click the Continue button.**

   Figure 6-11 shows an example of these settings.

   As a best practice, use the master's IP address on this screen. By doing so, you can avoid future problems with DNS resolution between the replica and the master; however, the fully qualified hostname also works for setting up the replica.

Figure 6-11: Settings in Open Directory Assistant when creating a replica.

7. **View and verify the replica settings and then click the Continue button.**

   During the replication process that follows, the master's LDAP server is temporarily stopped and its database copied to the replica. The same also happens for the Password Server database and the Kerberos realm. Although the interruptions are brief, you may want to avoid creating replica servers during times of heavy network use because users may see delays or failed logins while the databases aren't accessible during the copying process.

   After you successfully create the replica, close Open Directory Assistant by clicking the Done button and return to Server Admin. In Server Admin, you see that the role of your server has changed to a replica, and just like the master, LDAP server, Password Server, and Kerberos are all running.

You just configured your first Open Directory replica. If you've followed along, you know that clients who connect to your shared domain now connect to either the master or the replica by determining which responds faster to ping requests.

Attaching a replica to another replica, which creates an Open Directory relay, is no different than creating a replica from the master. Instead of specifying the master's IP address or the hostname in Step 6 of the preceding list, you enter the IP address or the hostname of a first-tier replica. After the replication process is complete on the second-tier replica, the first-tier replica is an Open Directory relay. See the section, "Master, replica, and relay servers," earlier in this chapter, for details about the rolls of Open Directory.

Creating a Primary Domain Controller for Windows Clients

For your Windows clients, you can use Server Admin to set up your Mac server as a Windows primary domain controller (PDC). This creates a Windows directory domain that can provide authentication for clients and provide home folders for Windows users. You can only create a PDC on a Mac that is serving as an Open Directory master. To create a PDC, do the following:

1. **In Server Admin, click the triangle to the left of your server to expand this list of services and select SMB.**
2. **Click the Settings icon in the toolbar and then click the General tab.**
3. **Click the Role pop-up menu and choose Primary Domain Controller (PDC).**
4. **Enter the appropriate information in the following fields:**
   - *Description* (Optional): On Windows client computers, this appears in the Network Places window.
   - *Computer Name:* This is the NetBIOS name for the server, which Windows users see when they connect. Use 15 characters or less, with no punctuation. The default is the server's (unqualified) hostname.
   - *Domain:* This is the name of the Windows domain that your server is hosting. This name is 15 characters or less, with no punctuation. Also, don't use the word "workgroup."

     Make sure you don't enter the name of a Windows domain on another PDC on the network, or you will create conflicts.
5. **Click the Save button.**
6. **In the dialog that appears, enter the name and password of an LDAP administrator and click OK.**

If your network already has a PDC running on another server, you may want to create a backup domain controller (BCD) instead. However, the Mac must be acting as an Open Directory replica. To create a BCD follow these same steps, except choose Backup Domain Controller (BCD) in Step 3.

To start the PDC or BDC, click the Start SMB button.

Backing Up and Restoring Open Directory with Archives

Open Directory contains several databases of critical information that, in heavily used domains, are constantly being accessed and modified. Open Directory includes the ability for you to easily create backup archives of the entire shared domain, including the LDAP directory, the Password Server database, and the Kerberos realm. During the archive process, which takes a matter of seconds, the open databases are closed and copied.

The downside to the Apple implementation of archiving in Server Admin is the lack of scheduling. The only way to schedule is with the command line.

Because the archive contains password information, the archive is encrypted in a disk image. Your password for the archive and the archives themselves need to be closely guarded like any sensitive data.

Creating an archive in Server Admin

Start by reviewing the options for archiving and restoring Open Directory domains in Server Admin. Work on the Open Directory master — you can't create an archive from a replica server. To create an archive:

1. **Open Server Admin and connect to the Open Directory master.**
2. **Click the triangle next to the server to expand the list of services and select Open Directory.**
3. **Click the Archive icon in the toolbar.**
4. **Type in a folder path or click the Choose button next to the Archive In field and select a location to save the archive.**

   You're browsing the file system of the server regardless of where you run Server Admin.

   In Figure 6-12, you can see the archive options in Server Admin with the archive being stored in a directory on the server's local hard drive.
5. **Click the Archive button and enter a filename and password for the archive. Click OK.**

   A progress bar indicates the archive progression when you click OK.

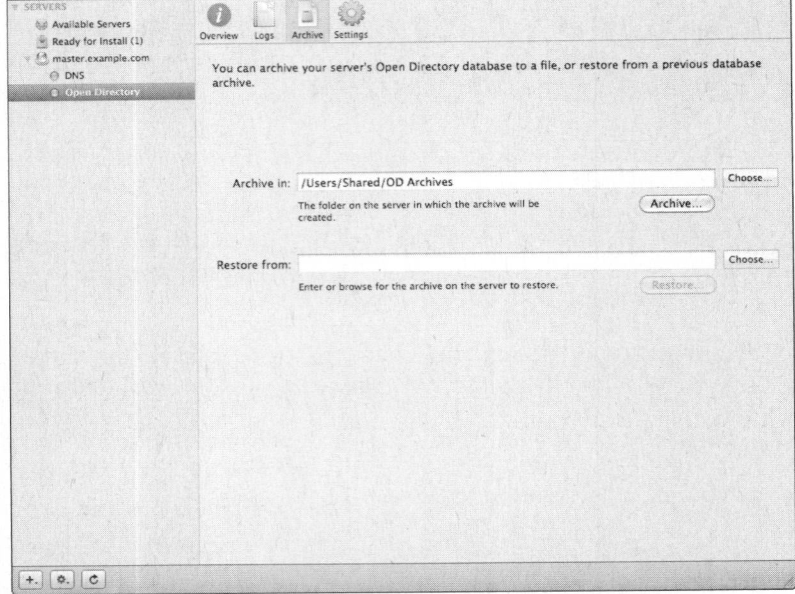

Figure 6-12: Creating an Open Directory archive in Server Admin.

Be extremely careful when you enter the archive's password. No confirmation field exists in the Server Admin interface; a mistyped password could leave you with a useless backup. After you complete the archive, you may want to verify the password by opening the archive disk image in the Finder. When you double-click the image, the Finder prompts you to enter the password you used to create the archive. Secure the image again by unmounting the disk image.

Figure 6-13 shows an open and mounted Open Directory archive in the Finder. Archive disk images always mount with the name `ldap_bk`.

Figure 6-13: An Open Directory archive mounted in the Finder.

After you create the archive, it's a good idea to copy the archive to another drive, server, or location where the archive will be safely stored. Many administrators also use their backup software to make historical backups of the archives and for off-site storage.

Restoring from an archive

In the event that your Open Directory domain becomes corrupt, or you lose user records, you can restore from an archive. The process is essentially the same as the backup, but in reverse.

Before you restore from an archive though, be cognizant of the conditions that restoring imposes. When you restore, you're prompted to either merge or to completely restore the directory data on the server:

- **If you click the Restore button,** the data in the archive completely destroys your existing directory data — all users, passwords, and KDC data is replaced from the archive.
- **If you click the Merge button,** the data in the archive is combined with the existing domain data.

Prior to restoring an archive, if your directory is still working, you may want to create an additional archive as a precaution.

You can also restore an archive to a newly promoted Open Directory master that has no user data. However, if this is your plan, make sure the new Open Directory administrator short name and numeric user ID match the old administrator's short name and user ID when you change the server's role from standalone to master.

Also realize that any Open Directory replica servers in your shared domain need to be demoted to standalone and then reconnected to the new master after you restore from an archive.

Figure 6-14 shows the process of restoring an archive in Server Admin, with the option to restore or merge the directory data.

You can only restore from an archive that's located on the local file system of the server. If your archives are stored elsewhere, copy them to the server's hard drive. Then follow these steps to restore the archive:

1. **Open Server Admin and connect to the Open Directory master server.**
2. **Click Open Directory in Server Admin's expanded list of services and then click the Archive button.**

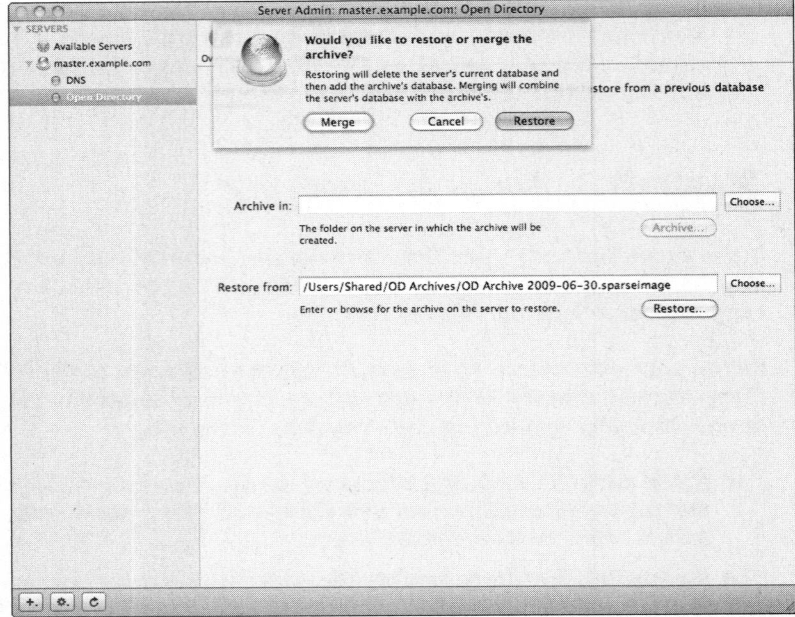

Figure 6-14: Using Server Admin to restore from an Open Directory archive.

3. **Click the Choose button next to the Restore From field to select the location of the archive disk image file and then click the Restore button.**

   Decide whether you want to destroy the existing directory or merge the archive with the directory.

4. **Click the Merge or Restore button, and then enter the password for the archive.**

   Server Admin processes the restoration or merger, and then enables the background directory services.

5. **Verify the directory contents by using Workgroup Manager to browse accounts and other elements of the directory.**

   See Chapter 16 for details on Workgroup Manager.

Binding Clients to the Shared Domain

You share the directory by creating a binding between the client and the Open Directory domain. *Binding* creates a connection between the server and the client, enabling the client to read the LDAP database, send authentication requests, and interact with the Kerberos realm for service tickets. Regarding authentication, you see this interaction most frequently from the login window in Mac OS X, and most of that interaction is transparent to the user.

Any version newer than Mac OS X 10.2 can bind to Open Directory running on Snow Leopard Sever. Your Mac OS X 10.6 client systems should not be bound to versions of Mac OS X Server previous to 10.6 in order to properly support the newest enhancements of Mac OS X. Snow Leopard Server supports Windows 2000 and later as clients.

Binding Mac OS X 10.6 clients

Unlike previous versions of Mac OS X, you can bind Mac OS X 10.6 clients by using System Preferences. Follow these steps to bind a Mac OS X 10.6 client:

1. **Select the Apple menu and choose System Preferences and then click the Accounts icon.**
2. **Click Login Options.**

   If the client has never previously bound to a directory, you will see a Join button next to Network Account Server at the bottom of the Login Options window. If a current binding exists, you will see an Edit button.
3. **Click the Join or Edit button and enter the Open Directory master's fully qualified hostname in the Server field, as shown in Figure 6-15.**

   If you've previously enabled service discovery on your Open Directory Master server, you can find it by clicking the down arrow to show the list of discovered servers on the network.

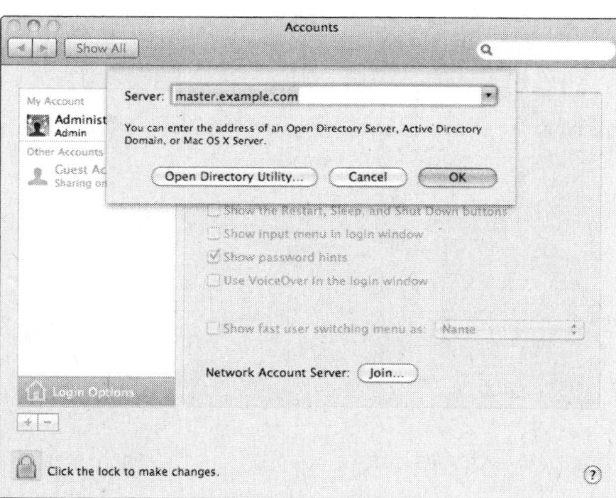

Figure 6-15: Joining the Open Directory master from a Mac OS X client.

4. **Click OK and if prompted, enter the local administrator username and password, authorizing changes to the local directory structure.**
5. **(Optional) Edit the Client Computer ID and enter the directory administrator's username and password, or leave those fields blank for an anonymous binding, as shown in Figure 6-16.**

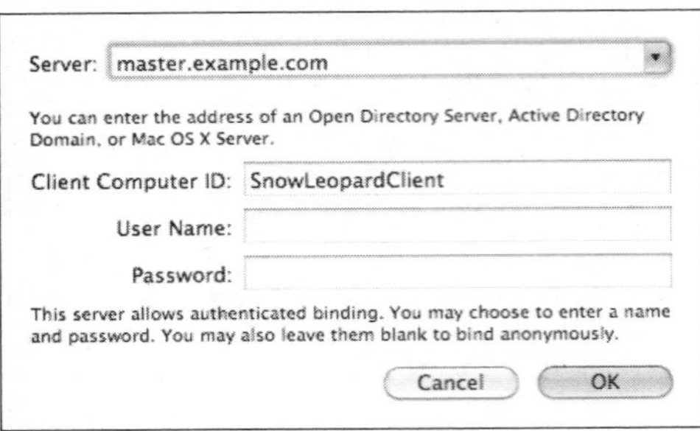

Server: master.example.com
You can enter the address of an Open Directory Server, Active Directory Domain, or Mac OS X Server.
Client Computer ID: SnowLeopardClient
User Name:
Password:
This server allows authenticated binding. You may choose to enter a name and password. You may also leave them blank to bind anonymously.
Cancel
OK

Figure 6-16: Options for binding to the Open Directory master.

After your client is bound to the server, the Accounts preference pane in System Preferences indicates this with a green dot and the server's hostname. You can click the Edit button to modify the settings, and you can also access Directory Utility (in /System/Library/CoreServices/) to make more advanced changes to the directory bindings.

Binding Mac OS X 10.5 and earlier clients

In previous versions of Mac OS X, Directory Utility is installed in the Utilities folder within the Applications folder. To bind a Mac OS X 10.5.8 or earlier client, open Directory Utility and do the following:

1. **Click the lock icon and enter an administrator name and password.**
2. **Click the Add (+) button and select Open Directory from the pop-up menu.**

   Select Active Directory to bind to an Active Directory domain.
3. **Enter the fully qualified hostname or IP address of the server hosting the domain and click OK.**

Binding Windows clients

To bind Windows clients to Mac OS X Server's directory services, you connect it to a PDC, a Windows domain. (See "Creating a Primary Domain Controller for Windows Clients" earlier in the chapter.) With Windows Vista and Windows 7, you can only bind the Ultimate and Business editions. You can also bind Windows XP clients. Here's how to bind them:

1. **Log in to Windows as an administrator.**
2. **Open the Control Panel from the Start menu, and then double-click the System icon.**
3. **Click the Change Settings button.**

   Note: Skip this step for Windows XP.
4. **Click the Computer Name tab, and then click the Change button.**
5. **Enter a computer name if none exists.**
6. **Click Domain and enter the Windows domain name of the Mac OS X Server PDC, and then click the OK button.**

   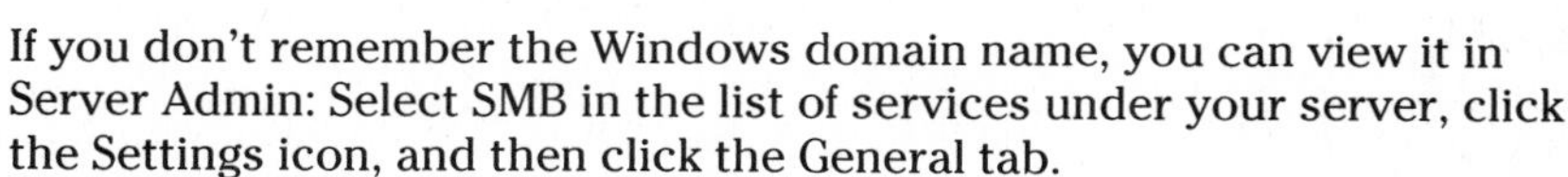

   If you don't remember the Windows domain name, you can view it in Server Admin: Select SMB in the list of services under your server, click the Settings icon, and then click the General tab.
7. **In the dialog that appears, enter the name and password for an LDAP directory administrator and click OK.**

Chapter 7

Integrating Open Directory with Active Directory

In This Chapter

- Understanding Active Directory and Open Directory integration
- Connecting a Mac OS X Snow Leopard server to Active Directory
- Leveraging Active Directory user and computer information
- Setting up Mac clients to be managed by Active Directory
- Configuring Open Directory to utilize Active Directory single sign-on
- Troubleshooting and getting help

Microsoft Active Directory is a fact of life for most corporate networks. Sure, having a homogeneous Macintosh world would make life easier (and would curtail many of the issues that keep IT folks up late at night, such as viruses running rampant through the network). But in reality, corporate networks are largely Microsoft territory. Fortunately you can use a Mac server to provide native services to Mac clients within a larger Windows network.

Adding a Mac OS X Snow Leopard Server to an existing Active Directory infrastructure is a bit less automated than setting up a homogeneous Mac network, but still relatively straightforward. Apple provides an LDAP (Lightweight Directory Access Protocol) plug-in and an Active Directory plug-in that allows a Snow Leopard server to access information from Active Directory, allowing for single sign-on and enforcement of user and computer policies. In this chapter, I show you how to integrate a Mac OS X Snow Leopard Server into an existing Active Directory implementation.

One of the great things about Apple's implementation of Open Directory services is that your Active Directory administrator doesn't need to do anything special to support a Mac OS X Server. The Mac server manages and stores the information about the Mac network and exchanges the information with Active Directory in the format that it likes. (For more information about setting up an Active Directory schema, check out *Active Directory For Dummies,* 2nd Edition by Steve Clines and Marcia Loughry, Wiley.)

Doing the Directory Services Two-Step

Directory services make a server administrator's life much easier by providing a centralized repository for information about users, groups, and computers. Using directory services, administrators can consolidate users and computing resources into groups and then apply and enforce security and permissions policies across those groups.

Snow Leopard Server uses Open Directory to provide directory services for Mac clients, though it also supports Windows clients (as described in Chapter 6). Windows servers use Active Directory to provide directory services on a network. Apple's Active Directory plug-in for Mac OS X allows a Mac server to maintain information about Mac clients and allows access to enforce Active Directory policies and authentication.

In an Active Directory environment, Mac servers actually provide authentication of both Open Directory and Active Directory to the Mac clients. This dual authentication role allows policies to be implemented on the Mac server for Mac clients that would be non-standard in an Active Directory environment (such as iChat services or Podcast Producer services) while allowing Active Directory to handle the network services that are common to Windows and Mac users on the network.

The Mac server's ability to manage both Open Directory and Active Directory separately (and never the twain shall meet) is known as implementing the *magic triangle,* as shown in Figure 7-1. (The magic triangle shouldn't be confused with a percussion instrument for productions of *The Magic Flute.*) The Mac server handles the Active Directory piece of the puzzle by using the Active Directory plug-in, which sets up a special account on Active Directory that translates network requests from Mac clients into the format that Active Directory expects from Windows clients.

Binding Your Server to Active Directory

The first step in integrating a Mac server into an Active Directory environment is to bind the Mac OS X Server to the Active Directory domain. *Binding,* in this case, means creating the link between the Mac server and Active Directory.

Prior to binding the Mac server to the Active Directory domain, you need to have ready the following information (some of which must come from your Active Directory domain administrator):

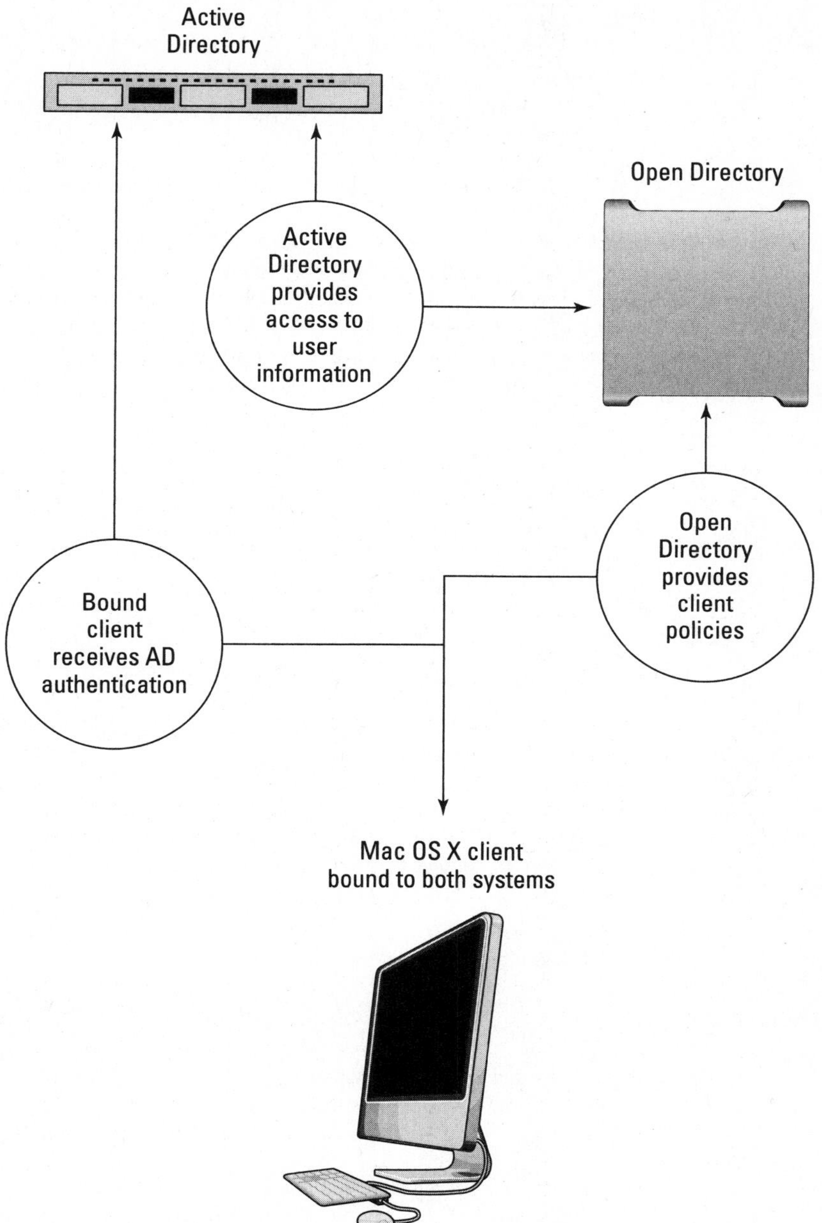

Figure 7-1: The Active Directory-Open Directory magic triangle.

- **Mac Server credentials:** You need to have your local server administrator login and password at the ready. But you have that memorized anyway, right?
- **Domain administrator login credentials or rights:** An administrator login and password for the Active Directory domain to which the server will be bound (or having your credentials added to this administrative group in Active Directory).
- **Fully qualified domain name for the Active Directory (AD) domain:** If you don't know the fully qualified AD domain name, ask your AD administrator. Generally the domain name is `domain.top-level-domain` for example, `mycompany.com` in a simple structure or `NorthAmerica.BigCompany.Com` in a larger network with multiple domains.
- **The hostname or IP address of the time server used by the Active Directory domain:** The time setting for the Active Directory server must be within five minutes of the time setting for the Mac OS X Server for the binding to be successful. The easiest way to ensure that the time settings are correct is to use the same time server for all servers and clients on your network. Select the same date and time server from the Date & Time System Preference pane.

Checking DNS configuration

Active Directory requires that domain name services (DNS) be working properly so that the Mac OS X Snow Leopard Server hostname and IP address are linked. The linkage should work both in forward and reverse (meaning that if you check the IP, it resolves to the server's hostname; and if you check the hostname, it resolves to the correct IP address).

To check that DNS is configured properly, open Terminal (in /Applications/Utilities/) to access the command line and type `NSLOOKUP` *`hostname`*. If configured properly, the DNS server reports the IP address of the server. To check the reverse, type `NSLOOKUP` *`ipaddress`*. If configured correctly, the DNS server reports the hostname for your Mac OS X Server. If either of these fail, DNS isn't configured properly for your server. (See Chapter 3 for more on DNS.)

Binding the server

After you have the required information in hand and have ensured that DNS is working properly (see the preceding section), you're ready to bind the server. To bind your server to an Active Directory domain, follow these steps:

1. **Launch System Preferences and click the Accounts icon.**

   The Accounts pane opens, as shown in Figure 7-2.

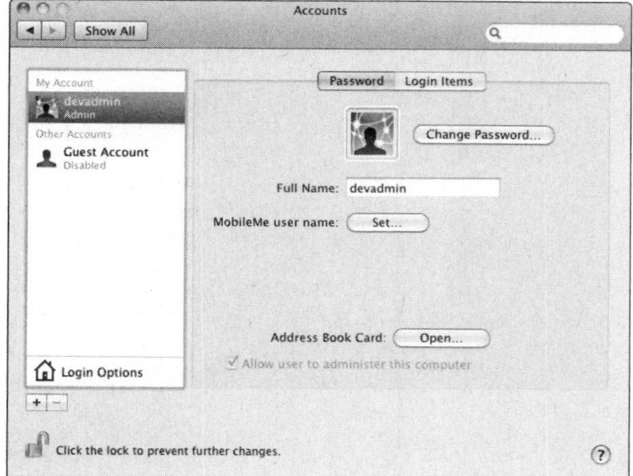

Figure 7-2: The Accounts pane.

2. **Click the lock icon (see Figure 7-2) to display a login dialog.**
3. **Enter your administrator login and password and then click OK to make changes to the Accounts pane.**
4. **Click the Login Options icon at the bottom left of the Accounts pane.**

   You see the available options, as shown in Figure 7-3. This pane provides access to set network directory configuration.

Figure 7-3: Configure network directories by clicking the Login Options icon.

5. **Click the Edit button.**

   A drop-down sheet opens that displays all network directories that the machine has been set up to access. The first time you bind a directory, you can see only the local directory server, as shown in Figure 7-4.

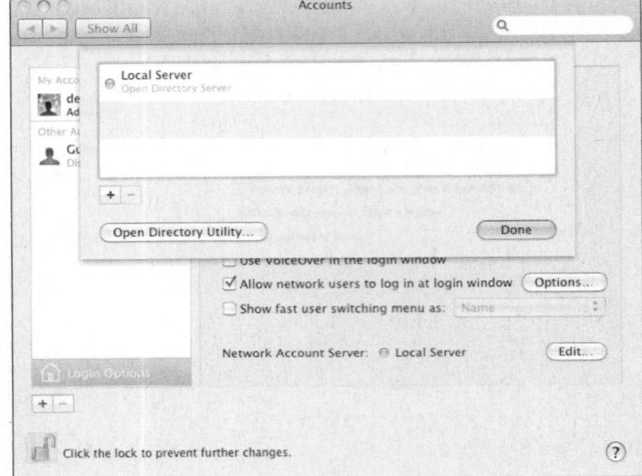

Figure 7-4: Before binding, you see only the local server in this list.

6. **Click the Open Directory Utility button in the drop-down sheet.**

   The Directory Utility application opens, as shown in Figure 7-5.

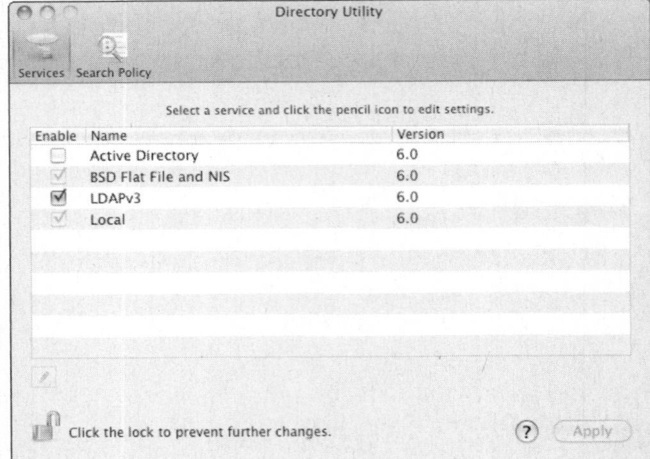

Figure 7-5: The Directory Utility application is where binding happens.

7. **Ensure that the Services icon is selected in the toolbar.**

   Services is the default.

8. **Click the lock icon at the bottom left of the Directory Utility pane to access the login and password dialog. Enter your administrator credentials again and then click OK.**

9. **Click the Active Directory line to *highlight* it.**

   Don't select the Enable check box at this time.

10. **Click the plug-in configuration button (the pencil icon, as shown in Figure 7-5).**

    A drop-down sheet appears, as shown in Figure 7-6.

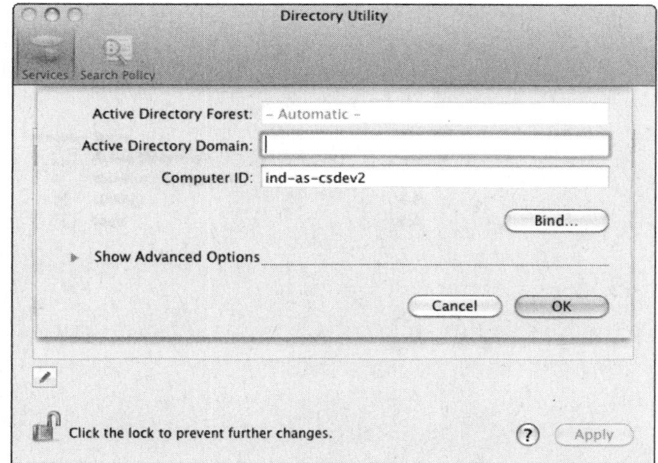

Figure 7-6: Active Directory plug-in configuration options.

11. **Type your fully qualified Active Directory domain name in the Active Directory Domain text box, as shown in Figure 7-7.**

12. **Click the Bind button.**

    The Network Administrator Required dialog opens, as shown in Figure 7-8.

13. **Enter a network domain administrator login and password, and then click OK.**

    This may not be the same as the local administrator credential you entered earlier. This must be a login and password that has rights to make changes to the Active Directory domain. If you are unsure, contact your Active Directory administrator.

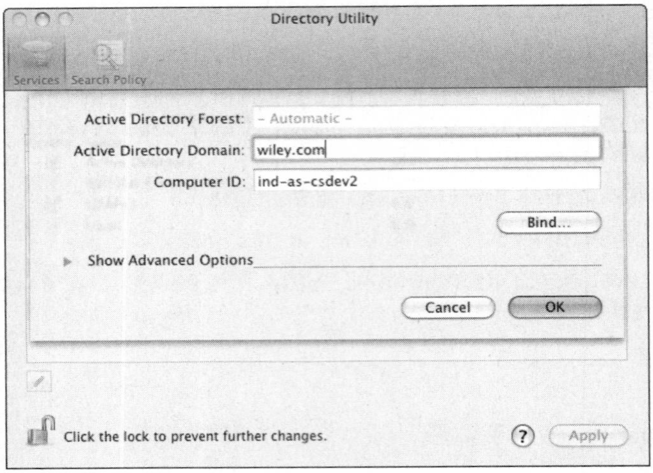

Figure 7-7: Fill in the Active Directory Domain text box and then click Bind.

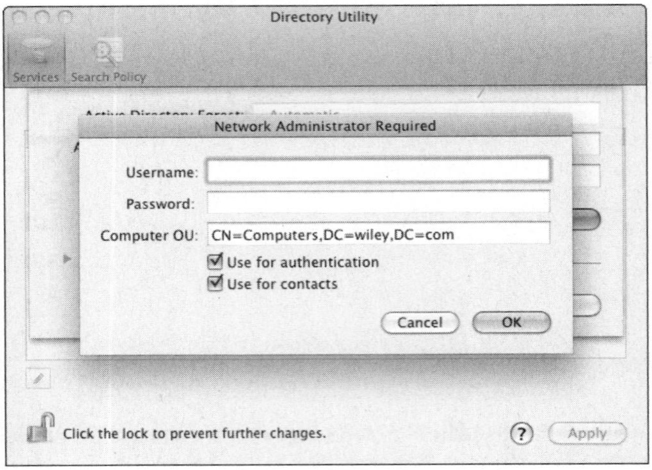

Figure 7-8: Enter the login credentials for a domain administrator.

The Computer OU (organizational unit) text box typically has the correct information by default. If you're unsure whether it's correct or if this text box is blank, contact your Active Directory domain administrator for the correct organizational unit to enter.

Another authentication dialog appears that asks for the local server administration credentials.

14. **Enter your Mac OS X Server administrator credential and password and click OK.**

    The Bind button in the Directory Utility dialog changes to Unbind, as shown in Figure 7-9. This tells you that the binding has succeeded; the server is now bound to the Active Directory domain.

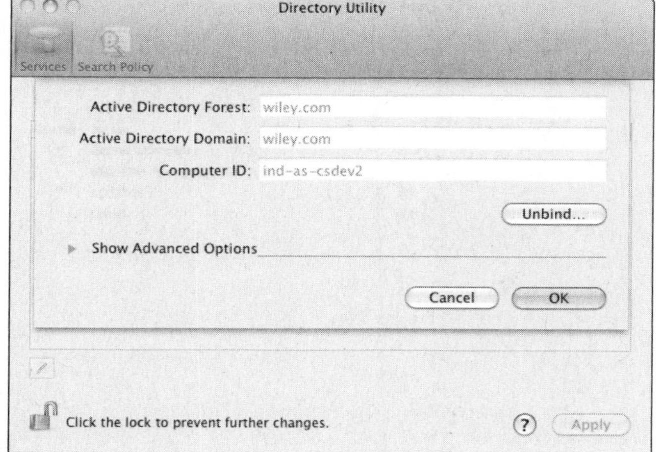

Figure 7-9: The appearance of the Unbind button signals success!

To test whether the binding is indeed successful, open a Terminal session to access the command line and type `id` *`AD user shortname`*. If the binding is successful, Active Directory returns the first 16 Active Directory groups of which the user is a member.

Deciding whether to Muck Around with Advanced Configuration

In some cases, Mac OS X administrators want to configure particular settings that appear in the advanced options of the Directory Utility to specify particular ways that the Mac OS X Server interacts with Active Directory. In many cases, the default settings are fine, but in some cases, particularly when the AD schema is for a large company, you may need to make some specific changes to these settings.

All the advanced options specify how the plug-in accepts information from Active Directory for the server itself. The configurations are not translated to clients and groups administered by the Mac OS X Server on the Active Directory domain.

To access the advanced options for configuring the Active Directory plug-in, follow these steps:

1. **Access the Directory Utility application by following Steps 1 through 10 in the previous section, "Binding the server."**
2. **Click the triangle next to Show Advanced Options at the bottom of the Directory to expand the advanced options, as shown in Figure 7-10.**

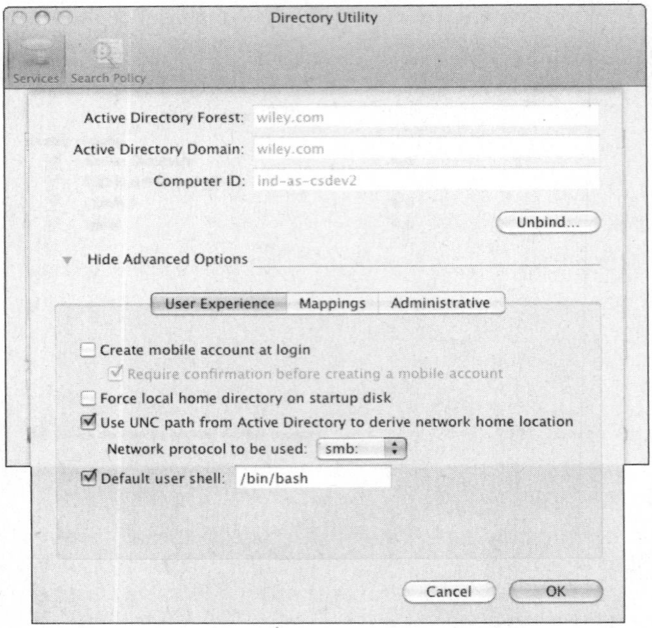

Figure 7-10: Advanced options for Active Directory integration.

Three tabs are available in the advanced options:

- **User Experience:** This tab lets you change some default settings for users, including changing the location of the home directory to point to an external file server rather than the hard drive on the local Mac OS X Server.
- **Mappings:** This tab allows the administrator to redirect default user and group ID settings to customized extensions in the Active Directory schema. These mappings may or may not come into play depending upon the configuration of the Active Directory schema. Contact your Active Directory administrator for details.
- **Administrative:** This tab allows the administrator to allow direct contact between the Mac OS X Server and Active Directory domain to a specific domain server, to allow or deny server administration by domain administrators or other groups without the need to log in with the Mac OS X Server's login credentials, and to allow the server to look up user and password information for domains administered by Active Directory outside the local domain (cryptically referred to as *other domains in the forest* in IT architecture parlance).

Managing User Groups with Workgroup Manager

The important thing to remember about managing users in an Active Directory environment is that you need to add the users from Active Directory into your Open Directory domain on the Mac server. Doing so is necessary because Active Directory manages the permissions and policies of the users in an Active Directory environment. Active Directory user information isn't directly translatable to a Mac client. Open Directory serves as the mechanism to implement client management policies similar to the policies that Windows clients enjoy from Active Directory.

Adding users from Active Directory is as simple as dragging and dropping users into Open Directory. Follow these steps:

1. **Open Workgroup Manager by clicking its icon in the Dock.**

   Workgroup Manager asks you to authenticate with your local server manager username and password to connect to the local server.

2. **Enter your local admin username and password, and then click OK.**

   Workgroup Manager opens.

3. **Click the lock icon to bring up an authentication dialog to allow changes to Open Directory.**

   An authentication dialog opens.

4. **Enter the username and password for the Open Directory administrator and then click OK.**

5. **Click the Accounts icon in the toolbar (the default) and then click the Groups icon directly below the Accounts icon.**

   The window now looks like Figure 7-11.

6. **Click the New Group icon in the toolbar.**

   Workgroup Manager creates a new group with a group ID (GID).

7. **Type a name for the group in the Name text box.**

   The name can include characters, numbers, and spaces. The short name is automatically created and will abide by Unix naming conventions, so you're free to name the group in any way you like. You can also supply a path to an icon by entering the path in the Picture Path text box and comment, but this isn't necessary.

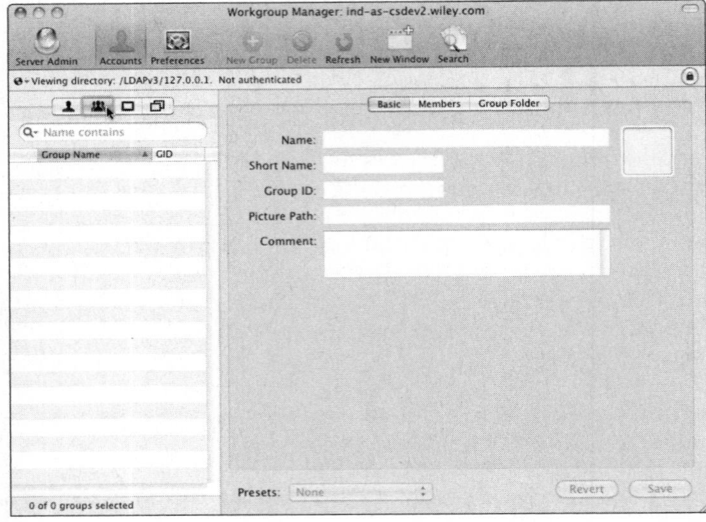

Figure 7-11: The Group accounts area of Workgroup Manager.

8. **Click the Members tab.**

   A blank members table opens.

9. **Click the Add (+) button, as shown in Figure 7-12, to display the Open Directory users list.**

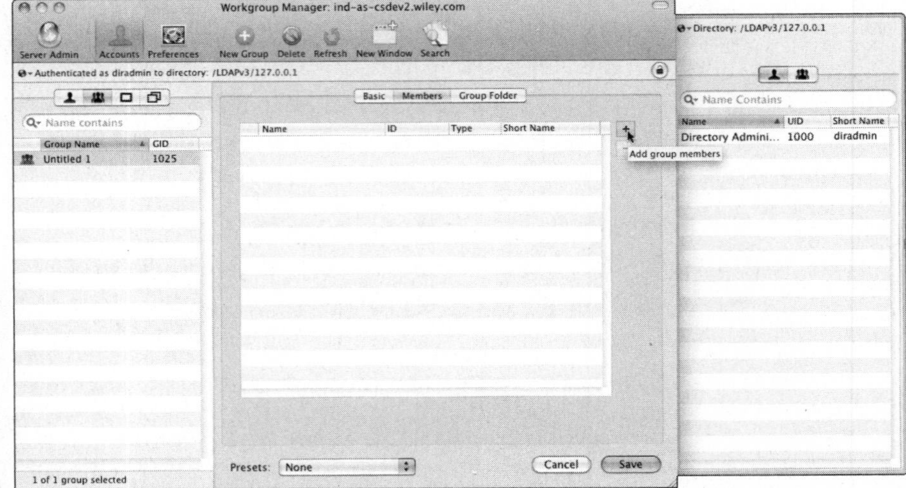

Figure 7-12: Accessing Open Directory users.

10. **Click the directory menu (refer to Figure 7-12) to access the Active Directory domain, as shown in Figure 7-13.**

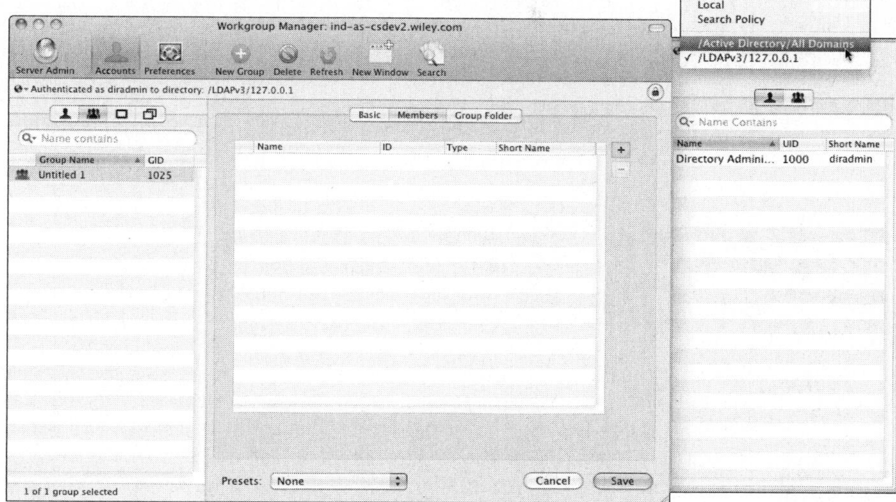

Figure 7-13: Selecting the Active Directory domain.

A list of Active Directory users for your domain is returned. All records may not show up in the list, but you can gain access to any user record in the domain via the search field.

11. **Drag the records you want to manage from the drawer list to the user list in the main window, as shown Figure 7-14.**

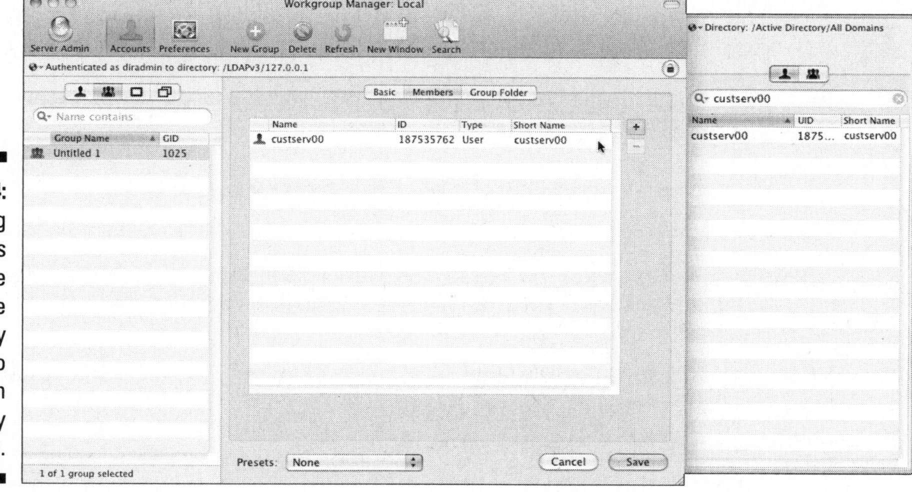

Figure 7-14: Drag records from the Active Directory domain to the Open Directory domain.

12. **After you identify all records that you want to manage, click the Save button.**

    At this point, Active Directory is managing authentication for the users in the groups. You can further specify user preferences under the Preferences pane for Open Directory access for these users. See Chapter 6.

Configuring Single Sign-On for Mac Clients

After successfully binding the Mac server to the Active Directory domain (see the section, "Binding Your Server to Active Directory," earlier in this chapter), another step to consider is to implement Kerberos on the server. Kerberos is used by both Active Directory and Open Directory for authentication across various applications so that after a user logs in to the network, the user can access all network assets and applications for which she has permission without the need for further authentication. Doing away with the need for multiple passwords and authentications is called *single sign-on.*

Single sign-on in Active Directory works by AD issuing a *ticket* when a user logs in to the domain. The ticket represents everything that the user can do. After logging in initially, all other authentication activities are handled automatically by the ticket.

Of course, for single sign-on to work for Mac clients on an Active Directory network, single sign-on must first be implemented in Active Directory. Single sign-on implementation in Active Directory is beyond the scope of this book.

To implement Kerberos and SSO for Mac clients in an Active Directory domain, follow these steps:

1. **Open Server Admin by clicking the icon in the Dock.**

   Server Admin opens.

2. **If necessary, connect to your Mac OS X Server by choosing Server⇨Connect and entering your server administrator username and password.**
3. **Click the triangle next to the server name and then select Open Directory.**
4. **Click the Settings icon in the toolbar.**
5. **Click the Kerberize button.**

The Kerberize the Open Directory Master dialog opens (as shown in Figure 7-15) and requests authentication. The credential you enter must have administrator rights over the Kerberos domain. Contact your Active Directory administrator to gain the necessary rights.

That's it!

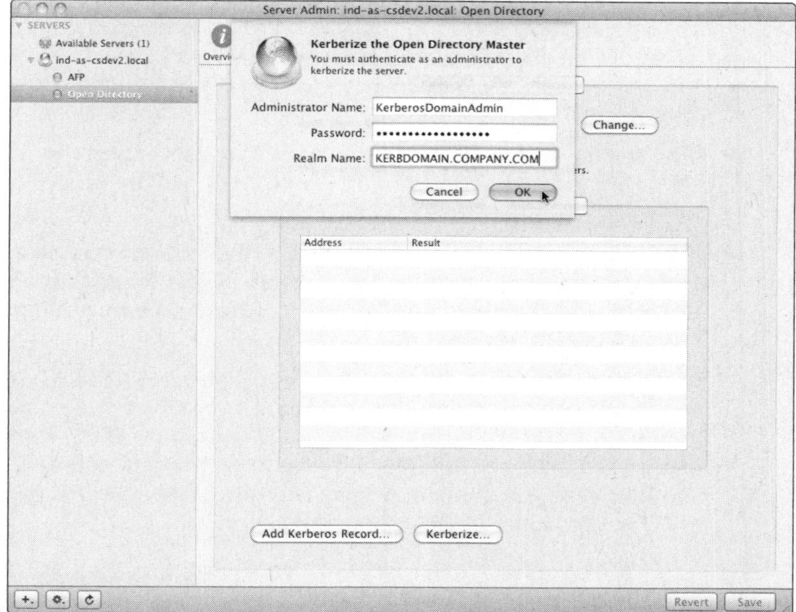

Figure 7-15: The Kerberize the Open Directory Master admin login.

Test that single sign-on is working properly by logging in as a user and attempting to access a resource to which the user has permission that's managed by Active Directory. In a working deployment, access is granted without the need to reauthenticate.

Troubleshooting and Getting Help

Having come to this section, I can only assume that something went wrong with implementing Mac OS X Server on Active Directory. This short section provides some areas known to cause problems and some troubleshooting tips. Because every Active Directory implementation is different, troubleshooting every possible scenario is impossible. But Apple stands behind its products and will help you to figure out what's going wrong if these tips fail. The most commonly reported issues are

- **DNS service problems:** The Mac client must use the same DNS servers as all the Windows clients on the network. To ensure that the correct DNS server is being used, open a Terminal session and type `dig -t SRV _ldap._tcp.`*`yourDomainDNS`*`.com`. If configured properly, you should receive in response, the IP address of your domain server. If this doesn't work, either the Mac systems are using a different DNS server than the Windows clients or DNS is set up improperly on your Mac server.
- **Time server issues:** If the times on the Mac server and the domain server are more than five minutes apart, you will be unable to join the domain.
- **.local domain issues:** It's possible that the .local domain used by Bonjour may conflict with a .local Active Directory domain. If this is a problem, add the .local domain to the search domain settings of the Network preferences pane.
- **Replication issues:** In the past, binding a Mac to a large AD domain has resulted in the computer account being created on one domain and the computer account's password on another domain. If the replication interval isn't fast enough, the set password request fails and the Mac isn't bound to the domain. Ensure that the same server is being used for both Kerberos and LDAP connections.

This book can't replicate your Active Directory schema to analyze uncommon problems. (Though, that would be a great trick!) You can access Apple's directory support at `www.apple.com/support/macosxserver/opendirectory`.

If you're having problems, check out John Rizzo's MacWindows.com. Up on the Web since 1997, MacWindows.com features lots of bug reports and tips regarding Mac integration with Active Directory, among other topics.

Part III
Serving Up Files and Printers

"Don't laugh. It's faster than our current system."

In this part . . .

Meat and potatoes.

For many, network file and print sharing makes up the basic work of a server. Snow Leopard Server's roots go back to file-sharing software, Apple's 1985 release of AppleShare. Apple thought it would help Mac sales to businesses by providing a central repository for files that all Mac users could access. Today, file and print sharing are only two of many functions that the server provides to users, but they still play a central role in networks. Snow Leopard Server's file and print services support client computers running any operating system with rich user and administration features and robust security.

You can easily share printers without a server, but print serving goes beyond giving users access to printers. It juggles multiple printing requests to any single printer and manages all your printers. You can set priorities for particular printers and place limits on how much users print. And it provides user features, such as sending a print job to a free printer rather than sitting in a queue.

But before I show you how all that works, I throw in a chapter on *permissions*, settings that determine who can do what to which files. Snow Leopard Server supports a set of easy-to-use permissions that you can configure in minutes. It also supports high-end, enterprise-level permissions for large and complex network situations. Use one or the other, or mix and match.

Chapter 8

Controlling Access to Files and Folders

In This Chapter

- Working with standard POSIX permissions
- Understanding access control list permissions
- Inheriting permissions
- Looking at the rules of precedence
- Controlling access to protocols with service access control lists

If you're a strict egalitarian, you may be inclined to give everyone on the network complete access to everything on the server. This might work with a small office with a handful of users, but can be confusing to users if they have to sift through numerous server folders or if they find that someone accidentally moved a needed file.

Snow Leopard Server lets you control access by users to shared folders, files, and applications. You do this by assigning permissions, which grant users the ability to perform certain actions, such as open a folder or edit a file. Snow Leopard Server has permissions for files, folders, and applications.

You assign or change these user and group entities and permissions in Sever Admin's File Sharing pane in the Permissions tab, as shown in Figure 8-1 for reference. (Chapter 9 describes how to use Server Admin to set these permissions for shared folders.) In this chapter, I focus on describing the different types of permission schemes and their options.

Figure 8-1: Server Admin File Sharing pane.

Owner, Group, and Others (Everyone)

In file sharing, you set permissions for three user categories: *Owner, Group,* and *Others.* There's also *Everyone,* which is similar to Others. (You can also find these user categories on users' Macs; ⌘-click or right-click any file or folder and then choose Get Info.) You can use the categories to restrict access to a certain set of users, provide different levels of access to different users, or prevent access. When you create shared folders (called *share points*), you assign permissions to these classes of users.

These user categories are hierarchical; a user gets the permissions of the highest level he's a member of. If a user is both the owner and in a group, the user gets Owner permissions.

Owners

The owner can be a user with a local account or one with a directory domain account. By default, the owner of a file or folder is the user who created it. The owner could also be the administrator.

The owner usually has the highest level of permissions. This could be the ability to do anything to a file, such as edit, delete, or copy it. The owner is the only entity that can change permissions for groups or for

Others/Everyone. The owner can also change the owner — that is, transfer ownership to another user.

The owner doesn't have to be a person — the owner can be entities of the operating system or the operating system itself. With the latter, this owner is `system`, the equivalent of the Unix `root` user.

Groups

A *group* is a collection of users that you create accounts for. When a folder on the server has permissions for a particular group, all members of the group can access the folder. In Chapter 5, I describe creating groups, which you can do with System Preferences or Workgroup Manager.

Everyone, Others, and Guests

Everyone, Others, and Guests are similar and can be treated as one category of user. For a particular shared file or folder, they all refer to *everyone else* — users who aren't an owner or in a group. This category is given the lowest level of permissions, which can be no access at all.

Others are users who are logged in to the file server but are not an owner or in a group for a particular file or folder. *Everyone* includes anonymous users not logged in to the file server. (Just to be different, the NFS file-sharing protocol refers to *Everyone* as *World*.)

Don't worry too much about it: You'll never have to choose between Others and Everyone in a dialog. They are used in different places.

You see a choice for *Guest* only in the settings for file services (not for individual share points), where you can choose to Allow Guest Access. Doing so allows anonymous users who aren't logged in to access that file service or protocol without using a password. Guests have access only to files and folders with privileges for Everyone.

Permission Schemes: POSIX permissions and ACLs

Snow Leopard Server offers two different types of permissions for files and folders: Portable Operating System Interface for Unix (POSIX) permissions from the Unix world and access control lists (ACLs) from the Windows world.

POSIX permissions are easier to use, but ACLs give you a finer degree of control over access to files and folders. Keep in mind, however, that ACLs are more complicated to manage.

POSIX permissions allow only one owner and one group setting for a shared folder. POSIX permissions don't provide different permissions to different individual users. ACLs allow multiple individuals and multiple groups. This can be useful if you have several departments in the organization that need different levels of access for the same shared folder.

Table 8-1 shows the permission types that each file-sharing protocol can use. Chapter 9 describes the file-sharing protocols in further detail, but here's the gist: Apple Filing Protocol (AFP) is the best to use for Mac clients, and Server Message Block (SMB) is the best to use for Windows clients. NFS (Network File Sharing) is provided in case you need it for certain Unix or Linux clients. Otherwise, Unix and Linux use SMB. FTP (File Transfer Protocol) is a special protocol for public or semipublic access with Web browsers or other common software.

Table 8-1 Permission Types Available to File-Sharing Protocols

File-Sharing Protocol	*POSIX Permissions*	*ACL Permissions*
AFP	Yes	Yes
SMB	Yes	Yes
NFS	Yes (files only)	No
FTP	Yes	No

You can use Server Preferences to set a limited set of POSIX permissions for AFP and SMB, using only a few mouse clicks. To take advantage of the full set of permission combinations that POSIX permissions offer, or to set ACLs, use Server Admin, which enables you to set all permissions that Snow Leopard Server provides.

The following sections look more closely at POSIX permissions and ACLs.

Standard POSIX Permissions

POSIX permissions are the standard that defines how Unix interacts with applications. Among other things, POSIX permissions define a permission structure for accessing files and folders. POSIX permissions are used not only in file sharing on a network, but also on the Unix computer itself. Because Mac OS X (and therefore Snow Leopard Server) has Unix at its core, POSIX permissions are used on all files and folders on every user's Mac.

Because these permissions are used throughout Mac OS X, POSIX permissions are sometimes referred to as *standard* permissions in Apple documentation and elsewhere.

For any given file, folder, or volume, Standard POSIX permissions have four types of access that you can set for Owner, Group, and Others/Everyone:

- **Read and write:** Full access to a shared folder or file. A user can open and save files located on the server-based folder and can copy files to the folder.
- **Read-only:** A user can open the shared folder and files as well as copy a file or folder to his computer. But users with read-only access can't save changes to files that they open in the shared folder, and they can't add files to the shared folder or delete files.
- **Write-only:** Users can only copy a file into a write-only folder. They can't open the folder to see what's in it or access the files. A write-only folder on a server is sometimes referred to as a *drop folder.*
- **No access:** The user has no access to the folder or file, and can't copy files to or from it.

In Unix, another POSIX permission is *execute.* This permission enables a user or group to run a program. In a Unix command-line shell, the execute permissions also allows you to list the files in a directory. This is similar to read permissions, which let you open folders to see what's inside. The execute permission isn't used in Server Admin or Server Preferences.

Propagating POSIX Permissions

When you configure file sharing, you generally set permissions for one or more shared folders (share points). Usually users can create new files or folders and can copy files into a folder. Rather than having to set Owner and Group permissions for every new file and folder, these *child folders* and files are automatically assigned based on rules.

All the file-sharing protocols can use the standard POSIX permissions behavior. The AFP and SMB protocols have another option for propagating POSIX permissions — dubbed *Inherit Permissions from Parent,* or just *Inherit Permissions.* With this method, new files and folders inherit certain permissions from the *parent* folder (the folder in which the files and folders are created).

Standard POSIX permissions behavior

In the standard behavior, permissions are assigned for new files and folders on a share point, regardless of what the permissions are on the parent folder. New files or folders get these permissions:

- **Owner:** The user who created the new folder or file becomes the owner and is assigned read/write permissions.
- **Group:** The new file or folder inherits the group assigned to the parent folder; however, the group is assigned read-only permissions.
- **Everyone/Other:** Is assigned read-only permissions.

Files and folders copied to the share point or duplicated don't inherit any permissions from the parent folder:

- **Owner:** The user who created the folder or file remains the owner and is assigned read/write permissions. This is just as with new files and folders.
- **Group:** Retains the group and permissions of the *original* file or folder.
- **Everyone/Other:** Retains permissions of the *original* file or folder.

Again, these are the default rules. The permissions of files and folders can be changed.

Inherit permissions from parent

In addition to standard POSIX permissions behavior, the AFP and SMB protocols also support another model for propagating POSIX permissions that can be more convenient. It's an *inheritance* model, where certain permissions are inherited from the parent folder. Here's how it works:

- **Folders:** New folders, folders that are copied into the share point (parent folder), and duplicated folders inherit the Owner, Group, and Everyone permissions from the parent folder.
- **Files:** New files, files that are copied into the share point, or duplicated files. For these, the Owner inheritance is different than for Groups and Everyone:
    - *Owner:* The owner/user who created the file or copied it to the shared folder remains the owner.
    - *Group and Other/Everyone:* The Group and Other/Everyone permissions are inherited from the parent folder. In other words, if a user

copies a file or folder into a share point that uses the inheritance model, the Group permissions change. This is different from the standard POSIX permissions behavior described in the preceding section.

The standard POSIX permissions behavior and the inheritance model rules are for POSIX permissions. ACLs have their own permissions propagation models.

Access Control Lists

For any share point, you can also create an *access control list (ACL)* to define permissions. An ACL is a list of users and groups that have access to a share point, and the permissions and inheritance settings that they have. Each entry in the list is an *access control entity (ACE)*. An ACE is a user or group and the associated permissions and inheritance settings.

Here's a simple ACL with two ACEs you might set for a share point:

	Permission	***Applies To***
User: ronmckernan	Read/write	This Folder
Group: students	Read	This Folder

This ACL is similar to a set of POSIX permissions for a folder. There's one user and one group with read/write permissions. Applies to This Folder means no inheritance, as with POSIX permissions.

A limitation of POSIX permissions is that you can assign only one group and one user (the owner) access to a shared folder. With an ACL, you can continue to add ACEs to the list. Here, I added a teachers group with read/write privileges and a second user with write-only access:

	Permission	***Applies To***
User: ronmckernan	Read/write	This Folder
User: Tim Constanten	Write	This Folder
Group: teachers	Read/write	This Folder
Group: students	Read	This Folder

Further deviating from POSIX permissions, you can further refine the ACL by setting more specific permissions, in addition to read and write and adding inheritance. Here I've done this for the first user:

	Permission	*Applies To*
User: ronmckernan	Read/Create Files/Create Folders/Write Extended Attributes	This Folder/Child Folders/ Child Files/All Descendents
User: Tim Constanten	Write	This Folder
Group: teachers	Read/write	This Folder
Group: students	Read	This Folder

I describe these more specific ACL permissions in the next section.

ACL permissions

ACLs provide finer shades of what read and write mean. For instance, you could set write permissions to enable a group to edit files but not to create new folders. You could also enable users to edit a file but not to delete it.

Thirteen permissions are in Apple's implementation of ACL, plus four types of inheritance you can define. Figure 8-2 shows the window in Server Admin where you can set ACL permissions. (Chapter 9 has a description of how to access this window in Server Admin. The short version is to click your server, click the File Sharing icon, select a share point, and then double-click an entry under ACLs.)

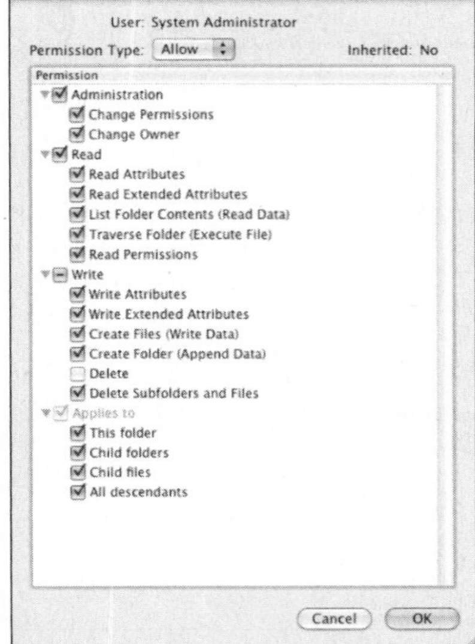

Figure 8-2: ACL permissions in Server Admin.

The 13 permissions are grouped by type, as follows:

- **Administration:**
  - *Change Permissions:* Users can change standard POSIX permissions even if they aren't an owner.
  - *Change Owner:* Users can change the file's or folder's ownership to themselves or to someone else.
- **Read:**
  - *Read Attributes:* Users can view the file's or folder's attributes, including filename, date created, and size.
  - *Read Extended Attributes:* Users can view the file's or folder's attributes, or metadata, added by third-party developers.
  - *List Folder Contents (Read Data):* Users can view the folder's contents and open files.
  - *Traverse Folder (Execute File):* Users can open subfolders and run programs in the folder.
  - *Read Permissions:* Users can view the standard POSIX permissions of the file or folder with the Mac Finder's Get Info window (choose Finder⇨Get Info) or with Terminal commands.
- **Write:**
  - *Write Attributes:* Users can change the file's or folder's standard attributes.
  - *Write Extended Attributes:* Users can change the file's or folder's other attributes.
  - *Create Files (Write Data):* Users can create and edit files.
  - *Create Folder (Append Data):* Users can create subfolders.
  - *Delete:* Users can delete a file or folder.
  - *Delete Subfolders and Files:* Users can delete subfolders and files within the selected folder. You set these permissions on folders only. Files inherit permissions from the folder they're in. I describe ACL inheritance in the following section.

You can use ACLs only on storage devices formatted in the HFS+ file system. If you want to use ACLs on a particular storage device that's formatted differently, you have to first reformat that drive in HFS+.

To take advantage of ACL permissions, you must use Server Admin. You can't set or manage ACL permissions with Server Preferences.

With this staggering array of permissions, you can easily lose track of who gets access to what and how. The best practice is to base your permission structure on group permissions. Don't set individual user permissions unless you need an exception, either with more permissive or more restrictive access. A good plan is to try to assign permissions to groups only once. Then if you need to change individuals' access, just add or remove them from groups.

ACL inheritance

You can apply one or more of the 13 permissions to a folder. ACLs use an inheritance model to propagate these permissions to files in the folder and to folders within the selected folder. The Applies To section of the ACL permissions in the Server Admin dialog in Figure 8-2 gives you four choices for inheritance. Each applies to a particular level of folder hierarchy:

- **This Folder:** Apply permissions to the selected folder (the folder you're setting the permissions for).
- **Child Folders:** Apply permissions to subfolders (folders that are one level below the selected folder).
- **Child Files:** Apply permissions to the files in the selected folder.
- **All Descendants:** Apply permissions to folders and files that are inside subfolders, that is, to items that are two or more levels below the selected folder. (See Figure 8-3.) By itself, this doesn't apply to the subfolders.

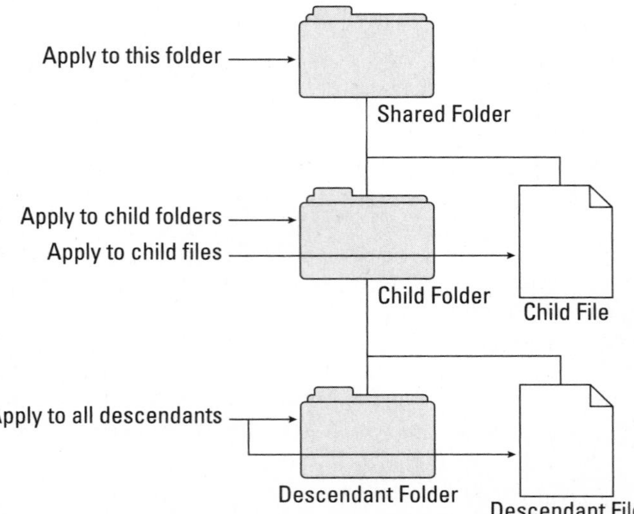

Figure 8-3: The ACL inheritance settings apply to different levels of folders within folders.

The four inheritance settings can be used in combination with each other. If you select Applies to This Folder only, the ACL permissions settings wouldn't propagate but would apply only to the selected folder.

If you check both Applies to Child Folders and Applies to Child Files, the permissions would apply to the files and folders inside the selected folder, but would not apply to the selected folder itself. Also, any folders inside the subfolders wouldn't get the permissions.

If you select Applies to This Folder and Applies to All Descendants, the permissions propagation would *skip a generation,* applying to the selected folder and to all folder levels below the first subfolder level.

Allow and Deny permissions

In Figure 8-1, the Permission Type pop-up menu is set to Allow. You can also choose Deny. *Allow* means that all the selected permissions are allowed, which is the normal situation. You can also create an ACE where you use the Deny setting to specifically deny a permission, such as write access, rather than simply assigning read-only access.

The difference is that the Deny setting overrides other permissions. If the server finds a Deny permission in the ACL, it stops looking for other permissions the user might have. In a complex situation with a lot of nested folders with different permissions settings and a user belonging to multiple groups, a Deny permission could cause access problems that might be difficult to track down. For this reason, it's best to limit the use of Deny permissions. Apple recommends keeping a list of any Deny permissions that you set so that you can undo them later if needed.

Using inherited and explicit ACEs together

You can use inheritance to automatically assign ACLs together with manually set permissions, which are called *explicit* permissions settings.

As an example, say you have a Publications share point. You've assigned a Marketing group with certain ACL permissions that propagate down through all the subfolders. For two subfolders, you want to add permissions for the Art Department group. For the contents of those two subfolders, both Marketing and Art Department groups can have permissions for the files and folders in those subfolders. Within other subfolders, only Marketing would have permissions.

Explicit permissions can also be propagated down through subfolders by inheritance settings. (Use the Propagate Permissions item in the gears icon under the permissions area, as shown in Figure 8-1.) This allows you to set permissions that propagate through a portion of the folder structure — useful for changing permissions for hundreds of folders and files all at once.

Rules of Precedence

If a user complains that she can't access a certain share or save a file, look at your permission structure and the inheritance. You may have one type of inheritance unexpectedly taking precedence over another. For instance, check the groups that the user belongs to and whether any Deny permissions are set. The issue is that if you have multiple sets of permissions and inheritance, only one can apply for any given shared folder and user or group. Some permissions take precedence over others.

Here are some of the rules that define which permissions take precedence:

- **Standard POSIX permissions apply automatically if no ACL exists for a certain file or folder.** If you don't specify any permissions to a newly created share point (and none are inherited), the default POSIX permissions and inheritance rules are applied.

- **Deny permissions rule.** When the server sees a Deny permission, it applies it regardless of other rules or precedence. This can unintentionally block access for a user.
- **ACL entries are first come first served.** The order in which users and groups are listed in the ACL matters. If a user belongs to multiple groups in the list, the group listed higher takes precedence over one listed lower. So, if the first entry doesn't give a user the right to delete a file even though another permission further down in the list does, the user can't delete a file in the folder.
- **Mac OS X Server adds all the Allow permissions.** Mac OS X counts all the permissions that allow the user to do things and gives them to the user. If a user has one set of permissions and belongs to a group that has different permissions, she gets the Allow permissions of both.

  After looking at all the ACL permissions that might apply to a user for a given folder, the server looks at the POSIX permissions for any Allow permissions that might apply. Mac OS X Server then adds them to create the access to the file for the particular user or group.

SACLs: Controlling Access to Protocols

I still have one more, even higher-level method of controlling access to touch upon: *service access control lists (SACLs).* SACLs control access to the file-sharing protocol services: AFP, SMB, and FTP. (SACLs don't affect NFS.) If you set an SACL permission for a protocol, all the folders shared with that protocol get that permission.

SACLs are another layer of permissions on top of POSIX permissions and ACLs. With SACLs, you can prevent certain users and groups from having access to share points that use one or more of the protocols. Removing a user or group from a protocol's SACL prevents him from accessing share points with that protocol, including home folders.

The use of SACLs is optional. The default setting of each protocol's SACL is to list all users as having access to all three protocols. If you don't want to bother with it, just pretend it doesn't exist. If you think SACLs are something you could use, check out Chapter 9.

Chapter 9

Setting Up File Sharing

In This Chapter

- Configuring file sharing easily
- Types of files sharing for Mac, Windows, and Linux clients
- Setting up file sharing in Server Admin
- Setting user and group permissions for share points
- Configuring AFP, SMB, FTP, and NFS file services

For many locations, file sharing is still the *raison d'etre* for a server. It enables users to quickly and securely move files between computers sitting next to each other or in different buildings. It doesn't matter what computers an organization has because Snow Leopard Server uses the native file-sharing methods of Mac OS X, Windows, and Linux/Unix. Apple refers to shared folders as *share points;* Microsoft calls them *shares.* But they're the same thing in Mac OS X Server.

Snow Leopard Server has two tools you can use to configure file sharing: Server Preferences, for simple tasks or workgroups, and Server Admin for larger or more complex networks. You can also use both: Start with Server Preferences and move to Server Admin when you need more control. Both are located in the /Applications/Server/ folder. You can use these tools on the server Mac or remotely from another Mac on the network.

This chapter starts with setting up file sharing with Server Preferences. The rest of the chapter describes the technology for more complex file-sharing configuration managed by Server Admin. This includes setting options for file-sharing protocols and creating user permissions to control access to files and folders. Chapter 8 describes the types of permissions and how they work.

Setting Up File Sharing the Easy Way

Server Preferences provides a simple way to quickly set up file sharing and grant users and groups access. You don't need to know anything about protocols or permissions, and you don't have to understand the differences among AFP, ACL, ACE, and other tech jargon. Server Preferences has limitations, but it might be all that you need. If that's the case, congratulations — you don't have to read most of this chapter.

When you use Server Preferences to turn on file sharing, it automatically turns on the file-sharing protocols for clients running Mac OS X (AFP) and Windows (SMB), and for universal access (FTP). If you want to run only one or two of these, or if you want to use NFS, use Server Admin. I describe these terms in the section, "Protocol Soup: AFP, SMB, and Other File-Sharing Methods," later in this chapter.

You can use Server Preferences from the server Mac or remotely from another Mac on the network (if you've installed the Server Administration tools, described in Chapters 1 and 3). In either case, Server Preferences is located in the /Applications/Server folder.

Turning on file sharing with Server Preferences

You may have already told Snow Leopard Server to turn on file sharing when you installed and set up the server. If not, turn it on and start it now:

1. **Launch Server Preferences from the Dock.**
2. **If Server Preferences presents a login dialog, type the server's DNS name or its IP address in the Server field.**

   The username and password are those of the administrator account, which is the account you created when you installed the server.

   If you've connected to this server recently, you can choose Connection➪Recent Connection to select a server.
3. **Click the File Sharing icon.**
4. **If the File Sharing switch is set to Off, click it to turn it on (see Figure 9-1).**

Notice in Figure 9-1 that several share points have been created already:

- **Backups:** This appears if you've enabled Backup to the server. You can't use the Edit Permissions or Delete buttons with this share point.

Figure 9-1: You can turn file sharing on and off by clicking the big switch.

- **Groups:** If you've set up group accounts (which I describe in Chapter 5), each group has a shared folder in the Groups folders. When you create a new group in the System Preferences Group pane and you select the Give This Group a Shared Folder check box, a shared folder is created in the Group folder. The users in the group have access to the corresponding group folder.
- **Public:** This is a read-only folder that administrators can use to distribute files to users. Ordinary users can open items in the Public folder and copy items from it, but they can't put files and folders into it.

If the automatically created group folders fulfill your needs, you're finished. To share another drive, partition, or folder, read the following section.

Sharing a folder with Server Preferences

In order to share a folder or a hard drive, create a share point. Here's how to do this in Server Preferences:

1. **If the folder you want to share doesn't exist, create it (on the server) in the Finder and give it a name.**
2. **Open Server Preferences and click the File Sharing icon.**
3. **Click the Add (+) button (refer to Figure 9-1).**
4. **In the new dialog that appears, navigate to the folder or drive you want to share; select it and click the Share button.**

   If you're working on the server (not remotely from another Mac), you can simply drag a folder or volume from the Finder into the Server Preferences File Sharing pane.

The new share point shows up in the Shared Folders list.

When you create a shared folder with Server Preferences or Server Admin, the folder is shared with the file-sharing protocols that both Mac and Windows computers can access. The difference is that Server Admin lets you turn off some of the file-sharing methods.

Changing user access to a shared folder

Every user who has an account can access the new share point. They have full read and write access to the shared folder. You can use Server Preferences to restrict access to certain users or groups, or to allow people to access the folder without logging in. Do the following:

1. **In the File Sharing pane, select a share point in the Shared Folders list and then click the Edit Permissions button.**

   A new dialog appears, as shown in Figure 9-2. The default setting is All Registered Users, which is everyone who has an account on the server.

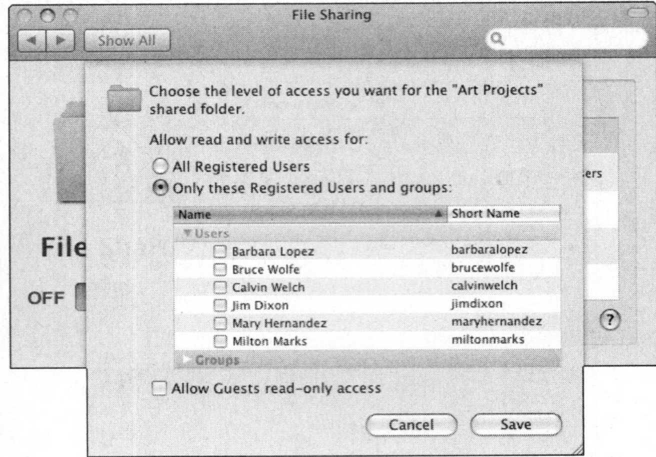

Figure 9-2: Giving users access to a share point with Server Preferences.

2. **To change from the default to specific users, click the Only These Registered Users and Groups option.**
3. **Click the triangle next to Users or Groups to expand a list.**
4. **Select the check box to the left of each user or group that you want to access the share point.**

   This gives read and write access to the folder.

5. **(Optional) To give non-registered users the ability to open and copy files, select the Allow Guests Read-Only Access check box.**
6. **Click the Save button when you're finished.**
7. **To completely disable access to the folder (unshare it), deselect it to the left of the folder in the Shared Folders area (refer to Figure 9-1).**

You can also change read or write access to a group from the Finder on the server using the Get Info window of the shared folder. In the Finder, click the folder to select it and then choose File➪Get Info. For more on read and write access of shared items, see Chapter 8.

Protocol Soup: AFP, SMB, and Other File-Sharing Methods

Mac OS X Server can share files using four standard *protocols* — sets of rules that the server and client use to share the files. Each protocol is known by its three-letter acronym. Because the acronyms are more widely used than the full names, acronyms are used in Mac OS X Server and in the Help system.

File-sharing protocols 101

The different protocols are native to different operating systems, though Macs have the ability to use all these protocols. You can use multiple file-sharing protocols at the same time to support different client operating systems:

- **Apple Filing Protocol (AFP):** AFP is the native file-sharing protocol for Macs. It's been used in the Mac OS for years, so even your most ancient, pre-OS X Macs use it. AFP should be your first-choice file-sharing protocol for Mac clients. It can be faster than SMB, and your Mac clients will have fewer file-sharing glitches. AFP also provides Mac users with special features that the other protocols don't support, such as the ability to search server folders with Spotlight. Windows clients don't use AFP.
- **Server Message Block (SMB):** SMB is the native protocol that Windows clients use to access file servers. Many Linux and Unix clients also use SMB. Mac clients can also access file servers using SMB, but they get better results with AFP.

SMB is also referred to as Samba or CIFS. Samba is used on Linux, whereas CIFS (Common Internet File System) comes from the Windows world. Although often used interchangeably, SMB and CIFS aren't actually the same thing, but the two technologies are often used together. Mac OS X Server's SMB service is technically SMB/CIFS.

- **Network File System (NFS):** A long-time native protocol of Unix operating systems, NFS is still a good protocol to use to serve files to Unix and Linux computers. By itself, NFS isn't as secure as SMB, but Mac OS X Server lets you use it with Kerberos authentication for increased security. You can also make NFS shares read-only to secure server data. You'll find differing opinions as to whether NFS or SMB is better for Linux clients, but NFS is there if you want it.
- **File Transfer Protocol (FTP):** FTP provides a simple method for moving files and is commonly used with any operating system. FTP is a different animal than AFP, SMB, and NFS. FTP volumes don't mount on a user's machine, and you can't open a document on an FTP server. A benefit of FTP is that any computer operating system can download files from an FTP server with a Web browser. Mac users can download with the Finder. For uploading to a server, you can choose from cheap or free FTP client applications. FTP is often used to serve files across the Internet, but it isn't secure. (There is also *SFTP — secure FTP* or *FTP with SSH.* It's only available from the command line in Snow Leopard Server.)

When Mac OS X Server runs these protocols, the user can't tell that the shared files are on a Mac. Snow Leopard Server's SMB server looks and acts just like a Windows server to Windows clients.

If you're looking for a good FTP client for users running Mac OS X, Windows, or Linux, try the free, open-source FileZilla (`http://filezilla-project.org`). FileZilla is dependable and easy to use. Plus, because it's available for multiple operating systems, you can provide user support easily.

Security in file-sharing protocols

The four file-sharing protocols support different levels of security to protect login passwords and transmitted files from snoopers or malware that may have infected users' computers.

There are two basic levels of security in file-sharing protocols: no encryption and encryption. No encryption, or *cleartext,* sends the straight characters of a password over the network. AFP is the most secure file-sharing protocol. FTP is the least secure. This is what each protocol provides:

- **AFP** provides the option of sending login passwords to the server as cleartext or with Kerberos encryption. You can also set AFP to encrypt all transmitted data between clients and the server.
- **SMB** supports sending passwords as cleartext or with Kerberos encryption, as well as some older Windows encryption methods. SMB does not support encryption of transmitted data, however.

- **NFS** authentication always uses Kerberos, but is less secure than the other three protocols. NFS doesn't ask the user for a username and password. Instead, the client computer tells the server what the computer ID is. This means that anyone using that computer has access to whatever the user account has. This makes NFS authentication less secure than AFP and SMB. Like AFP, NFS file transmission can either be cleartext or use Kerberos encryption.
- **FTP** sends all data as cleartext. It doesn't provide for encryption of passwords or data transmission.

This doesn't mean you should always use AFP or never use FTP. The protocol you choose depends on the situation and the need for security.

Setting Up File Sharing with Server Admin

Although file-sharing configuration in Server Preferences is largely automated, Server Admin gives you the ability to control all the file-sharing settings. You can use Server Admin from the server Mac itself or remotely from another Mac on the network. With either method, you're prompted to enter a name and password the first time you use Server Admin to connect to a server.

When Server Admin launches, it displays a list of Mac OS X servers in the column on the left. In Figure 9-3, only one server is shown. Server Admin first opens to the Overview icon. File sharing uses the File Sharing and Settings icons in the toolbar.

The first task in setting up file sharing with Server Admin is to designate a drive, partition, or folder to share as a *share point.* After that, you can configure one or more of the file-sharing protocols and set permissions.

Creating a share point with Server Admin

To designate a folder or drive to share with Server Admin, use the software to browse for a folder and then select it:

1. **In Server Admin, click your server listed in the column on the left.**
2. **Click File Sharing in the toolbar.**

   If you want to share a drive, partition, or volume, go to Step 3. If you want to share a folder, go to Step 4.

   The File Sharing pane defaults to having the Volumes and List headings selected, as shown in Figure 9-4.

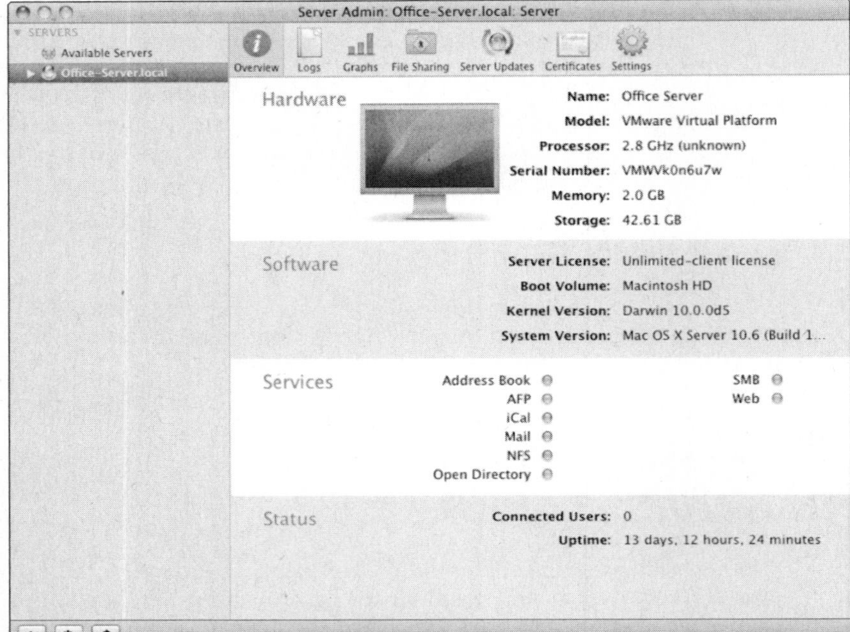

Figure 9-3: The Server Admin Overview screen.

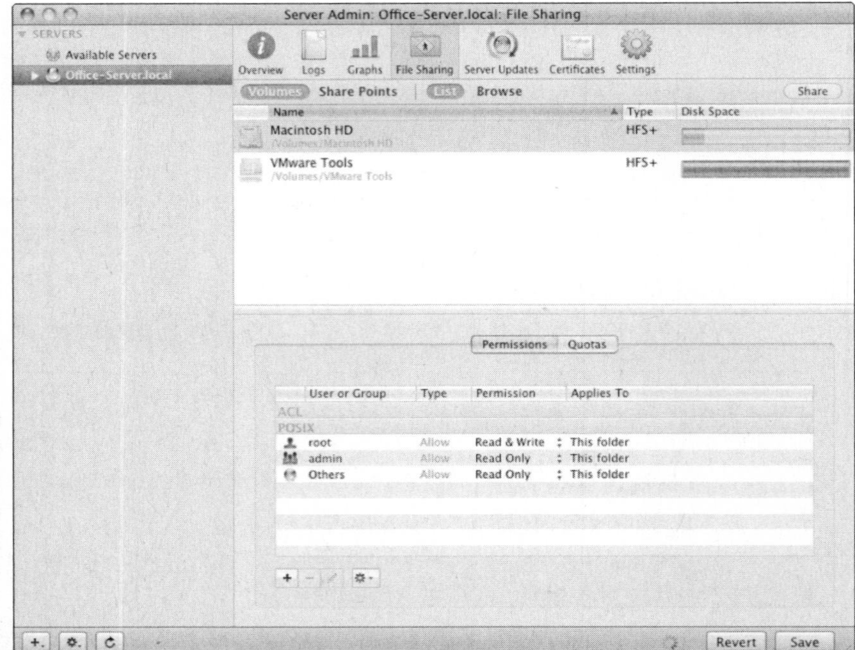

Figure 9-4: Create share points in Server Admin's File Sharing icon.

3. **If a partition or drive that you want to share is displayed here, follow these steps to share it now:**

   a. *Click a volume to select it.*

   b. *Click the Share button in the upper right.*

   c. *Click Save.*

   If that's all you need, you're done.

4. **To share a folder, click the Browse button, navigate to a folder (see Figure 9-5), and then click that folder to select it.**

   If you want to create a new folder, navigate to where you want the folder to be, click the New Folder button in the upper right (see Figure 9-5), and give the folder a name.

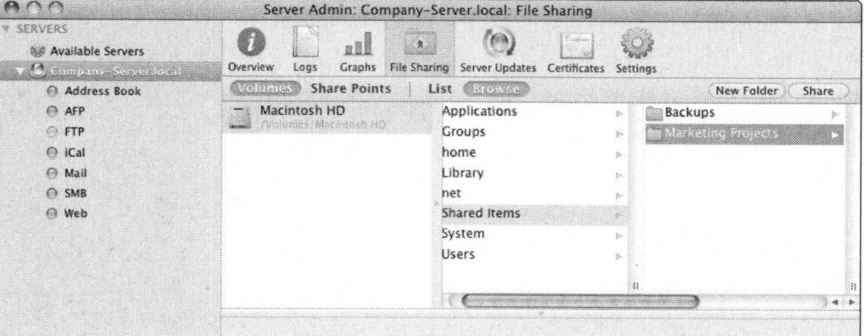

Figure 9-5: Navigate to a folder you want to share, or create a new folder.

5. **With your folder selected, click the Share button in the upper right.**

6. **Click the Save button.**

You can modify the protocol and permissions settings for this share.

Assigning file-sharing protocols to a share point

When you create a share point, it's shared automatically with the AFP, SMB, and FTP file-sharing protocols. For any share point, you can turn off any of the default protocols or turn on NFS file sharing.

I recommend turning off file-sharing protocols you're not using for any given share point. So if you have a folder that only your Windows users access, turn off AFP and FTP for that folder.

To enable and disable file-sharing protocols for any given share point:

1. **In Server Admin, select your server listed in the left column.**
2. **Click File Sharing in the toolbar and then click the Share Points heading just below the toolbar (see Figure 9-6).**
3. **Click your share point to select it.**
4. **In the bottom half of the screen, click the Share Point tab and then click the Protocol Options button.**

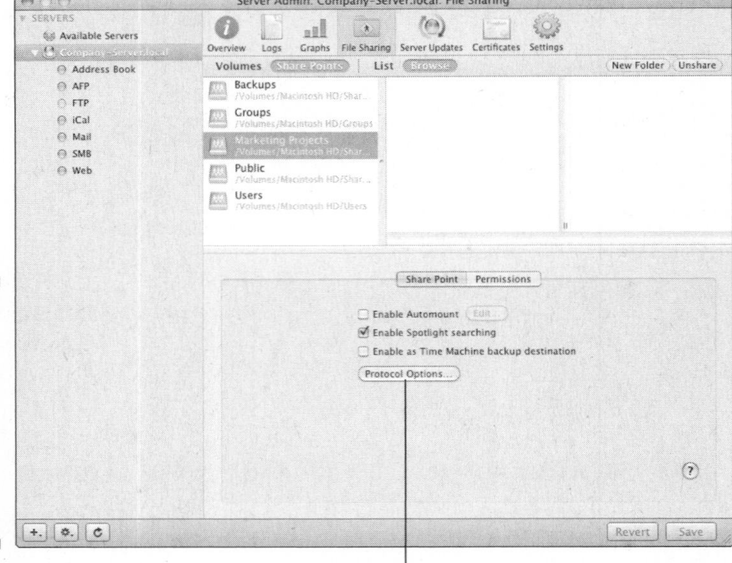

Figure 9-6: Select a share and click the Protocol Options button to get to the settings.

A new dialog (see Figure 9-7) slides down to present four tabs, one for each of the file-sharing protocols.

5. **Turn off a protocol for the share point you selected in Step 4 by clicking the appropriate tab and deselecting the Share This Item Using *AFP* (or *SMB* or *FTP*) check box.**

NFS is off by default, but the tab is a little different. Instead of a Share This Item check box, NFS says Export This Item and Its Contents To. (For more on NFS, see the section, "Configuring NFS for Unix clients," later in this chapter.)

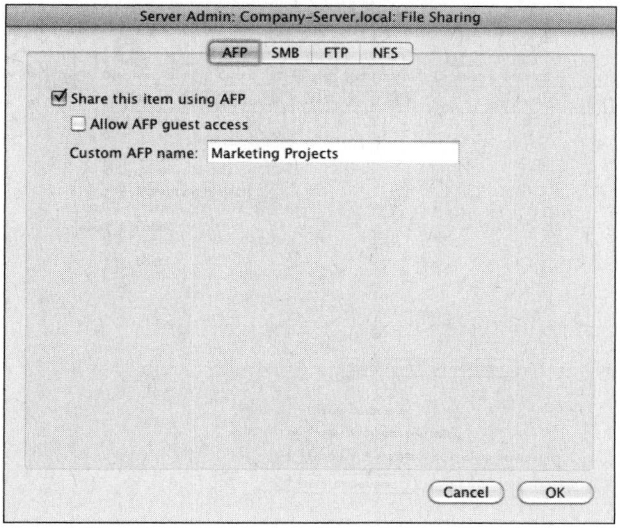

Server Admin: Company-Server.local: File Sharing

AFP | SMB | FTP | NFS

Share this item using AFP

Allow AFP guest access

Custom AFP name: Marketing Projects

Cancel OK

Figure 9-7: This dialog appears when you click the Protocol Options button.

6. **Click OK.**

The AFP tab (refer to Figure 9-7) and the FTP tab are simple. They each contain a check box to allow guest (anonymous user) access and a field to type a new name for the share point. The SMB and NFS tabs contain a number of other settings relevant to those protocols.

Setting permissions for a share point

In Figure 9-8, the window has a Permissions tab in the lower half. This is where you define the levels of user access to the selected share. (Chapter 8 describes the types of permissions and how they work.)

When you first create a share point, Mac OS X Server assigns it standard POSIX permissions for Owner, Group, and Others (see Chapter 8). You can change the owner and group as well as change the permissions for all three entities.

For share points shared with AFP and/or SMB, you can also add permissions with an access control list (ACL). An ACL is the server's list of all permissions for all users and groups and for a share point. You add names of users and groups to the list and then use a pop-up menu to assign permissions.

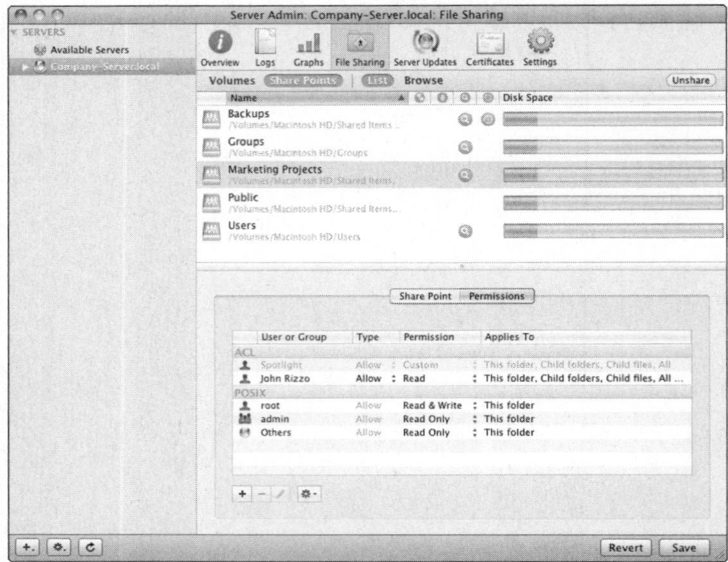

Figure 9-8: Set permissions in the lower half of this window.

In this section, I first describe how to set standard POSIX permissions and how to create an ACL for a share point. This section ends with setting service access control lists (SACLs) to control access to protocol services. (I describe POSIX permissions and ACLs in Chapter 8.)

Setting standard POSIX permissions with Server Admin

Standard POSIX permissions are easier to set than ACLs and may be all that you need. You can change the default owner and group as well as set read and write, read-only, write-only, and none permissions for Owner, Group, and Others. Permissions apply to the share point and the files and folders inside.

To set standard permissions on a share point:

1. **In Server Admin, select your server listed in the left column.**
2. **Click File Sharing in the toolbar and then click the Share Points heading just below the toolbar.**
3. **Click a share point to select it and then click the Permissions tab below the list of shares.**

   The Server Admin window looks like Figure 9-8. Note that the lower half of the window has an ACL section and a POSIX section.
4. **Click the Add (+) button to open the Users & Groups palette.**
5. **To change the folder owner, drag a name from the Users & Groups palette to the first line in the POSIX section, which is `root`, as shown in Figure 9-9.**

The owner has a single-person icon.

The username you drag replaces the original owner name.

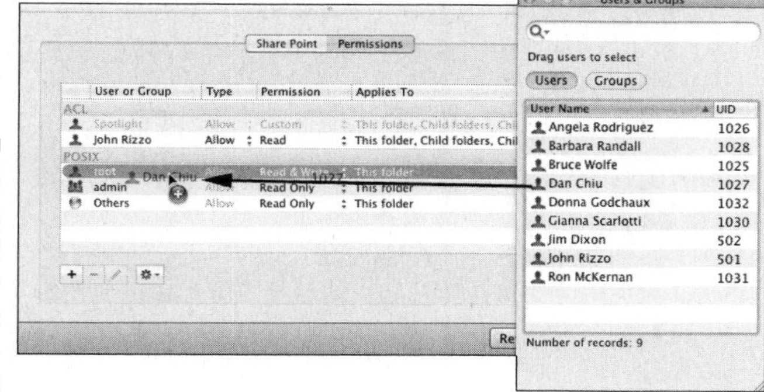

Figure 9-9: Change the owner of a folder by dragging a new name.

6. **Click the Groups button in the Users & Groups palette to change the group access to this folder. Then drag a group from the palette to the second line under POSIX.**

   The Owner permissions are read and write by default. The Group permissions and the Others permissions are read-only.

7. **Change the POSIX permissions by selecting the Owner, Group, or Others and then clicking the arrows in the Permission column.**

   A pop-up menu appears with permissions, as shown in Figure 9-10.

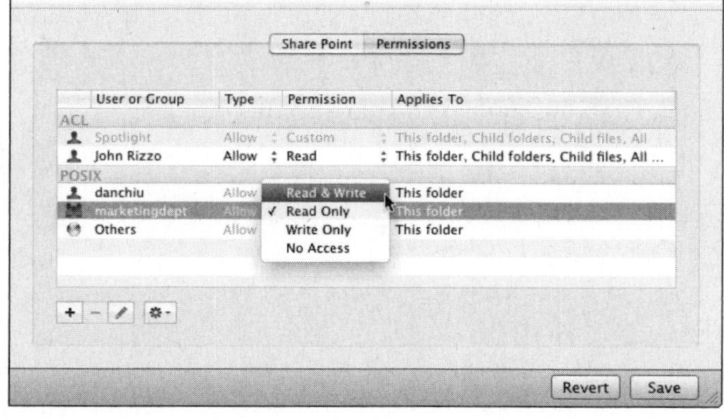

Figure 9-10: Change the marketingdept group permission to Read & Write.

8. **Click the Save button in the lower-right corner.**

Setting ACL permissions with Server Admin

You can also create an ACL for a share point. Each entry in the ACL is an *access control entry (ACE)*. An ACE is a user or group and the associated permissions settings. ACLs are more complicated than POSIX permissions because they give you many more choices, as I describe in Chapter 8.

Setting ACL permissions is similar to setting POSIX permissions, described in the previous section. The main differences are as follows:

- You can have more the three user and group items (ACEs).
- Dragging in a new user or group doesn't replace one of the existing items — it adds the new item to the list.
- The pop-up menus in the Permission column give you access to not just read and write permissions, but the full set of 17 ACL permissions.

The procedure starts the same as for standard permissions:

1. **Perform Steps 1–4 in the preceding section.**
2. **Drag users and groups from the Users & Groups palette to the ACL portion of the window. (See Figure 9-11.)**

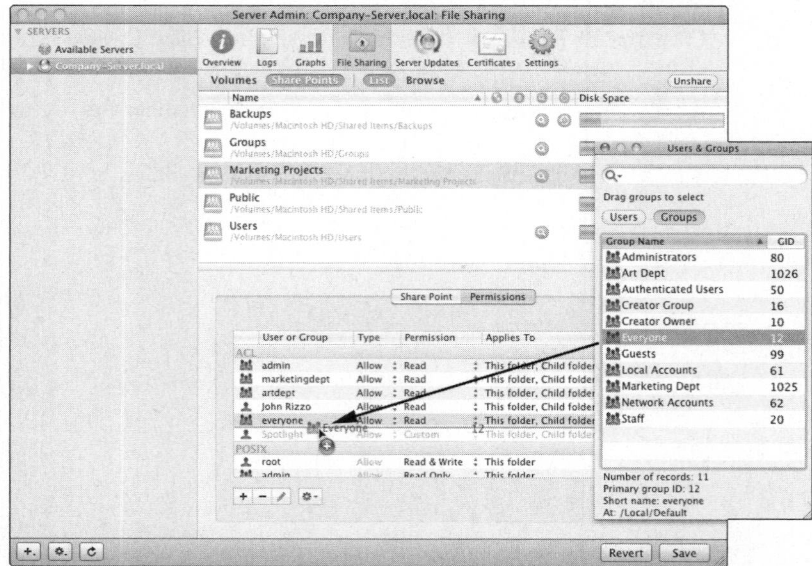

Figure 9-11: Create an ACL for a share point by dragging users and groups into the list.

3. **Drag the ACEs up and down to arrange them in order of precedence.**

   The order of the ACEs is important, as items higher in the ACL list take precedence when there are conflicting permissions.

4. **(Optional) If you want to change the default permissions, click the arrows in the Permission column.**

   The default permissions for each ACE that you create is full read and inheritance for the user or group, but not write.

5. **In the pop-up menu (see Figure 9-12), choose one of the five, high-level views of ACL permissions. If that's all you need, click the Save button.**

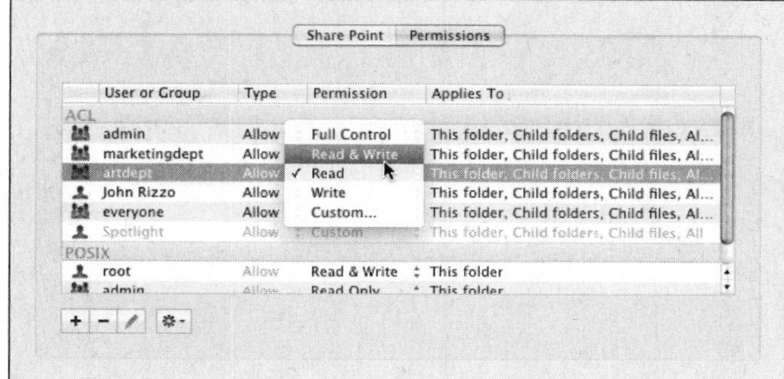

Figure 9-12: The first level of ACL permissions.

6. **To set more detailed ACL permissions, click Custom in the pop-up menu.**

   A new window opens with four choices: Administration, Read, Write, and Applies To (see Figure 9-13). You can make choices here. (A hyphen [–] in a check box means that some, but not all, of the subordinate items for that category are selected.)

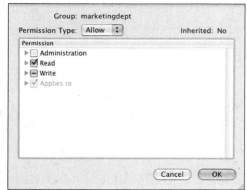

Figure 9-13: The second level of ACL permissions.

7. **(Optional) If you want to go even deeper in ACL permissions, click the triangles next to the choices to expand them.**

   The fully expanded window is shown in Figure 9-14. (I explain the ACL permission choices shown in this window in Chapter 8.)

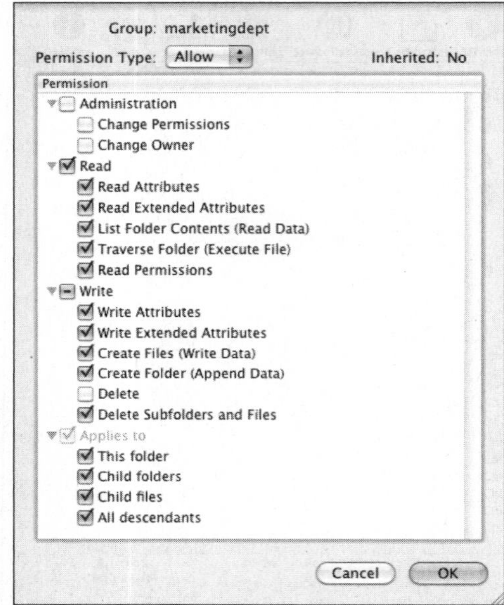

Figure 9-14: The fully expanded ACL permissions.

8. **Make any change that you need, click OK to close this window, and then click Save.**

In Figure 9-14, the Permission Type pop-up menu is set to Allow. The other choice is Deny. If the server finds a Deny permission in the ACL, it stops looking for other permissions, blocking the user's access to all the checked items. Using Deny permissions could create problems that might be difficult to track down. Apple recommends keeping a list of any Deny permissions that you set so that you can undo them later if needed.

Checking ACL permissions with the Permissions Inspector

Server Admin provides an easy way to check the permissions of any user for any share point: the Permissions Inspector. Here's how to access and use it:

1. **With the File Sharing and Share Points icons selected (refer to Figure 9-6), click a share point.**

2. **In the Action pop-up menu (the gear icon at the bottom of the window), choose Show Effective Permissions Inspector.**
3. **Click the Add (+) button to bring up the Users & Groups palette.**
4. **Drag a user from the Users & Groups palette to the Permissions Inspector to see the permissions for that user on the selected share point (see Figure 9-15).**

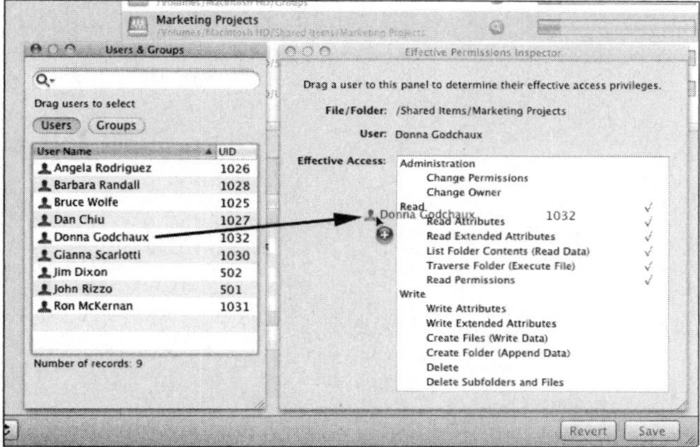

Figure 9-15: Drag a user to the Permissions Inspector to see the assigned permissions.

Setting SACL permissions for limiting access to protocols

You can prevent certain users from accessing AFP, SMB, and/or FTP protocol services using access control lists (ACLs). Removing a user or group from an SACL listing for SMB, for instance, prevents that user or group from accessing *all* share points shared with SMB.

To configure SACLs, do the following:

1. **In Server Admin, select your server listed in the left column.**
2. **Click Settings in the toolbar, click the Access tab, and then click the Services tab.**

   The window in Figure 9-16 appears.
3. **Select one of the two radio buttons on the left to restrict services:**
   - *For All Services* limits access to all services listed.
   - *For Selected Services Below* limits access for individual services.

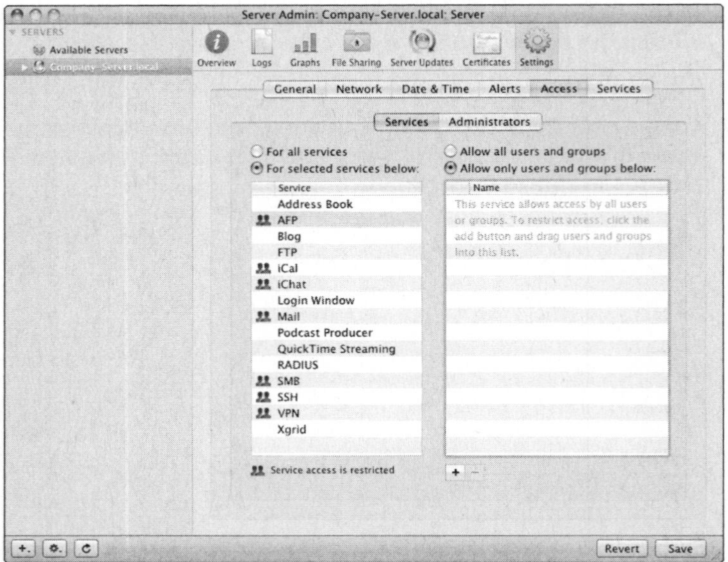

Figure 9-16: Setting SACL permissions.

4. **Select one of the two radio buttons on the right to choose a level of restriction for users and groups:**

   - *Allow All Users and Groups* allows access to the service(s) by all.
   - To restrict access, click *Allow Only Users and Groups Below.* Then click the Add (+) button to bring up the Users & Groups palette, and drag users and groups to the list.

5. **Click Save.**

To restrict access to services for administrators, click the Administrators tab. Here, you can also turn users and groups of users into administrators for a particular service. Drag a user and group over to the Allow to Administer or Monitor list.

Configuring AFP for Mac users

The Apple Filing Protocol (AFP) has some special features for Mac users that the other file-sharing protocols don't provide:

- **Spotlight searches of AFP share points on the server:** Users can search for files for which they have read permissions.
- **Automatic Reconnect:** When a Mac client goes into sleep mode, Mac OS X Server disconnects its AFP session. You can set AFP to automatically reconnect to Mac clients after they wake, enabling users to pick up working on open files from where they left off.

AFP also supports Kerberos authentication, access control lists, and the resource forks and extended attributes of Mac files.

If you're interested in using Server Admin to tweak AFP and take advantage of some of the these advanced (and quite useful) settings, read on.

Turning on and starting AFP service in Server Admin

You must turn on AFP service before configuring it. If AFP service is already turned on, skip to the next section. If not, you can do it now:

1. **In Server Admin, select your server listed in the left column.**
2. **Click Settings in the toolbar and then click the Services tab.**
3. **Select the AFP check box and then click the Save button.**

You can also turn SMB, FTP, and NFS on or off in this dialog, along with other services.

You'll still need to start AFP service to get it running. Here's how:

1. **In Server Admin, click the triangle to the left of your server's name to expand the list of services.**
2. **Select AFP from the list of services.**
3. **Click Settings in the toolbar and then click the Start AFP button on the lower left.**

Configuring AFP

To bring up the configuration window for AFP, do the following:

1. **In Server Admin, click the triangle to the left of your server's name to expand the list of services.**
2. **Select AFP from the list of services and then click Settings in the toolbar.**

   You now see four tabs, as shown in Figure 9-17:

   - *General:* This tab lets you create a login greeting for users. The Encoding for Older Clients pop-up menu lets you set a language for filenames, for use by Macs with pre-Mac OS X operating systems.
   - *Access:* This tab lets you set a type of authentication, guest access, and the maximum number of client connections.
   - *Logging:* Here you can turn on logging for the AFP service.
   - *Idle Users:* The tab lets you have the server disconnect users after a certain amount of inactive time. You can also allow clients to reconnect after sleeping using Automatic Reconnect.

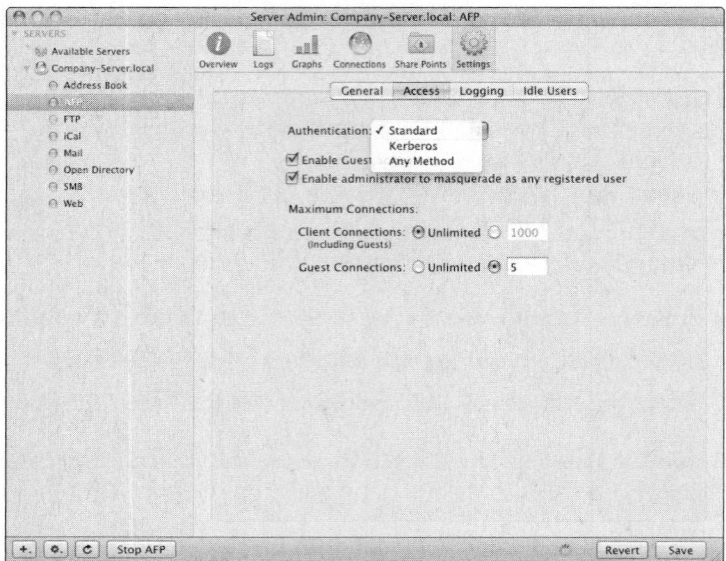

Figure 9-17: The Settings icon for AFP service.

General and Logging are pretty simple. Here's some more about the Access and Idle Users tabs.

AFP's Access settings

Figure 9-17 shows the Access tab. The Authentication pop-up menu presents three choices:

- **Standard** transmits a user's password as non-secure clear-text.
- **Kerberos** encrypts the password sent to the server.
- **Any Method** uses whatever the client machine uses.

To enable users to access the server without logging in with a password, check Enable Guest Access. Even with guest access enabled, you can disable it in the permissions for individual shares. If you enable guest access, the Guest Connections radio button lets you set a maximum number of simultaneous guest connections as a security measure.

You can also set a maximum number of connections for all AFP clients, which is useful if you have a large number of Mac clients that are bogging down the server. If you have the ten-user version of Snow Leopard Server, ten is the maximum number of client connections you can set.

The Enable Administrator to Masquerade as Any Registered User setting lets an administrator log in with another user's name, but with the administrator's password. This is useful for testing and troubleshooting, as it lets the administrator experience the server as the user does.

Click the Save button when you're finished with the Access tab.

AFP's Idle Users settings

Figure 9-18 shows the Idle Users tab; it lets you tell the server to disconnect users after a certain amount of time of inactivity. You can exempt certain users — it's certainly a good idea to exempt idle users who have open files to prevent file corruption. You can also have the server send a message to users when it disconnects them.

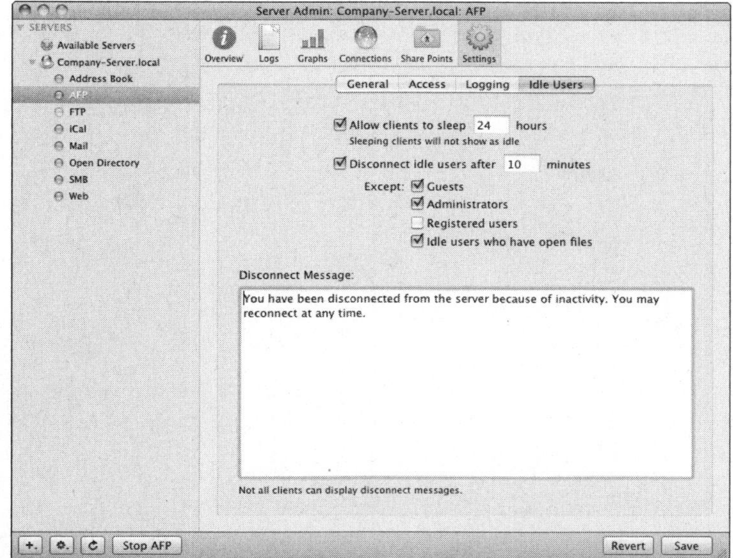

Figure 9-18: The Idle Users tab for AFP service.

The Allow Clients to Sleep check box enables Macs to automatically reconnect when waking (without a password) if they wake within the set time limit. In Figure 9-18, the limit is set to 24 hours. During the 24 hours, clients that wake up before the 24-hour period can reconnect automatically after waking. If the client Mac wakes after 24 hours, the user will need to log in.

Click the Save button when you're finished.

Configuring AFP guest access for individual share points

You may remember earlier in the chapter that when you create a share, you can turn a file-sharing protocol on or off. That window, as shown in Figure 9-6, also lets you configure AFP settings that apply only to that share.

Here's how to get there:

1. **In Server Admin, select your server in the left column.**
2. **Click File Sharing in the toolbar and then click the Share Points heading (see Figure 9-6).**
3. **Click your share point to select it.**
4. **In the bottom half of the screen, click the Share Point tab.**
5. **Click the Protocol Options button.**

   A new dialog (see Figure 9-7) presents four tabs. The AFP tab lets you enable AFP access for the share point and provides two other settings:

   - *Allow AFP Guest Access:* Lets you disable guest access for this share point even if you have it enabled globally for AFP.
   - *Custom AFP Name:* This provides a name for the share point that users will see. It doesn't change the name of the volume or directory on the server.

Configuring SMB for Windows users

Just as the AFP service provides Mac clients with some special features, Snow Leopard's SMB service provides features needed to support Windows clients on a network. These include

- **Windows Internet Naming Service (WINS):** This enables Windows clients to find Windows servers and other Windows clients across multiple subnets. WINS resolves the Windows network computer names (called NetBIOS names) to IP addresses.
- **Windows domain browsing:** This enables Windows clients to browse for Windows servers across subnets. Snow Leopard Server makes itself appear to be a Windows server to Windows clients.
- **Domain login:** This enables Windows users to log in with the same username, password, roaming profile, and network home folder on any Windows (or Snow Leopard Server) computer that can log in to a Windows domain.
- **Windows-style authentication:** Snow Leopard Server provides authentication of Windows clients via NTLMv2, NTLM with Kerberos, and LAN Manager, which are Windows authentication standards.

Snow Leopard's SMB service also provides Windows-style file locking, which prevents multiple users from editing the same portion of a file at the same time. And it provides Windows users with the ability to print to queues on the server (see Chapter 10 for more on printing).

If you're interested in using Server Admin to tweak SMB and take advantage of some of the more advanced (and quite useful) settings, read on.

Turning on and starting SMB service with Server Admin

There's a good chance you turned on SMB service when you first installed and configured Snow Leopard Server. If not, you can do it now:

1. **In Server Admin, select your server listed in the left column.**
2. **Click Settings in the toolbar and click the Services tab.**
3. **Check the SMB check box and then click Save.**

You need to start the SMB service so that it is actually running. Here's how:

1. **In Server Admin, click the triangle to the left of your server's name to expand the list of services.**
2. **Select SMB from the list of services.**
3. **Click Settings in the toolbar and then click the Start SMB button on the lower left.**

Configuring SMB

To bring up the main configuration window for SMB, do the following:

1. **In Server Admin, click the triangle to the left of your server's name to expand the list of services.**
2. **Select SMB from the list of services and then click Settings in the toolbar.**

You now see four tabs, as shown in Figure 9-19. The first three tabs have the same names as those for AFP, but different content. All four tabs are specific to serving Windows clients:

- **General:** This tab lets you set the server name and workgroup as Windows clients will see them.
- **Access:** This tab is similar to that of AFP; it lets you set authentication, guest access, and a maximum number of simultaneous client connections. The authentication selection is different than AFP. Here, the choice is NTLMv2, NTLM with Kerberos, and LAN Manager.

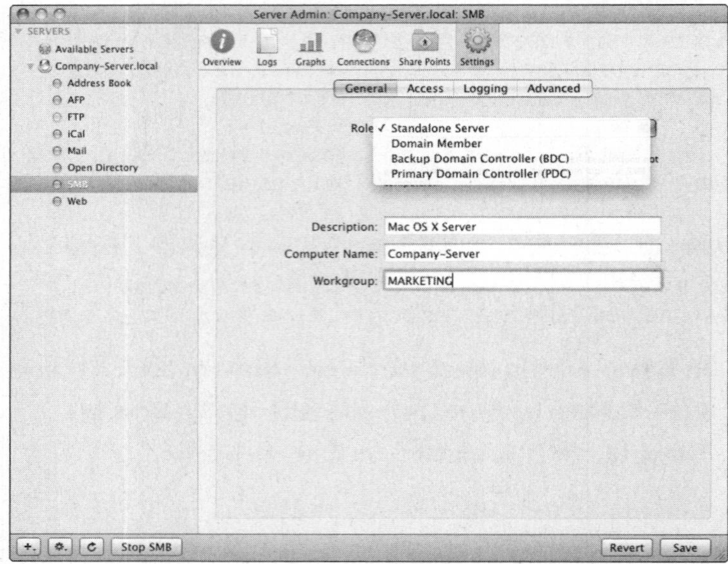

Figure 9-19: The General tab of the SMB setup window sets NetBIOS information.

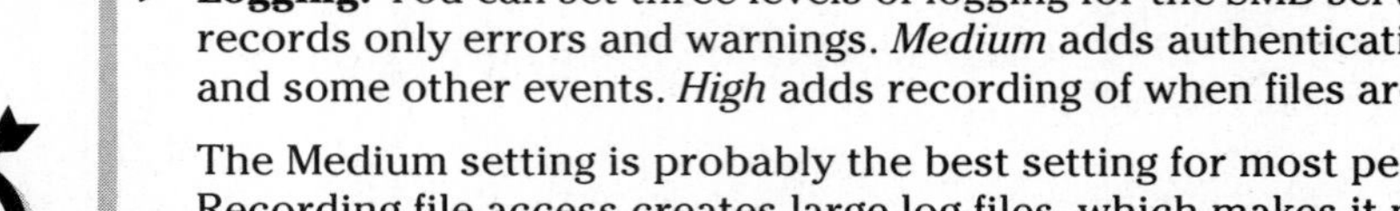

- **Logging:** You can set three levels of logging for the SMB service. *Low* records only errors and warnings. *Medium* adds authentication errors and some other events. *High* adds recording of when files are accessed.

  The Medium setting is probably the best setting for most people. Recording file access creates large log files, which makes it more difficult to scan them to look for problems.

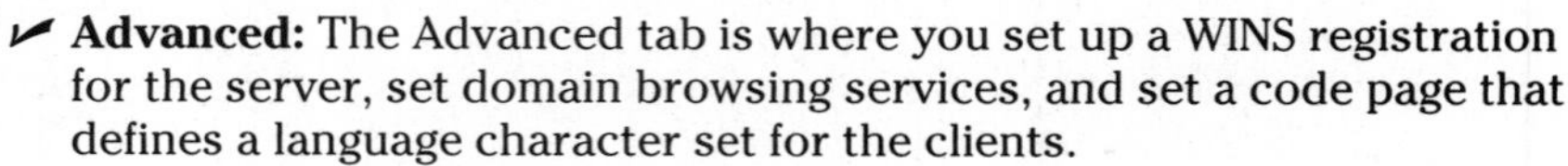

- **Advanced:** The Advanced tab is where you set up a WINS registration for the server, set domain browsing services, and set a code page that defines a language character set for the clients.

The Access and Logging tabs are simple; this description pretty much covers them. The General and Advanced tabs have some different options that are worth looking at more closely. If your Mac server is on a Windows network, consult your network administrator before using these settings.

General tab: Setting server NetBIOS name, workgroup, domain role

The General tab of Figure 9-19 is mostly about NetBIOS: identifying Snow Leopard Server to Windows clients and making it look like a Windows server. The terminology and technology here are those of Windows networks.

The Computer Name acts as the NetBIOS name for the Windows clients. It's set automatically from the Mac computer name you set when you first installed and configured Snow Leopard Server. This should be 15 characters or less, with no punctuation.

Before you change this name, make sure that the new NetBIOS name is the same as the server's hostname and DNS hostname. (If the DNS hostname is `jerry.acme.com`, you might use `jerry` as the NetBIOS name.) If it's not, a computer accessing the server via SMB and DNS might get inconsistent information that could cause problems.

Workgroup is the name that Windows users will see in the My Network Place or Network Neighborhood window. This name must be 15 characters or less, with no spaces or punctuation. If you already have Windows domains with workgroups configured on the network, enter one of those. Mac OS X Server will join that workgroup.

The Role pop-up menu defines whether the server offers authentication services for Windows users. The name refers to the role the Mac server will play on a Windows network. There are four choices representing standard roles for servers in Windows network domains:

- **Standalone Server:** This default setting provides SMB file and print service, but doesn't offer authentication services for Windows PCs logging in to Windows domains. The server is *standalone* in the sense that it is not an active participant in a Windows domain.
- **Domain Member:** When acting as a domain member, the server offers file and print services by authenticating a Windows client against a Windows domain controller running on another server on the network. The Windows client could be logging in to an Active Directory domain.
- **Primary Domain Controller:** This setting enables Windows clients to authenticate directly to the Mac server. Snow Leopard Server stores the user and group information for the Windows clients, and it hosts user profiles and network home folders. The Mac server must be configured as an Open Directory master in order to act as a primary domain controller. (See Chapter 6 for information about Open Directory.)
- **Backup Domain Controller:** With this setting, the Mac server automatically acts as a primary domain controller if another fails. This setting applies only if your Mac server is an Open Directory replica.

Advanced tab: WINS registration, enabling virtual share points

The General tab has some fairly advanced settings in it; so does the Advanced tab. (Apple might have called them Advanced 1 and Advanced 2.) The Advanced tab focuses on talking to the Windows clients.

The Advanced tab is shown in Figure 9-20. Here's what the settings do:

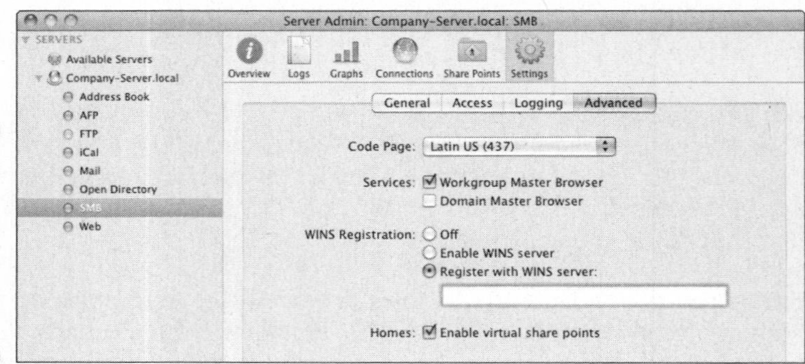

Figure 9-20: The Advanced tab of the SMB setup window.

- **Code Page:** Code page is an old IBM term that defines a character set — basically, a language — for use with the Windows clients. Latin US is the default for the United States and Canada.
- **Services (Workgroup and Domain Master Browser):** This setting determines how the server will enable Windows clients to discover and browse for the Mac server over the network. There are two choices:
  - *Workgroup Master Browser* enables browsing on a single subnet.
  - *Domain Master Browser* provides discovery and Windows browsing for servers across multiple subnets.

  If you already have a Windows server acting as a domain controller, don't make the Mac server a domain master browser.

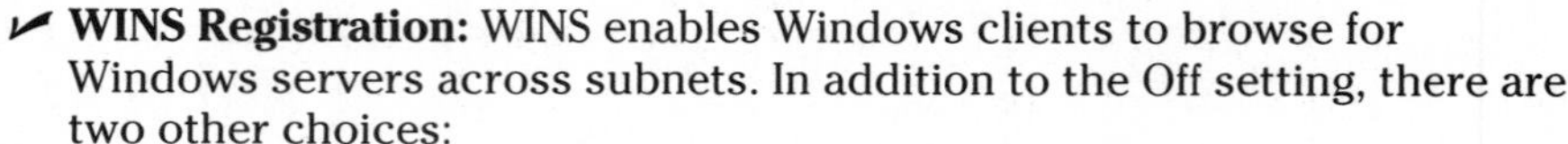

- **WINS Registration:** WINS enables Windows clients to browse for Windows servers across subnets. In addition to the Off setting, there are two other choices:
  - *Register with WINS Server* lets you specify the IP address or name of a WINS server already on the network.
  - *Enable WINS Server* turns your Mac into a WINS server. Select this option if Mac OS X Server is the only server on your network.
- **Homes: Enable Virtual Share Points:** This setting needs to be on if you're hosting home folders for Windows users on the Mac server. But this setting goes even further, allowing a user to access the same home folder whether he logs in from a Windows or Mac computer.

Changing SMB file-locking settings for individual share points

You may remember earlier in the chapter that when you create a share point, you can turn a file-sharing protocol on or off. This window, shown in Figure 9-21, also has some settings that apply only to that share point. These are

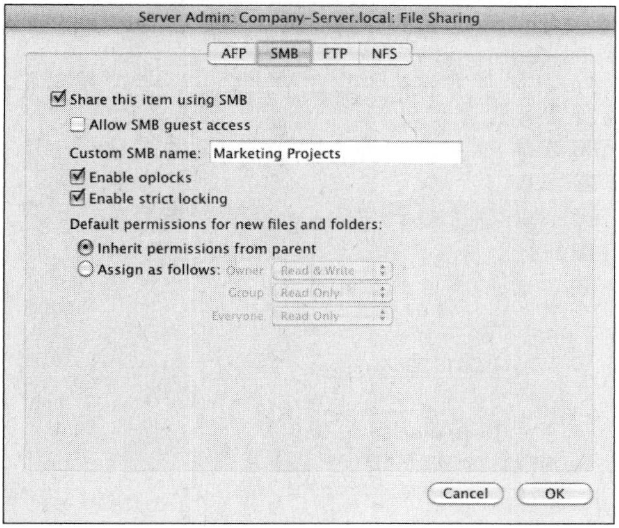

Figure 9-21: The SMB protocol options dialog applies to a single share point.

- **Allow SMB Guest Access:** As with AFP, SMB guest access allows users to log in anonymously, without a password.
- **Custom SMB Name:** This is the name of the share as Windows clients will see it. It doesn't affect the actual name of the folder.
- **Settings for file locking:** Prevents multiple clients from editing the same file at the same time. A file that a client opens will be locked out to other users, giving access solely to the client. *Strict locking* (the default) is a simple locking out of an open file to other users. *Oplocks,* short for *opportunistic locking,* enables the client to cache changes on the client computer. This improves server performance over strict locking.
- **Default Permissions for New Files and Folders:** You can set POSIX permissions for the Owner, Group, and Everyone, or set the share point to inherit permissions from the parent folder. (POSIX permissions are described in Chapter 8.)

Here's how to get to the dialog shown in Figure 9-21:

1. **In Server Admin, select your server in the left column.**
2. **Click File Sharing in the toolbar and then click the Share Points heading.**

   (Refer to Figure 9-6 earlier in the chapter.)
3. **Click your share point to select it.**

4. **In the bottom half of the screen, click the Share Point tab.**
5. **Click the Protocol Options button.**

   A new dialog presents four tabs.
6. **Click the SMB tab.**

Configuring FTP service

FTP is a handy method for people to send and retrieve files over the Internet, including files that may be too big to e-mail. Any client operating system can use FTP.

FTP authentication and anonymous users

FTP supports authenticated users (those with a username and password) and anonymous users who don't have accounts on the server. FTP anonymous users are similar to guest users in AFP and SMB.

In Mac OS X Server, FTP can have Kerberos authentication for secure login, but users will have to run an FTP client that supports it. The Mac Finder doesn't support FTP Kerberos authentication.

The default settings for anonymous users allow them to upload files to an upload folder located in the `root` FTP folder. By default, anonymous users can't delete, rename, or overwrite files and can't change permissions. You need to create the `upload` folder yourself.

Turning on and starting FTP service

You may have turned on FTP service when you first installed and configured Snow Leopard Server. If not, you need to do it now. This is the same procedure as turning on AFP and SMB:

1. **In Server Admin, select your server listed in the left column.**
2. **Click Settings in the toolbar and click the Services tab.**
3. **Select the check box next to FTP under Select the Services to Configure on This Server.**
4. **Click the Save button.**

You also need to start SMB service so that users can access it. Here's how:

1. **In Server Admin, click the triangle to the left of your server's name to expand the list of services.**

2. **Select FTP from the list of services and then click Settings in the toolbar.**
3. **Click the Start FTP button on the lower left.**

Configuring FTP

To bring up the main configuration window for FTP service, do the following:

1. **In Server Admin, click the triangle to the left of your server's name to expand the list of services.**
2. **Select FTP from the list of services and then click Settings in the toolbar.**

You now see four tabs, as shown in Figure 9-22:

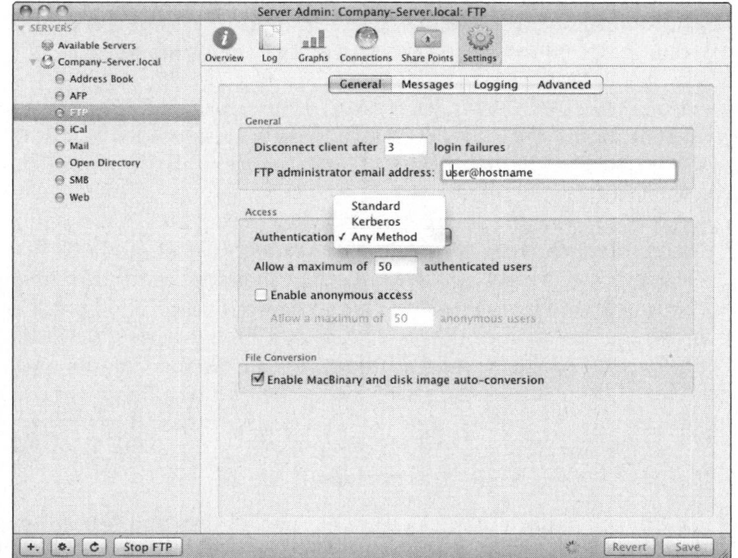

Figure 9-22: The General tab of the main FTP setup window in Server Admin.

- **General:** Here you can provide an administrator e-mail address and limit the number of users and number of login attempts. You can also enable MacBinary file conversion.
- **Messages:** Here you can write two messages to greet users. A banner message appears to users when they first contact the server before logging in. A welcome message appears to users after they log in.

- **Logging:** Logging access by authenticated and anonymous users is turned on by default. You can turn one or the other off, and add logging of FTP commands and of rule violation attempts.
- **Advanced:** This tab lets you specify folders that authenticated FTP users can access. You can also change the FTP `root` folder here.

The Messages and Logging tabs are simple to use. The General and Advanced tabs are worth some more explanation.

The General tab: Security and limiting the number of FTP users

Figure 9-22 shows the FTP General tab. Several items deal with security. Disconnect Client after *XX* Login Failures is aimed at thwarting people or programs attempting to continually try passwords. The Authentication pop-up menu gives you a choice of Standard (unencrypted cleartext) or encrypted Kerberos. Any Method uses Kerberos if the client supports it.

Select the Enable Anonymous Access check box to set a maximum number of simultaneous users for authenticated and anonymous users.

Anonymous users can log in by typing `anonymous` or `ftp` in the username field of their client software. They can leave the password blank, but Mac OS X Server asks for an e-mail address. Nothing prevents the user from typing a fake e-mail address, however.

The Enable MacBinary and Disk Image Auto-Conversion check box enables the FTP service to automatically encode, compress, and archive files as they're requested for download. This works with an FTP client, such as a Web browser, that allows the user to type a filename or a path. If a user adds `.tar` to the end of the requested file path, the server creates and downloads an archive. If the user adds `.z` or `.gz` to the end of a file path, the server compresses the file. The server can also decompress: If the user requests a `work.doc` file but only the compressed `work.doc.z` file is on the server, the FTP service decompresses it and sends it to the user.

If the FTP server detects a pre-Mac OS X file containing a resource fork, it will encode it using MacBinary (`.bin`) before sending it to the users. (There are a few Mac OS X applications that contain resource forks, but that is rare.)

The FTP Advanced tab: Adjusting the FTP root

The Advanced tab (shown in Figure 9-23) lets you change settings related to the FTP `root` folder, which is the highest level that a user can access.

The FTP service uses Unix symbolic links (similar to Mac aliases or Windows shortcuts) to make share points appear in the FTP `root` folder.

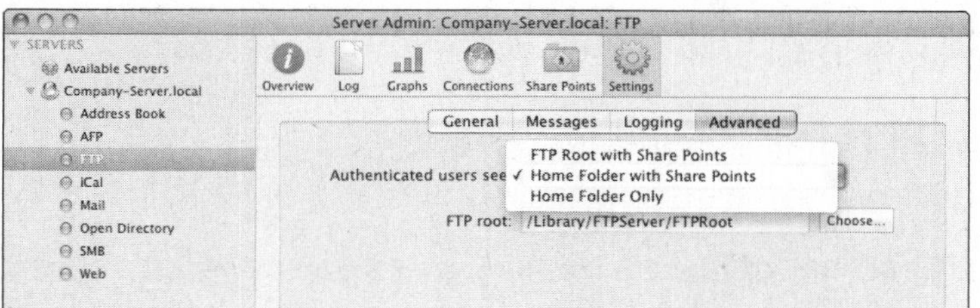

Figure 9-23: The FTP Advanced tab lets you change the FTP root and how it's viewed.

The Authenticated Users See pop-up menu gives you three choices for how authenticated users see and access share points with FTP:

- **FTP Root with Share Points:** With this setting, users see share points as residing in the FTP `root` folder. These share points could be located anywhere, including on other hard drives, and could be shared with AFP or SMB as well as with FTP.

  Worth noting, anonymous users and users who don't have server-based home folders are always connected with the FTP Root with Share Points setting, regardless of the setting of this pop-up menu.

- **Home Folder with Share Points:** Authenticated users with home folders on the server see FTP share points in their home folders. The actual location of the share points can be anywhere on the server.
- **Home Folder Only:** Users will see only their server-based home folders, if you have them set up. Users don't have access to the FTP `root` folder or other FTP share points.

Configuring NFS for Unix clients

If you have Unix or Linux clients that need to access share points using the NFS protocol, you can add NFS to an existing or new share point. Mac clients can also access the NFS file service if needed.

Macs connect to NFS servers by specifying the path to the share point in Connect to Server, accessible from the Finder's Go menu. The form is like this: `nfs://DNSname/path/`. For example: `nfs://acmeanvils/sharedfolders/myproject/`.

By itself, NFS is not secure, but Snow Leopard Server lets you add Kerberos authentication to an NFS-shared folder. This enables you to have server-based home folders via NFS. In order to use Kerberos and NFS, client computers must be running NFS client software that supports it. Clients running Mac OS X 10.5 and later can use Kerberos with NFS.

To set up NFS in Snow Leopard Server, you must use Server Admin to turn on and start NFS and export and configure share points. I describe these tasks in the following sections.

Turning on and starting NFS service

Turning on NFS uses the same procedure as turning on AFP, SMB, and FTP:

1. **In Server Admin, click your server listed in the left column.**
2. **Click Settings in the toolbar and then click the Services tab.**
3. **Check the box next to NFS under Select the Services to Configure on This Server and then click the Save button.**

You've now turned on NFS, but users can't access it yet. You need to start the NFS service so that it is actually running. Here's how:

1. **In Server Admin, click the triangle to the left of your server's name to expand the list of services.**
2. **Select NFS from the list of services, click Settings in the toolbar, and then click the Start NFS button on the lower left.**

   While you're here, you can also change some settings. For most people, the default settings should be fine. But if you're having performance issues with NFS service, there are a couple settings you can change:

   - *Use XX Server Threads:* An NFS *thread* is a bit of code that processes read and write requests from clients. Increasing the number of threads increases the number of clients that can simultaneously access the NFS service. Consider increasing this number if you have a lot of NFS clients accessing the server or you find that file transfers are slower. I wouldn't increase it by more than 8 to start with, or you can run into other problems.
   - *TCP and UDP:* The default setting is both TCP and UDP. You can change this to only UDP, which puts less load on the server Mac, so it's better for heavily used services. You could also use only TCP, which is faster for clients than is UDP, and also adds error correction, which is good for remote clients.

3. **Click Save when you're done.**

Exporting and configuring an NFS share point

In the older Unix terminology, sharing a folder using NFS is called *exporting* a share point. Server Admin uses the NFS terminology.

With NFS, computers, not users, get access to items shared with NFS. The NFS service identifies the computers by their IP address. Specifically, you tell the NFS service which IP addresses (or range of addresses) are allowed to log in.

On any single volume, you can't nest exported (shared) NFS folders. That is, you can't have an exported folder inside another exported folder. Just export the highest-level directory or the volume itself.

The next few subsections describe the process for exporting a share point. You need to follow these directions in sequence, so the numbering of the steps continues through the subsections. The various choices for settings are explained as you go along.

Selecting a share point for NFS

1. **In Server Admin, click your server listed in the left column.**
2. **Click File Sharing in the toolbar.**
3. **Click the Share Points heading and click a share point from the list. (Click the Share button if it isn't already shared.)**

   If you need to create a new share point, follow the procedure in the section, "Creating a share point with Server Admin," earlier in this chapter.
4. **In the bottom half of the screen, click the Share Point tab and then click the Protocol Options button.**

   A window appears with AFP, SMB, FTP, and NFS tabs.
5. **Click the NFS tab (see Figure 9-24).**

   You can also deselect AFP, SMB, or FTP under the respective tabs.

Figure 9-24: *Exporting* a folder is NFS-speak for *sharing.*

Specifying client computers for access

6. **Select the Export This Item and Its Contents To check box and then click the pop-up menu.**

You're presented with three permission choices that will decide which computers will get access to the shared folder: World, Client List, and Subnet. This terminology is specific to NFS:

- *World:* Allows any IP address/computer to access this share via NFS, including computers on the Internet. Exporting to World is similar to sharing to Everyone in POSIX permissions.
- *Client List:* This option lets you create a list of computer IP addresses that will be granted access. When you choose this option from the menu, a new field appears (see Figure 9-25). Click the Add (+) button to add an IP address.

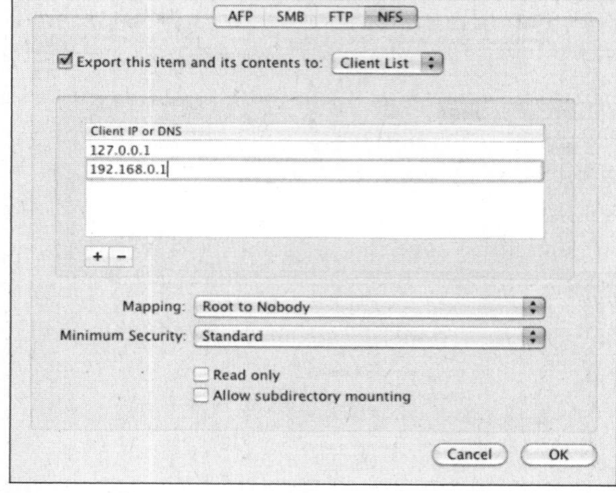

Figure 9-25: Creating a list of computer IP addresses to be granted NFS access.

- *Subnet:* This allows computers connected to a particular subnet to access the NFS share. The subnet address is the IP address of the subnet, not of the client computers. An IP address of a subnet corresponds to a subnet mask determined by the range of IP addresses of the clients on the network.

If you don't know what subnet mask to use, you can use a network (or subnet) calculator. There's an online version here:

```
www.subnet-calculator.com
```

The Mapping pop-up menu (refer to Figure 9-25) lets you map either all users or the Unix `root` user (with permissions for everything). Mapping the permissions of all users or the `root` user to Nobody is a security setting to compensate for the lack of user passwords.

7. **Choose one of these options from the Mapping pop-up menu:**

   - *Root to Root:* This sets the Unix `root` user to have all the `root` privileges to read, write, and carry out commands.
   - *All to Nobody:* This setting gives all users the minimal read/write permissions that you've set for Everyone. This would be a good choice if you're using the Export to World selection in Step 6. This is similar to AFP's Guest access.
   - *Root to Nobody:* This gives the `root` user on a client the minimal permissions that you've set for Everyone. This is a secure setting, used to block someone who might be pretending to be the `root` user.
   - *None:* This option doesn't map user privileges. It trusts the client that the user is who the client says and applies POSIX permissions.

Selecting authentication

8. **Select a method of authentication from the Minimum Security pop-up menu (refer to Figure 9-25).**

   You have five choices:

   - *Standard:* This means that there's no authentication. The computer user types in a path and connects to the server much like connecting to a Web site.
   - *Any:* The server will accept any method of authentication.
   - *Kerberos v5:* The NFS server requires Kerberos encrypted authentication for this share point. Clients can't connect without it.
   - *Kerberos v5 with Data Integrity:* In addition to authentication, NFS will do a checksum validation of the data during transmission.
   - *Kerberos v5 with Data Integrity and Privacy:* In addition to encrypting authentication, this setting adds encryption of user data as it is moved between server and client.

9. **(Optional) Select the Read Only check box to prevent NFS users from making changes to the share point.**
10. **(Optional) Select the Allow Subdirectory Mounting check box to allow users to directly mount folders inside the NFS share point.**
11. **Click OK.**

Chapter 10

Sharing Printers Over a Network

In This Chapter

- Understanding printer service
- Creating print queues and printer pools
- Publishing printer queues to Open Directory
- Helping Mac and Windows clients print

Printer sharing, or print serving, is a useful feature for both users and network administrators. For users, a print server eliminates waiting for a printer when it's busy. Administrators get management tools that can keep track of how often different printers are used and who's using them, as well as keep track of print errors.

Mac OS X Server allows you to set up a shared print queue for any printer. When users hit their Print buttons, the print job doesn't go to the printer, but instead goes to the shared print queue on the server. The print server feeds print jobs in the queue to the printer one at a time. You can also schedule printing and assign priority.

Mac OS X Server also allows you to set up a *printer pool,* which is basically a queue that can feed print jobs to multiple printers. This is useful for where there's a lot of printing is going on, such as in a school's computer lab.

A Second Helping of Protocol Soup: IPP, LPR, and SMB

One great thing about Snow Leopard Server's print service is that any client can print to any printer connected to the server. Without a server, the user's computer communicates directly with the printer, and the computer and the printer both need to support the same technology. When you throw a print server into the mix, here are the two steps of communication: client to server and server to printer. The two steps don't have to use the same technology.

It starts with the printer. Snow Leopard Server supports a variety of types of printers. But in printing parlance, *printer type* can mean different things: USB, LPR (Line Printer Remote), inkjet, Ethernet, PostScript, IPP (Internet Printing Protocol), or laser printer. These sometimes cryptic terms aren't equivalent, however. We're talking apples and oranges, with some cherries and pomegranates thrown in for good measure.

Communicating with the printer

Snow Leopard Server works with hundreds of new and old printer models. Here are the printer types that Mac OS X Server supports:

- **Printer technology (laser, inkjet, others):** Mac OS X Server doesn't really care about how the ink's put on the paper. More exotic technologies, such as dye sublimation, may also work, depending on drivers and the other factors noted later in this list. Inkjet printers typically use USB to connect to the server.
- **Physical connection (USB or Ethernet):** You can share a printer that's plugged into the server Mac or a printer that connects directly to the network with its own Ethernet port.

  Ethernet printers use a print protocol to communicate with the server over the network; directly connected USB printers do not. USB printers are easier to configure in Mac OS X Server, but Ethernet printers are more convenient because you can locate them where the users are, not just where the server is located.

  To make things a little more confusing, you might be able to connect a USB printer to a box that puts it on the network. Apple's Time Capsule does this, as do some DSL modems. For the purposes of the Mac OS X Server's print service, these are treated as Ethernet printers.
- **Page description language (PostScript, raster, or proprietary):** This is what the client uses to describe the page; the printer reads the description to re-create the page in printed form. PostScript is the most standard page-description language for Ethernet printers. Some inkjet printers also use PostScript, though many describe a page with *raster* printing, which simply defines where dots are applied on a printed page. HP's PCL (Printer Command Language) is another common page description language. Proprietary page description languages are also used for specific printers.
- **Network printing protocol:** Snow Leopard Server uses Line Printer Remote (LPR) to communicate with printers and servers. These network protocols aren't used for USB printers. In that case, the USB data transmission standards are used to move print data from server to printer.

Previous versions of Mac OS X Server supported another network printer protocol, AppleTalk, which ran over standard IP networks, supported PostScript, and was self configuring. Because Apple dropped AppleTalk in Snow Leopard Server, you won't be able to use an older AppleTalk printer if it doesn't also support LPR.

The printing protocol that the server uses to communicate with the printer doesn't have to be the same one it uses to communicate with clients.

Communicating with the client

The print service in Mac OS X Server can communicate with user client computers with one of three network printing protocols. You set up a print queue with one more of these print protocols:

- **Internet Printing Protocol (IPP):** Mac, Windows (XP and later), and Unix/Linux clients can all use IPP to print. When Mac OS X clients print to a non-PostScript printer, they can use the printer's native driver installed on the client to have access to the printer's special features. This isn't available with LPR.
- **Line Printer Remote (LPR):** Mac, Windows (XP and later), and Unix/Linux clients can all use LPR to print.
- **Server Message Block (SMB):** Windows clients only, including older versions of Windows.

Client computers can use any of these protocols to transfer PostScript print jobs to the server. If you have a printer that uses a proprietary, non-PostScript print driver, it will use IPP to send print job data with.

A USB printer connected to the server Mac is a network printer as far as the client computers are concerned. So although a USB printer doesn't use a network printing protocol to talk to the server, the clients do use a network printing protocol to send jobs to the server. If the USB printer is a raster (non-PostScript) inkjet printer, the client computers can use any printing protocol to send a PostScript job to the server. The server converts the PostScript job to what the inkjet printer expects to receive.

Paving the Way to Painless Printing

This section describes how to set up print service in Snow Leopard Server. I include directions for creating a print queue for each printer and combining printers into a printer pool. For these tasks, you use Server Admin. (You can't use Server Preferences to configure print sharing.)

This section also describes setting quotas for individual users to limit the number of pages they print; it also describes publishing printers via Open Directory. You use Workgroup Manager for both of these tasks.

Printing and print serving in Mac OS X Server uses the Common Unix Printing System (CUPS), a Unix standard. If you're so inclined or are familiar with using CUPS to configure printers, you can use the CUPS Web-based administration tools and the CUPS command-line tools. Just open a Web browser and type `http://localhost:631/admin`.

Before you start: Set up your printers

Before you configure print services in Mac OS X Server, make sure your printers are connected to the network or plugged into the server. You also need to set up and configure your printers according to the manufacturer's directions. For network printers, it's a good idea to configure them using a static IP address so that they have a consistent location on the network.

Some printers have print serving or spooling features built into the printer. Turn off these features if you want your users to go through the Mac OS X Server. Using two print queues (one in the printer and one on the Mac OS X Server) can cause users to wait longer before their documents are printed.

A good idea is to print to the printer from a Mac and a Windows PC (if you have them) before you configure printer sharing on your server. This way, you can spot any trouble that might be caused by the printer.

Turning on and starting print service

You need to turn on the print service before you choose settings. Turning on Mac OS X Server's printer is similar to turning on file services (which I describe in Chapter 9). Here's how:

1. **In Server Admin, select your server listed in the left column.**
2. **Click the Settings icon at the top and then click the Services tab.**
3. **Select the Print check box.**

   Figure 10-1 shows the Server Admin window as it now appears.
4. **Click Save.**

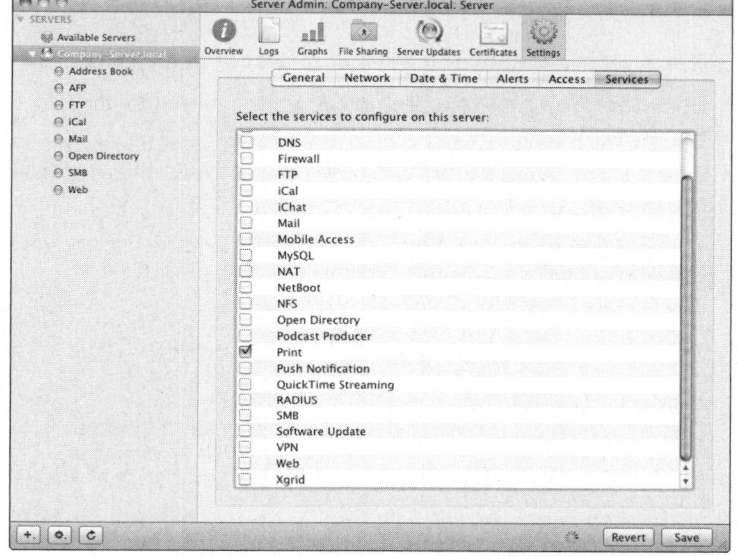

Figure 10-1: In Server Admin, select services you want to turn on.

Although you've turned on the print service, it isn't available to users — you still need to start it. You can configure the print service before starting, or you can start the service now. To start the print service:

1. **In Server Admin, click the triangle to the left of your server's name to expand the list of services.**
2. **Select Print from the list of services.**

   If the circle next to Print is filled in, the print service is already running.
3. **Click the Settings icon and then click the Start Print button on the lower left.**

Setting up print queues

To share a printer with Mac OS X Server, the printer needs a print queue configured for it. You do this with Server Admin. For printers connected to the network via Ethernet, you need to create the print queues. If you have a printer connected to the server via USB, you don't need to create a print queue: The server creates one automatically and displays it in Server Admin.

If you don't see a print queue for your USB printer, choose System Preferences⇨Print & Fax. If it's not there, delete it in System Preferences and then add it again. This may force the USB printer's queue to be regenerated in Server Admin.

Creating a print queue for a network printer is a fairly simple task:

1. **Open Server Admin and click your server listed in the left column.**
2. **Click the triangle to the left of the server name to display the list of services.**
3. **Select Print from the list of services and then click the Queues icon in the toolbar.**

   The Queues pane appears. Figure 10-2 shows the list of queues at the top of the window with one queue created already.

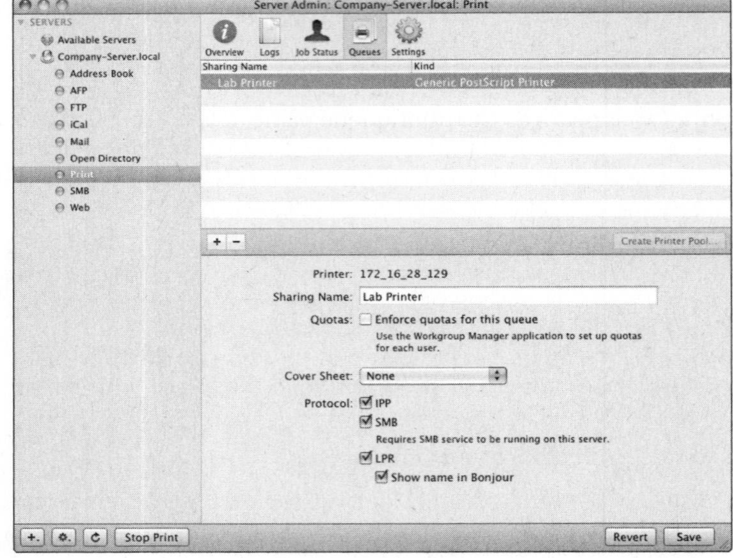

Figure 10-2: The Queues pane of Server Admin, with a print queue created already.

4. **Click the Add (+) button.**
5. **In the dialog that appears, click the pop-up menu and then choose between LPR and Open Directory (Figure 10-3):**
   - *Choose LPR for most network printers.* (LPR refers to the protocol used by the printer to connect with the server.) Type an IP address or a DNS name in the Printer's Address field.
   - *Choose Open Directory for printers that are listed in Open Directory as a directory record.* Open Directory could be running on this Mac server or another server. (For more on Open Directory printers, see "Publishing a printer to Open Directory," later in this chapter.)

Figure 10-3: The LPR print queue name you set is the name the users see.

6. **(Optional) If you choose LPR, select the Use Default Queue on Server check box (refer to Figure 10-3) if this is a printer with a built-in print server supporting multiple queues.**

   When you select this check box, the name of the default queue in that printer appears as the print queue name. If you don't want to use the in-printer queue or if the printer doesn't have this feature, leave this check box deselected and type a name for the queue. The queue name should be descriptive of the printer or the location of the printer. For users, the queue name and printer name are the same.

7. **Click OK to return to the main Queues pane.**

   Your new queue appears in the list.

8. **Select your queue and notice that the name you entered is in the Shared Name box.**

   This is the name the users see. You can keep the name or create a new one. Here are some rules for naming print queues:

   - If you're sharing to clients with LPR or SMB, use only letter and number characters and underscores. The names of print queues shared with SMB must be 15 characters or less.
   - LPR Unix/Linux clients may have trouble with spaces in the name.
   - Older Windows clients (before XP) require queue names to be 12 characters or less.

9. **Select the protocols that you want to use with your client computers.**

   The printer doesn't need to support these protocols; this is for communication between the clients and the print server. (See "Communicating with the client," earlier in this chapter for more on these choices.)

   If you use SMB, the SMB service needs to be running. Select SMB from the list of services and click Start SMB.

10. **(Optional) If you choose LPR in Step 5, select Show Name in Bonjour to enable Bonjour clients to browse for print queues.**

    (Mac clients and Windows clients with Bonjour for Windows installed.)

11. **(Optional) Select the Enforce Quotas for This Queue check box if you plan to use quotas, and choose a coversheet from the pop-up menu if you desire.**

    If you choose to enforce quotas for users, you need to create them in Workgroup Manager. I describe this later in this chapter.

12. **Click Save.**

Creating a printer pool

In a situation when a printer is heavily used, you might want to group together two or more printers in a pool. A *print pool* is basically a queue that contains multiple printers in it. When users print to the pool, the job gets printed to the first available printer. Often, administrators place the pooled printers next to each other so that users can easily find their printout.

It's best to use printers of the same model in a printer pool to insure that printouts from the machines are the same and the printer features are consistent. If you have printers with different features, a user could select a print feature in her Print dialog that doesn't exist in one of the printers. This could lead to a situation in which a print job won't print on one of the printers in the pool.

Before you create a printer pool, you have to create print queues for the printers you want to include in a pool. Setting up a printer pool is very similar to creating a print queue:

1. **Open Server Admin and select your server in the left column.**
2. **Click the triangle to the left of the server name to display the list of services.**
3. **Select Print from the list of services and then click the Queues icon in the toolbar.**
4. **In the list at the top of the window, select two or more print queues.**
5. **Click the Create Printer Pool button (as shown on the right side in Figure 10-2).**

    A dialog asks you to enter a name for the pool. This is the name that users see as the shared printer name.

6. **Enter a print pool name and click OK.**

    At this point, you can set the same options that you can for creating a print queue (start at Step 9 in the preceding section). You can choose protocols, enforce quotas, and print cover sheets.

7. **Click Save when you're done.**

You can see the new pool in the print queue list (as shown in Figure 10-4). This pool has two things that differentiate it from print queues: The pool has a triangle to its left and is identified in the Kind column as Local Printer Class.

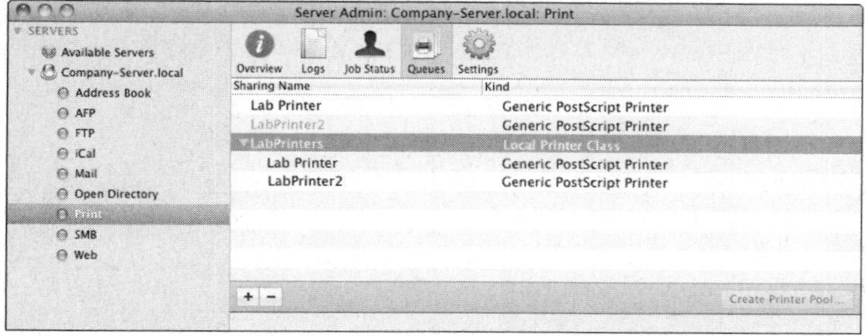

Figure 10-4: The print pool shows up in the print queue list with a triangle next to it.

Click the triangle next to the pool to see the print queues in it. The individual queues are listed twice: once inside the pool, and once outside it. If you've previously enabled sharing of these queues, users can still print to the individual printers in the pool, bypassing the pool and its advantages.

To prevent this, you can disable the sharing of the individual queues that make up the pool so that users can choose only to print to the pool and not to the printers individually. To do this, select a queue outside the pool and turn off all the protocols you previously set to share it (IPP, LPR, and SMB).

Setting print quotas

It can be frustrating to see users printing e-mails to high-end color printers that use expensive ink and paper. The same is true when users print reams of pages of PDF documents that they might only glance at, or print 30 copies of a document for a meeting with 10 people attending.

You can prevent superfluous printing by assigning quotas to users for specific printers. A *print quota* limits the number of pages a user can print in a day or a number of days. Quotas can make users think about the use of paper and ink and toner. If a user has a quota of 20 pages a day on a color printer, he's less likely to print all his e-mail to it. If a user hits her quota but still needs to print, the administrator can reset the quota to allow further printing.

Before you set a quota, create a print queue for the printer (which I describe in "Setting up print queues" earlier in this chapter). You then assign print quotas for specific print queues in the users' Open Directory accounts.

To create a print quota for one or more users, use Mac OS X Server's Workgroup Manager:

1. **Open Workgroup Manager and click the Accounts icon in the toolbar.**
2. **Choose the name of a user from the list.**

   If you want to set the same quota for multiple users, Command-click the names of each user.
3. **Click the Print tab.**

   The window looks like Figure 10-5.

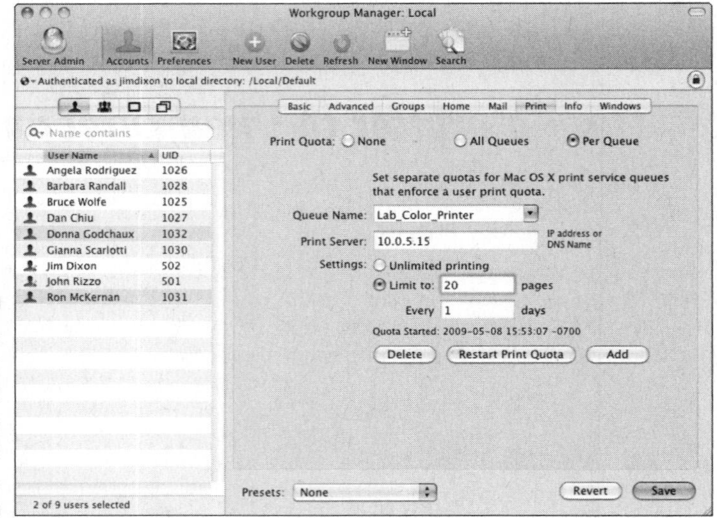

Figure 10-5: Setting a print quota with Workgroup Manager.

4. **To set a quota for a particular printer, select Per Queue and then choose a queue from the pop-up menu.**

   If you don't see your queue in the list, click the Add button, enter the queue name in the Queue Name field, and type the IP address or DNS name of the server.
5. **To set a quota for all printers, select All Queues.**
6. **Click Limit To and then type the number of pages you want to use as the quota.**
7. **Type the number of days you want for the quota period and click Save.**

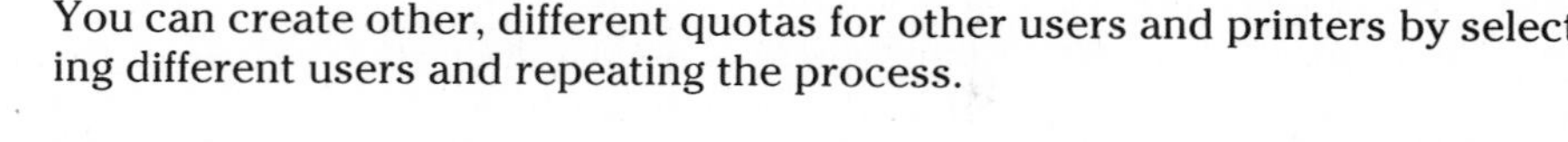

You can create other, different quotas for other users and printers by selecting different users and repeating the process.

To enable a user to print after reaching his or her quota, click the Restart Print Queue button. This button resets the quota, as if the user hadn't printed anything yet.

The preceding procedure creates the quotas, but they aren't yet active. To activate a quota, you need to tell Mac OS X Server to begin enforcing it. You do this in Server Admin for each queue.

First, follow the steps in the section, "Setting up print queues," earlier in this chapter, to get to the Queues pane, as shown in Figure 10-2. Select the Enforce Quotas for This Queue check box and then click Save.

Publishing a printer to Open Directory

Publishing a printer to Open Directory enables Open Directory to make the printer visible to users. You can use it as an alternative to Bonjour for enabling a printer to appear in the user's default printer list. The advantage is that you don't have to add Bonjour for Windows to PCs. (Although, they may be using Bonjour for other network resources.) Another benefit of publishing a print queue to Open Directory is that you can limit discovery of the printer to clients that are bound to a single domain. (See the following section, "Don't Forget Your Clients," for more on Bonjour and printer discovery.)

Before you start, make sure you've created a print queue for the printer and shared it with LPR.

To list a print queue in Open Directory, do the following:

1. **Open Workgroup Manager.**
2. **Click the Workgroup Manager menu and select Preferences.**
3. **Make sure the Show 'All Records' Tab and Inspector check box is selected and then close Workgroup Manager Preferences.**
4. **On the left side of the screen, click the bull's-eye icon.**

   If you hover your cursor over it, the words All Record Types appear.
5. **Click the pop-up menu below the bull's-eye and choose Printers.**
6. **Click the New Record icon in the toolbar.**
7. **In the main field, click RecordName (as shown in Figure 10-6) and then click the Edit button.**

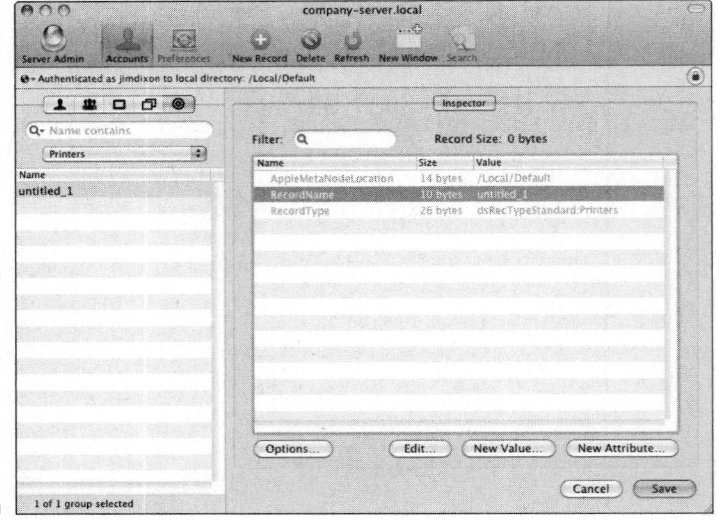

Figure 10-6: Creating a new record for a print queue in Workgroup Manager.

8. **In the new dialog that appears, type a printer name that you want your users to see when browsing for a printer and then click OK.**

   You return to the screen in Figure 10-7, except the queue name you typed is displayed instead of Untitled_1 in the Name column on the left.

9. **Enter the server that hosts the print queue:**

   a. *Click the New Attribute button.*

      A new dialog slides down.

   b. *In the Attribute Name pop-up menu, choose PrinterLPRHost.*

   c. *Type the IP address or DNS name of the server that hosts the print queue in the text box and click OK.*

10. **If the queue you want to publish isn't the default queue on the server, define the print queue that you're listing in Open Directory:**

    a. *In the main window, click the New Attribute button.*

    b. *In the Attribute Name pop-up menu, choose PrinterLPRQueue.*

    c. *In the text box, type the name of the print queue and click OK.*

11. **(Optional) Specify the printer model:**

    a. *Click the New Attribute button in the main window.*

    b. *Choose PrinterType from the Attribute Name pop-up menu.*

    c. *Type the printer model name in the text box.*

You must enter the model name exactly as it appears in the PPD (PostScript Printer Description) file for that printer. One way to find out is in System Preferences, in the Print & Fax pane. Click the Add (+) button to see the model name.

Another way to find the model name is to look in the PPD files in this folder: /Library/Printers/PPDs/Contents/Resources/. Option-drag the PPD file to the desktop to copy it. Double-click to decompress and then Control-click (or right-click) and open with TextEdit. The correct name is identified by "ModelName."

d. Click OK.

12. Click Save.

Figure 10-7 shows what the Workgroup Manager window now looks like.

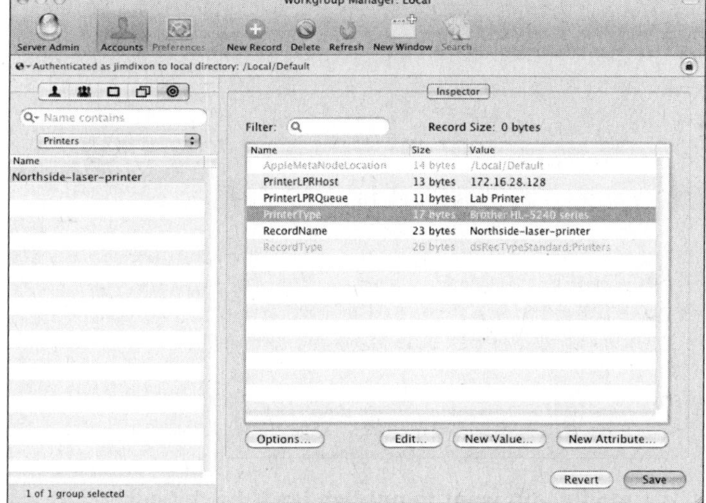

Figure 10-7: A print queue is fully configured to be listed in Open Directory.

Don't Forget Your Clients

You probably know how to enable your Mac and Windows clients to print. In this section, I point out a few things that are helpful to know when your clients connect to Mac OS X Server. I also mention some things you might want to remember for Mac and Windows clients.

PPD files

It's helpful for the server and client computers to have the correct PostScript Printer Description (PPD) files for the specific network printer models. The PPD files enable a user to choose special features, such as double-sided printing and the ability to select specific paper trays. Mac OS X Server and Mac and Windows clients come with plenty of PPD files installed.

When adding a print queue to a client computer, you or the user chooses the PPD on the client by selecting the printer model from a list. If you don't see the PPD file on the client or if the Mac OS X server doesn't have it, check with the printer manufacturer or the software that came with the printer.

If you don't have a PPD file on the clients or server for a network printer, the user can probably still print to that printer. Mac OS X identifies the printer as Generic PostScript Printer. Users probably won't have access to special features of that particular printer model.

On a Mac server and on Mac clients, you can check for a PPD file by looking in this folder: /Library/Printers/PPDs/Contents/Resources/.

Enabling printer discovery

You can more easily set up printing on client computers if the clients can discover the print queues. You can enable the print server to advertise print queues over the network. You can do this in Server Admin with the settings for the protocols you use to share your print queue (refer to Figure 10-2):

- **Sharing with SMB:** The SMB protocol automatically advertises print queues to Windows computers. The SMB service must be enabled. Unlike SMB file service, Mac clients can't access SMB print service.
- **Sharing with LPR with Bonjour enabled:** By itself, LPR doesn't advertise the existence of print queues. You need to select the Show Name in Bonjour check box in Server Admin (refer to Figure 10-2).

  Bonjour is a protocol that Apple created for the advertising and discovery of computers, printers, and other services over a network. Outside of Apple, Bonjour is called ZeroConf or Multicast DNS. (It was also once called Rendezvous.)

  TIP

  Mac OS X 10.2 and later clients have Bonjour built in, but Windows doesn't. Apple offers Bonjour for Windows as a free download here:

  ```
  http://support.apple.com/downloads/Bonjour_for_Windows
  ```

- **Sharing with IPP:** When you share a queue with IPP, the queue appears on the Mac client's System Preferences's Print & Fax pane (in the default browser list), as well as in the Print dialog of Mac OS X applications.
- **List the print queue in Open Directory:** This works for any client computers that are bound to a directory domain. I describe the procedure to list a print queue in Open Directory in "Publishing a printer to Open Directory," earlier in this chapter.

Some printers also come with protocols that can advertise the printer over the network, such SMB and Bonjour. You may consider turning off these features in these printers to prevent users from directly accessing the printers and avoiding the server-hosted print queues.

Helping Mac clients print

Since the earliest models, Macs have been good at printing, with easy setup and few printing errors. Today, connecting to network printers is done in System Preferences, in the Print & Fax preference pane. You can also add a printer in the Print dialog of any application, in the Printer pop-up menu.

When a Mac client prints to a queue that's shared with IPP, the user can monitor the progress of the printing in the Print & Fax pane of System Preferences. The user can also delete a print job from the queue.

On a Mac OS X client, to add a print queue that's shared with LPR and advertised with Bonjour or Open Directory, do the following:

1. **Open the Print & Fax pane of System Preferences.**
2. **Click the Add (+) button and then click the Default icon in the toolbar (as shown in Figure 10-8).**
3. **Click a print queue in the list and then click the Print Using pop-up menu to select a PPD file for the printer model.**

   Usually, the correct PPD file is chosen for you. If you can't find it or don't know the printer model, choose Generic PostScript Printer.
4. **Click the Add button.**

If Bonjour isn't used with the LPR protocol, choose the protocol from the Protocol pop-up menu. You also need the IP address or the DNS name of the *server* (not the printer). You may also have to know the queue name. To avoid all this, just enable Bonjour on the server (see the preceding section).

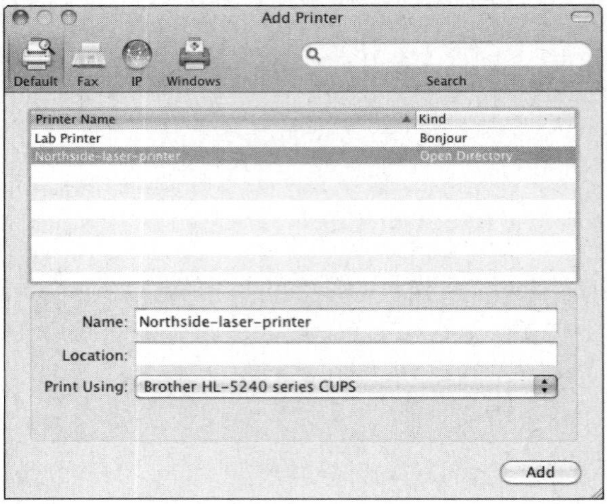

Figure 10-8: The Mac OS X client Print & Fax preferences.

For *really* old Macs running Mac OS 8 and Mac OS 9, add LPR printers with the Desktop Printer Utility, which is located in the Utilities folder inside the Applications folder, or in Apple Extras⇨LaserWriter Software. Mac OS 8 and 9 don't support Bonjour, so you need the server's IP address or DNS name.

Helping Windows clients print

Most versions of Windows can send print jobs to the server with SMB. Windows XP, Vista, and Windows 7 support SMB, IPP, and LPR. To connect to print queues on Mac OS X Server, you can use the Add Printer Wizard (see Figure 10-9). To find this wizard, choose Start⇨Printers and Faxes and then click Add a Printer.

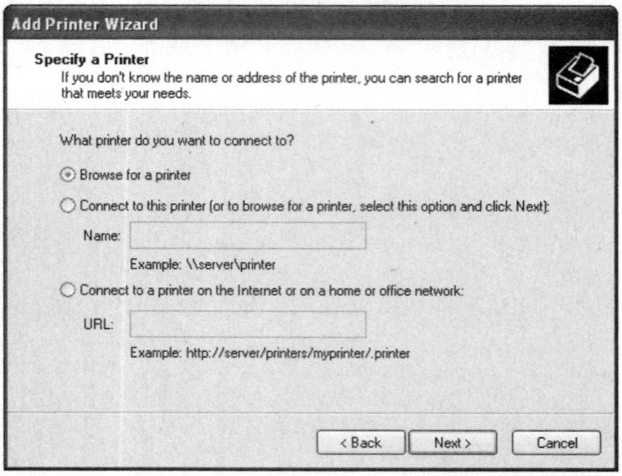

Figure 10-9: The Add Printer Wizard in Windows XP.

Here, you can either browse for a discoverable print queue or type in a printer address. The latter takes this form: `\\servername\printqueuename`.

Keep in mind that the server name is actually the NetBIOS name or a Windows domain server. The print queue name is the sharing name you gave to the print queue, which I describe in, "Setting up print queues," earlier in this chapter.

You can check the NetBIOS name of the Mac server with Server Admin:

1. **Click the triangle to the left of the server and then choose SMB from the list.**
2. **Click the Settings icon and then click General.**

   The Computer Name field has the NetBIOS name.

If you have trouble finding a print queue shared with SMB, check the name of the print queue. If it's longer than 15 characters, that's a problem. SMB print queues need to be 15 characters or less.

Keeping Track of Network Printing

Server Admin includes some management tools for monitoring current print jobs and other activity of server-based print queues:

1. **In Server Admin, select your server listed in the left column.**
2. **Click the triangle to the left of the server name to display the list of services.**
3. **Select Print from the list of services.**
4. **Click the Jobs Status icon in the toolbar.**

You can do several things here. The top of the window shows a list of print queues that you've configured on this server. In the list of print queues, the number in the Jobs column is the number of print jobs in the queue. Here you can pause a print queue (and all the jobs in it) by selecting the print queue and clicking the Pause button. You might do this if you need to attend to a paper jam, change a toner cartridge, or perform some other service on the printer. The Resume button starts the queue again.

In the lower half of the window, you will see a list of print jobs in a particular queue. This list tells you the name of the user, the job name, and the status. To change the queue to look at, choose another from the pop-up menu. You can pause and resume these queues by selecting a queue and clicking the Pause and Resume buttons at the bottom of the list. You can also remove a print job from the list with the Remove button.

When you click the Logs icon in the toolbar, you view the print log for the server. The print log records the sizes of print jobs and the user who submitted them. The print log also lists when a print queue was put on hold, as well as when the print service was started and stopped.

Part IV
Facilitating User Collaboration

"As a candidate for network administrator, how well-versed are you in remote connectivity protocols?"

In this part . . .

In the year 1624, John Donne wrote compellingly that "no man is an island, entire of itself." Of course, Donne was talking about collaboration software, also known as *groupware*: e-mail, group scheduling and calendars, text chat, and user-editable Web pages.

But Donne wrote his profound reflection *before* Apple shipped Snow Leopard Server. He didn't know about some of the stuff that other servers don't provide: a wiki-based collaborative environment, already built when you turn on Snow Leopard Server; Address Book Server, an interactive contact manager that users can safely edit without tampering with directory services; Podcast Producer, an automated video workflow system; and iChat, which adds video conferencing to instance messaging.

And Donne didn't know that iPhone can access it all.

Well, I know it, and I'm sharing it with you in Part IV. It's not profound like *Meditation XVII*, but it does help you serve humankind — or at least, your users — with groupware.

Chapter 11

Sharing Contacts with Address Book Server

In This Chapter

- Considering clients for Address Book Server
- Configuring Address Book Server
- Importing contacts from Mac OS X Server 10.5
- Setting up the Address Book client

Address Book Server is a new service that enables users to share contacts in Snow Leopard Server. Address Book Server binds to a network directory, such as Open Directory or Active Directory, and then makes the contacts in the network directory available to Mac OS X 10.6 users through the Address Book application. People can use the Address Book client to search the global address list of the network's directory service. Address Book Server makes contacts available to other Mac applications, including Mail, iCal, and iChat, in Mac OS X 10.6. (See Chapters 5 and 6 for more on directory services.)

That's all nice, but here's the key benefit to Address Book Server: It enables *users* to modify contacts and add their own contacts to the server. This usually isn't possible (or desired) in Lightweight Directory Access Protocol (LDAP)-based directories, such as Open Directory. Users can also create their own fields for contacts, such as for Twitter names or company-specific information — an unheard-of thought with an LDAP directory. Because Address Book Server acts as kind of a gateway to the directory server, you don't need to give users write permissions to the network directory, and you don't need to modify the LDAP schema.

Address Book Server stores contacts as standard *vCards,* or electronic business cards. The cards are stored outside the Open Directory or other LDAP directory. vCards can be e-mailed or dragged to the desktop for sharing. Address Book clients connected to Address Book Server are authenticated from Open Directory and Kerberos.

iPhone users also get two-way access to Address Book Server data by syncing contacts from the Address Book client that's in contact with the server.

Clients for Address Book Server

Address Book Server uses a fairly new open standard, *CardDAV,* to communicate with clients. Like CalDAV for iCal Server, CardDAV is based on WebDAV and HyperText Transfer Protocol (HTTP). As I write this, the only contact client that supports CardDAV and works with Address Book Server is Address Book 5, which comes with the Mac OS X 10.6 Snow Leopard client. Because the server is based on open standards, you may eventually see CardDAV clients for older versions of Mac OS X, as well as for Windows and Linux.

Some of the other collaboration applications in the Snow Leopard client also support Address Book Server. For instance, Mail 4 and iChat 5 can access the contacts supplied by Address Book Server. In Mail 4, you configure Address Book Server connections in the Mail Preferences Composing pane. iChat 5 can locate users and groups provided by Address Book Server.

To configure Address Book 5, see the section, "Setting Up a User's Address Book 5 Client," later in the chapter.

A Prerequisite

You don't really need to do much to your network to make Address Book Server available to users. You don't even have to alter the directory. The one requirement is that the Mac you run Address Book Server on needs to be configured as an Open Directory master. See Chapter 6 for more on this.

This is necessary because Address Book client users are provisioned in Open Directory. This means that the directory services provide the authentication and access privileges.

Turning on Address Book Server

If you chose Address Book Server during the initial setup of Snow Leopard Server, Address Book Server is configured and running when you first log in. If you didn't choose Address Book Server during installation or want to shut it off, the easiest way is to use Server Preferences. Click the Address Book icon and then click the big switch to the On (or Off) position. You're done.

You can also use Server Admin. You first enable the service and then turn it on. This is the same procedure for all services:

1. **Enable the service:**
   a. *Select the server in the left column.*
   b. *Click the Settings icon in the toolbar and click the Services tab.*
   c. *Make sure the check box next to Address Book is selected and then click Save.*
2. **Start the service:**
   a. *Click the triangle next to your server in the left column to expand the list of services.*
   b. *Select Address Book from the list.*
   c. *Click the Start Address Book button.*

Changing Address Book Server's Default Settings

Use Server Admin to change the default settings of Address Book Server:

1. **In Server Admin, click your server name in the left column to expand the list of services and then click Address Book from the list.**
2. **Click the Settings icon in the toolbar and then click the General tab, as shown in Figure 11-1.**

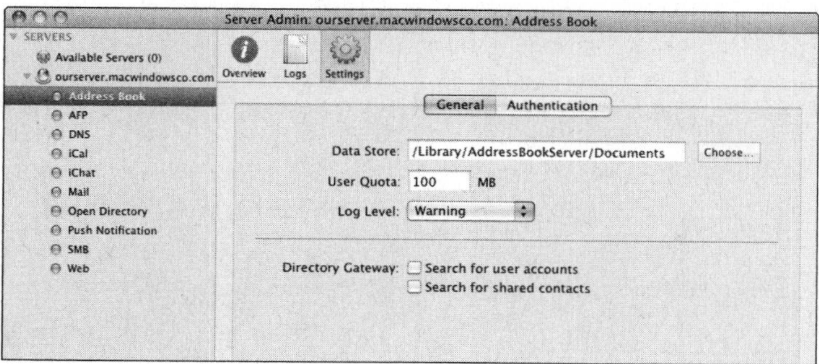

Figure 11-1: The General tab of Address Book Settings, with default settings.

You now change the following settings:

- **Data Store:** This is the directory in which Address Book Server stores the vCards for the contact. The default location is /Library/AddressBookServer/Documents. If you want to store this data on a RAID, Xsan, or other storage device, you can enter the path here. You can also click the Choose button to browse and select a new location.
- **User Quota:** This is the largest allowable total size for a user's vCards. vCards can contain photos, which can drive up the size. Individual vCards without photos are very small, however, under 1KB. The default 100MB quota can hold quite a few vCards, even with photos.

  You can also set a user quota in the Server Preferences Address Book pane.
- **Log Level:** This is the amount of information recorded in the log. These are arranged on the pop-up menu from the lowest amount of information recorded (the Error setting) to the highest (the Debug setting).

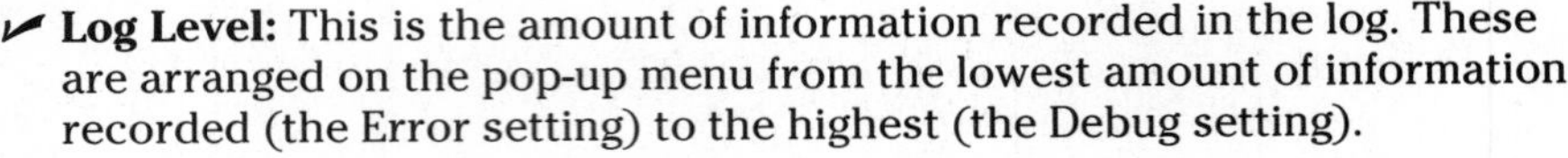

Click Save. A message appears asking you to restart the service. Click Restart; however, before doing this, two more groups of settings are worth going into more detail: the Directory Gateway check boxes and the Authentication tab.

Enabling users to search directories with Address Book using Directory Gateway

The Directory Gateway settings under the General tab of Address Book Settings (refer to Figure 11-1) enable users to employ the Address Book client to search the directory service that Address Book Server is bound to. This can be Open Directory on Snow Leopard Server, directories on Mac OS X Server 10.5 that were configured with Directory Utility, or Active Directory and LDAP directories on the network.

Here are the two settings that you can employ:

- **Search for Users Accounts:** This setting allows users to search for contacts in directory services that Address Book Server is bound to.
- **Search for Shared Contacts:** This setting enables users to search for contacts stored in the Mac OS X Server 10.5 directory.

You can also convert the older contacts, which I describe in the section, "Upgrading Contacts from Mac OS X Server Version 10.5," later in the chapter.

Security: SSL and Authentication

Click the Authentication tab (see Figure 11-2) to set an authentication type for password encryption or to turn on SSL (Secure Sockets Layer) data encryption. You can choose an authentication method with or without SSL.

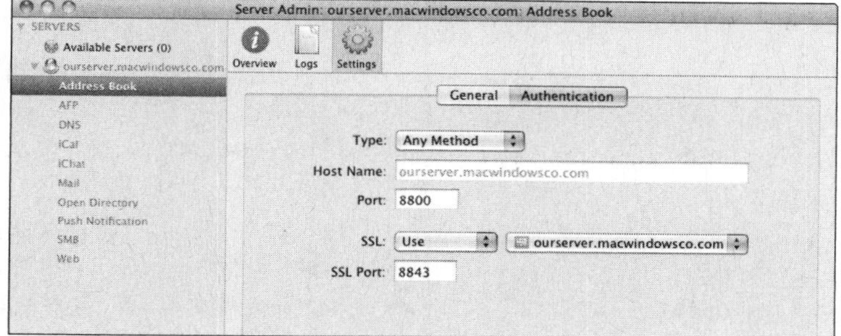

Figure 11-2: Enabling SSL encryption and authentication for iCal Server.

In the Type pop-up menu, Digest and Kerberos both provide encryption of passwords, but Kerberos is stronger. The Any Method selection uses whichever one the client can support.

SSL is off by default. The SSL pop-up menu encrypts the data moving between the server and the clients. The SSL pop-up menu gives you choices of Don't Use (no SSL), Use, and Redirect. With Use, Address Book Server can accept connections from both the unencrypted port and the encrypted SSL port. With Redirect, Address Book Server accepts connections over the SSL port only, while redirecting connection requests that come over the HTTP port to the secure HTTPS port. You can choose an SSL certificate from the second pop-up menu next to SSL.

The default for the Port field is 8800. If you're using SSL, use 8843 for the port number. (For more on security issues, see Chapter 18.)

When you're finished, click Save and restart Address Book Server.

Upgrading Contacts from Mac OS X Server Version 10.5

Mac OS X Server 10.5 didn't have Address Book Server but instead had something called Shared Contacts. If you've upgraded the server, you can convert these to Address Book Server in Snow Leopard Server 10.6. The only way to do this is from the command line within Terminal (in the /Applications/Utilities/ folder). Here's how:

1. **Log in to the server and launch Terminal.**
2. **Type the following command on one line:**

```
/usr/sbin/ContactsMigrator -s /LDAPv3/serverName -d http://
        yourserverName:8800/addressbooks/groups/mygroup/addressbook/ -u
        username -p password
```

The server name is the fully qualified domain name of your Address Book Server. The username and password are those of the system administrator. Note also that in this example, 8800 is the port number; if you're using another port number (such as 8843 for SSL), type that number.

Setting Up a User's Address Book 5 Client

Enabling a user's Address Book to access Address Book Server is referred to as *binding* the client to the server. After you do this, users are authenticated from Open Directory or Kerberos. To bind from the user's Address Book client:

1. **Launch Address Book 5 on the Snow Leopard client machine.**
2. **Click the Address Book menu and select Preferences.**
3. **Click the Accounts icon in the toolbar and then click the Add (+) button.**

   The Add Account dialog slides down, as shown in Figure 11-3.
4. **In the Account Type pop-up menu, choose CardDAV.**
5. **Type the username, password, and server hostname.**

   For example, type `ourserver.macwindowsco.com`.
6. **Click the Create button.**

The account is now in the Accounts list in the left column of the Preferences window, as shown in Figure 11-4. When selected, the window displays the account information.

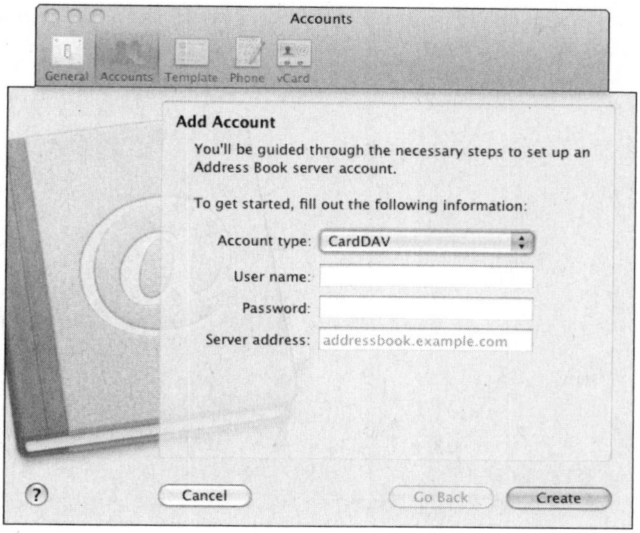

Figure 11-3: Setting up a user's Address Book for Address Book service.

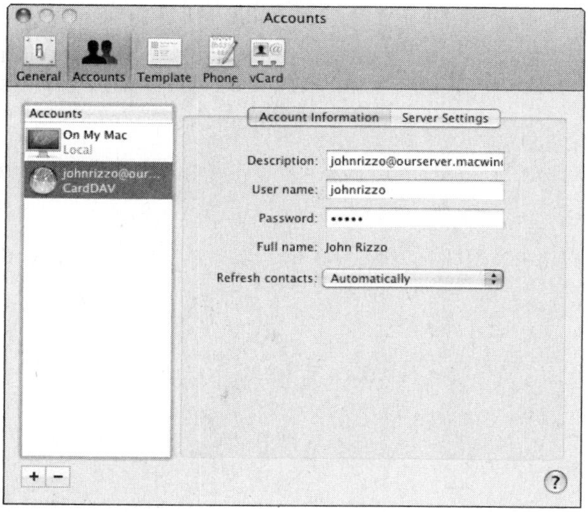

Figure 11-4: The Address Book client's Preferences window shows the server binding.

If you click the Server Settings tab, you can turn on SSL for this client's connection to Address Book Server. You can also change the port number (use 8843 for SSL).

Figure 11-5 shows the Address Book 5 client. The Address Book Server appears as a group with the user's name. The user can select it and click the Add (+) button in the Name column. The other users can now see this contact.

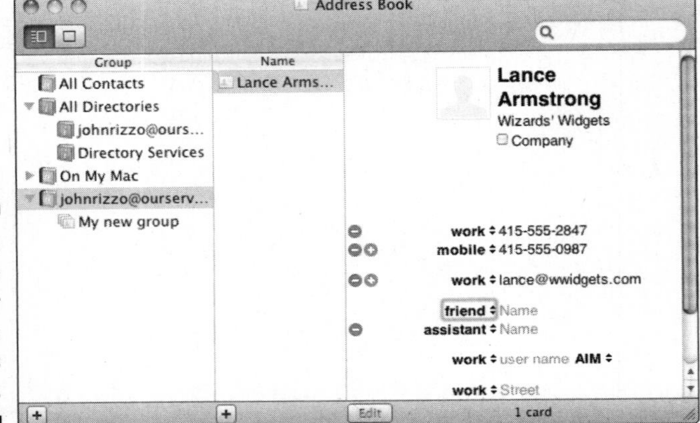

Figure 11-5: Address Book Server appears in the Address Book client.

Additionally, an All Directories group appears with the new group (on Address Book Server) and the network directory. These will be colored blue. You use these for searching. Click Directory Services, and you can search Open Directory from the search field. Pretty neat.

Chapter 12

Sharing Calendars with iCal Server

In This Chapter

- Choosing clients for iCal Server
- Getting your network ready for iCal Server
- Using Server Admin to customize settings and enable SSL
- Creating resources to reserve
- Setting up iCal 4 clients

Snow Leopard Server beefed up the calendar server from the previous version of Mac OS X Server. iCal Server 2 is a collaboration tool, enabling users to share calendars, schedule meetings and tasks, and include attachments. When scheduling an event, a user can check whether people invited are available.

The biggest new feature is Push Notification Server, which lets users (including iPhone users) instantly know about calendar changes that other users make. Notification Server pushes out just what's changed to all the clients who have subscribed to the update system (and who have been authenticated to receive updates). In some respects, the Notification Server is like a Twitter feed, with iCal Server sending tweets to listening iCal clients to keep them abreast of changes.

At publishing time, the only clients that can use the push features are iPhone and the iCal 4 client in Mac OS X 10.6. To make up for that, Snow Leopard Server has another new feature, e-mail notification of invitations to non-iCal 4 users — or even to users who don't have calendar accounts. And, with Snow Leopard Server's Wiki Server (see Chapter 13), users with Web browsers on any computer can access iCal Server's calendar.

iCal Server has even more new features. Event attendees can add private comments to events that only they and the event organizer can see. Invitations are now processed by the calendar server, freeing up the client's resources.

iCal Server is simple to set up. The calendar and notification servers set up automatically if you choose iCal during installation. Directory compatibility is also simpler than before, but domain name service (DNS) setup is more complicated due to the push notification feature.

Clients for iCal Server

The best client for iCal Server 2 is iCal 4, which comes with the Snow Leopard client, Mac OS X 10.6. Other clients that support the open CalDAV standard (Calendaring Extensions to WebDAV) will also work. There are CalDAV clients for Windows, Linux, and older versions of Mac OS X that work with iCal Server to various degrees. The following clients support the CalDAV standard:

- **eM Client:** From E&S Software Ltd, this is a commercial messaging client for Windows. In addition to CalDAV and Google Calendar, it supports e-mail, contacts, and tasks.

  `www.emclient.com`

- **Outlook Connector Project with Microsoft Outlook:** This is an open source plug-in for Outlook for Windows. However, at press time, it hasn't been updated in a year.

  `http://sourceforge.net/projects/otlkcon`

- **Mozilla Sunbird and Lightning:** These are two open source clients available for Mac OS X, Windows, Linux, and Unix. Sunbird is a standalone calendar client. Lightning is an extension for the Thunderbird e-mail client.

  `www.mozilla.org/projects/calendar`

- **Chandler:** From the Open Software Application Foundation, Chandler is an open source calendar and tasks program for Windows, Mac OS X, and Linux.

  `www.chandlerproject.org`

- **Mulberry:** An open source e-mail and calendar client for Mac OS X, Windows, and Linux.

  `www.mulberrymail.com`

- **GNOME Evolution:** For Linux and Unix, this is an e-mail, calendar, and contact client for users of the GNOME desktop interface. Evolution requires the CalDAV plug-in to be installed.

  `http://projects.gnome.org/evolution`

At publishing time, only Snow Leopard's iCal 4 client supported discoverability of servers and push notifications. The other clients (including iCal 3) require the server to send e-mail for invitations. However, some of these clients will likely acquire this discoverability at some point.

That's because iCal Server 2 and Push Notification Server are based on open standards. The calendaring functionality uses CalDAV, which is based on WebDAV, which is based on HyperText Transfer Protocol (HTTP). The push-subscriber technology uses the Extensible Messaging and Presence Protocol (XMPP), which is based on Extensible Markup Language (XML). XMMP sends a small-sized message (like a tweet) to the client telling it that new data exists. The client then fetches that data.

Setting Up the Network for iCal Server

iCal Server sets up itself. If you selected iCal Server during installation, it's turned on and running when Snow Leopard Server first boots, along with the Push Notification Server. The Web-based calendar for Snow Leopard Server's wiki service is also enabled automatically.

If you didn't select iCal Server during installation, a few mouse clicks gets it running:

1. **In Server Preferences, click the iCal icon.**
2. **Click the big switch to the On position (see Figure 12-1).**

   You're done.

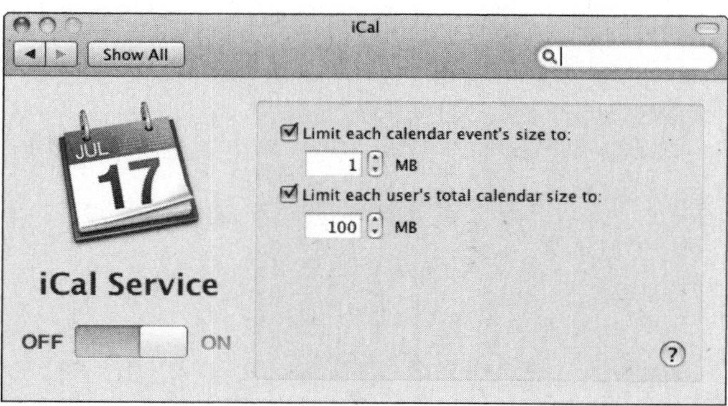

Figure 12-1: This switch turns on iCal and lets you set limits to attachments to calendars.

But here's a catch: iCal Server needs more than to just be turned on. Keep the following in mind:

- If a firewall is between iCal Server and your users, it needs to be configured to allow traffic on TCP port 8008 (or 8443 for Secure Sockets Layer [SSL] encryption).
- iCal Server needs directory service.
- iCal Server needs a DNS system with full reverse lookups running on the network.

Sound simple? Maybe yes, maybe no.

Directory service for iCal service

iCal Server must be connected to a directory server of some type on the network. This could be Open Directory running on the same server as iCal Server. Directory compatibility is simpler than in Mac OS X 10.5 Server because you no longer need to modify LDAP (Lightweight Directory Access Protocol) and Active Directory systems to designate calendar users.

If you choose Open Directory during installation, it's set up automatically and any users you add are signed up automatically for iCal service. Open Directory could be located on the same Mac server or on another server computer (Mac OS X 10.5 Server or later), or the directory could be another non-Apple LDAP server or Microsoft's Active Directory.

Setting up DNS for iCal service

Unfortunately, DNS for iCal isn't as simple as directory services, especially if your DNS server is running on Mac OS X Server. iCal Server 2 has a new requirement that wasn't in the previous version. For push notifications, clients use DNS to keep track of iCal Servers, a self-discovery feature. To enable this, you need to create a *Service (SRV)* record in each DNS zone that has the CalDAV calendar service. The SRV record needs to be in a special format as well, which I describe in the following section.

With all the automation of Snow Leopard Server, you'd think that it would automatically configure DNS if you choose to use the server for DNS and iCal at installation. After all, iCal and DNS zones are auto-configured. But no, Snow Leopard Server doesn't do this. And it gets worse.

Surprisingly, Apple tells you that you can't use Server Admin to configure Snow Leopard Server DNS for iCal Server's automatic detection feature. Server Admin can't do it correctly. You have to edit the zone record configuration file by hand. And, to make it even worse, Apple recommends *against* doing this if you don't have "previous experience administering DNS BIND 9 on Mac OS."

This is a major hole, and my major complaint with all of Snow Leopard Server. I can only hope that this section of this book quickly becomes obsolete, and Apple plugs the hole.

DNS SRV record format for iCal Server

On any DNS server, the SRV record needs to be in this format (on one line):

```
_caldav._tcp.example.com. 86400 IN SRV 0 0 8008 calendar.example.com.
```

The `caldav._` term is for a standard connection. If you're using a secure SSL connection, use `caldavs._` instead.

The standard port number is `8008`. For SSL connections, use port `8443`.

The `0 0` after SRV represent the priority and weight. These are 0 if only one CalDAV server is on the network. If multiple CalDAV servers are on the network, use numbers other than 0.

The `86400` represents the DNS time-to-live number, in seconds. `86400` is one day, but you can use another time period.

Sample DNS zone record file for Snow Leopard Server

The DNS zone file that you edit is in the/var/named/ directory. The file has the form db.*domainname* such as db.ourserver.macwindowsco.com. To access it in the Finder, choose Go➪Go to Folder and then type `/var/named/`. Open the file and type your additions *after* a line that begins with `$INCLUDE /var/zones/db`. *Do not* delete or change this line.

This INCLUDE line inserts your additions into another similarly named file in `/var/named/zone/`. Although you don't edit this file directly, here's a sample of the file in `/var/named/zone/` to give you an idea of what the final looks like. This file contains the DNS entities called "A records" that are referenced in the SRV records. The text after the semicolons (;) are in-code comments.

```
;GUID=<GUID here>
$TTL 10800        ; default expiration time of a record
abc.com. IN SOA ns.abc.com. username.abc.com. (
2009031903    ;Serial
```

```
     86400          ;Refresh
     3600           ;Retry
     604800         ;Expire
     345600         ;Negative caching TTL
     )
abc.com.  IN  NS    ns.abc.com.  ;ns.abc.com is the name server for abc.com
abc.com.  IN  A     10.0.0.1     ;this is the IP address of  abc.com
ns                A     10.0.0.2 ; IP address of ns.abc.com
name              CNAME ns       ;"name.abc.com" is another name for "ns.abc.
              com"
calendar      IN  A     10.0.0.12   ; the IP address for "calendar.abc.com"
                  TXT   "The iCal Server that we're using"
ical          IN  CNAME calendar.abc.com. ;"ical.example.com" is another name
              for "calendar.example.com"
_caldav._tcp.abc.com.  86400 IN SRV 0 0 8008 calendar.abc.com.
```

If you have a backup server to use when the first is down, add another `calendar` line:

```
calendar2     IN  A     10.0.0.13
```

Plus another SRV line at the end:

```
_caldav._tcp.abc.com. 86400 IN SRV 1 0 8008 calendar2.abc.com.
```

For SSL, the CalDAV line(s) is

```
_caldavs._tcp.abc.com. 86400 IN SRV 0 0 8443 calendar.abc.com.
_caldavs._tcp.abc.com. 86400 IN SRV 1 0 8443 calendar2.abc.com.
```

Using Admin Server for Administration

If you want to use Server Admin to set up iCal and tweak the settings, turning on iCal and Push Notification Server is a little more complicated than with Server Preferences, but you can do more. With Server Preferences, the only settings you can change are the attachment size for an individual calendar event and the size of each user's total calendar attachments. Server Admin lets you change those settings as well as enable SSL encryption, change the location of the data store, and disable/enable wiki calendaring and e-mail invitations.

Starting iCal and Push Notification with Server Admin

If you selected iCal Server while you installed Snow Leopard Server, the iCal and the Notification Servers are up and running, and you can skip this section. If you need to turn it on manually, in Server Preferences, click the iCal icon and then click the big switch to the On position.

If you plan to use iChat Server, it needs to be started before Push Notification Server. If you ever need to start the iChat Server, you have to restart the Push Notification Server by turning it on and off. This is why it's good to turn on iChat Server now if you're going to use it.

To enable iCal Server with Server Admin, click your server name in the left column, click the Settings icon, and then click the Services tab. Select the iCal and Push Notification check boxes. If you're going to use iChat Server, make sure to select it now.

To start these services, click the triangle next to your server in the left column to expand the list of services. Follow these steps:

1. **Click iChat in the left column and then click the Start iChat button in the lower left.**
2. **Click Push Notification in the left column and then click the Start Push Notification button in the lower left.**
3. **Click iCal in the left column and then click the Start iCal button in the lower left.**

Now test the push notification functionality of iCal Server. Open the iCal client on the server or on a Snow Leopard user machine. Open iCal Preferences and click Accounts. You should see "Push" as the polling interval.

If Push Notification Server is running on a different server computer, you have to tell iCal Server where it is. To do so, click iCal in the left column, click the Settings icon in the toolbar, and then click the General tab. Click the Add button next to Push Notifications and type the full DNS hostname of the server running Push Notification Server. Click the Save button and restart the service when prompted.

Changing iCal Server's default settings

To change the default settings of iCal Server:

1. **In Server Admin, click your server name in the left column to expand the list of services and then click iCal in the list.**

2. **Click the Settings icon in the toolbar and then click the General tab (see Figure 12-2).**

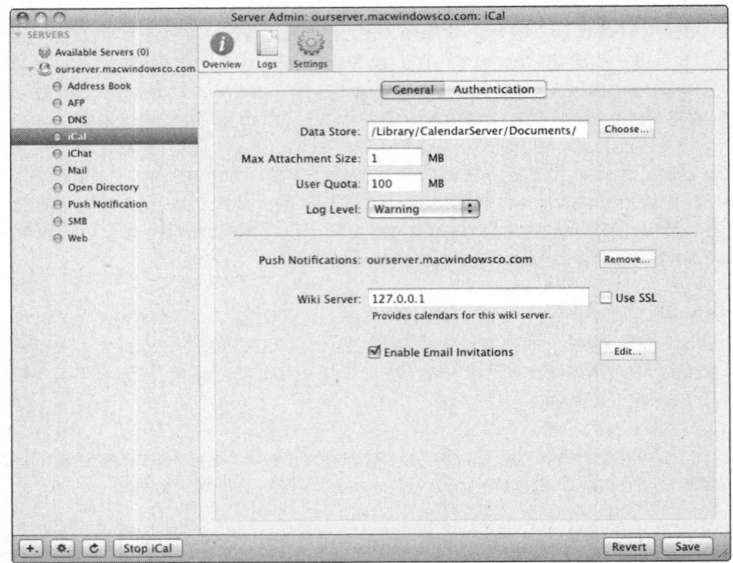

Figure 12-2: The General tab of iCal Settings, with default settings.

You can now change the following settings:

- **Data Store:** The default location is /Library/CalendarServer/Documents. If you have a RAID, Xsan, or other storage, you can enter the path here.
- **Max Attachment Size and User Quota:** The former is the largest allowable attachment to a calendar event. The latter is the maximum size of all the attachments a user may use.
- **Log level:** This is the amount of information that will be recorded in the log. These are arranged on the pop-up menu from the lowest amount of information recorded (the Error setting) to the highest (Debug).
- **Push Notifications:** This is the server on which the Push Notification Server runs. You can assign the hostname of another Mac running Snow Leopard Server by clicking the Remove button and adding a new host.
- **Wiki Server:** Calendars also appear in Snow Leopard Server's automatically created wiki site. This setting defaults to the Wiki Server running on this server. You can specify another IP address.

When you are finished making changes, click the Save button and then stop and restart the service. However, two more groups of settings deserve further explanation.

Enabling e-mail notification

The Enable Email Invitations check box enables the sending and accepting of meeting invitations by e-mail. This is available for users who don't have an iCal Server account, but not for those who do. Users of iCal 4 (Mac OS X 10.6) use iCal client for sending and accepting invitations.

To enable e-mail invitations, you have to create an e-mail account for the server. This is a two-step process, starting with the Server Admin window (shown in Figure 12-2):

1. **In Server Admin, click the Edit button next to Enable Email Invitations.**

   A dialog appears with POP, SMTP, and port information of the e-mail server on this Mac server. (You can change this to another server if you like.) Also notice a User field filled with `com.apple.calendarserver` and an e-mail address with this "user" name. This is an e-mail user that represents the iCal Server. You can change this to something else (iCalServer, for instance). Type an e-mail address in the field of that name.

2. **Open Workgroup Manager or Server Preferences and create a user account and e-mail address with this username:**

   a. *Go to the User Accounts section and add a user to represent the iCal Server, with the same name as in Step 1.*

   b. *Assign this user the e-mail address that you used in Server Admin.*

Security: SSL and Authentication

In Figure 12-2, notice the Use SSL check box next to Wiki Server. This provides SSL encryption for traffic between users and the wiki calendar. You can also set SSL for the CalDAV clients by clicking the Authentication tab (see Figure 12-3) in the iCal Settings window. SSL is off by default. You can also choose an authentication method, with or without SSL.

In the Type pop-up menu, Digest and Kerberos both provide password encryptions, but Kerberos is stronger. The Any Method selection uses any method that the client can support.

The SSL pop-up menu gives you the choice of Don't Use (no SSL), Use, and Redirect. With Use, iCal Server can accept connections from both the unencrypted port and the encrypted (SSL) port. With Redirect, iCal Server accepts connections over the SSL port only, while redirecting connection requests that come over the HTTP port to the secure HTTPS port.

When you're finished, click the Save button and then restart the iCal service.

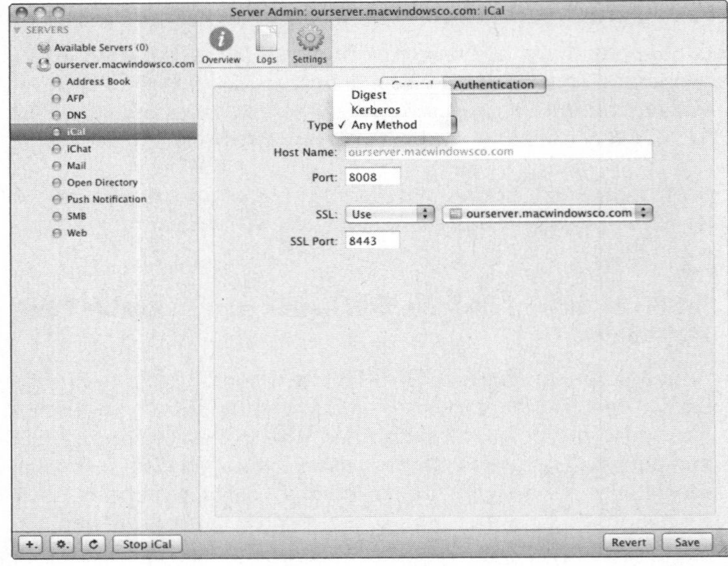

Figure 12-3: Enabling SSL encryption and authentication for iCal Server.

Creating Schedule Resources and Locations

In addition to creating events and inviting people to them, users can also reserve locations, such as meeting rooms, or resources, such as projectors or other equipment. In iCal Server, resources and locations share some of the attributes of users and groups. Recourses and locations each get their own calendar. When booking a room, iCal Server checks whether the time period is free and accepts the booking like an event invitation. Users can include resources and locations in invitations.

You use iCal Server Utility (new to Snow Leopard Server) to add resources and locations. When you open it, it authenticates you to Open Directory. The resources and locations are stored in an Open Directory master. If your users are authenticating to Active Directory, you need an Open Directory master that's bound to Active Directory:

1. **Open iCal Server Utility.**

   iCal Server Utility asks for your Kerberos identity, which is your e-mail address and your account password.

2. **Click the Add (+) button in the lower left and choose New Location or New Resource from the pop-up menu.**

3. **Enter descriptive information in the fields.**

   For a new resource, choose an item from the Resource Type pop-up menu (see Figure 12-4). For a new location, you can attach a graphics file of a map. For a new resource or a new location, you may type a contact name.

4. **Click the Save button.**

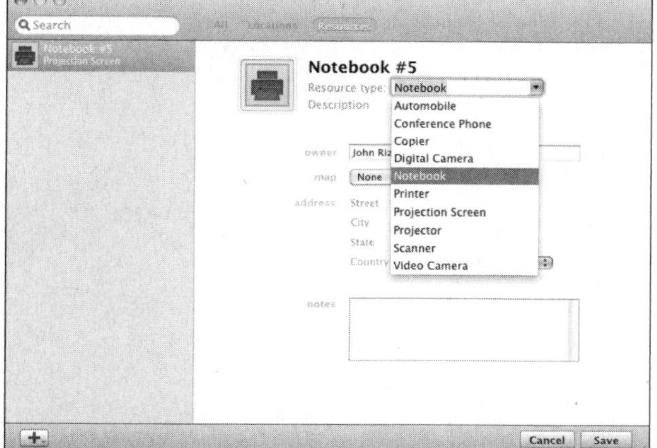

Figure 12-4: Use the iCal Server Utility to add resources and locations.

Supporting iCal 4 Clients

Users with Mac OS X 10.6 get the iCal 4 client, which is Apple's most advanced client for iCal Server 2. This section describes how to get the client running with the server.

Adding an iCal Server account to an iCal client

To connect the iCal 4 client to the server, you add an account in the client. On the user's Mac, open iCal and do the following:

1. **Choose Preferences from the iCal menu and click the Accounts icon.**
2. **Click the Add (+) button at the bottom left of the window.**

   The Add an Account dialog slides down.

3. **In the Account Type pop-up menu, choose CalDAV.**

4. **Type a username (the short name), password, and the server address (`myserver.domain.edu`, for instance).**
5. **Click Create.**

You can now change some of the default settings in the main Account Information tab, as shown in Figure 12-5:

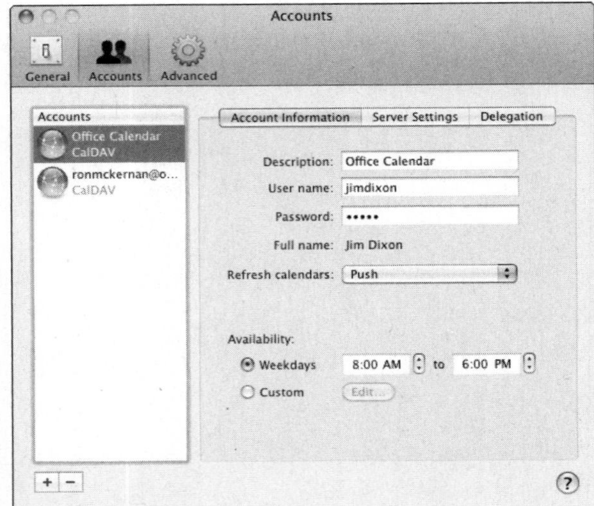

Figure 12-5: The Account Preferences window of the iCal 4 client.

- **The Description field** lists the user's e-mail address. You can change this to something more descriptive, such as Office Calendar.
- **The Refresh Calendars pop-up menu** sets how the client Mac updates calendar information (including invitations) with the server. The default is Push, which means the server contacts the client. You can change this to a time interval or manually.
- **The Availability area** lets you set the times when the user is available for events. The Weekdays radio button lets you specify a time span during the day. The Custom radio button lets you choose specific days of the week along with different times for each day.

Creating another server-based calendar using an iCal client

When you create an account, which I describe in the preceding section, you'll see it when you close iCal Preferences. In the left column of iCal is a Calendars heading, with two default calendars — Home and Work. These are local calendars. Below all this is a heading with the name of the Description field you typed in the preceding section. Below the Description field is a server-based calendar that was created and dubbed Calendar by default. To add another server-based calendar here:

1. **Click the server-based calendar to select it.**
2. **Click the Add (+) button at the bottom left of the window.**
3. **Enter a name for the new calendar.**
4. **Press Return.**

   Your server-based calendar is added.

Setting a delegate using iCal client

You can set another user to be a delegate, or proxy, for one of your calendars. Delegates can be read-only delegates or read/write delegates. A read-only delegate can see everything that the main user can. Delegates for resources or locations can see everything about them, not just whether they're available. A read/write delegate can also make changes to another user's calendar. To create a delegate:

1. **In the iCal client, choose Preferences from the iCal menu and click the Accounts icon.**
2. **Click an account to select it, and on the Delegation tab, click the Edit button.**
3. **Click the Add (+) button in the dialog that appears.**
4. **Type the account name of the user who will be the delegate.**
5. **(Optional) Select the Allow Write check box if you want the delegate to be able to edit your calendar.**
6. **Click the Done button.**

Delegates must have user accounts in the same authentication directory as the user.

Chapter 13

Hosting Web Sites and Wikis

In This Chapter

- Using and managing the built-in wikis, logs, calendars, and Webmail
- Managing and hosting Web sites with Server Preferences
- Hosting Web sites with Server Admin

Any server can host a Web site, but Snow Leopard Server creates a complete, dynamic site for you, prebuilt. By merely turning on Web services, every user gets an automatically updated Web portal called *My Page*. Users get access to a collaborative environment that includes wikis, blogs, Web calendars, Webmail, and mailing lists. Users can edit these with a few mouse clicks. The site uses *wiki* technology, which enables group editing of content with a Web browser. Wiki Server 2, introduced with Snow Leopard Server, enables all this.

Mac OS X Server can also host Web sites for use in your organization and for publishing to the Internet. At the heart is the powerful, industry standard open-source Apache Web server. You can set up Apache, fine-tune it, and administer it from Server Admin software. But, you can also do a lot with Server Preferences to set up Web sites.

This chapter doesn't tell you how to design or build a Web site. I can't even tell you everything that you can do with Snow Leopard Server's Web services — that'd fill a whole book by itself. So, first, I describe the Web site that Snow Leopard creates for you and how to alter it. I then describe using Server Preferences to manage the Web services, as well as show you what you can do with Server Admin for more advanced tasks.

The Prequel

Before hosting a Web site, you need to do a few things:

- If you want your Web site to be visible on the Internet, you need to own your domain name and register it with a domain name service, such as Network Solutions. (You can find a complete list at `http://internic.net`.)

- Have domain name service (DNS) configured so that your domain name resolves (or points to) the IP address of the Web server. This could be on a DNS server on your network or on the Mac server itself, if it's acting as the network's DNS server.

  If DNS isn't set up, users have to enter the IP address of the server in their Web browser. There is some information on DNS throughout this chapter and in Chapter 3.

This chapter assumes you've done these things.

The Automatically Created Web Site

Snow Leopard Server can set up a sophisticated wiki-based Web site containing collaboration tools for your user accounts. No HTML coding or design layout is required. If you selected Web services when you installed Snow Leopard Server (or turned it on later), the site is waiting for you.

The built-in Web site is dynamically created and updated, and is user-configurable. You can limit users' access to features, or you can give them the whole ball of wax. Users of Macs, Windows, Linux, and Unix can create their own pages, wikis, and blogs; upload pictures, movies, and audio; and change the way it looks and feels — all in a Web browser, without any coding. And, if users want to edit some HTML, they can — again, from the Web browser. You can also turn on a mailing list with a single click.

Here's what Snow Leopard Server creates for you automatically when you have Web services turned on:

- **A home page:** Lets users get to the Web features (see Figure 13-1).
- **A wiki-based Web portal called My Page for each user account:** When a user clicks the My Page link (see Figure 13-1) and then signs in, his Web portal appears, as shown in Figure 13-2. The portal contains links to the wikis, blogs, and Web calendars of other users and groups, and links to the user's own pages. Users can also access Webmail here if it's been enabled. The portal also creates links to updates, displaying what's changed or has been added and who changed it.

  Any time you add new user accounts to Snow Leopard, each account automatically gets its own My Page portal.
- **Blogs with design templates:** Each user can create blog entries. In an organization, people can use blogs to distribute FYI-type information rather than clogging e-mail inboxes. This information can later be linked to rather than buried in a mail folder.

Figure 13-1: The default Web home page in Mac OS X Server.

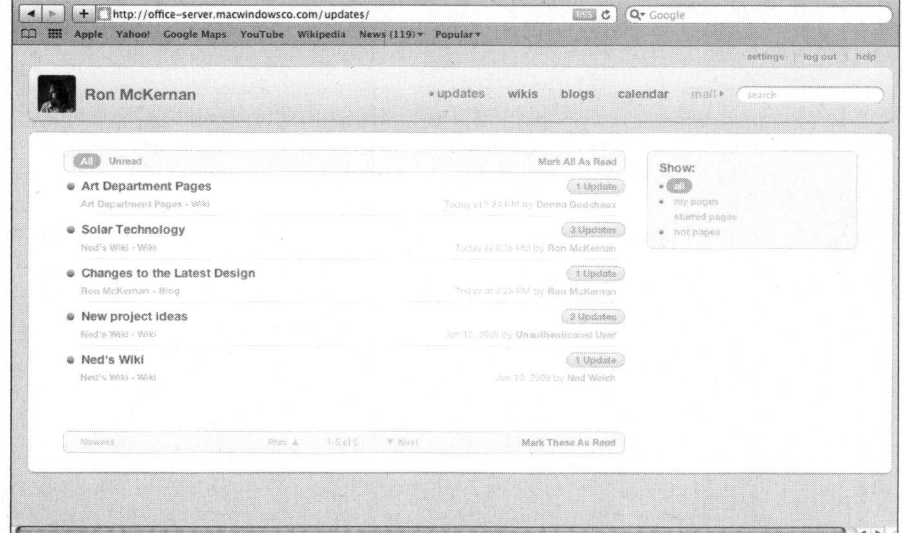

Figure 13-2: A user's My Page Web portal, automatically updated with the latest changes.

- **Wikis with design templates:** Each user can create a wiki. Even better, when you create a group, you can select a check box to have Snow Leopard Server automatically create a wiki for the members of that group. Users outside the group can have access if you wish.
- **Web calendar:** Individual users get their own personal calendars and also have access to shared calendars for groups. Users can choose to create multiple calendars on either.

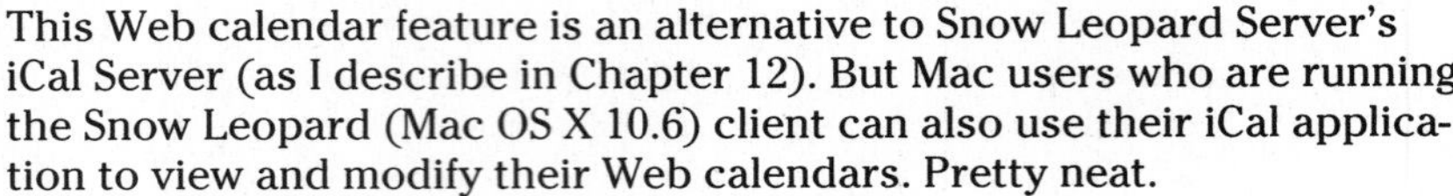

This Web calendar feature is an alternative to Snow Leopard Server's iCal Server (as I describe in Chapter 12). But Mac users who are running the Snow Leopard (Mac OS X 10.6) client can also use their iCal application to view and modify their Web calendars. Pretty neat.

- **Themes:** Figure 13-2 shows one theme, but users can choose from any of several dozen to change the look.
- **Navigation links:** Get to anything from anywhere.
- **A Help system for the site:** Readers can learn how to navigate as well as create, edit, and administer content.
- **Podcasts:** Users can easily turn on this feature from their Web browser.
- **iPhone support:** Users can access and use the wiki controls from an iPhone. This area is improved over Mac OS X 10.5 Server.

You get all this simply by turning on Web services. You can choose to disable features you don't need or to customize the site. You can designate a group wiki as the home page. However you change it, Snow Leopard Server creates the navigation links, the auto-updates, and the relevant Help system.

To create a mailing list , simply select a check box in a group wiki's settings area. The server creates an e-mail address for the mailing list, and everyone who can access the wiki becomes a member of the mailing list. (See the section, "Administering a wiki site from a browser," later in this chapter.)

You don't need to choose between the preconfigured Web site and your own site. Snow Leopard Server can host multiple Web sites.

Navigating My Page

Figure 13-2 shows a My Page portal for a user who's logged in to the Web site. In the main area are links to recent updates to other pages that belong to users or groups. On the left, you see who created the wiki or blog; on the right, you see who last edited it and when, as well as how many times it's been updated since you last read it. The Show box on the right filters which pages are displayed in the updates section. Users can mark pages as Hot.

The toolbar has the site navigation and a search field for the site. To add a page or go to an existing page, click the Wikis or Blogs link. Above the toolbar on the right, you can click the Settings link to change the look of your personal site, or click the Help link for more info on how to use and edit the site.

A Tags link, which appears on other pages, is another way to filter pages. Users can tag pages that are related for easy location and then filter pages by a tag. You might tag pages with a project name or some common identifier.

My Pages is also optimized for iPhone users. From an iPhone, you can log in and view content, comments, and files. iPhone users can also tag pages. The automatic updates that are posted to My Page are visible from an iPhone, as are changes and comments to documents.

Creating a personal wiki

From My Page, you can create a wiki that all users or just certain users can edit. Doing so takes only a few mouse clicks:

1. **From My Page, click the Wikis link in the toolbar and then click the Create a Wiki link on the right.**

   An assistant appears, providing a three-step process for creating a wiki.
2. **Type a name for the wiki and a description; click Next.**
3. **Choose a theme that determines what the wiki looks like; click Next.**
4. **From the third screen asking you to set wiki access, choose one of the following:**
   a. *Choose Public to give anyone access to edit the page.*

      You can require them to log in. If you don't, their changes are identified as anonymous.

   b. *Choose Private to add individuals and groups who will have access to your wiki.*
5. **Click Create.**

You now have a new wiki. You can make further changes by using the Settings link, as I describe in "Administering a wiki site from a browser," later in this chapter.

Navigating a group wiki page

Group wikis can be created automatically when you create a group account in Server Preferences.

Figure 13-3 shows a simple group wiki Web page that took only a few minutes to create. The photo, text, and links were added with the tools I describe in the following section. Note that the Click for Full-Size Image link is created automatically.

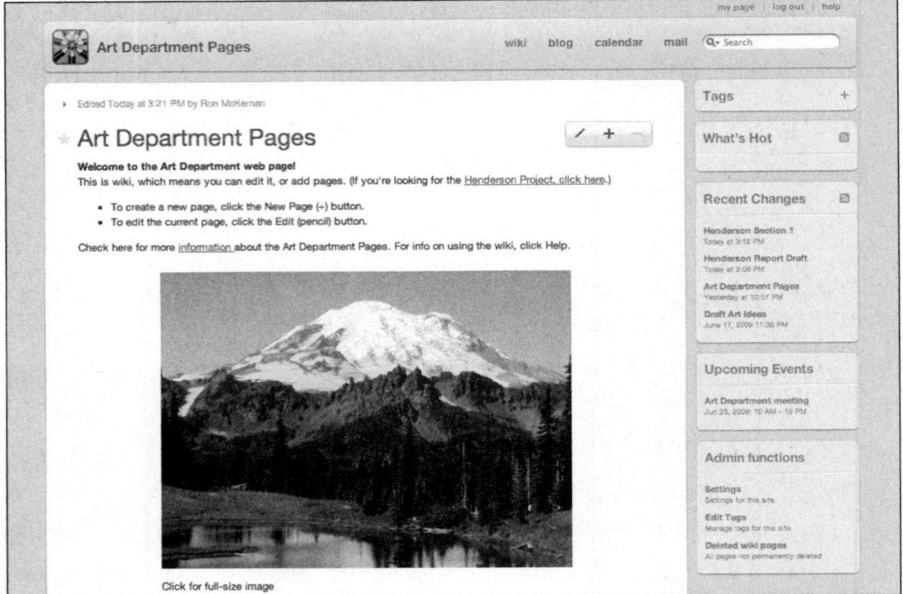

Figure 13-3: A group wiki page with a photo, text, and links added.

A wiki page for a group of users has some added navigation features to enable collaboration. These are in the sidebar at the right of the page:

- **Recent Changes:** Links to recently changed wiki pages that are within the group site.
- **Upcoming Events:** These are links to calendar items on the group's Web calendar.
- **Admin Functions:** There are three links:
  - *Settings:* For administering the built-in Web site.
  - *Edit Tags:* This lets you change the name of tags, which link to other pages.
  - *Deleted Wiki Pages:* Pages that users delete are removed automatically from all links but remain stored on the server.

Editing the built-in Web site

Users can add and edit wiki pages and blogs that belong to them, other users, or groups that they're members of. To do this from a Web browser, follow these steps:

1. **From your My Page, click the Wikis or Blogs link in the toolbar to bring up a summary page.**

   Figure 13-4 shows the wiki summary page, which lists the user and group wikis and when they were last updated. (In this figure, I used an Internet Explorer browser in Windows.) The blogs summary page looks almost exactly the same, except showing a list of blogs.

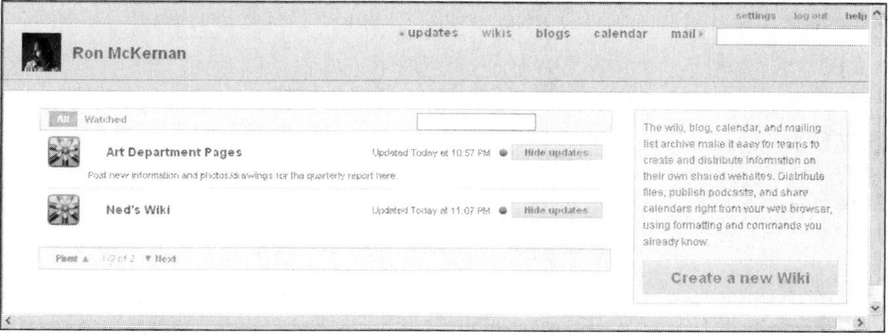

Figure 13-4: The wikis page lets you edit user and group pages, or create your own.

2. **Create a new wiki (or blog) page by clicking the Create a New Wiki button (or by clicking the Create a New Blog button if you're on the blog summary page).**

   You're asked to name the page and provide a description.

3. **Edit the page by clicking its name in the summary list and then clicking the pencil icon to take you into edit mode.**

   The plus icon adds a page; the minus icon deletes the current page.

   When editing a wiki page or creating a new page, a new toolbar appears above the text, as shown in Figure 13-5. This toolbar gives you the following options:

   - The text field on the left is where you name or rename the page.
   - The left three icons are tools for formatting text.
   - The curved arrow icon lets you create a link for selected text.
   - The musical notes icon inserts pictures, movies, or audio.
   - The paperclip icon lets you attach a file to the page.

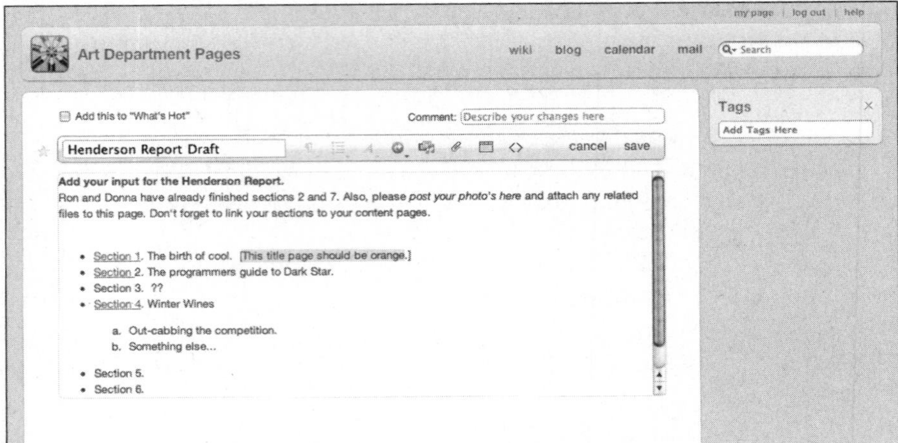

Figure 13-5: The editing toolbar lets you edit text, add links and photos, and more.

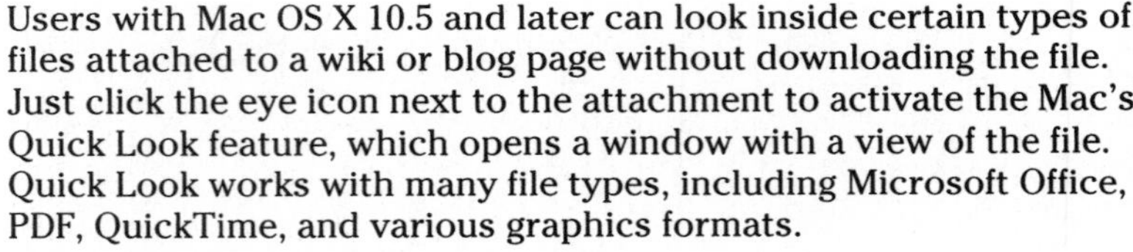

Users with Mac OS X 10.5 and later can look inside certain types of files attached to a wiki or blog page without downloading the file. Just click the eye icon next to the attachment to activate the Mac's Quick Look feature, which opens a window with a view of the file. Quick Look works with many file types, including Microsoft Office, PDF, QuickTime, and various graphics formats.

- The square icon inserts a table.
- The brackets icon displays the HTML code for the page's section that contains your content. You can edit anything you like with standard HTML tags.

4. **Click the Save link on the editing toolbar when finished.**

   The toolbar slides out of sight.

Administering a wiki site from a browser

Users can administer wikis they create as well as group wikis from a Web browser within the wiki. They can change the look of a site, create a mail list with the click of a button, turn on a group calendar, and perform a number of other tasks. Users can also assign other users as site administrators.

This is all accomplished through the Settings link on the main wiki page of the user or group site. You can see the Settings link in Figure 13-3 in the lower right of the window below Admin Functions.

When you click this link, the Settings page appears with the General settings displayed. In the left sidebar are five links to different types of settings. Most users see only four links in the sidebar. You see the Advanced link only if you're a *server* administrator with access to Server Preferences and System Admin.

Changing the site theme, name, and contact

The General page lets you change the look and name of the wiki site:

- **Wiki icon:** Click the Wiki icon at the top to change the default icon to any picture you might have. This is the icon that appears in the list of wikis.
- **Theme:** Click the Change Theme icon to bring up a list of themes.

  You can add your own banner to the top of the site's pages. In the list of themes, click the Banner Image pop-up menu and choose Upload New.
- **Wiki Name:** Type a new name in this field. This name appears on the top of every page of this wiki site, including related calendars and blogs.
- **Description and Contact:** These can be anything you like.

When you're finished, click the Save button in the lower right of the screen.

Although you make these changes from the main wiki page, they apply to all the pages related to a wiki, including blogs, calendars, the mail list archive page, and other wiki pages.

Turning blogs, calendars, mailing lists, and podcasts on and off

The Services link on the Settings page takes you to a page for turning features on and off: namely blogs, calendars, mailing lists, and podcasts.

The Services page is shown in Figure 13-6. (I applied a different theme than shown in the earlier figures.)

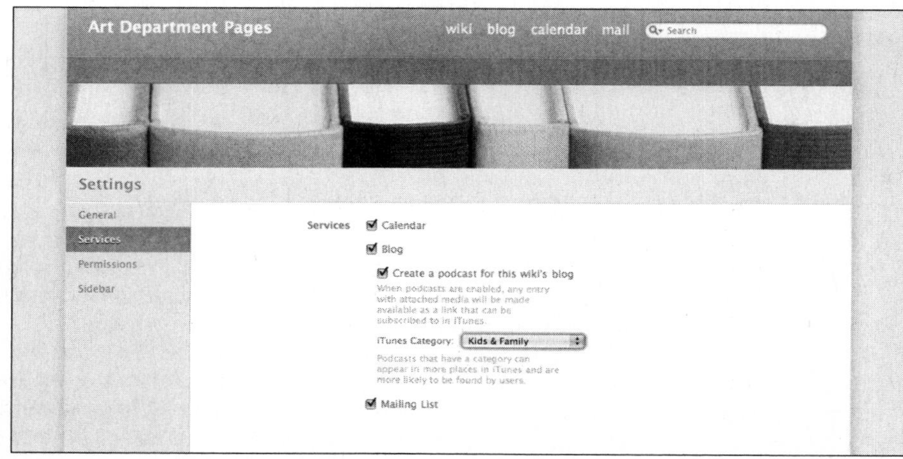

Figure 13-6: The wiki Services configuration page.

Wiki calendars

If you turned on calendars in the Web pane of Server Preferences or in Server Admin, a Web calendar is created for you. If calendars aren't turned on, selecting the Calendar check box (see Figure 13-6) creates a new calendar, as shown in Figure 13-7. (I used another snazzy theme, just to show off.) Group wikis have a group calendar that everyone in the group can access.

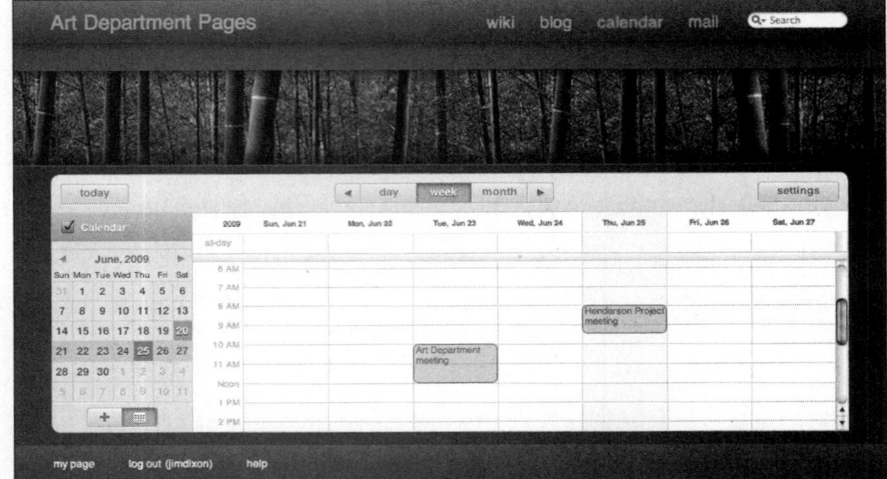

Figure 13-7: A group calendar for a group wiki.

To create a new calendar to be displayed on the calendar grid, click the plus (+) icon at the bottom left and give it a name.

Mac users can use iCal Server with the iCal software that comes with Mac OS X. One reason to use a wiki-based calendar is that it grants access to Windows and Linux users as well.

Snow Leopard Server uses iCal Server for its Web calendars. Deselecting the Calendar check box in Figure 13-6 doesn't turn off iCal Server. This turns off the Web calendar for this group's or individual's wiki site.

Blogs and podcasts

The Blog check box (refer to Figure 13-6) is pretty straightforward: If it's deselected, users can't create blogs for the group or individual wiki site.

The really interesting and powerful check box is Create a Podcast for This Wiki's Blog. With this enabled, a Subscribe in iTunes link appears on the wiki's blog page. Clicking the link opens the user's copy of iTunes and places the podcast in iTunes's Podcast playlist. Additional entries in the podcast are uploaded automatically to the user's copy of iTunes. To place the podcast content on the server, simply create a blog entry and attach an audio or video file with the paperclip button in the editing toolbar (refer to Figure 13-5). Every time you create a new blog entry and attach a media file, the user's podcast subscription is updated automatically.

If you're using Podcast Producer (described in Chapter 15) to distribute videos, they will also automatically be added here.

Creating and using a mail list for the wiki

By selecting the Mailing List check box, Snow Leopard Server creates a mail list (or a *listserv*) and an e-mail address for the list. Users e-mail to this address to send a message to other users on the list. The e-mail address looks like this: `WikiName-wiki@WebAddress`.

In this example, the mail list looks like this:

```
artdepartmentpages-wiki@Office-Server.macwindowsco.com
```

Everyone who has access to the group or individual wiki is a member of the mail list. For a group wiki, members of the group are subscribed to the mail list. For an individual's wiki, the people that user gave access to are subscribed.

An archive of all e-mail messages appears on a Mail List Archive page. Users can get to this page by clicking the Mail link at the top right of any of the site's Web pages.

Defining user permissions and site administrators

The third link on the wiki Settings page is Permissions, as shown in Figure 13-8. This page provides two basic functions: changing access by users and defining administrators.

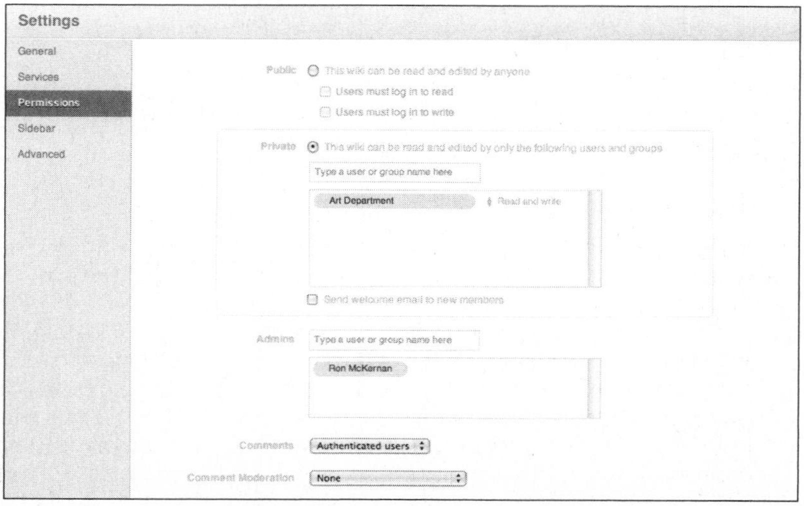

Figure 13-8: Setting user access and assigning site administrators.

In the top half, you have the same choices you have when you create a new individual site: Public (all users) versus Private (designated users and groups). Figure 13-8 shows the default setting for group wiki sites: Private with one group assigned. You can add other groups and individual users by typing their names in the field, and then use the pop-up menu to give them read-and-write or read-only privileges.

One great thing about built-in wiki-based Web sites that the server creates is that you don't have to bother with them if you don't want to. Users can create and administer sites from a Web browser and make changes. The Admins section in the lower portion of the screen lets you designate users or groups as site administrators.

There is a difference between site administrators and server administrators:

- **Server** administrators use Server Preferences or Server Admin to turn services on and off and to configure them.
- **Site** administrators use only a Web browser to change settings to the built-in Web site. They don't have the ability to turn Web services on or off or to configure services.

Server administrators are also site administrators for the built-in Web site.

You can designate multiple site administrators by typing their names in the Admins field. You can also type a group name, which gives everyone in the group administrator privileges.

To remove a user or group from the user or administrator list, hold the cursor over the name and click the small X that appears next to the left of the name.

Click the Save button in the lower right when you are finished.

The sidebar setting

The Sidebar link on the wiki Settings page lets you create a custom title for the sidebar that appears on all the wiki pages. You can also specify a tag so that all pages with the tag appear in the sidebar.

Configuring virtual hosts

A *server* administrator has an additional option in wiki settings that *site* administrators don't have: the Advanced link. If your server has several host-names with the same IP address (called *virtual hosts*), the Advanced setting lets you select one or more URLs that bring up the site. For instance, a server or network might have DNS set up for `www.acme.com`, `library.acme.com`, and `wiki.acme.com`. The Virtual Hosts setting could enable the site to appear in a Web browser with any one, any two, or all three of these URLs.

The default is for the site to respond to all the hostnames, but a site administrator can change that. Here's how:

1. **Click the Advanced link on the left in the wiki Settings window.**
2. **In the Virtual Hosts pop-up menu, choose Specific Hostnames.**
3. **Type in the hostname (or names) you wish to use.**

   To delete a hostname, hold the cursor over the name and click the small X that appears next to the left of the name.
4. **Click the Save button.**

Server Preferences versus Server Admin

Outside the built-in Web site that Snow Leopard Server creates is much more that you can do with Web services. As with other services in Snow Leopard Server, you can use Server Preferences or Server Admin, or both, to configure and manage your Web site. Server Preferences can actually do a lot, and much of the basic work is automated.

Here's what you can do with Server Preferences:

- Turn Web services on and off.
- Use and view a pre-built, wiki-based Web site that Apple supplies as the server's Web site.
- Assign your own Web site (if it uses static pages) as the default Web site for the server.
- Tell the server to automatically create wikis for your group accounts, complete with snazzy user features.
- Use one of the wikis as the default server Web site.
- Automatically enable blogs for individual users.
- Host multiple Web sites with the same IP address (virtual hosts).

Server Admin can do everything that Server Preferences can, plus more. Here are just a few of the things you can only do with Server Admin:

- Host your own dynamically generated Web content via Server Side Includes (SSI) and other standards. (Server Preferences lets you host only static pages, other than Snow Leopard Server's built-in site.)
- Change the default theme for the built-in wiki-based Web site.
- Enable Secure Sockets Layer (SSL) security.

- Enable Common Gateway Interface (CGI) scripts for a particular site.
- Enable WebDAV to use a Web site as a file server.
- Host multiple Web sites with different IP addresses.
- Use multiple aliases to point to one Web site.
- Use redirects to take a user to a different page than entered in the browser.
- Monitor usage of the site in terms of Web traffic.

You can use both Server Preferences and Server Admin. Use Server Preferences to get things running and then employ Server Admin to add more features, tweak settings, troubleshoot, or monitor usage.

You can run Server Preferences and Server Admin either from the server Mac or from another Mac that has Admin Tools installed. Either way, the utilities ask you to log in to your server's admin account.

The following section describes what you can do with Server Preferences. After that, I describe how to use Server Admin for more advanced tasks.

Managing Web Services with Server Preferences

If you enabled Web services during installation, the default Web page (shown in Figure 13-1) is turned on and wikis, blogs, and a Web-based calendar are enabled. You can get access to this immediately after you install by launching Server Preferences. When you open Server Preferences and click the Web icon, the window shown in Figure 13-9 appears. As with other services, you can turn Web services on and off with the big switch.

Figure 13-9: The Server Preferences Web pane.

Turning wikis, calendars, blogs, and Webmail on and off

The four check boxes in Figure 13-9 refer to the built-in Web site that Snow Leopard Server creates (which I describe in earlier sections):

- **Wikis:** Makes all wikis available, including the My Page Web portal for each user. Notice that if you turn off wikis, the Home Page pop-up menu grays out. That's because the built-in Web site uses the wiki server.
- **Calendar:** Adds a calendar to users' My Page Web portals. Users can also include calendars in wikis they create with a Web browser. If wikis aren't enabled, a group calendar can act as a home page.
- **Blogs:** Enables users to add automatically created blogs — again, with their Web browsers.
- **Webmail:** Lets users use the automatically created Web site to access e-mail from Snow Leopard Server's Mail service.

The arrows next to these settings launch your default Web browser and take you to the corresponding server-created Web page. Here's where each arrow takes you:

- **Open Home Page:** (`http://`*`yourserver`*), in which *yourserver* is the server's DNS name. This might be in the form of `myserver.abc.com`. Clicking this link takes you to the server-created home page. However, if you set the default Web site to your own custom site or another of the server-created wiki pages, that page opens instead.
- **Wikis:** (`http://`*`yourserver`*`/groups`) This takes you to a list of wikis currently created by users or automatically created for groups.
- **Calendar:** (`http://`*`yourserver`*`/ical`) Clicking this arrow brings up a login dialog. Logging in takes you to the user's individual calendar.
- **Blogs:** (`http://`*`yourserver`*`/users`) This brings you to the wiki page that lists the user blogs — the same page that users get to by clicking the Blogs button in the toolbar.
- **Webmail:** (`http://`*`yourserver`*`/Webmail`) Clicking this arrow opens the built-in Webmail site.

If you've used Server Admin to delete the automatically created Web site, an additional Create the Wiki button appears in Server Preferences (not shown in Figure 13-9) in place of the Home Page pop-up menu. Clicking this button re-enables the automatic wikis.

Don't panic if you see a Reveal Custom Site button instead of the Home Page pop-up menu and the Web Services check boxes in Figure 13-9. That button means that you or someone has created a custom Web site that uses the same port number and DNS name as the built-in wiki-based Web site. The built-in Web site, by default, uses Snow Leopard Server's DNS name and uses port 80. You can't change these from within Server Preferences. But, if you click the Reveal Custom Site button, it shows you the custom site and lets you delete it. If you don't want to delete it, clicking this button at least lets you know where the custom site is.

Creating a group wiki

You can use Server Preferences to create a group wiki for you. All user accounts in the group have access to the wiki. Assuming you have wikis turned on (which I describe in the preceding section), here's how to create a group wiki:

1. **Open Server Preferences and click the Groups icon.**
2. **Select a group from the list on the left.**

   You can also create a new group.
3. **Click the Create a Group Wiki button.**

   Your Web browser opens and guides you through a series of steps to define what you want in the wiki.
4. **Select a theme and set permissions for group members.**

By default, the created group wiki includes a blog and Web calendar that group members can see and edit. A mailing list *(listserv),* which includes all the group member accounts, is also created and configured for you.

Changing the default home page

You can use the Home Page pop-up menu in the Server Preference's Web pane to change the home page from the default home page shown in Figure 13-1 to something else. Figure 13-10 shows what you might see. You can choose from a group or user wiki page created with the built-in wiki tools I describe in the section, "The Automatically Created Web Site," earlier in this chapter. If you created your own static, custom page (as I describe in the following section), you see that in the pop-up menu as well.

Figure 13-10: Changing the default home page with Server Preferences.

Adding Web Sites with Server Preferences

With Server Preferences, you can host Web sites that you've created with other Web tools and copied onto the server Mac. This is easy to do with Server Preferences, but you do have one proviso: The Web site has to use static HTML pages. If you want to publish a dynamic site with a content management system, you need to use Server Admin.

You can also host multiple Web sites on one server, each with a different domain name. If these multiple sites share an IP address, they are called *virtual hosts;* however, if they have different IP addresses, the process is called *multihoming.*

To publish a custom Web site with Server Preferences, do the following:

1. **Launch Server Preferences and click the Web icon.**
2. **Click the Custom Sites tab (as shown in Figure 13-10) and then click the Add (+) button.**
3. **(Optional) To specify a custom location, choose a folder where your Web site files will be in the Store Site Files In pop-up menu.**

   If you leave the setting Default Location, Server Preferences creates a folder for you in this location: /Library/WebServer/Sites/.
4. **In the Domain Name field (see Figure 13-11), type the site's *fully qualified DNS name.***

   This is a unique identifier for the site. For example, two different fully qualified DNS names might be `homework.abc.edu` and `teachers.abc.edu`.

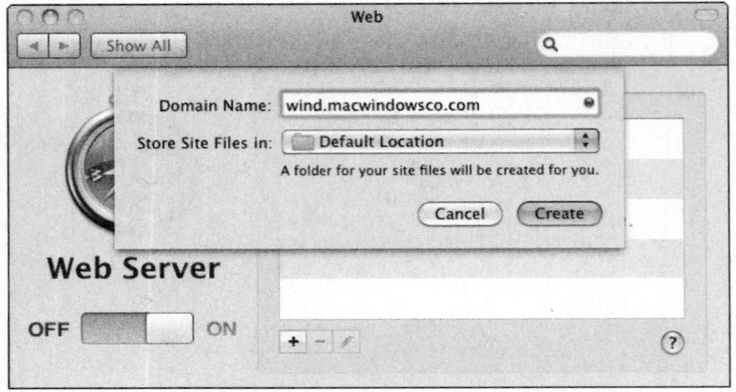

Figure 13-11: Type the fully qualified DNS name for your new site.

5. **If the dot next to the domain name in Figure 13-11 is green, click the Create button.**

   Server Preferences creates a placeholder index page in the location created or specified in Step 4.

   If the dot is red, proceed to the next section.

6. **Replace this index file with your own Web site files and make sure the new site's home page is index.html or index.pgp.**

Running into DNS problems

If the dot next to the domain name in Figure 13-11 is red, you have a problem: Server Preferences can't resolve the DNS name to your server's IP address. To fix it, try one of these options:

- **Change the domain name to something that will resolve.**
- **Assign another available IP address.** To do this, click the Create button. An error message appears saying, "Server Preferences doesn't have enough information to automatically setup this domain name." Click the Manual Setup button. The screen in Figure 13-12 appears. Choose an IP address from the pop-up menu and then click the Create button.

If these don't work, something is wrong with the DNS service. You need to use Server Admin to adjust Snow Leopard Server's DNS service or the DNS service running on another server on the network.

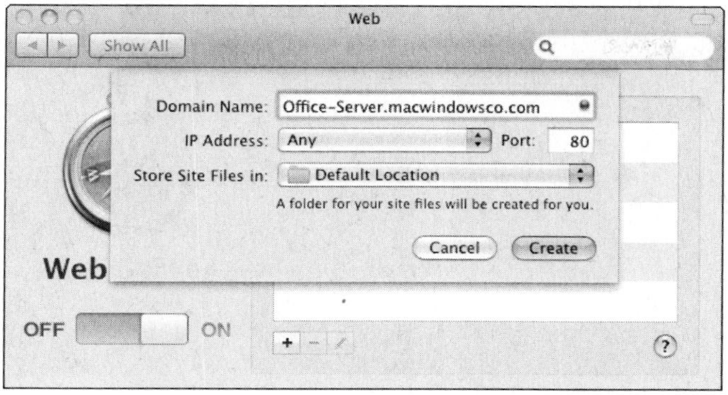

Figure 13-12: Manual Web site setup in Server Preferences.

If you click the Create button and you see the error message shown in Figure 13-13, you already are using this DNS name for the automatically created Web site (wikis, blogs, calendar, or Webmail). In this case, you have two choices to retain the existing site:

- **Click the Change Domain Name button:** This takes you back to the screen in Figure 13-11. Type a new fully qualified DNS name.
- **Click the Manual Setup button to change the port number:** This takes you back to the screen in Figure 13-12, where you can type in a different port number. The default port setting is 80. Choose a port number that isn't being used by another service. You may be able to use port 8080, which is another port the server uses as a default. Port numbers 81–87 are generally safe to use.

Dozens of port numbers are reserved for different Mac OS X services. To see a list, open Server Admin, click the Help menu, and search for TCP and UDP port reference.

Figure 13-13: If you see this, you're already using this DNS name and port.

You see the Web site(s) you added in Server Preferences, as shown in Figure 13-14. The location of the Web site files displays under the DNS name for the site. Select the check box next to the Web site in order for it to be available.

Figure 13-14: Custom Web sites added in Server Preferences.

Configuring Web Services with Server Admin

Sever Admin gives you access to more settings and capabilities than does Server Preferences. This section looks at some of the more important settings.

You can more easily turn Web services on and off with Server Preferences, but if you want, you can also use Server Admin. As with other services, you first enable Web services and then turn it on.

To enable Web services, click the server name in the left column, click the Settings button, and then click the Services tab. Finally, make sure the Web check box is selected.

To turn on Web services, click the triangle next to your server in the left column to expand the list of services. Click Web and then click the Start Web button in the lower left. If the button says Stop Web, Web services is running.

There are two icons in the toolbar that you use to configure Web sites: the Settings icon and the Sites icon. Here's a clear distinction between the two:

- **Settings:** These settings apply to all Web sites on your server.
- **Sites:** These settings apply to individual Web sites that you host.

Creating one or more Web sites

With Server Admin, you can host multiple Web sites. Here, I assume that you're retaining the created wiki-based site that Snow Leopard Server creates automatically. To host your own Web site, follow these steps:

1. **Copy a folder containing your Web site documents to your server.**

   The default location is /Library/WebServer/Documents/. You can put it anywhere, however. You just have to tell Server Admin where it is.

2. **Open Server Admin to the Sites General pane:**

   a. *Click the triangle to the left of your server's name to expand the list of services and then select Web.*

   b. *Click the Sites button in the toolbar and then click the General tab.*

3. **Click the Add (+) button.**

   The window in Figure 13-15 appears, with some of default settings.

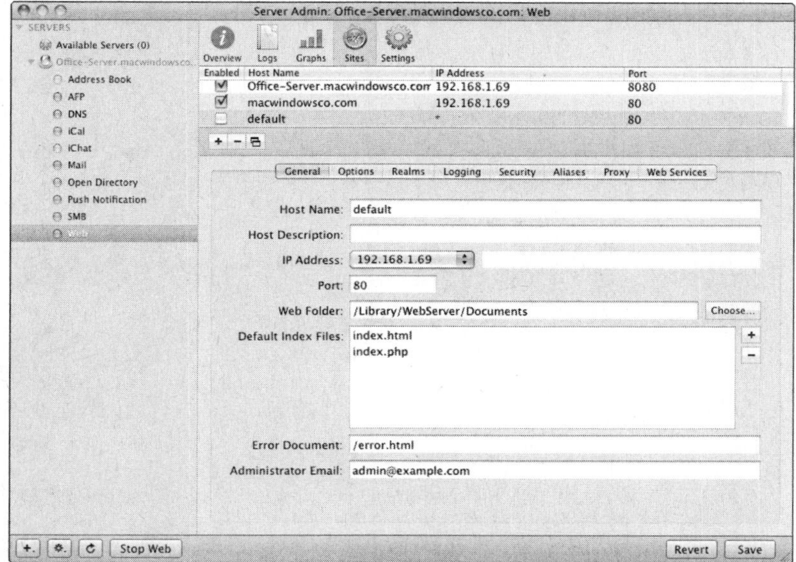

Figure 13-15: Defining a new Web site in Server Admin.

4. **Enter the server's domain name in the Host Name field.**

   This needs to be a fully qualified domain name, such as office-server. macwindowsco.com, in which *office-server* is the host computer located in the domain *macwindowsco.com.*

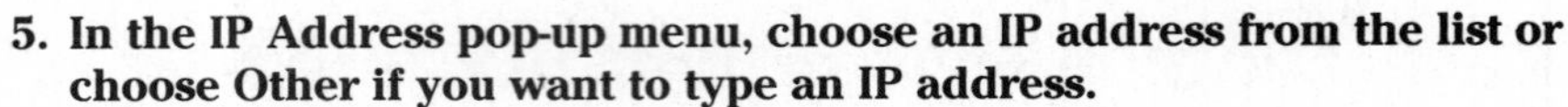

5. **In the IP Address pop-up menu, choose an IP address from the list or choose Other if you want to type an IP address.**

   In the Port field, use the default 80 number or type something else, such as **8080** or **443** if you're using SSL encryption (enabled in the Security tab). Don't use a port number used by another service on the server.

   If you're hosting more than one Web site on a server, each site must have a unique combination of domain name, IP address, and port number. Web sites can share any two of these three items but not all three.

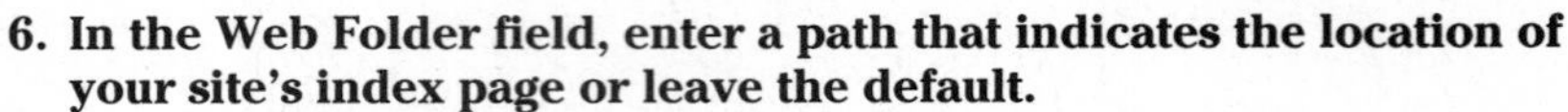

6. **In the Web Folder field, enter a path that indicates the location of your site's index page or leave the default.**

   Instead of typing the location, click the Choose button to browse to your Web site's folder to ensure that you don't making any typing errors.

7. **Enter the e-mail address of the site administrator.**
8. **Enable the site you just created by selecting the check box next to it in the list at the top and then click the Save button.**

You also have a number of optional settings. With many, the default settings work. There's no particular reason to change the entry for Error Document, which sets the location of the file (within your Web folder) that appears when browsers ask for a page that doesn't exist. Default Index Files also work for most sites.

Logging of access and errors is enabled by default. To disable or to change the default settings, click the Logging tab.

Using Server Admin for wikis, blogs, calendars, and Webmail

Earlier in the chapter, I show you how to use Server Preferences to turn the individual built-in services on and off: wikis, blogs, calendars, and Webmail. You can also do this from Server Admin for each individual Web site:

1. **Click Web in the left column list of services, click the Sites button in the toolbar, and then click the Web Services tab.**
2. **Select a Web site from the top of the page.**

The interface you see looks a lot like that of Server Preferences, as shown in Figure 13-10, with Wikis, Blogs, Calendar, and Webmail check boxes. Click the arrow that appears to the right of each item, and your Web browser launches taking you to the corresponding Web page that the server creates.

Server Admin can also do some things that you can't do from Server Preferences. These are in the Settings icon on the toolbar, which means they apply to all your sites. After you click the Settings icon, click the Wiki tab, as shown in Figure 13-16.

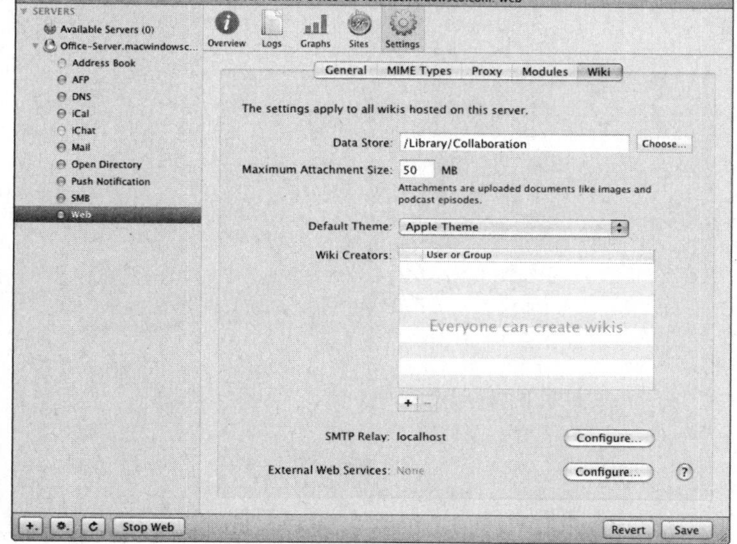

Figure 13-16: Server Admin has additional settings for the built-in wiki-based Web pages.

An useful feature here is the Default Theme pop-up menu. This lets you set the default theme of the automatically created pages (wikis, blogs, calendars, and Webmail). Users can still change the theme from within the wiki. You can also limit who can create new wiki, blog, and calendar pages with the Wiki Creators field. The default is that everyone can create wiki pages. To restrict this, click the Add (+) button. In the dialog that appears, drag over the names of users and/or groups. Only those users can create new wiki pages.

Some other settings are

- **Maximum Attachment Size:** Limits the size of files that users can upload to wiki and blog pages.
- **SMTP Relay:** Lets you change the mail server that delivers e-mail notification and change the e-mail address of the sender or administrator.
- **External Web Services:** Lets you specify calendar and mail servers other than those running on your server to deliver these services to the wiki-based calendar and Webmail.

Aliases and redirects

Aliases and redirects are ways to enable users to go to your Web site by using a different name than the hostname. An *alias* is an alternative DNS name for your site. You can create multiple aliases for a single Web site. Aliases must be in the form of DNS names. For example, if your primary DNS name is `myschool.edu`, you might create aliases for `www.myschool.edu`, `www.myschool.com`, and `www.myschool.org`.

Of course, you have to own the DNS names that you're using. And they must resolve to the Web site's IP address on a DNS server, either on your network or on your Mac server.

A *redirect* takes a Web browser to a different file or folder than entered in the browser, as long as they have valid URLs. With redirects, the browser actually makes a connection with the URL in the Address field. The server of that page sends the browser to another host. With aliases, the browser connects only to the destination URL.

Server aliases versus URL aliases and redirects

The Server Admin Aliases pane is shown in Figure 13-17. Click Web in the left column, click the Sites icon in the toolbar, and then click the Aliases tab. This pane groups aliases and redirects into two areas:

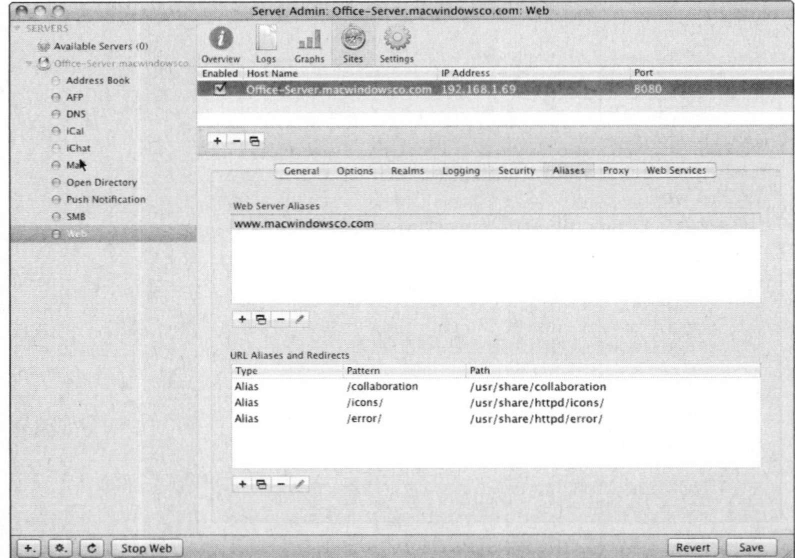

Figure 13-17: Here I added an entry under Web Server Aliases. The bottom items are defaults.

- **Web Server Aliases:** You add domain-name-level aliases here, such as `www.myschool.edu`.
- **URL Aliases and Redirects:** These are aliases and redirects that point to a file or folder on the Web server with a path. These are more specific than Web server aliases.

  Which one to use? URL aliases map the URL term to another location on the server. Use redirects to redirect to a location on another server.

  You can also use the asterisk (*) as a wildcard term in URL aliases and redirects; these are *match* aliases and redirects. But, for these, you need to use a specific computer syntax called *regular expression patterns,* which represent all JPEG files as (.*)\.jpg.

When you enter URL aliases and redirects, you must provide a *pattern* (which is what a Web browser will request) and a *path* (which is where the Web browser will be sent).

Some example entries are

- **Web server alias:** `server.myschool.edu`
- **URL alias:** Pattern: `/images`; Path: `/Volumes/newharddrive/images`
- **URL redirect:** Pattern: `/images`; Path: `http://newserver.abc.edu/images`
- **URL alias match:** Pattern: `(.*)\.jpg`; Path: `(.*)\.jpg`
- **URL redirect match:** Pattern: `(.*)\.jpg`; Path: `http:// other server.myschool.edu/images$1.jpg`

Redirect paths start with http or https because they're being redirected to another server.

Figure 13-17 shows three URL aliases. These are created by Snow Leopard Server for the built-in wiki-based site.

Configuring aliases and redirects

You create both aliases and redirects in the same Server Admin window:

1. **Open Server Admin to the Web Sites Aliases pane:**

   a. *Click the triangle to the left of your server's name to expand the list of services and then select Web.*

   b. *Click the Sites icon in the toolbar.*

   c. *Click the Aliases tab.*

   The window in Figure 13-17 appears.

2. **Select your Web host near the top of the window.**

   If you're hosting more than one site, select the one for which you'll create aliases or redirects.

3. **If you see an asterisk (*) character in the Web Site Aliases field, delete it by selecting it and clicking the Minus (–) button.**

4. **If you're adding a server alias, click the Add (+) button under the Web Server Aliases field.**

   If you're adding a URL alias or redirect, skip to Step 8.

5. **Type the server alias in the dialog that slides down and click OK.**

   You can add additional server aliases by repeating Steps 4 and 5.

6. **To create a URL alias or redirect, click the Add (+) button under the URL Aliases and Redirects field.**

   A new dialog slides down, as shown in Figure 13-18.

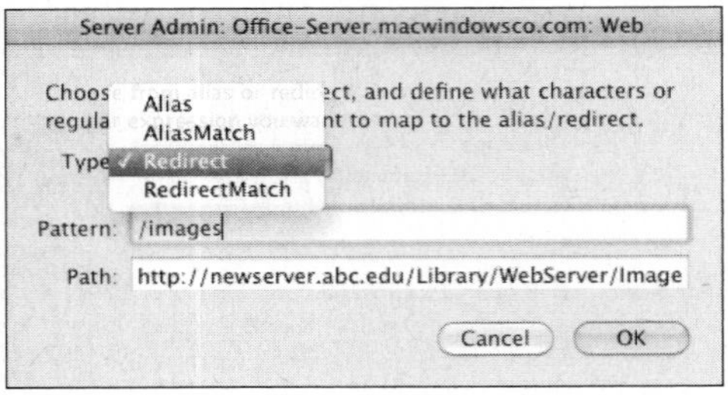

Figure 13-18: Adding a URL alias or redirect.

7. **Choose from Alias, AliasMatch, Redirect, and RedirectMatch from the Type pop-up menu.**

8. **In the Pattern field, enter the pattern that comes from the users' Web browsers.**

   (See preceding section for examples.)

9. **In the Path field, enter the path that the user is sent to.**

10. **Click OK and then click the Save button.**

To edit an alias or redirect, select it and click the pencil icon.

Tuning performance of your Web server

For most people, the default parameters that govern the performance of all your Web sites work just fine. But worth knowing is that you can change these settings if you find your server bogging down. You can access these settings on Server Admin's Web Settings General pane:

1. **Click the triangle to the left of your server's name to expand the list of services and then select Web.**
2. **Click the Settings icon in the toolbar and then click the General tab.**

Here are a number of settings that can enhance performance:

- **Maximum Simultaneous Connections:** The default is 1024 connections. This doesn't refer to users: A Web browser loading a single Web page from your server can create multiple connections. If your server is accessible to the Internet, a lot of traffic can slow down the server. By lowering this number, you prevent the server from being overburdened. Users receive a Server Is Busy message.

  On the flip side, if users are getting to many Server Is Busy messages and your server isn't slowing, you can raise the default setting.

  This number is the total number of connections for all the Web sites hosted on the server.

- **Connection Timeout:** This is the amount of time before an inactive user is disconnected from the server. The default is 300 seconds. A shorter timeout can free up resources for other users.
- **Minimum and Maximum Spare Servers:** This refers to the number of idle service processes running. Idle server processes can increase performance by being ready when users need them but can bog down the server if there are too many. If the number of spare server processes drops below this Minimum number, the server creates them. After the maximum is reached, the server stops adding spare server processes.
- **Number of Servers to Start:** This is the number of spare server processes that are created at server startup. The default is 1.
- **Allow Persistent Connections:** This is on by default because it reduces network traffic. It enables a Web browser to make multiple server requests over a single connection. You can also change the maximum allowed persistent connections and the timeout length.

One setting that isn't related to performance is the Enable Tomcat check box. Tomcat is a Sun technology that lets you add Java *servlets* (server-based Java programs) and JavaServer Pages for dynamic Web sites. JavaServer Pages let you embed Java servlets in your HTML Web pages. For information on JavaServer Pages, see `http://java.sun.com/products/jsp`.

Where Mac OS X Server Puts Web Files

In this chapter, I mention the location of the Web site files in Snow Leopard Server's file system. For some people, it might also be useful to know the location of some of the other related files, including cascading style sheets and wiki themes as well as the Apache Web server modules and configuration files. Few people need to edit or replace them, but if you know what you're doing, go for it.

Table 13-1 shows the folder path in which Snow Leopard Server's Web-related files reside.

Folders with paths starting with /etc/ and /usr/ aren't visible in the Finder. To access these folders, in the Finder, choose Go⇨Connect to Server and then type the folder path. (In a Unix shell, open Terminal in /Applications/Utilities/.)

Table 13-1 Location of Web Files in Snow Leopard Server

Description	*Location*
Auto-created wiki, blog, Web calendar, and mailing list pages	/Library/Collaboration/
Custom sites created with Server Admin	/Library/WebServer/Documents/
Custom sites created with Server Preferences	/Library/WebServer/Sites/
Temporarily disabled virtual hosts (Sites turned off but not deleted)	/etc/apache2/sites_disabled/
CGI scripts	/Library/WebServer/CGI-Executable
Configuration files for Web service	/etc/apache2/
Configuration files for sites	/etc/apache2/sites/
Apache and Apple plug-in modules	/usr/libexec/apache2
Web access and error logs	/var/log/apache2/
Wiki cascading style sheet (`.css`) files	/usr/share/collaboration/css/required/
Wiki themes (`.plist`, `.xsl`, `images`, `.css`)	/Library/Application Support/Apple/WikiServer/Themes/
Compressed subfolder for themes	/usr/share/collaboration/themes/theme_name/

More Services

There's much more to Snow Leopard Server's Web services than I could squeeze into this chapter. Before ending, I want to point out one more settings pane that offers some powerful features. Click the Sites button, click the Options tab, and then you see several options that are turned off by default:

- **Folder Listing and WebDAV:** WebDAV is a file-sharing method that enables users of any operating system to mount a share and to copy files to and from the server. This requires a WebDAV client, such as Goliath. Mac users can also use the Finder. Set permissions for files and folders as you would for any type of file sharing (as I describe in Chapter 9).
- **CGI Execution:** This enables the use of Common Gateway Interface (CGI) scripts on your Web site. When this is enabled, you can place script files on the server.

To make scripts available to all your sites, place them here: /Library/WebServer/CGI-Executable. When you do this, a link to the script needs to include `/cgi-bin/`, such as `www.abc.edu/cgi-bin/script.cgi`. You can also place scripts in the Documents folders for each site, without the `/cgi-bin/` requirement.

If you click the Realms tab, you can add realms to limit access to a Web site. A *realm* can be a collection of files or directories in the Web site. You could create a realm that includes a portion of a Web site that only a group can access. Realms are often used with WebDAV.

For more on these and other topics, see Server Admin Help in the Help menu.

Chapter 14

Running an E-Mail Server

In This Chapter

- Understanding Mail protocols and technologies
- Setting up mail service
- Configuring the DNS server for mail
- Tightening security with Server Admin
- Blocking spam and viruses
- Configuring mail user accounts on the server
- Creating new user e-mail addresses and mailing lists

There are advantages to hosting your own e-mail server over using an outside provider. It gives you flexibility, letting you customize the e-mail options whenever you need to. If you have confidential data in your e-mail, storing your messages on your own server will give you peace of mind.

When using an outside e-mail server, such as an Internet service provider or an off-site host, users in your building that e-mail each other send traffic out through your Internet connection and back. This can slow the Internet connection in organizations with limited Internet bandwidth. Using your own e-mail server keeps internal e-mail traffic off your Internet connection.

This chapter describes setting up e-mail service with all the trimmings, including spam and virus blocking and domain name service (DNS).

Growing Your Own E-Mail

Setting up your own e-mail service isn't all that complicated. There are some things you need to know, however. This section describes the technologies involved. If you're already familiar with mail protocols and DNS, you can skip ahead to the section, "Setting Up Your E-Mail Server."

Mail protocols

There are three protocols used for sending and receiving mail:

- Users send e-mail with the *Simple Mail Transfer Protocol (SMTP).*
- Users receive e-mail with either the *Post Office Protocol (POP)* or the *Internet Message Access Protocol (IMAP).*

You can set SMTP to require authentication to prevent spammers from using your server to relay spam to others.

POP and IMAP each provide benefits. You can enable both on the server (this is the default setting) and have different computers using different methods. The basic difference between the two is whether the user reads e-mail from the client or from the server. Each approach has different ramifications.

With POP, e-mail is downloaded to the client computer and deleted from the Mail server. The client disconnects from the server as soon as the last message is downloaded. Because clients are connected to the server for only short periods, there's minimal use of the server's processor and RAM. This allows large numbers of users to access the server with minimal impact. And because e-mails are deleted from the server, POP has the advantage of using less server storage space than IMAP. All this makes POP an attractive alternative for a slower server Mac with limited RAM and hard drive space.

IMAP requires more server resources but can provide more benefits for the user. An IMAP connection to the server can last as long as the user needs, allowing the user to download content on demand. This can provide faster response times, and users can read one large message at a time without waiting for a whole batch to download.

IMAP also retains messages on the server even after they're read. It's up to the user to delete the messages from the server. This requires a lot more hard drive space than POP, as the amount of stored e-mail is growing constantly. (You can put a cap on the total amount of e-mail a user stores on the server.) But, this allows IMAP users to access e-mail from more than one computer or device, such as a home machine, a work machine, and an iPhone. IMAP permits users to have a mail folder structure on the server, which appears the same from any computer they use.

Snow Leopard Server's e-mail service uses the open source Postfix as the *mail transfer agent (MTA)* to send SMTP e-mail to the Internet. Snow Leopard Server uses the open source Dovecot for POP and IMAP e-mail.

If your users are sending e-mail to each other only, then SMTP, POP, and IMAP are all you need to configure. But if you're like most people and want to exchange e-mail with users on the Internet, you need to configure DNS.

In case you're wondering for purposes of backup, Snow Leopard Server temporarily stores mail going to the Internet in this location: /var/spool/postfix/.

Incoming IMAP e-mail is stored in directories for each user in this default location: /var/spool/imap/dovecot/mail/*username.* Messages stay here until the user deletes them from the client e-mail application. You can change this location with Server Admin.

Mail service and the Internet: DNS

In addition to mail protocols, a few more elements need to be in place in order to send mail to destinations on the Internet. Domain name service (DNS) helps determine who will eventually receive a sent e-mail by looking up the domain name of the e-mail recipient (the `acme.com` in `bob@acme.com`) and finding an IP address to send it to.

The DNS service can be running on your Snow Leopard Server Mac or on your ISP's server. If you want to run DNS on your Mac for use on the Internet, your organization needs to own a registered domain name.

MX records

The DNS server also uses mail exchange (MX) records to help route incoming e-mail to your server. An MX record contains a list of Mail servers that handle mail for a particular domain name. MX records help other Mail servers find your e-mail users.

An SMTP server sending a message looks at the domain name of the e-mail message and asks a DNS server for the corresponding IP address of an e-mail server, either the final destination server or an intermediate e-mail server on the Internet. The DNS server looks up the domain name in an MX record and then sends the IP address back to the SMTP server. The SMTP server can then send on the e-mail message. MX records can list multiple IP addresses for a given domain name, ranked in order for the SMTP server to try.

The "Configuring DNS for Use with E-Mail" section, later in this chapter, describes creating MX records.

Relay servers

You may also need to connect your e-mail server to the Internet by specifying a *relay server,* which is another Mail server that you'd forward outgoing mail to. Your Internet service provider may require that you relay e-mail to one of their servers. Or, you may need to relay e-mail to another server in your organization if you have a server designated to send outgoing mail through a firewall. In this case, you wouldn't be using MX records on your server. You can specify a relay server with either Server Preferences or Server Admin.

Don't specify a relay server without telling the operator of the server. You may look like a spammer and could get your server blacklisted.

Setting Up Your E-Mail Server

You may have chosen e-mail service during the initial setup of Snow Leopard Server. This procedure set up a basic e-mail server. The main limitation of the automatic setup is that it isn't configured for delivering mail to the Internet.

Here's how mail service is configured if you selected it during installation:

- SMTP, POP, and IMAP protocols are turned on.
- SMTP authentication is turned off.
- User POP and IMAP passwords are set to be transmitted as unencrypted cleartext.
- Relaying of mail to another server is turned off.

If you have an ISP that requires you to relay mail to their server, you can turn on mail relay to enable Snow Leopard Server to send e-mail to the Internet. If you're not using an ISP that offers mail relay, you need to have DNS running on your server or another server on your network.

Mail tools: Server Preferences versus Server Admin

From default settings provided with Snow Leopard Server's installation, you can use either Server Preferences or Server Admin to further configure Mail service. For basic e-mail service, both are pretty easy to use. Both tools let you turn on some additional e-mail features, but Server Admin gives you access to more advanced features.

Server Preferences lets you set up a relay to an Internet service provider to send e-mail to the Internet, but doesn't enable you to create an MX record. Server Preferences also lets you blacklist known e-mail servers (spammers) as well as filter spam and viruses. Server Preferences doesn't let you turn off either POP or IMAP.

Server Admin gives you some additional options for dealing with spam and lets you change settings for authentication. It also lets you set up mail lists, or *listservs,* and set maximum message sizes. You can create MX records with Server Admin, as well as configure Mail server *clustering,* in which multiple servers act as one Mail server.

Server Admin also gives you a choice of using two different user interfaces: the standard setup windows or the Configuration Assistant, which takes you through the configuration with explanations of what you need to do.

The Configuration Assistant is like a wizard in Windows.

Setting up mail with Server Preferences

Server Preferences may be all you need to start mail service. If you're using an Internet service provider that offers a relay server, a few mouse clicks may be all that you need. Here's what you do:

1. **Launch Server Preferences and click the Mail icon.**

   The window shown in Figure 14-1 appears.

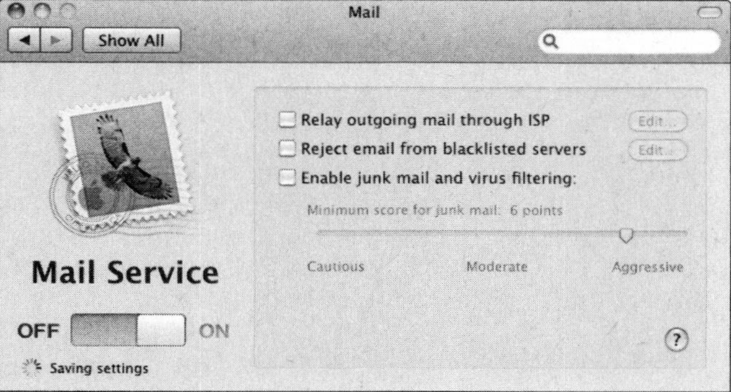

Figure 14-1: Mail configuration in Server Preferences.

   If you configured mail when you first set up Snow Leopard Server, the big switch is set to On.

2. **If off, click the switch to the On position.**
3. **If you are using an Internet service provider to relay mail to the Internet, do this:**
   a. *Select the Relay Outgoing Mail through ISP check box.*

      This could be a server in your own organization.

      A new dialog appears, as shown in Figure 14-2.

   b. *Enter an IP address or a DNS name for the relay server.*
   c. *If your ISP requires authentication for its SMTP relay, enter a user-name and password.*
   d. *Click OK.*

Figure 14-2: Specifying a mail relay server in Server Preferences.

4. **Select the Reject Email from Blacklisted Servers check box to specify a blacklist server to prevent spam from known spam servers from reaching you.**

   If you select this option, the default is `zen.spamhaus.org`. You can change this if you like.

5. **Select the Enable Junk Mail and Virus Filtering check box to activate the slider for the severity of filtering.**

   The higher you set the slider, the higher the chance that junk e-mail is detected. Any messages that are deemed to be spam are marked as JUNK and forwarded to the user. This setting also tells the Mail server to remove all e-mail messages it suspects of containing viruses and to place them in this folder: /var/virusmails/.

For more on spam and virus filtering, see the section, "Blocking Spam and Other Nasty Bits," later in this chapter.

Turning on and starting Mail service with Server Admin

If you configured mail service during startup, it's up and running. If not, you have to turn it on and then start it running.

You can tell if Mail is turned on and running in Server Admin by going to the left column and clicking the triangle to the left of your server to expand the list of services. If Mail isn't included in the list, it isn't turned on. If Mail appears but the circle is empty (as shown in Figure 14-3), Mail is turned on but isn't started.

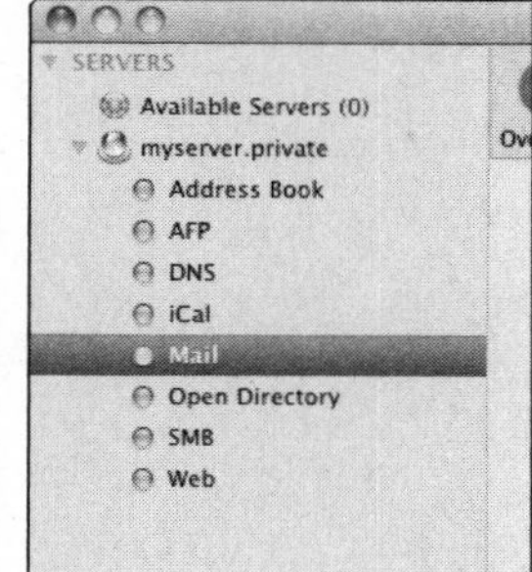

Figure 14-3: Mail service is enabled but isn't running.

You can turn on Mail service in Server Preferences by clicking the big switch, as shown in Figure 14-2. You can also use Server Admin to turn on Mail service. The procedure is the same as for file sharing and other services:

1. **In Server Admin, click your server in the column on the left.**
2. **Click the Settings icon in the toolbar; then click the Settings tab.**
3. **Select the Mail check box and click Save.**

To start the Mail service:

1. **Click the triangle to the left of your server to expand the list of services and then click Mail.**
2. **Click the Start Mail button in the lower left of the screen.**

Using Configuration Assistant to configure mail service

Server Admin gives you two ways to configure or edit your mail service settings: the Configuration Assistant or the Settings window. This section looks at the former. The subsequent section looks at the latter.

The Configuration Assistant is good to use if you aren't sure where to find a setting or if you need some more information about the settings. The Assistant brings up what you need to configure without you having to look for it — just click through any screens until you find what you need. The Configuration Assistant also provides instructions. Here's how to use it:

1. **In Server Admin, click the triangle to the left of your server to expand the list of services.**

2. **Click Mail from the list and then click the toolbar's Overview icon.**
3. **Click the Configure Mail Service button in the lower right (see Figure 14-4).**

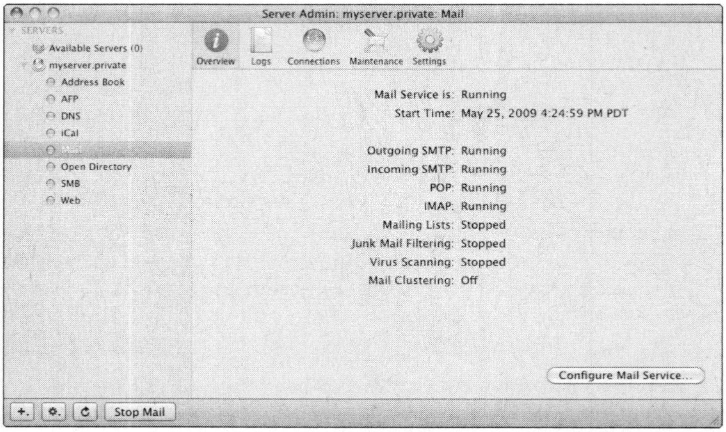

Figure 14-4: The Configure Mail Service button brings up the Configuration Assistant.

4. **When the Configuration Assistant opens to an introduction screen, click the Continue button.**
5. **In the Mail Service: General window that opens (as shown in Figure 14-5), select or deselect the POP, IMAP, and SMTP protocols.**

   All are on by default.

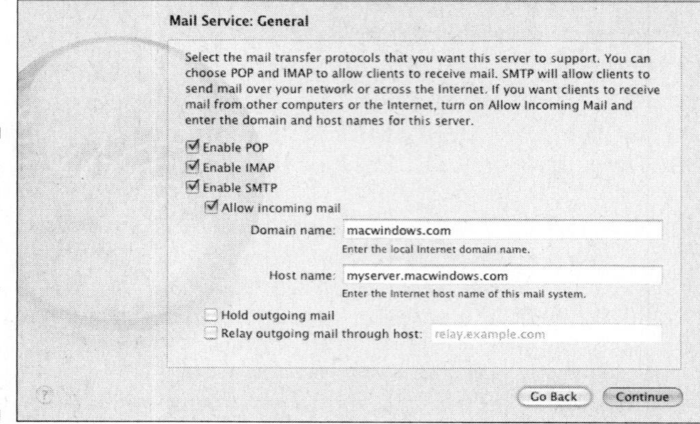

Figure 14-5: The Mail Service: General window of Configuration Assistant.

6. **Select the Allow Incoming Mail check box to enable Internet e-mail, and then type your domain name and server name.**
7. **Select the Relay Outgoing Mail through Host check box if you have an SMTP relay.**

   The Hold Outgoing Mail check box is a setting you can use for troubleshooting or to queue mail until you solve another problem. The queued mail is sent when you deselect this setting.

8. **Click the Continue button.**

   The next window is Filters, for blocking spam and viruses. It is similar to that of Server Preferences (see Figure 14-1). (For more on spam and virus filtering, see the section, "Blocking Spam and Other Nasty Bits," later in this chapter.)

9. **Click the Continue button.**

   The Security window appears with choices for encrypting passwords.

10. **Use Kerberos and/or CRAM-MD5 for SMTP and IMAP; for POP, use Kerberos or APOP; click the Continue button.**

    See the section, "Security with Server Admin Settings," later in this chapter for more information on these settings.

11. **(Optional) In the next screen that appears, change the default location for IMAP mail messages.**

    Most people can ignore this.

12. **Click the Continue button.**
13. **In the confirmation screen that appears listing your settings, click the Go Back button to change your settings or click the Continue button to have your settings configured.**

You can come back to the Configuration Assistant any time to make changes. Or, you can use the Settings window, described in the following section.

Configuring e-mail with Server Admin's Settings window

In addition to the Configuration Assistant, Server Admin offers a Settings window that you can use to set up e-mail. The section describes the General tab, where you make or change basic e-mail server settings.

There are a few more setting changes that you can make here that you can't make in the Configuration Assistant, including assigning a Push Notification Server and limiting the maximum amount of simultaneous IMAP connections.

Here's how to use the Settings window for configuring e-mail service:

1. **In Server Admin, click the triangle to the left of your server to expand the list of services.**
2. **Click Mail in the list, click the Settings icon in the toolbar, and then click the General tab.**

   The window in Figure 14-6 appears.

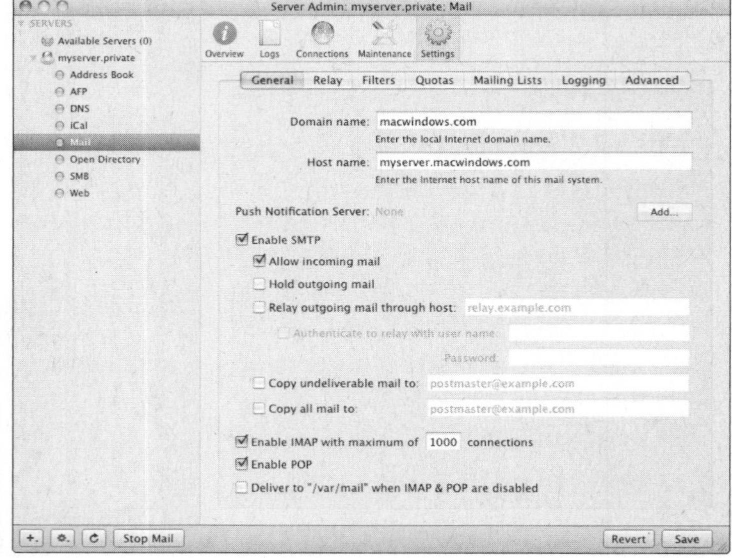

Figure 14-6: Server Admin's Mail Settings window, General tab.

3. **Type your domain name and hostname in the fields near the top.**
4. **Select the Enable SMTP and Allow Incoming Mail check boxes if not checked already.**
5. **If your ISP or organization requires that you use a mail relay server, select the Relay Outgoing Mail through Host check box and type the domain name of the host. If a name and password are required for the relay server, type those in.**
6. **Select the Enable IMAP or Enable POP check box, or both, if not selected already.**
7. **Click the Save button in the lower right.**
8. **Click the Start Mail button if Mail isn't already running.**

   Your Mail service is now configured.

A few other options are also shown in Figure 14-6:

- **Push Notification Server:** This is useful for iPhone and notebook clients. Instead of requiring the user to check for e-mail, push notification goes to the iPhone to tell it that mail has arrived. Before you select this option, you need to have the Push Notification Server turned on.
- **Hold Outgoing Mail:** This is a setting you can use for troubleshooting or to queue mail while you solve another problem. Users can still send mail, but the server holds it, so mail won't be sent to their destinations. Queued mail is sent when you deselect this setting.
- **Allow Incoming Mail:** Block inbound messages by deselecting this option. Incoming e-mail messages are bounced back to the servers they came from.
- **Copy Undeliverable Mail To:** Selecting this sends problem outgoing e-mail to an e-mail address, typically for an administrator. Copy All Mail To copies all mail to an e-mail address — something you might want to do if you want a single place to search for e-mail for all your users.

Configuring DNS for Use with E-Mail

DNS service set up with mail exchange (MX) records allows mail to be sent to the correct host on your network. Whether you need to set this up depends on your situation:

- **Your Internet service provider supplies the DNS server for your network:** If this is the case, your ISP can set up and host MX records for you. All you do is let them know your Mail server's IP address and domain name.
- **Your network has DNS service running on a non-Mac server:** In this case, the server administrator creates an MX record for your Mail server that's hosted on the DNS server.
- **The DNS service is running on one of your Mac OS X Servers:** Use Server Admin to access any of these servers to create an MX record.

If you're in the last case, you actually *can* do without MX records if you really want to. To do this, you need to include the Mail server hostname in the e-mail addresses of your users. For example, with MX records configured, a user's e-mail address might look like this: `fred@acme.com`.

Without MX records, you must include the mail hostname: `fred@our-server.acme.com`.

The problem with this is that if you ever change your Mail server, you have to change all your users' e-mail addresses.

If you're going to use MX records, you also need to make sure DNS has a *machine record,* a DNS entry that identifies your Mail server on the network. This section looks at creating an MX record. After that, I look at how to create a DNS machine record for the mail host. But first, make sure DNS Service is turned on.

Turning on DNS service

If you enabled DNS when you installed Mac OS X, it's turned on. If not, turn it on the way you turn on other services, including Mail:

1. **In Server Admin, click your server in the upper left of the window.**
2. **Click the Settings icon in the toolbar and then on the Services tab, select the DNS check box.**
3. **Click the Save button at the bottom right.**

Creating an MX record

To create an MX record, do the following in Server Admin:

1. **Click the triangle to the left of the server running the DNS service.**

   If you don't see DNS listed, you need to turn it on.

2. **Select DNS from the list of services under the server and then click the Zones icon in the toolbar.**
3. **Select a zone from the list near the top of the window (as shown in Figure 14-7).**

   If you don't have a zone, create one with the Add Zone drop-down menu. This is the zone to which you create the MX record.

   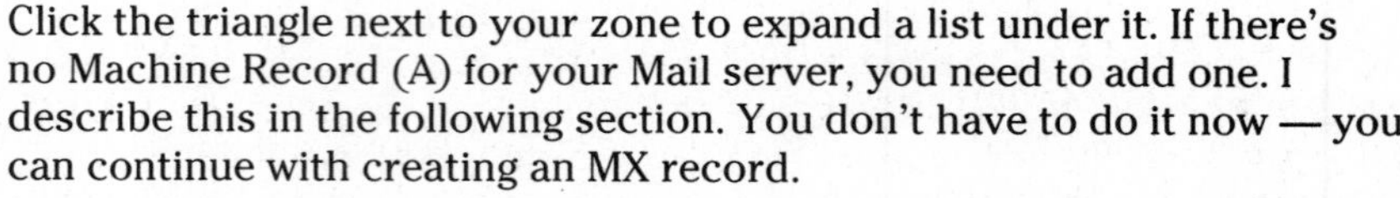

   Click the triangle next to your zone to expand a list under it. If there's no Machine Record (A) for your Mail server, you need to add one. I describe this in the following section. You don't have to do it now — you can continue with creating an MX record.

4. **With your zone selected, go to the bottom of the window and click the Add (+) button next to the Mail Exchangers box.**

   MX stands for *mail exchange.*

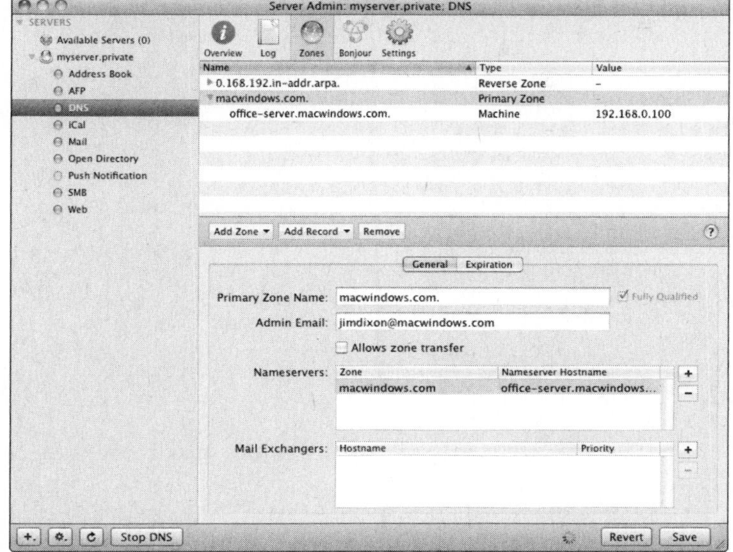

Figure 14-7: Selecting a DNS zone in Server Admin.

5. **Type the hostname of the Mail server in the Mail Exchangers box, as shown in Figure 14-8.**

   If you type just `mail` without the domain (as shown in Figure 14-8), `.macwindows.com` is added when you click the Save button.

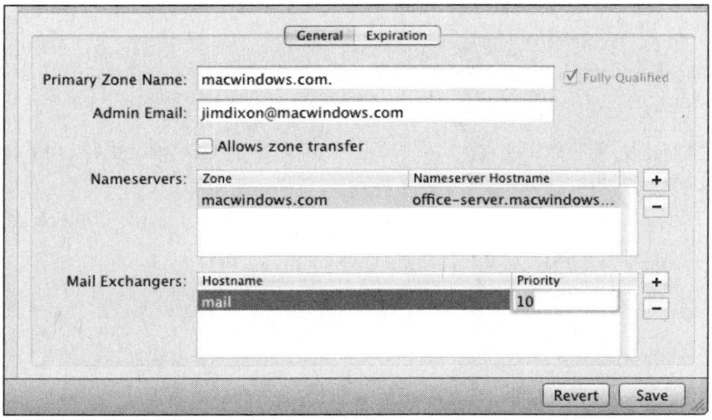

Figure 14-8: The hostname and priority are essentially the MX record.

6. **Type a priority number in the Priority column.**

   If this is your only Mail server, type `10`. If this is a backup Mail server, the priority number should be higher than that of your primary Mail server.

7. **(Optional) If you have other Mail servers for redundancy, you can add more MX records by clicking the Add (+) button.**

   Typically the priority numbers are in multiples of 10 (10, 20, 30) to enable you to add other servers later in between those numbers.

   Priority numbers tell the DNS server which Mail server to route incoming mail to. The highest priority has the lowest number, which is 10 in this example. If that server is out of commission, the mail is routed to the next priority number, 20.

8. **Click the Save button.**

Creating a DNS machine record for the Mail server

In addition to an MX record, the DNS zone needs to have an entry called a Machine Record (A) defined for the mail service, using the same Mail server hostname that you used in the MX record.

Start from the same DNS Zones window, shown in Figure 14-7, described in Steps 1–4 of the preceding section.

1. **Click the triangle to the left of the selected zone to display the list of records for that zone.**

   If there's already an entry for your mail host, you're done.

   In the example in the preceding section, you want to see an entry for `mail.macwindows.com`.

2. **Click the zone to select it and, in the Add Record pop-up menu just below the zone list, choose Add Machine (A) (see Figure 14-9).**

   A record called newMachine is added to the zone (see Figure 14-10).

3. **With the newMachine record still selected, go to the Machine Name field below and type the hostname of the server.**

   In this example, the hostname is `mail`.

4. **Click the Add (+) button and enter the IP address of the Mac server.**

5. **(Optional) Enter the hardware and software information about your server in the boxes.**

6. **(Optional) Use the Comment box to include the location of the server or any other information that might identify it.**

   Figure 14-11 shows what the window looks like.

7. **Click the Save button.**

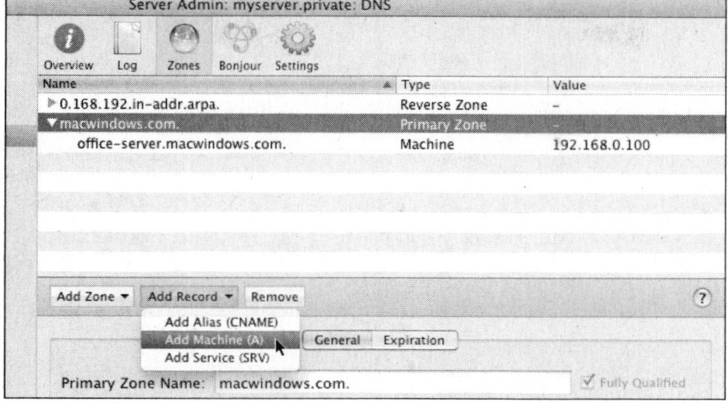

Figure 14-9: The Add Record button brings up a pop-up menu.

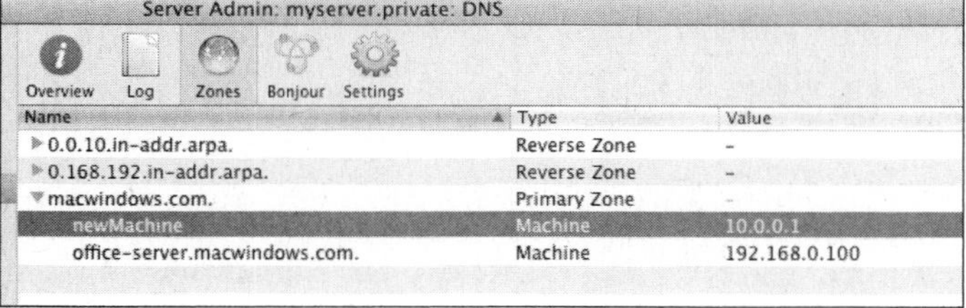

Figure 14-10: The newly created machine record.

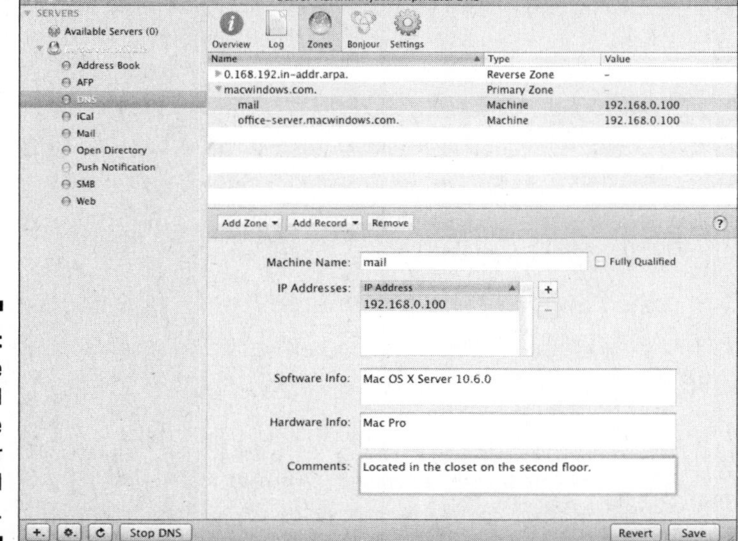

Figure 14-11: The completed machine record for the Mail server.

If you like, you can add *aliases* for this server — additional names for the server that will resolve to the server's IP address. To do this, click the Add Record button and choose Add Alias (CNAME) from the pop-up menu. Then add the additional name for your server in the Alias Name field and add the actual hostname in the Destination field; click the Save button.

If you add an alias, you have to go back to the Mail settings:

1. **Click Mail in the left column under your server, click the Settings icon in the toolbar, click the Advanced tab, and finally, click the Hosting tab.**
2. **Click the Add (+) button and type the alias name; click Save.**

When you're finished, make sure the DNS service is running. With DNS selected in the left column, if DNS isn't running, the button on the bottom left of the window says Start DNS. Click it to start.

E-Mail Security with Server Admin

Snow Leopard Server lets you require clients to encrypt passwords when they sign in to the e-mail server; it can also encrypt e-mail messages with the Secure Sockets Layer (SSL) standard. The earlier section, "Using Configuration Assistant to configure mail service," describes how to do this with Configuration Assistant. This section describes Server Admin.

Password authentication is useful if users connect to your e-mail server over the Internet from home or when traveling. Mac OS X Server offers different methods of authentication because not all mail clients support the same methods.

In Server Admin, you can find these under the Advanced tab of the Mail Settings window:

1. **In Server Admin, click the triangle to the left of your server to expand the list of services.**
2. **Click Mail from the list; then click the Settings icon in the toolbar.**
3. **Click the Advanced tab in the upper right and then click the Security tab in the second row of tabs.**

   You see the window in Figure 14-12.

Here you can set encryption for authentication (usernames and passwords) and for e-mail messages. The following two sections describe what these settings mean and when you might use them.

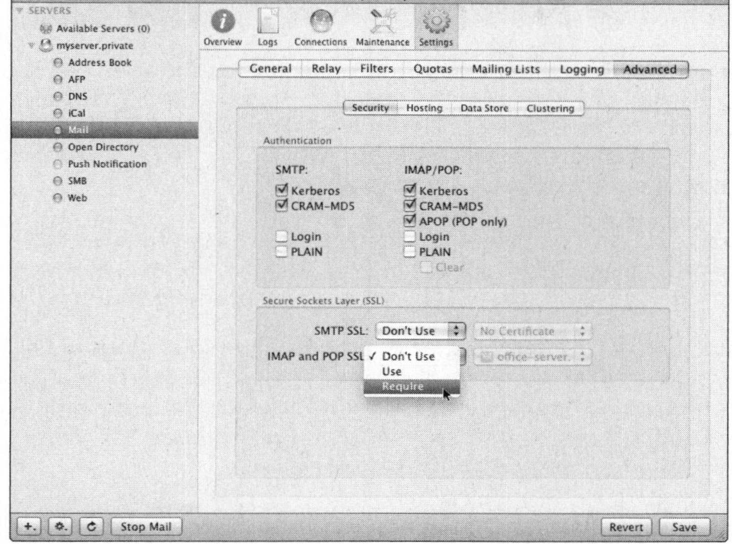

Figure 14-12: Mail password protection settings in Server Admin.

Securing mail authentication

In the Authentication section, there are choices for password encryption for SMTP and IMAP/POP. Which you choose depends on what your e-mail clients support. You can choose multiple authentication methods to support multiple e-mail clients. It's a good idea to disable any authentication method that your clients aren't using. If you need only one type for all your clients, use that. Using only one authentication requires clients to use it.

Here's the lowdown on your choices:

- **Kerberos and CRAM-MD5** are the most secure authentication methods. To use Kerberos for mail, you need Snow Leopard set up for Kerberos authentication in Open Directory or on another server. Of the two, Apple recommends Kerberos.
- **APOP** is an encryption type used only for POP clients.
- **Login, Clear, and Plain** are unsecure authentication methods that send passwords unencrypted. If you choose these in addition to the more secure authentication methods, clients that don't have the more secure methods set up are allowed to log in without encryption. If you deselect these unencrypted options, these clients can't log in until they're configured for encryption.

Securing e-mail messages with SSL

The preceding methods encrypt only passwords and usernames. You can also encrypt e-mail itself with the Secure Sockets Layer (SSL) section in the lower part of the window in Figure 14-12. For POP and IMAP, SSL encryption is between your server and your clients. For SMTP, SSL encryption is between your server and other e-mail servers.

To use SSL, click the pop-up menu for SMTP or the menu for IMAP and POP, as shown in Figure 14-12. If you choose Require, the mail service won't connect if the client or other Mail server isn't supporting SSL.

If you choose Use, SSL encryption is used if a POP or IMAP client asks for it. If a client isn't set up to request an SSL connection, the Mail service can still deliver mail to that client. The Use setting works the same with SMTP and other Mail servers: For Mail servers that don't request SSL, Snow Leopard Server's mail service sends mail unencrypted.

In the pop-up menus to the right, you can choose to select a certificate or to not use a certificate. You can use the Certificate Manager in Server Admin to import a certificate from a certificate authority or create a certificate signing request and a keychain. To access the Certificate Manager in Server Admin, click your server in the left column and then click the Certificate icon in the toolbar. See Chapter 18 for information about certificates.

Blocking Spam and Other Nasty Bits

Using Server Admin's Mail Settings window to set spam and virus blocking is similar to using Configuration Assistant, but it gives you more choices than in Server Preferences.

Here's how to bring up the Settings window for configuring filtering:

1. **In Server Admin, click the triangle to the left of your server to expand the list of services.**
2. **Click Mail from the list; then click the Settings icon in the toolbar.**
3. **Click the Filters tab.**

   You see the window in Figure 14-13.

The following sections describe the choices here and give some advice. Remember to click the Save button after you configure your settings.

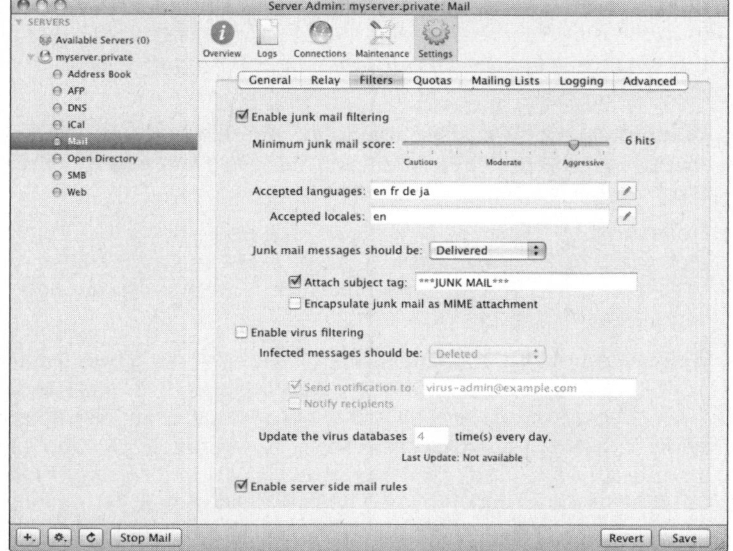

Figure 14-13: Server Admin's spam and virus filter window.

Statistical spam filtering

At the top of the Server Admin Filters window (refer to Figure 14-13) is the Minimum Junk Mail Score slider bar, the same one you see in Configuration Assistant and Server Preferences. How you set it is really a matter of philosophy. Setting the slider toward the left (Cautious) lets more spam get through to users, where their own spam filters deal with it. Setting it toward the right (Aggressive) sends fewer junk mail messages to users but could trap more legitimate e-mail (false positives). If the server filters legitimate e-mail, users don't know about it. I tend to be conservative in setting server-based spam filtering, but it might be more secure to accept more false positives and prevent phishing e-mail from getting to users.

Snow Leopard Server's junk mail filtering uses a statistical method known as *Bayesian filtering.* For example, instead of stopping every message with the word *loan,* it takes into consideration the context of the message and the frequency of the word used in known spam. Bayesian filtering assigns a probability that's calculated on past history based on a mathematical formula. This results in high accuracy in detection and low false positive IDs.

What you do with filtered mail can help you decide how aggressive you want to get with filtering. The Junk Mail Messages Should Be pop-up menu in Figure 14-13 gives you four choices:

- **Bounced:** Sends the message back to the sender. I don't recommend this because it usually doesn't help and could invite a malicious attack. With this setting, you have the option of sending a notification to an e-mail address.
- **Deleted:** Saves hard drive space but eliminates the possibility of ever retrieving false positives. This setting also gives you the option to send a notification to an e-mail address.
- **Delivered:** Delivers the message to the user with a warning in the subject (such as ***JUNK MAIL***). I like this setting because it lets the user look through it for false positives. You can also encode the message as an attachment for extra security.
- **Redirected:** Sends the e-mail to another address. This could be an address for an administrator, who could look through it for false positives. The downside is that this takes a lot of hard drive space, given the flood of spam that everyone gets.

You can also block all e-mail from a known spam server. In the left column of Server Admin, under your server, click Mail, click the Settings icon in the toolbar, and then click the Relay tab. You can then type in the IP address of one or more known spammers.

Spam filtering exceptions by country or language

Below the slider in the Server Admin spam and virus filter window are settings for accepted languages and locales (refer to Figure 14-13). These are exceptions to the Bayesian filtering rules. For instance, the spam filter often categorizes all e-mail with non-roman typefaces as junk mail. If you routinely get legitimate e-mail in the Korean language, you can use the Accepted Locales setting to enable e-mail with a Korean country code to get through. The Accepted Languages list lets through e-mail written in different specific languages that you might receive.

Click the pencil icon to bring up a new window for selecting additional languages or locales.

Virus filtering

The Enable Virus Filtering setting in the Server Admin spam and virus filter window (refer to Figure 14-13) looks at e-mail using a different method than it uses for spam. It uses the open source ClamAV (`www.clamav.net`) software to keep track of known malicious e-mail viruses, worms, and other malware and is automatically updated regularly. You can set how often the virus database is updated in the Update the Virus Databases box at the bottom of the window.

You can tell the server what to do with the virus e-mail in the Infected Messages Should Be pop-up menu. You get three of the four options that are found in the junk mail filtering section:

- **Bounced:** I don't recommend the Bounced setting because it usually doesn't help and could invite a malicious attack.
- **Deleted:** Lets you notify the user or any e-mail address that a suspected virus has been deleted. Most people should use this setting.
- **Redirected:** Sends the suspected infected e-mail to an e-mail address.

For whatever reason, fewer viruses are written for Macs than for Windows PCs. However, your Mac e-mail server can just as easily pass malware to your Windows clients as any other server. And, you don't want to risk your Mac clients getting infected with the viruses that do exist.

Configuring User Accounts for E-Mail

If you've finished setting up the mail and DNS services, congratulations. But don't rest just yet. You need to enable user accounts to access mail. If you're using Server Preferences, do this:

1. **Click the Users icon and then select a user.**

   Server Preferences doesn't let you select more than one user.

2. **Make sure the Mail check box is selected.**

If you're using Workgroup Manager to manage users, you need to open Workgroup Manager and enable the user accounts to send and receive e-mail:

1. **In Workgroup Manager, click the Accounts icon in the toolbar.**
2. **Click the Mail tab and then select the multiple users you're mail enabling.**

   You can use standard Mac methods for selecting multiple names:

   - ⌘-click each name you want to select.
   - Double-click a name to select it and then press the ⌘-A keys to select all the names. Then ⌘-click any names you want to deselect, such as administrators or user accounts previously configured.

3. **In the Mail tab, click the Enabled option (as shown in Figure 14-14).**
4. **In the Mail Server field, type the domain name of the server (`myserver.acme.com`, for instance).**
5. **Select Both POP and IMAP, POP Only, or IMAP Only.**
6. **Click the Save button in the lower right.**

In the Mail Quota box, you can set the maximum amount of storage space that you want to allow for each user.

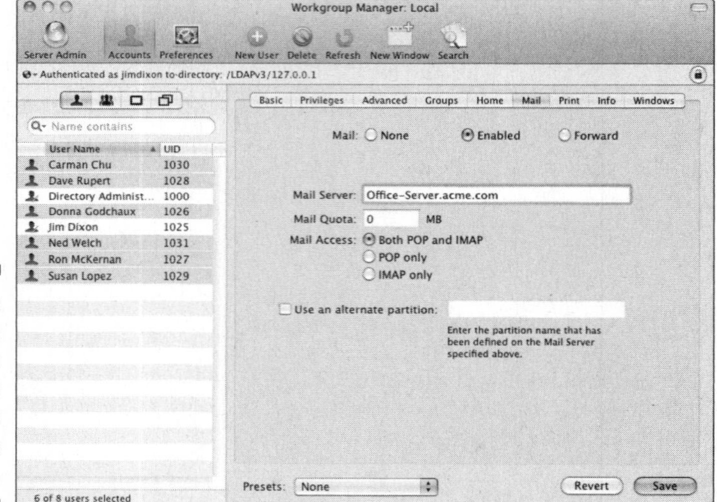

Figure 14-14: Enabling users to access e-mail in Workgroup Manager.

Creating New User E-Mail Addresses

When you create a user account, Snow Leopard Server automatically creates an e-mail address based on the short name followed by the domain name; for instance: `ronmckernan@acme.com`.

You can create additional e-mail addresses for any user. For instance, you might assign `info@acme.com` to a user responsible for a public Web site.

To create an alternate e-mail address for a user, you must use Workgroup Manager. Here's how:

1. **In Workgroup Manager, click the Accounts icon in the toolbar.**
2. **Click the globe icon below the toolbar on the left and select the account's directory domain.**

3. **Select the user from the list on the left.**
4. **Click the Basic tab.**
5. **Double-click in the empty space in the Short Names list box, as shown in Figure 14-15, and then type an alias that you want to use in the e-mail address for the selected user.**

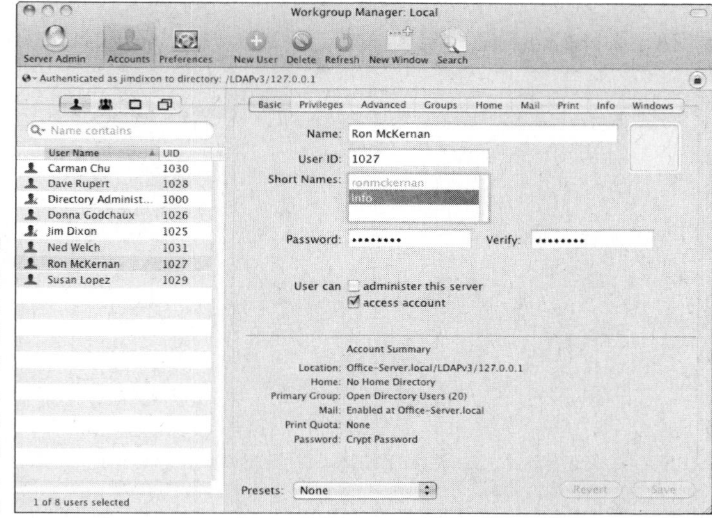

Figure 14-15: To create a new e-mail address for a user, create an additional short name.

If virtual host is enabled, type the full e-mail address (for instance, `info@acme.com`).

6. **Click the Save button.**

Setting Up a Mailing List

Mailings lists, or *listservs,* are a good way to enable group discussions via e-mail. When a member of the listserv sends a message to the list address, it gets delivered to all the members. To create a listserv, use Server Admin:

1. **In Server Admin, click the triangle to the left of your server to expand the list of services.**
2. **Click Mail from the list; then click the Settings icon in the toolbar.**
3. **Click the Mailing Lists tab and select the Enable Mailman Mailing Lists check box.**

4. **In the new dialog that appears (see Figure 14-16), type a master password and the e-mail addresses of users who can administer the mailing lists set up on this server.**

   List administrators don't have to have access to Server Admin: They administer the list by going to this Web page:

   yourserver.yourdomain.tld/mailman/listinfo

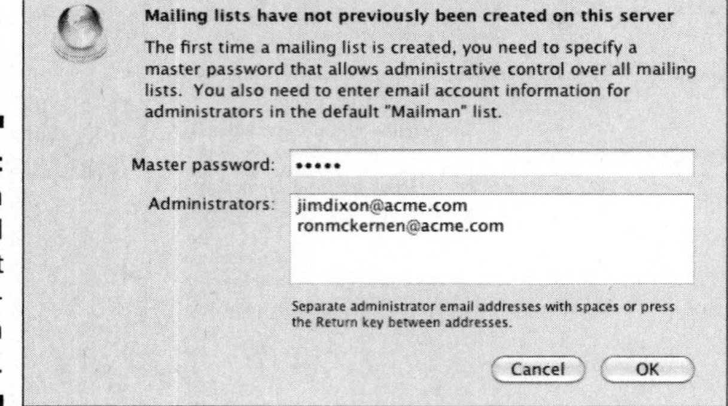
Mailing lists have not previously been created on this server
The first time a mailing list is created, you need to specify a master password that allows administrative control over all mailing lists. You also need to enter email account information for administrators in the default "Mailman" list.
Master password: •••••
Administrators: jimdixon@acme.com
ronmckernen@acme.com
Separate administrator email addresses with spaces or press the Return key between addresses.
Cancel
OK

Figure 14-16: Setting a password and list administrators for a mailing list.

5. **Click OK and then click the Add (+) button below the Mailing Lists list box to add a mailing list.**
6. **In the new dialog that appears (see Figure 14-17), type a list name and an administrator.**
7. **(Optional) Enable users to self-subscribe and choose a language.**

   The Maximum Length of a Message Body is, by default, set to 40KB, which is a bit limiting. Keeping this low saves hard drive space.

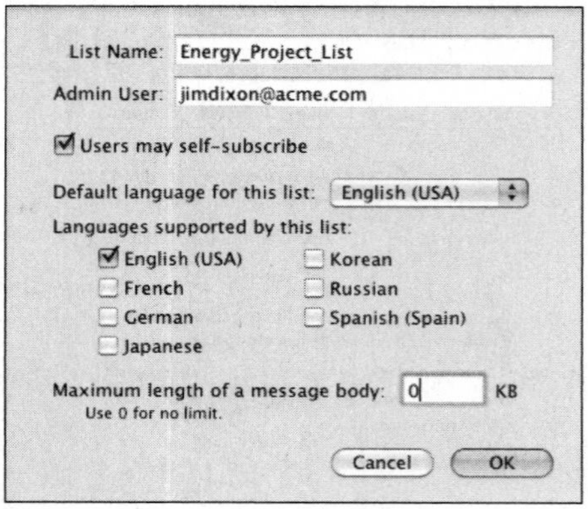

List Name: Energy_Project_List
Admin User: jimdixon@acme.com
Users may self-subscribe
Default language for this list: English (USA)
Languages supported by this list:
English (USA)
Korean
French
Russian
German
Spanish (Spain)
Japanese
Maximum length of a message body: 0 KB
Use 0 for no limit.
Cancel
OK

Figure 14-17: Naming the mail list and setting how it works.

8. **Click OK.**

   The new list appears in the main Mailing Lists pane (see Figure 14-18).

9. **Select it and click the Users & Groups button in the lower right.**

10. **When the Users & Groups window appears, drag the names of people you want to be members of the list into the main window.**

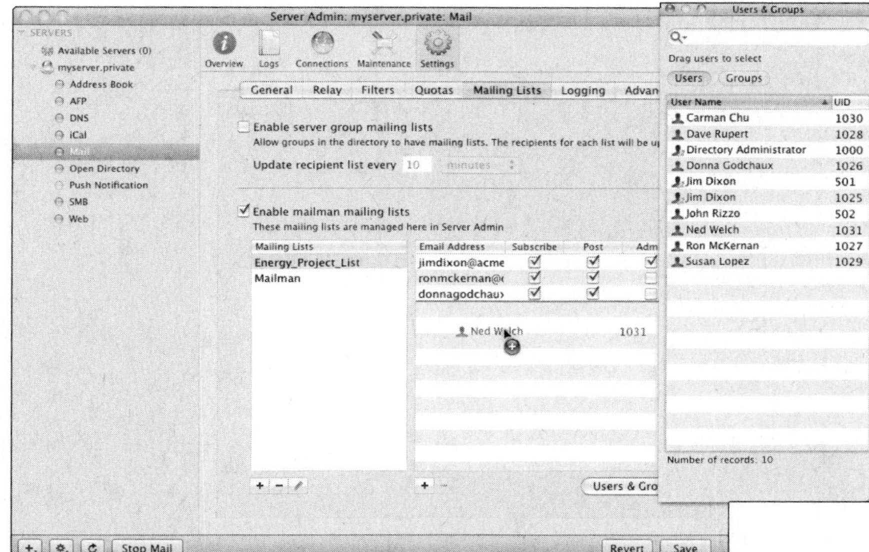

Figure 14-18: Drag users from the list into the main window to add them to the listserv.

11. **Click the Save button.**

Snow Leopard Server uses Mailman open source software to provide mailing lists. For more information about the features and roles for users, list administrators, and server administrators, check here: `www.list.org/docs.html`.

Chapter 15

More Collaboration: iChat and Podcast Producer

In This Chapter

- Getting ready for iChat Server
- Customizing iChat Server
- Understanding and setting up Podcast Producer

Some of Snow Leopard Server's built-in goodies may not be central to everyone's mission, but can be of great value to groups who can use them. If you take a look at this chapter, you may find yourself in the latter group, as we explore iChat Server and Podcast Producer.

iChat Server is a collaborative tool for brainstorming sessions, virtual meetings, video conferencing, and file sharing. One way to think of iChat Server is as a live version of the wiki tools I describe in Chapter 13.

Podcast Producer has been revamped and supercharged in Snow Leopard Server. But don't let the *Pod* in *Pod*cast Producer fool you — it's not about iPods. Podcast Producer is an automated video production system that yields professional results. Use it to create training videos, classroom projects, or tech support resources and to distribute your work automatically.

iChat Instant Messaging and More

iChat Server provides instant messaging, audio and video conferencing, and file transferring; it supports Mac, Windows, and Linux clients as well as mobile phones. iChat works on a person-to-person basis and in multi-user situations. iChat Server can also create *persistent chat rooms,* which let participants leave or log off. When they return, they can see everything that happened in their absence. Users can send chat messages to other users who are offline. iChat also acts as a kind of automatic note-taking service because users can generate chat transcripts. On the server, you can log chat text so that the administrator can read it or forward it to a group that needs it.

iChat service is private and secure, using Secure Sockets Layer (SSL) encryption. Users have accounts in (and are authenticated by) the Open Directory domain, which means they can use iChat services from any computer and still see their buddy lists, groups, and other information.

Snow Leopard Server's iChat service is compatible with a number of instant messaging servers and clients. iChat service is based on the open standard Extensible Messaging and Presence Protocol (XMPP), also called Jabber, which is used in the Jabber and Google Talk servers. This compatibility enables iChat Server to communicate (or federate) with other XMPP servers or domains, including Google Talk, to enable users of both to interact. XMPP support also means that the server supports Jabber clients on any platform.

Clients for iChat Server

For Macs, the iChat client application is the best to use and most trouble free, seamlessly accessing all iChat's features. iChat Server works with older versions of the iChat client as well as the latest and greatest. There are also a number of other clients for Macs as well.

For Windows, Linux, Unix, and mobile phones, you can use any instant messaging client that supports XMPP or is Jabber compatible. Instant messaging clients often support multiple protocols. There are a lot of XMPP clients, and more are popping up all the time. If you're looking for an open source client for Mac OS X, Windows, and Linux, try Pidgen (`www.pidgin.im`) or Spark (`www.igniterealtime.org/projects/spark/index.jsp`). Trillian (`www.ceruleanstudios.com`) is a Windows commercial product with a free version and a $25 pro version.

For longer lists of XMPP-compatible clients, check out `http://xmpp.org/software/clients.shtml`.

Reality check: Not all XMPP clients and servers communicate as smoothly with iChat service. You may find versions of XMPP software that have some issues, and you may find some that work more smoothly than others. Do a little testing before distributing a chat client to all your users.

Prerequisites

Before you set up iChat service, you need to take care of several network items. Quite likely, your network already has some of these things:

- **Open Directory configuration:** To authenticate users, iChat uses Open Directory (or another Lightweight Directory Access Protocol [LDAP] server) bound to the iChat server. iChat Server doesn't directly access the LDAP server. iChat users must have directory accounts in a directory domain. (See Chapter 6 for information on Open Directory.)

  You also need an Open Directory master to allow authentication with Kerberos or to use a Kerberos domain controller on another server. If you use the latter, the Kerberos realms of the controller and the iChat Server must match.
- **Firewall ports:** If your iChat users are crossing a firewall to get to the server, you have to open some firewall ports. This is true for any service, but iChat requires a relatively large number of firewall ports to be open. (See Chapter 18 for more on firewalls.)
- **Internet routers:** If you want Internet users to access iChat service on your server and you have a DSL, cable router, or other Internet router, you need to configure it for port forwarding.

Turning on iChat service

Before you adjust any settings for the iChat service, you need to turn it on. You can use Server Preferences or Server Admin to do this. The easiest way is to use Server Preferences. Just click the iChat icon and click the big switch to the On position. Server Preferences offers two settings: Log and Archive All Chats and Enable Server-to-Server Communication.

In Server Admin, the procedure is the same as with other services:

1. **Open Server Admin and select the server in the left column.**
2. **Click Settings in the toolbar and then click the Services tab.**
3. **Make sure the iChat check box is selected and then click Save.**

To enable user access, you need to start iChat service to get it running:

1. **In Server Admin, click the triangle next to your server in the left column to expand the list of services.**
2. **Select iChat from the list.**
3. **Click the Start iChat button in the lower left of the window.**

The server automatically assigns chat names (or Jabber names) to users. These are in the form of `*shortname@host.domain*`, such as `jimdixon@server.ourshcool.edu`. You can view the Jabber names by choosing Server Preferences⇨Users⇨Contact. You can also click the Add (+) button to add names for AIM, MSN, ICQ, and Yahoo.

Changing iChat service's default settings

To change the default settings of iChat Server, you mostly use Server Admin. Most of iChat configuration is in the General tab of iChat Settings:

1. **In Server Admin, click the triangle next to your server in the left column to expand the list of services and then select iChat.**
2. **Click the Settings icon in the toolbar and then click the General tab.**

   You see the window shown in Figure 15-1.

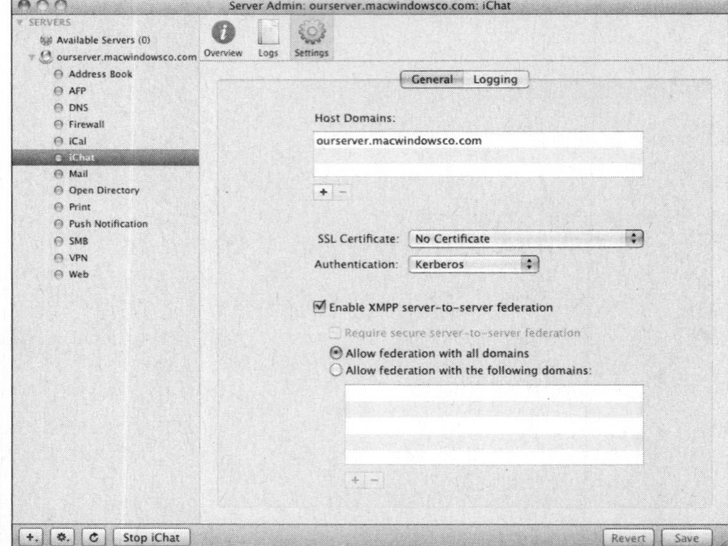

Figure 15-1: The General tab of iChat Settings, with default settings.

The next few sections use this General tab. After that, I describe using Server Preferences for autobuddy support.

Adding host domains

The default entry in the Host Domains field is the server host. You can use the Add (+) button to add other hostnames for use by iChat, as long as DNS is configured to resolve the names to the iChat Server IP address. (You can also add IP addresses in this field if you need to resolve a problem.)

Security and authentication

The SSL Certificate pop-up menu lets you select an SSL certificate for data encryption. The default is No Certificate. (See Chapter 18 for information on certificates.)

The Authentication pop-up menu gives you three choices: Standard provides for CRAM-MD5, a type of password authentication; Kerberos means iChat Server accepts only Kerberos; and Any Method means the server will accept either, depending on what the client is configured for.

If users authenticate with Active Directory credentials (iChat Server is bound to Active Directory), iChat clients can't authenticate with CRAM-MD5. One way around this is to set iChat Server's Authentication pop-up menu to Kerberos (not Any Method or Standard). However, this doesn't work if you have chat clients that don't support Kerberos (such as Mac OS X 10.4 Tiger). If that's the case, you have to set the Authentication pop-up menu to Any Method and disable CRAM-MD5 to force plain text authentication. Disabling CRAM-MD5 requires you to edit a file (`/etc/jabberd/c2s.xml`) and use Terminal to restart the jabberd service. Also, if you make a change after you do this and restart iChat, CRAM-MD5 is re-enabled. Apple has details here: `www.info.apple.com/kbnum/n306749`.

Saving and archiving chat messages

When you click the Logging tab (*not* the Logs icon in the toolbar) in Figure 15-1, you see an option to automatically save chat messages. This is the same setting as in Server Preferences. The difference here is that you can change the location of the files (the default is `/var/jabberd/message_archives`). The other option, Archive Saved Messages Every *x* Days, is an additional step that compresses older chat files.

Server-to-server federation

Server-to-server (S2S) communication, known as *S2S federation,* enables communications with other XMPP servers, including Google Talk, Jabber, and other iChat Servers, as long as the servers are visible to the Internet. Users of each federated server can communicate with each other.

Selecting the Enable XMPP Server-to-Server Federation check box turns on S2S (see Figure 15-1). You then have a choice of Allow Federation with All Domains, which lets your users connect to a user on any XMPP server, or Allow Federation with the Following Domains. The latter choice restricts access to domains or complete server hostnames that you add with the Add (+) button. (You can have both domains and server names in this list.)

You can require S2S sessions to use encryption by selecting the Require Secure Server-to-Server Federation check box and choosing an SSL certificate. With this setting, iChat Server blocks a user from connecting to a user in another domain if the latter doesn't support encryption. The other server must also be using a public key certificate.

Turning autobuddy support on and off

With the autobuddy feature turned on, all iChat Servers in a particular group are added automatically to everyone else's buddy list. The upside is that users don't have to add buddies manually. The downside is that if users remove buddies from their list, autobuddy adds them back. You can use only Server Preferences to turn autobuddy on:

1. **Open Server Preferences and click the Groups icon.**
2. **Select a group that will use autobuddy.**
3. **Select the iChat Autobuddy List check box.**

If you start autobuddy while iChat users are logged in, they can't communicate with the added buddies until the user first logs out and in again.

Podcast Producer

Podcast Producer is an automated video and audio workflow system that you can use to create and distribute lectures, presentations, training, tech support videos, classroom projects, and software demos. When I say automated, I'm not exaggerating. After Podcast Producer is set up, users can record video, send it to the server, and then wait for it to appear on a Web site or in iTunes's podcasting section. Educators can have Podcast Producer publish to Apple's iTunes U, part of the iTunes store, for mass distribution to students. (For more on iTunes U, see `www.apple.com/support/itunes_u`.)

Podcast Producer is an assembly line: Users put in raw video, and it gets processed and published. While processing, Podcast Producer can encode video in formats for computers or iPhones. Podcast Producer automatically adds introductory and closing videos, titles, and effects; it can even add watermarks or overlays, such as logos or graphics, to the video.

What the assembly line does to the video or audio is defined in *workflows,* which are lists of tasks that the system will perform on the inputted content. You can edit default workflows or you can create your own. The workflow also defines the encoding and output.

Because Podcast Producer is server-based, multiple users can input audio and video content over the network. The server can control access to cameras on the network. Snow Leopard Server's Xgrid service can farm out video encoding tasks to multiple Macs on the network. Podcast Producer can publish the finished video to network resources, including Snow Leopard Server's wiki-based Web site and its QuickTime Streaming Server.

New features

Snow Leopard Server comes with Podcast Producer 2, which is greatly enhanced over version 1. To start with, setup is more automated than before. Users of Windows, Linux, and older versions of Mac OS X can now input content with a Web browser, as can iPhone users. Users can now have two video sources and place a video inside a box *(picture-in-picture)* with a canned template or one you create. Also, a new graphical workflow editor creates workflows. Another major new feature is Podcast Library, which stores and organizes content.

What's in Podcast Producer

Podcast Producer 2 is a collection of software, some of which does have a user interface, and some of which doesn't. Knowing about the bits that you don't see is helpful in understanding what Podcast Producer does and how it does it:

- **The Podcast Producer service:** This ties everything together; it passes authentication to the directory service that receives content from users and forwards information to where it needs to be.
- **Podcast Capture application:** This is software for Mac OS X 10.6 clients to use to record audio and video and to send them to the server. You can record from a remote camera controlled by the server or from the built-in camera on the Mac. Podcast Capture can also record what's happening on the computer screen. Podcast Capture can also send QuickTime movies and audio to Podcast Producer for processing and distribution. You can find it in the /Applications/Utilities/ folder.
- **Podcast Capture Web application:** This server-based technology enables users of any operating system to record video and then send it to the Podcast Producer service. The Podcast Capture Web application can't record the computer screen activity. There is nothing to install on users' computers. Users simply access a Web page on the server.
- **Podcast Composer application:** Podcast Composer is what you use to create and edit workflows; it guides you through the steps needed. You can choose intro titles, intro and ending videos, watermarks, and effects, or you can add your own. You specify the workflow and the publishing and distribution method: wiki, iTunes U, or Podcast Library. Look for Podcast Composer in the /Applications/Server/ folder.
- **Podcast Library:** Podcast Library is a shared file system that holds the workflows and job submissions as well as a set of software routines. The Library stores the content submitted by users as well as the rendered content generated by Xgrid. Podcast Library organizes all this based on information about the job that the user supplies in Podcast Capture.

Podcast Library is also a server that distributes content to the viewers — customers, employees, or students. Podcast Library sends out lists of updates as feeds viewable in Safari, Mail, or any RSS reader. Podcast Producer can also send Atom feeds to iTunes or iTunes U, which are visible in the iTunes Store but leave the content on your server. An Atom feed contains multiple versions of the podcast that have been encoded for different devices (computer, iPod, Apple TV, and audio-only). The viewer's device chooses what it needs.

- **The Xgrid service:** Xgrid does the grunt work of Podcast Producer — putting together the pieces, rendering transitions, and encoding the video. Because video encoding is a processor-and-memory-intensive task, Xgrid can send the jobs out to an Xgrid cluster that you set up, which consists of one or more Macs on the network.

The workflow that you create in Podcast Composer is actually a property list (`.plist` file) containing tasks for Xgrid to execute. The Xgrid service creates an Xgrid user that has privileges for certain files and folders. The Xgrid user is the owner of the Podcast Library shared file system.

Xgrid is actually a service apart from Podcast Library and is designed to be used for any processor-intensive task. Podcast Producer puts it to practical use for you without any heavy lifting on your part.

In the following sections, I cover some of the major points about getting Podcast Producer up and running on your server.

Prerequisites

Podcast Producer requires a couple things to be set on your network. First, it needs DNS reverse lookup, either on this server or on another server on the network.

If you don't mind typing a one-line command in the Terminal utility, you can verify easily that DNS forward and reverse lookup is configured correctly. Type this, exactly:

```
sudo changeip -checkhostname
```

If forward and reverse DNS is working correctly, you see this, but with your server information:

```
Primary address      = 192.168.1.69
Current HostName     = ourserver.macwindowsco.com
DNS HostName         = ourserver.macwindowsco.com
The names match. There is nothing to change.
dirserv:success = "success"
```

The second thing Podcast Producer needs on the network is Open Directory, Active Directory, or another LDAP server to authenticate users. This requires your server Mac to be running an Open Directory master or to be bound to a kerberized directory.

To support Active Directory, you need to edit a `.plist` file. To see how to do this, see the section "Mac OS X Server 10.5.6 or later" in the following Apple article: `http://support.apple.com/kb/HT3289`.

Turning on and setting up Podcast Producer service

The procedure for getting Podcast Producer running is different than for other services. You turn it on like other services, but you can't start the service until you run Setup Assistant. The Podcast Producer Setup Assistant configures the Podcast Producer settings, starts the Library file system and the Xgrid service, assigns an Xgrid username, and connects to the directory.

Enable Podcast Producer using the same procedure as other services:

1. **Open Server Admin and select the server in the left column.**
2. **Click the Settings icon in the toolbar and then click the Services tab.**
3. **Make sure the Podcast Producer check box is selected and click the Save button.**

Launch the Podcast Producer Setup Assistant by starting the service:

1. **In Server Admin, click the triangle next to your server in the left column to expand the list of services.**
2. **Select Podcast Producer from the list.**
3. **Click the Start Podcast Producer button.**

   A dialog slides down asking if you want to use the Setup Assistant or just start without running the assistant.
4. **Click the Start Assistant button to launch Producer Setup Assistant.**
5. **Click through the introductory window.**

   You now have a choice between Express or Standard setup, as shown in Figure 15-2. Express automatically configures and turns on the needed services. With Standard setup, you have to type in information. I recommend using Express and making changes later.

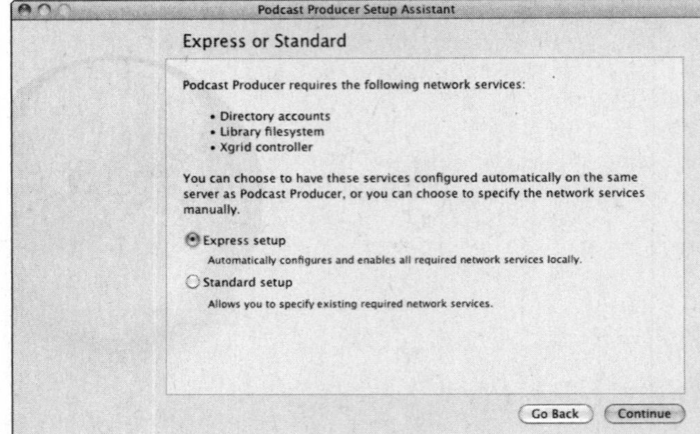

Figure 15-2: The Podcast Producer Setup Assistant.

6. **Click the Express Setup option.**

   With either the Standard or Express choice, Podcast Producer Setup Assistant checks your directory to see whether a Kerberos-supported directory service exists.

7. **Take the appropriate action in one of two screens that you may see:**

   a. *Click Continue if the assistant reports that it has found an Open Directory master on the server or if it detects that your server is bound to a kerberized directory.*

      This enables Podcast Producer to use the directory service.

   b. *If you're prompted to set up an Open Directory master or Kerberize your directory, enter a directory administrator name, short name, and password and then click the Continue button.*

8. **Click Continue at the Confirm window, which display the settings the Assistant has made.**

   Podcast Producer Assistant tells you whether the setup succeeded or failed.

9. **Click OK to one of the two possible responses from the Assistant:**

   a. *A dialog says it succeeded.*

   b. *A dialog says it failed and asks whether you want to try to fix the problem or run the assistant again.*

When complete, a Summary screen appears telling you that Podcast Producer has been configured and started.

To bring back the Podcast Producer Setup Assistant later, click the Overview icon in the toolbar and then click the Configure Podcast Producer button.

Managing cameras

After Podcast Producer is set up and running, you can add cameras and restrict access to them. The cameras are plugged into Mac OS X 10.6 computers on the network or are built-in cameras in Macs. The process of adding the cameras to the Podcast Producer server is *binding* the Macs to the server. You do this from the Podcast Capture application on the Macs. (You can't use the Podcast Capture Web interface.)

Binding Macs to the server

To bind a Mac to the Podcast Producer server, open Podcast Capture on the Mac that has the camera you want to use and do the following:

1. **Choose the Podcast Producer server when prompted, and enter a username and password.**
2. **Open Preferences from the Podcast Producer menu.**
3. **Click the Audio/Video icon in the toolbar.**
4. **Choose a Mac camera from the Video Source pop-up menu.**

   Make sure you see an image from the camera in the preview area.
5. **Choose an audio source from the Microphone pop-up menu and then click the Start Sharing button.**
6. **In the dialog that appears, enter a name for the camera.**

   The server and your username display in the dialog.
7. **Click the Start Sharing button in the dialog.**

You can do this for multiple cameras on a Mac and for multiple Macs. The cameras you add appear in Server Admin.

Limiting access to cameras

By default, all server users have access to all cameras listed in Server Admin. For Macs used by one person, you may want to restrict access to that person. You can limit access to cameras in Server Admin:

1. **Click the triangle next to your server in the left column to expand the list of services.**
2. **Select Podcast Producer from the list and click the Cameras icon on the toolbar, as shown in Figure 15-3.**
3. **Select a camera from the list.**
4. **Select Allow Access to *Camera Name* for the Following Users and Groups.**

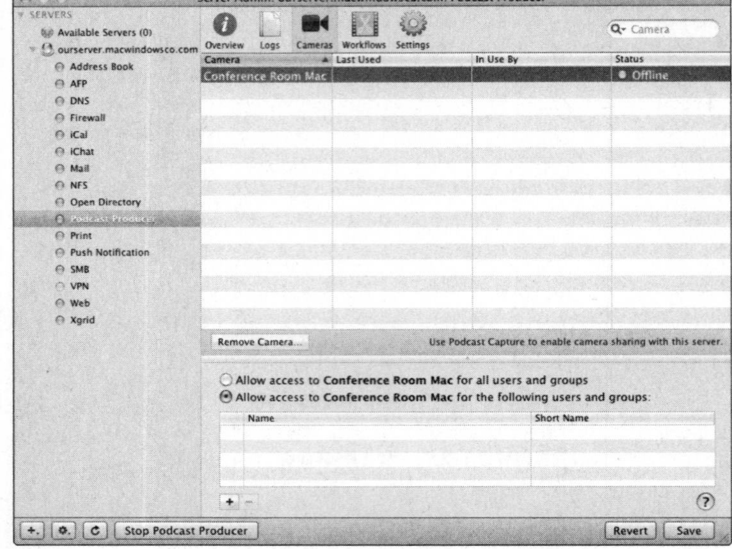

Figure 15-3: Server Admin's Podcast Producer Cameras window.

5. **Click the Add (+) button to add users and groups to the list.**
6. **Click the Save button.**

You can re-enable all users to access a selected camera by selecting Allow Access to *Camera Name* for All Users and Groups.

Opening the Web-based Podcast Capture

After Podcast Composer is set up, Podcast Capture is one of the four items on the home page of the built-in Web site, which I describe in Chapter 13. (The others are My Page, Wikis, and Blogs.) If you haven't disabled the home page, a user can get to it by typing the server's IP address or domain name in a browser's address bar. Click Podcast Capture, and you see the same interface as the standalone Podcast Capture application.

Another way to access the Podcast Capture Web application from a Web browser is to enter `https://`*`server`*`:8170/podcastproducer/capture`, where *server* can be the server's IP address or full domain name.

Part V
Managing Clients

"Sales on the Web site are down. I figure the server's chi is blocked, so we're fudgin' around the feng shui in the computer room, and if that doesn't work, Ronnie's got a chant that should do it."

In this part . . .

The more computers you have in your organization, the more there is the need to manage them centrally. You can keep accounts up-to-date and keep track of notebook computers. Central enforcement of policies can prevent troubleshooting of clients.

But it's not about authoritarian control and being the big network boss. Well, okay, there is some of that. But client management also has user benefits. A server-based home folder allows a user to access a home folder from any computer. Notebook computer users can get the benefits of a directory domain even when not connected to the network.

Client management is based on directory services, which I describe in Part II. You may want to review those chapters if you haven't yet set up your directory.

In this part, I cover the concepts for managing desktop and mobile accounts and take you through the steps you need to make it all work.

In Chapter 18, I switch gears a bit, moving on to secure remote client access to the network and other security issues. This is client management in the sense of keeping control of security, which protects the client computers as well as the server. Kind of like your own homeland security, but without having to take off your shoes.

Chapter 16

Managing Client Accounts

In This Chapter

- Types of accounts on Mac OS X Server
- Looking at Server Preferences versus Workgroup Manager
- Creating, managing, and deleting accounts in Server Preferences
- Managing various accounts in Workgroup Manager
- Importing and exporting accounts in Workgroup Manager
- Setting managed preferences for Mac OS X clients

When you install Snow Leopard Server, Server Assistant creates a local directory of accounts containing the initial local administrator account. After the initial account, you can create more local accounts with System Preferences — this process is identical to managing accounts in Mac OS X clients.

After you decide to move on to a shared directory of accounts, you can create an Open Directory shared domain, as described in Chapter 6. After a shared directory is created in Mac OS X Snow Leopard Server, use Server Preferences or Workgroup Manager to create and manage accounts.

User, Group, and Computer Accounts

Snow Leopard Server has three types of accounts: user, group, and computer accounts. User accounts aren't necessarily individual people; more than one person may have access to a particular user account, such as a shared administrator account. A user account, identified by a single silhouetted person's bust, has a long name, a short name, a password, and a user ID (UID) number. Depending on the type of user account, you can assign other attributes, such as the user's home folder location.

In the local directory of the Mac OS X client, the first UID is 501. In a network Open Directory domain, the first UID is 1025. System-level users, like `root` (UID 0) or the directory administrator default (UID 1000) generally have lower level numbers.

A number of individual user accounts, when combined, become a group account. Group accounts have Group IDs (GID). Groups make it possible to better manage access to resources on a larger scale. In Snow Leopard Server, many collaboration services, including wikis, blogs, and shared folders, can be accessed with group accounts.

Computers bound to the shared directory can have associated computer accounts. Putting computer accounts together creates a computer group, similar to a group of users. The importance of computer accounts and computer groups is evident in the section, "Setting Managed Preferences for Mac OS X Clients," later in this chapter.

Server Preferences versus Workgroup Manager

Snow Leopard Server has two types of functions to manage: services and accounts. You can use the simple Server Preferences tool to manage both. Server Preferences has a simple interface that hides details that you may not need to bother with. For more advanced management, you can use Server Admin for services and Workgroup Manager for accounts.

Workgroup Manager provides access to settings that aren't available in Server Preferences and allows for editing the raw data in the Lightweight Directory Access Protocol (LDAP) database (see Chapter 5). Workgroup Manager manages user and group accounts, computer accounts, and computer lists and manages preferences for accounts in the shared domain.

Unlike Mac OS X Server 10.5, Snow Leopard Server lets you use both Server Preferences and Workgroup Manager. But although Apple has endeavored to make the two interoperable, not all the settings in Workgroup Manager translate to the simplified interface of Server Preferences.

After your Open Directory domain grows to a master server and one or more replica servers, connect Server Preferences or Workgroup Manager to the master server only. Replicas and bound servers contain read-only user databases that can't be modified by the server tools.

Managing Accounts in Server Preferences

In Snow Leopard Server, Server Preferences is preconfigured to connect automatically to the server it's installed on. If you're running Server Preferences from another system or you've changed the hostname of the server post-installation, do the following in Server Preferences:

1. **Choose Connection⇨New Connection and type the hostname of the server in the Server field.**
2. **Enter the administrator's username and password.**
3. **Click the Connect button.**

For best results, always enter the server's fully qualified hostname in the Server field, usually in the form of `server.example.com`, or `server.local` if you entered this form when you installed Snow Leopard Server because DNS isn't running on your network. The `.local` domain denotes *Bonjour* networking, Apple's zero-configuration host-to-host networking protocol.

Creating, deleting, and managing user accounts in Server Preferences

To create and manage user accounts in Server Preferences, click the Users icon. For group accounts, click the Groups icon. You see the window shown in Figure 16-1.

Figure 16-1: The list of user accounts in Server Preferences.

If you haven't yet set up an Open Directory domain, clicking either the Users or Groups icon displays a screen you use to set up an Open Directory master; see Chapter 6. To add user accounts, do the following:

1. **In Server Preferences, click the Users icon.**
2. **Click the Add (+) button in the lower-left corner to add a new user.**
3. **Enter the new user's name, as shown in Figure 16-2.**

   A short name is generated automatically, but you can edit it. Short names don't contain spaces, although they can contain punctuation including periods, underscores, and hyphens.

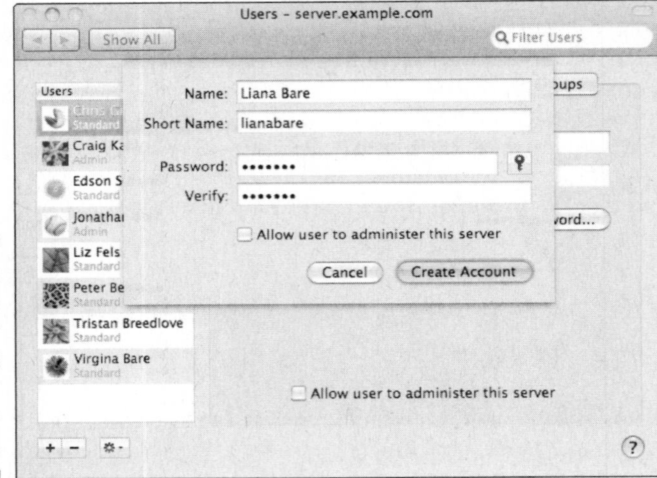

Figure 16-2: Adding a new user account in Server Preferences.

4. **Enter a password.**

   You can click the key icon next to the Password field to open the Password Assistant, which generates random passwords and tests password strength.

5. **(Optional) Select the Allow User to Administer This Server check box if you wish to grant the user full administrative privileges to control services, modify accounts, change passwords, and install software on the server.**

   You can create limited administrators with Workgroup Manager, as I detail in the section, "Creating user accounts with Workgroup Manager," later in this chapter.

6. **Click the Create Account button.**

The Users pane of Server Preferences gives you the option to view or change some additional settings. Many of these settings are created automatically:

- **Account tab:** To change the user's account icon, click the white square to the left of the Name and Short Name field. Select a picture from the pop-up list, or click Edit Picture... to select a custom icon for the user.
- **Contact Info tab:** This lets you add a street address, phone numbers, and other information about a user. If you enabled mail and chat during server setup, the user's e-mail and chat addresses are shown here. The Add (+) button under the Contact field lets you add new fields. Contact info is added to the database record for the user.
- **Services tab:** This displays seven services (File, iCal, Address Book, iChat, Mail, VPN, and Time Machine). Selecting or deselecting these boxes grants or denies (respectively) a user's ability to access a service. To add or remove a user from a service that isn't listed here, use Server Admin to configure service access control lists (SACL). I describe how to do this in Chapter 9.
- **Groups tab:** As shown in Figure 16-3, here you can manage group membership for each user in this tab or for each particular group. Click the Edit Membership button and then select the check box for each group that the user should be a member of.

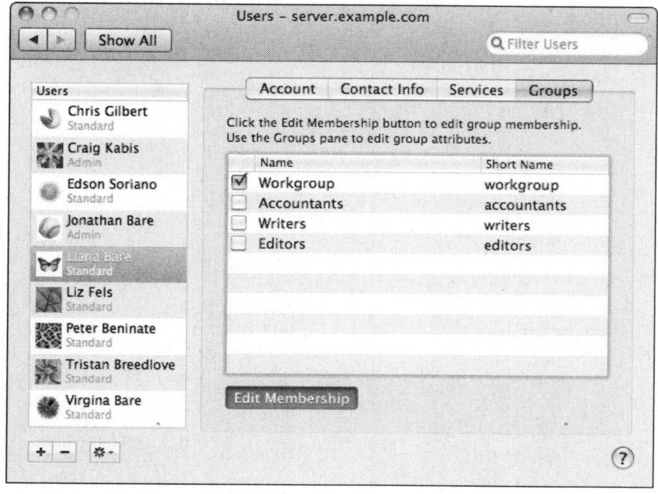

Figure 16-3: Editing group membership for a user in System Preferences.

To delete a user, just click the user in the Users list on the left and then click the Delete (–) button. Server Preferences asks you to confirm the action.

Unlike Mac OS X's System Preferences, deleting a user account in Server Preferences doesn't delete the user's home folder or any files the user created on the server.

Click the Show All button to return to the main Server Preferences window.

Creating, deleting, and managing group accounts in Server Preferences

Managing groups is very similar to managing user accounts, although you have fewer options to choose from in Server Preferences for groups. Follow these steps to create a group:

1. **In Server Preferences, click the Groups icon.**

   Figure 16-4 illustrates the Groups pane in Server Preferences with group accounts already created.

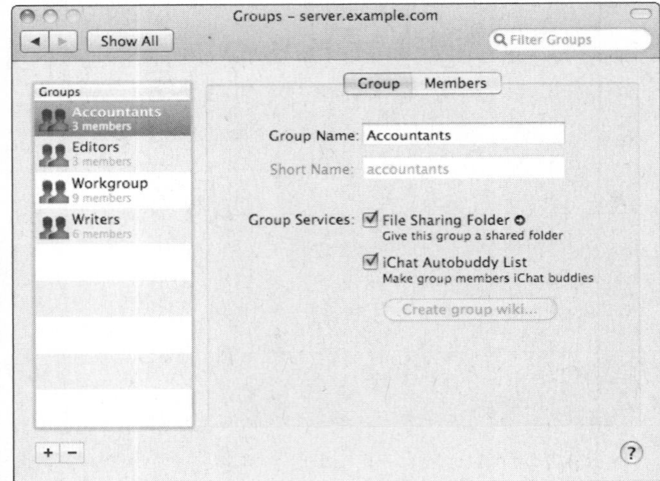

Figure 16-4: The Groups pane in Server Preferences.

2. **Click the Add (+) button in the lower-left corner under the Groups list to add a new group and then enter a group name in the dialog.**

   The short name for groups is created automatically.

3. **Click the Create Group button.**

4. **(Optional) Select the check boxes (or button) for Group Services:**

   • Selecting *File Sharing Folder* enables a shared server folder with access privileges for members of the group. File services must be running.

   • Selecting *iChat Autobuddy List* makes all group members buddies of each other in iChat. iChat services must be running.

   • Clicking the *Create Group Wiki button* sets up a collaboration wiki for the group.

5. **Click the Members tab to view the current membership of the group and then click the Edit Membership button to add or remove user accounts from this group by selecting/deselecting the check box next to the account name.**

   See Figure 16-5.

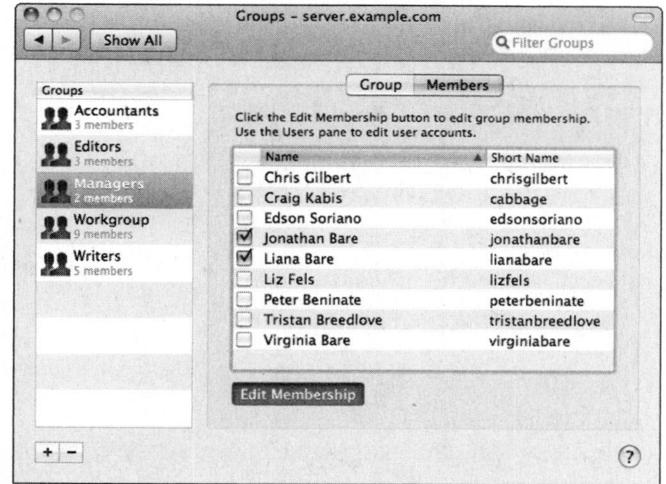

Figure 16-5: Editing group membership in Server Preferences.

6. **Click the Edit Membership button again when finished.**

Deleting a group is the same process as deleting a user, except you do it in the Groups pane. Select the group from the Groups list and then click the Delete (–) button. Deleting a group removes the ability for users to connect to common collaboration resources associated with that group, including shared folders, wikis, blogs, and group calendars.

All new users created in Server Preferences are, by default, members of the Workgroup group. This is a group for all users to collaborate and have common access to shared folders, wikis, blogs, and calendars in Snow Leopard Server. As with other groups, you can disable the Workgroup group.

Managing Accounts in Workgroup Manager

As Uncle Ben Parker reminds fans of *Spider-Man,* "With great power comes great responsibility." Workgroup Manager has great power for modifying the directory databases in Snow Leopard Server, so care in understanding the ability of this server tool is critical to healthy account management.

You can open Workgroup Manager installed on any Mac OS X 10.6 computer connected to the same network as the Open Directory master (see Chapter 6). For the most consistent results in Workgroup Manager, connect directly to the Open Directory master. Don't connect to replica servers or any server bound to the directory. Replica servers contain read-only copies of the directory databases that are periodically synchronized from the master, so editing accounts on replicas forces directory updates on the master from the replica; instead, the master needs to update the replicas.

Open Workgroup Manager from the Dock or from the /Applications/Server/ folder. Workgroup Manager is preconfigured to connect to the server it's installed on. In the Workgroup Manager Connect screen, enter the address, username, and password of the server's local administrator created when you installed Snow Leopard Server.

If you're running Workgroup Manager from another system or you've changed the hostname of the server post-installation:

1. **Choose Server⇨Connect and type the hostname of the server in the Server field.**
2. **Enter the administrator's username and password in each field.**
3. **Click the Connect button.**

You could also click the Browse button to locate available servers on the network, but for the most consistent results, enter the server's fully qualified hostname, such as `server.example.com`, in the Address field.

Workgroup Manager loads the default screen, as shown in Figure 16-6. In this example, a number of users have already been created.

Figure 16-6: Workgroup Manager's default screen after connecting to a server.

Becoming familiar with the Workgroup Manager layout

Workgroup Manager has several areas of browsing and control. The Server Admin icon in the toolbar is a shortcut to launching Server Admin. Next, selected by default, is the Accounts icon, which I describe in the following section. The Preferences icon controls managed account preferences (which I describe in the section, "Setting Managed Preferences for Mac OS X clients," later in this chapter).

The next set of icons (from left to right) allows for creating new accounts, deleting accounts, refreshing the window (data shown in Workgroup Manager is cached on the server), opening a new window in Workgroup Manager, and searching the directory.

As with many windows in Snow Leopard Server, you can customize Workgroup Manager's toolbar. Hold the Control key and click the toolbar; then choose Customize Toolbar from the shortcut menu.

Just below the toolbar is a small globe icon followed by text indicating the status of the directory you're browsing. The first time you connect to an Open Directory master, the status displays `Viewing directory: /LDAPv3/127.0.0.1. Not authenticated`. This indicates that you're browsing the shared directory on the server itself but you haven't yet authenticated to modify the directory.

Clicking the globe icon allows you to change the directory you're browsing. A lock icon on the right side of this row is used to authenticate to the directory, as I describe in the following section.

Just below the globe icon and directory information are four icons on tabs: Users (single silhouetted figure), Groups (three silhouetted figures), Computers (a square), and Computer Groups (two overlapping squares). Click each icon to view the accounts of each type in the directory.

On the right side of the window are the details for each account type. Clicking a particular user account reveals the username, user ID (UID), short names, and other details in the Basic tab.

As you create and edit accounts, click the Save button (in the lower-right corner) to save your changes to the directory. Clicking the Revert button undoes any unsaved changes in all Workgroup Manager tabs.

To change settings on many accounts at once, hold the ⌘ key while clicking accounts one by one. You can then modify settings for all the selected accounts at once. Keep in mind, though, that a mistake made when 50 users are selected instead of one causes you many more headaches.

Creating user accounts with Workgroup Manager

After you launch Workgroup Manager and connect, you need to authenticate to modify the directory. You can then add, remove, and modify accounts. Follow these steps to authenticate and create a new user:

1. **In Workgroup Manager, click the lock icon on the right side of the window to authenticate as the directory administrator (which you create in Chapter 6).**
2. **Enter the username and password of the directory administrator in the dialog shown in Figure 16-7 and then click the Authenticate button.**

   The status next to the globe icon changes to `Authenticated as diradmin to directory: /LDAPv3/127.0.0.1`, and the lock icon changes to an open lock.
3. **Click the Accounts icon.**

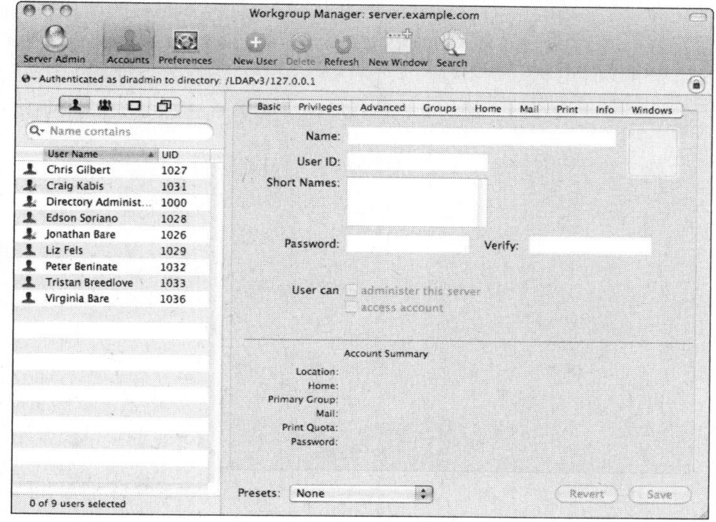

Figure 16-7: Authenticating as the directory administrator in Workgroup Manager.

4. **Select the Users tab just below the globe icon and then click the New User icon in the toolbar.**

   A new user is created named Untitled 1. If Untitled 1 already exists, the new user is Untitled 2, and so on.

5. **In the screen for the Basic tab, enter the username in the Name field.**

   A short name is generated automatically based on the name.

6. **Enter a password.**

   The user ID (UID) is automatically generated based on the first available number higher than 1025 — the first UID used for regular directory accounts.

6. **Click the Save button.**

Changing default account settings

With Workgroup Manager's Accounts icon selected in the toolbar, you can select any account from the list of users and modify its settings.

The initial short name is the only user attribute that can never be changed. Additional short names, or *aliases,* can be added by clicking the field below the existing short names under the Basic tab of Workgroup Manager, but some services require the user to enter the original short name.

After a user is created and her UID is set, don't change the number for it. Permissions and access to various services are tied to the particular UID for the user; changing the UID could have unintended consequences and make it impossible for a user to access her data.

Setting server administrators and directory administrators

By default, new user accounts aren't administrators. You can enable users to be server administrators and/or directory administrators. Server administrators can use Server Admin to modify services and settings of Snow Leopard Server. Directory administrators have privileges to change user and group settings.

To enable a user to be a server administrator:

1. **Log into Workgroup Manager.**
2. **Click the Accounts icon in the toolbar and then click the Basic tab.**
3. **Select a user and then select the User Can Administer This Server check box to allow users to administer this server.**

To give a user administrative privileges over the directory, click the Privileges tab and choose Limited or Full from the Administration Capabilities pop-up menu. For a limited administrator, you can add users or groups that the account will manage by clicking the Add (+) button. A list of users and groups slides out the side of the window. Drag users and groups from the slide-out list to the User Can Administer field.

You can also set the levels of administration by selecting the Manage User Passwords, Edit Managed Preferences, Edit User Information, and Edit Group Membership check boxes for each user or group added to the limited administration list, as shown in Figure 16-8.

Editing group membership

You can set group membership for the user in the Groups tab, which has several options. By default, all new users created in Workgroup Manager are members of the Open Directory users, or staff group. Staff has a group ID (GID) of 20.

A users and groups drawer slides out of the Workgroup Manager window when you click the Add (+) button. Change the primary group by dragging a group from the slide-out list over one of the three fields — Primary Group ID, Short Name, or Name.

Additional group membership can be added by dragging groups to the Other Groups list.

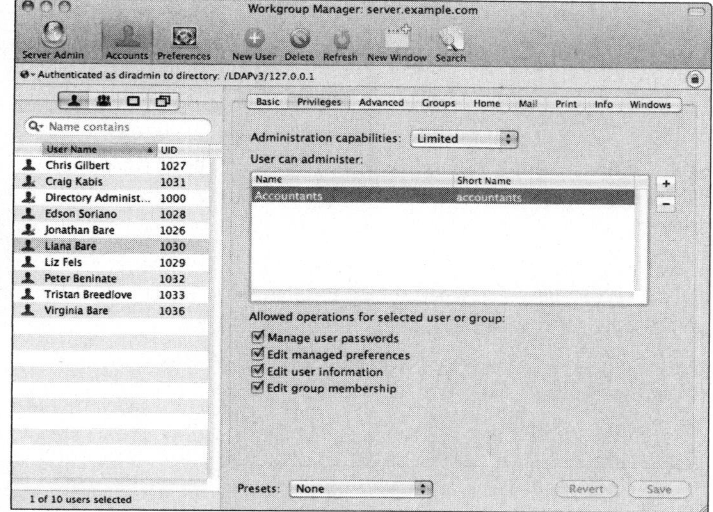

Figure 16-8: Setting limited administration capabilities of a user in Workgroup Manager.

Because groups can be members of other groups (called *nested groups*), click the Show Inherited Groups button to see additional groups the user is a member of via nested groups. Figure 16-9 shows the Groups pane for a user account that has membership in multiple groups.

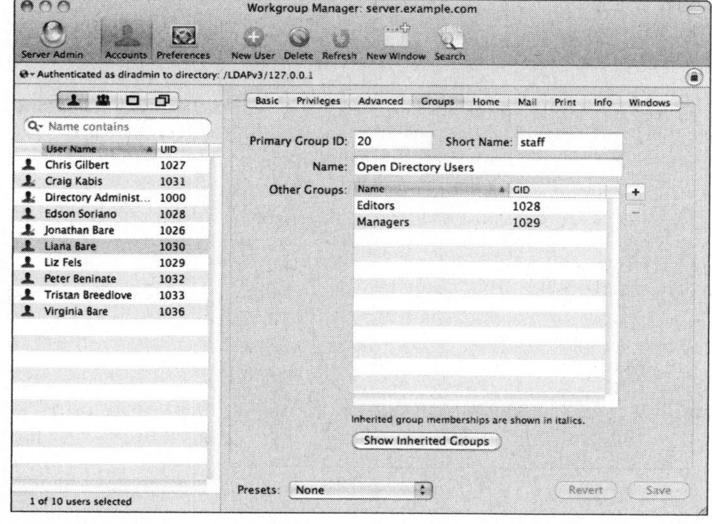

Figure 16-9: User account group membership in Workgroup Manager.

Setting the location of a user's home folder

The Home tab gives you various options for setting the location of a home folder. For Windows users, you also need to use the Windows tab.

- Select None if the user shouldn't have a home folder on the server. Select this option if the user doesn't need to log in to a home folder — useful for an account that accesses only sharing or collaboration resources.
- If you previously configured file sharing on this server or another server bound to the directory to act as an auto-mounted home folder share point, you see that share point listed.

  Select the share point to store the user's home folder in that location, as shown in Figure 16-10.
- Click the Add (+) button to add a new location for user home folders. In the dialog that appears, enter the Mac OS X Server/share point URL (this may be another server besides Snow Leopard Server), the path to the home folder, and the full path the Mac OS X client will use to access the home folder. The new location will be available to all users in the directory.
- If users store only their home folders on the local Mac OS X computer, set the home folder to /Users/. By doing so, regardless of where the user logs in, his home folder is in the local Users folder.

  You may need to add a new home folder location for the Users folder by clicking the Add (+) button and then entering */Users/short name* in the Full Path field, where the *short name* is the account's short name. Leave the Mac OS X Server/Share Point URL and Path to Home Folder fields blank.
- Next to the Add (+) button, three additional buttons exist for managing home folder locations. The double window button duplicates a home folder location. The Minus (–) button deletes a home folder location for all users in the directory but leaves the data intact in the home folders. The pencil button allows you to edit home folder locations.
- Click the Create Home Now button to immediately generate a new home folder at the specified location. This process doesn't overwrite an existing home folder with the same short name. The home folder is created automatically the first time a user logs in if this button isn't clicked, so creating a home folder from Workgroup Manager isn't required.
- Enter a disk quota for the user if required. The disk quota applies to all data created by the user on the volume where her home folder exists, not just on the share point where her home folder is stored.

For Windows users, the Windows tab provides details to configure the user profile, login script, and Windows Home Directory. These options require running the Server Message Block (SMB) file-sharing service, which I detail in Chapter 9.

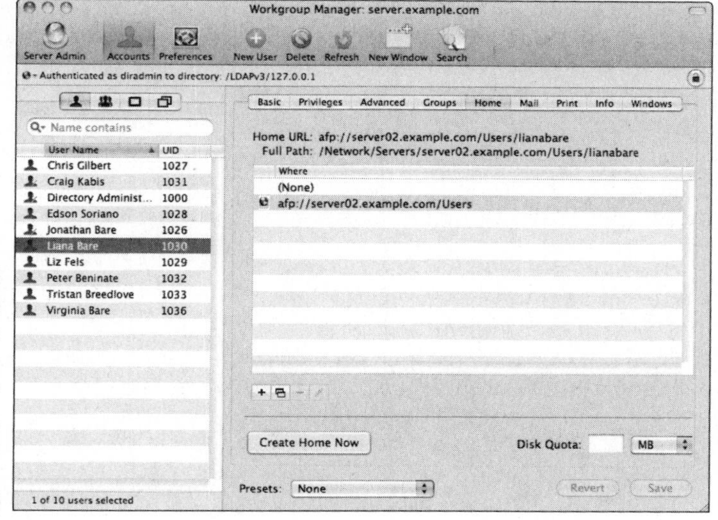

Figure 16-10: Setting the home folder for a user account in Workgroup Manager.

Other user account settings

Workgroup Manager's User Accounts pane has a few more areas you can edit.

The Mail tab

If you're using Snow Leopard Server's Mail service (as I describe in Chapter 14), the Mail tab lets you set four options for the selected user:

- **Mail** gives you the choice of None, Enabled, and Forward. If you installed Snow Leopard Server with Mail service, the Enabled setting is on, with the fully qualified hostname of the server. The Forward selection lets you enter a forwarding e-mail address for the user.
- **Mail Quota** is the maximum size of e-mail and attachments for a user. A 0 indicates unlimited storage for the user's e-mail account.
- **Mail Access** lets you change the e-mail protocols (POP and/or IMAP) that the user can access.
- **Use an Alternate Partition** lets you specify a special location for the e-mail data. You can also use Server Admin to do this.

The Print tab

If you're running Snow Leopard Server's print service, click the Print tab to set print quotas for the user account. The None button prevents the user from printing to queues that enforce quotas. For more specifics, see Chapter 10.

The Info tab

This area is the equivalent of Server Preferences' Contact Info tab. The Info tab lets you add a street address, phone numbers, and other information about a user. Details entered in this tab become part of the account record in the user database and can be viewed by the Address Book client on Mac OS X Snow Leopard, if Address Book Server (see Chapter 11) is running.

The Advanced tab

You can find several unrelated settings here:

- Deselecting **Allow Simultaneous Login** prevents a user from logging into the server from more than one computer at the same time.
- The **Comment and Keyword fields** can help you quickly locate accounts based on similar comments or keywords
- The **User Password Type pop-up menu** allows you to assign the user to a different password database. You can change from Open Directory to Crypt Password for backward compatibility with users connecting from Mac OS X 10.1 and earlier. When managing other types of directories, such as the unshared local directory of users, another choice is Shadow Password, the standard password type for local accounts in Mac OS X.
- **Login Shell** selects which Unix shell environment the user has when connecting to the server from Terminal. To disallow Terminal access on the server, choose None from the pop-up menu.

Disabling and deleting user accounts with Workgroup Manager

An alternative to immediately deleting a user account is to disable access to the account by deselecting the Access Accounts check box in the Basic tab of a user account in Workgroup Manager (as I explain in Step 4 in the section, “Creating user accounts with Workgroup Manager,” earlier in this chapter). Disabled accounts are shown in the Users list in Workgroup Manager with a red X through their icons.

However, the more disabled accounts you have, the more difficult it becomes to manage a large group of users. After a while, deleting a defunct user is the best option to keep your directory tidy.

After authenticating by clicking Workgroup Manager’s lock icon and typing a directory administrator’s name and password, click the Users tab just below the globe icon. Click to select a user and then click the Delete (–) button.

Files in shared and home folders created by deleted users remain on the server. However, data in Mail, iCal, Address Book, and blogs is removed from the server when the user account is deleted.

Creating group accounts with Workgroup Manager

Although the number of options and settings is far simpler, creating a group account with Workgroup Manager is much the same as creating a user account. Group accounts contain one or more user or group accounts. Group accounts that are members of another group are *nested accounts.*

To create a new group account with Workgroup Manager, follow these steps:

1. **Click the lock icon on the right side of the Workgroup Manager window and enter the username and password of the directory administrator in the dialog; click the Authenticate button.**
2. **Select the Groups tab just below the globe icon and then click the New Group icon in the toolbar.**

   A new group is created named Untitled 1, as shown in Figure 16-11. If Untitled 1 already exists, the new user is Untitled 2, and so on.

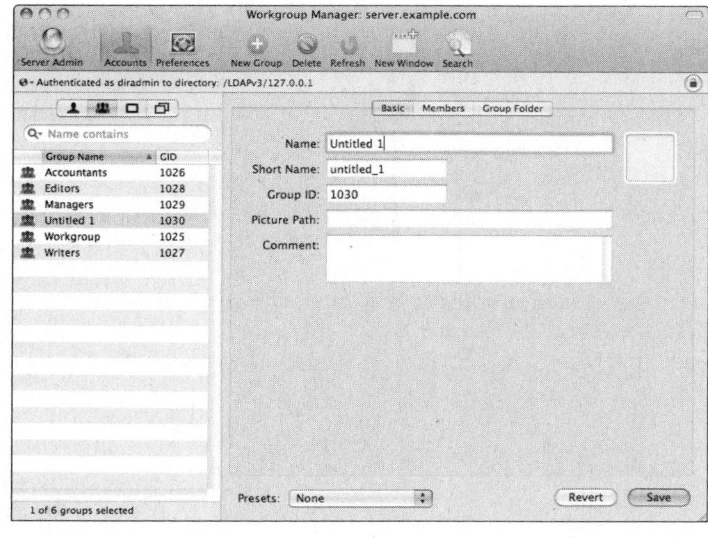

Figure 16-11: A new Untitled 1 group created in Workgroup Manager.

3. **In the screen for the Basic tab, enter the group's name in the Name field.**

   A short name is generated automatically.

   The group ID (GID) is generated automatically based on the first available number higher than 1025 — the first GID used for regular directory accounts. In this example, the account GID is 1030 because other groups already exist in the directory.

The Basic tab includes a field to enter a picture path, used to set a custom picture to identify this group. A Comment field can be used for human-readable comments regarding this group account.

4. **Add users and groups to the group account membership by clicking the Members tab (see Figure 16-12) and then the Add (+) button.**

   A users and groups drawer slides out the side of the Workgroup Manager window. Users are shown under a User icon (a single silhouetted figure) and groups under a Group icon (three silhouetted figures).

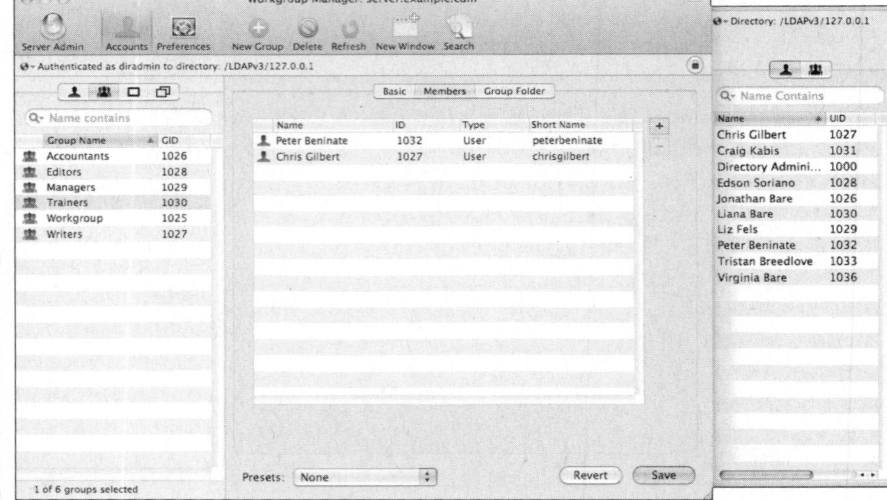

Figure 16-12: Adding user accounts to a group account in Workgroup Manager.

5. **Drag user and group accounts to the Members tab to add them to the new group.**

   To remove a user or group, click the account name in the Members tab and then click the Delete (–) button.

Like a user account, a group can have its own auto-mounting folder on a share point. Click the Group Folder tab (as shown in Figure 16-13) to set the share point and folder. Users can access the shared folder as well as save and edit content, subject to permissions set for the shared folder. (See Chapter 8 for details on setting file-sharing permissions.)

If you select a share point for a group folder, you must also specify an owner of the folder. Click the Ellipsis (. . .) button next to the short name to select a user that will become the group folder's owner. This can be a member of the group or an administrator. The owner can create, edit, or delete any file or folder in the group folder. Figure 16-13 shows the process for selecting a group folder location and adding the owner of the folder.

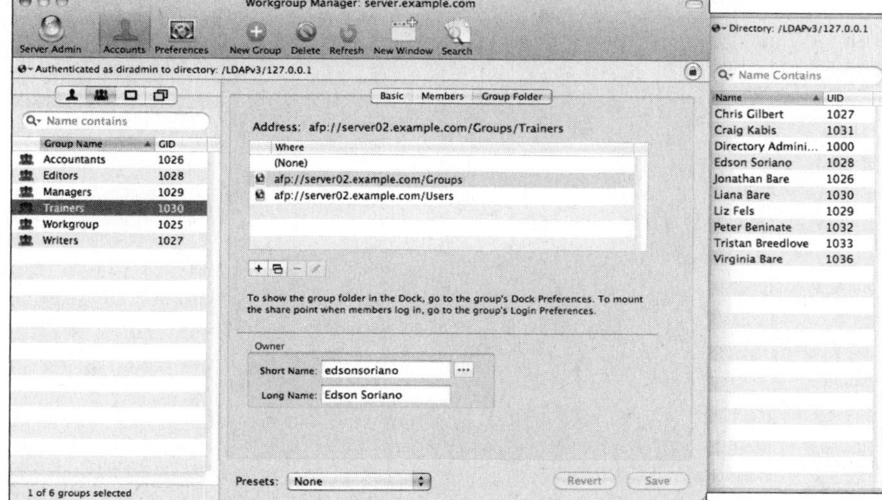

Figure 16-13: Setting the location and ownership of a group folder in Workgroup Manager.

Editing and deleting group accounts with Workgroup Manager

Although you can't change the short names of user accounts, you can modify any aspect of a group account within Workgroup Manager. Simply access an existing group account in the same way you would for a new account. (See "Creating group accounts with Workgroup Manager," earlier in this section.)

Like a user account's user ID, the group ID (GID) shouldn't be changed after a group is created. The GID is tied to file permissions and other resources in Snow Leopard Server; changing it may have unintended consequences and make data and resources unavailable to users.

Group accounts can't be disabled like user accounts; however, removing all members of a group effectively disables anyone from accessing the group resources. To permanently remove a group, do the following:

1. **Click the Groups tab just below the globe icon and then click the group to be deleted in the list of accounts.**
2. **Click the Delete icon in the toolbar and then confirm the deletion of the group account by clicking Delete in the dialog that appears.**

Files in shared folders created by deleted groups remain on the server. However, data, such as blogs, wikis, and group calendars, in other services are removed from the server when the group account is deleted.

Importing and Exporting Accounts

Chapter 6 describes how Workgroup Manager can archive and restore the entire Open Directory domain. You can also use Workgroup Manager to import and export account records. Periodically exporting accounts can help you restore your Open Directory domain if the worst should happen and your archive won't restore the databases.

When exporting user accounts from the archive process, user passwords aren't ever exported from Workgroup Manager. In addition, the Kerberos Key Distribution Center (KDC), which controls single sign-on, can't be exported.

Importing accounts can make a large influx of new users easier to manage. For example, a school may have a list of new students each fall taken from the registrar's database, manipulated, and imported into Workgroup Manager. Third-party utilities, such as Passenger from MacinMind Software (`www.macinmind.com/Passenger`), can help massage the raw data into a format compatible with an Open Directory domain.

To import users in Workgroup Manager, choose Server➪Import; then select a file and click the Import button. Chapter 6 describes how to import users and groups from another directory server using Server Preferences.

Exporting accounts is more straightforward. Follow these steps to export a list of accounts in Workgroup Manager:

1. **Click the lock icon on the right side of the Workgroup Manager window and enter the username and password of the directory administrator in the dialog; click the Authenticate button.**
2. **Depending on the type of account you plan to export, click the Users, Groups, Computers, or Computer Groups tab below the globe icon.**

3. **Select the accounts from the list you plan to export.**

   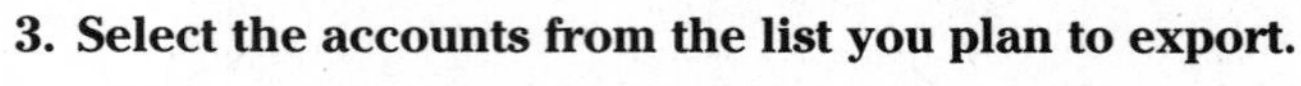

   Hold the Shift or ⌘ key to select more than one account.
4. **Choose Server➪Export.**

   A Save As dialog appears, allowing you to enter a name for the exported list of accounts and to select the location to save the file.
5. **Click the Export button.**

   Repeat this process for each type of account — users, groups, computers, and computer groups — you're exporting.

If you need to delete a number of accounts, you could also export the account lists before they're deleted. This saves you time if any of the accounts are deleted in error or need to be added again later.

Setting Managed Preferences for Mac OS X Clients

Managed Preferences for Mac OS X (MCX) is a feature that allows Snow Leopard Server to manage system, user, and applications preferences on Macs connected, or bound, to an Open Directory domain. MCX can manage any preference by storing a *manifest,* one or more preference files, on the Mac. Managed preferences can be set for almost any system, user, or application preference that uses Apple's standard preference list (`.plist`) files. Many system and user settings are preconfigured for easy management in Workgroup Manager under the Preferences icon.

Inheriting, combining, and overriding preferences

You can set managed preferences for all types of accounts in an Open Directory domain: users, groups, computers, and computer groups. A group with managed preferences is referred to as a *workgroup.* Managed preferences can't be controlled for computers that aren't bound to the domain, but users in the domain also can't log in at those computers with directory accounts until they're bound.

Because managed preferences can be applied to all types of accounts, you have a specific hierarchy for inheritance, combining, and overriding preferences. Some settings, such as controlling which items are opened at login, are cumulative because no one particular setting overrides another — any number of items can be opened at login.

Some settings are inherited from workgroups to the user level or from within nested workgroups. Settings with only one ultimate outcome — such as the position of the Dock onscreen — use an order of priority to override the same setting for different account levels. The prioritization of conflicting preferences to override the same setting also applies for inheritance. The order of inheritance and overriding preferences is

- Workgroup (the least specific level)
- Computer group
- Computer
- User (the most specific level)

For example, a preference set at the workgroup level can't override the same preference set for the computer group, computer, or user level. In this sense, a preference set for the user always wins when overriding other levels.

However, setting preferences at the user level can be time-consuming and complicated to manage. Managing at the workgroup or computer group level saves time and energy, and making your life a little easier is one of the reasons you bought this book.

Enforcing managed preferences

You can set managed preferences with four different restrictions:

- **Always:** The preference is enforced continuously. Users can't change the preference.
- **Once:** The directory sets the preference one time. The user is then free to change the setting.
- **Often:** The Often setting isn't present in Workgroup Manager's Overview tab for preference management, but it can be set within the raw preference manifests with the Details tab.

  Often sets the preference when the user logs in. During the user session, the preference can be changed, but it's reset on subsequent logins to the managed setting.
- **Never:** Effectively, Never means preference management for that setting is disabled, and the user can set whatever preferences are desired.

These settings appear when you select the Preferences icon, select an account, select the Overview tab, and then select a preferences icon. This is described in the "Working with managed preferences" section, later in this chapter.

Creating computer and computer group accounts

Managed preferences makes apparent the importance of computer and computer group accounts. Specific computer and computer group preferences streamline management of Energy Saver settings, mobile accounts, and hardware-specific preferences, for example.

You don't need to create computer or computer group accounts in Workgroup Manager unless you plan on using managed preferences. You could use the list of computer and computer group accounts to help you organize and manage large deployments of Mac OS X systems, but Workgroup Manager isn't a great replacement for a simple spreadsheet or database of systems.

You could create a new computer account by selecting the Computer tab (square icon) in Workgroup Manager and then clicking the New Computer icon in the toolbar. However, you then need to type in the Ethernet ID to identify the computer. It's easier to first create a computer group and then browse the list of bound computers to add the computer to the list, creating a computer account by default.

Here's how to create a computer group and add computer accounts to it:

1. **In Workgroup Manager, click the lock icon to authenticate as the directory administrator (which you create in Chapter 6) and enter the username and password of the directory administrator in the dialog; click the Authenticate button.**
2. **Click the Computer Groups tab (two overlapping squares) below the globe icon and then click the New Computer Group icon in the toolbar.**

   A new computer group named Untitled 1 is created. If Untitled 1 already exists, the new group is named Untitled 2, and so on. Figure 16-14 shows an example of a new computer group. Much like a group of user accounts, a computer group has Name, Short Name, Group ID (GID), and Comment fields in the Basic tab of Workgroup Manager.

   Enter a name for the computer group; the short name is generated automatically based on the Name field. The GID will be the first available number greater than or equal to 1030.
3. **To add computers to the group, click the Members tab.**

   Click the Add (+) button in the Members tab to add computers or existing computer groups to the new group, or click the Ellipsis (. . .) button to select computers already bound to the directory to add to the computer group.

   A search field can help you find particular computers in the list, as shown in Figure 16-15.

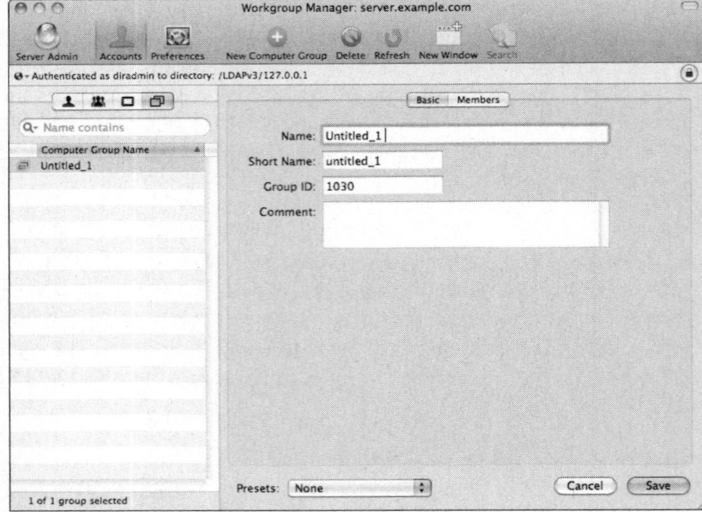

Figure 16-14: A new computer group created in Workgroup Manager.

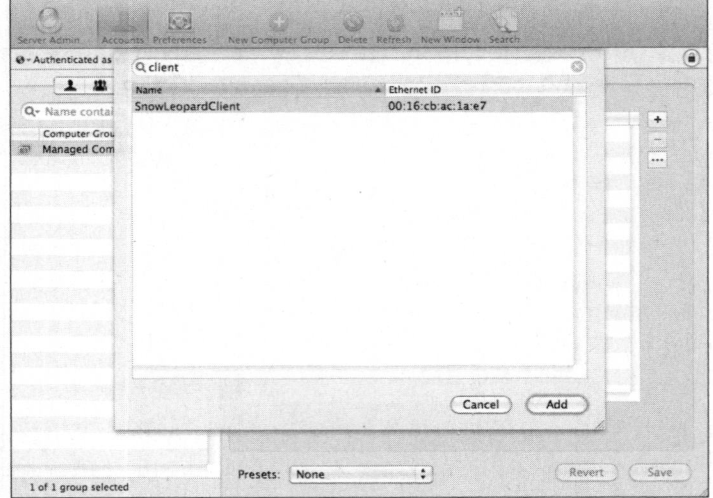

Figure 16-15: Adding a bound computer to a computer group in Workgroup Manager.

4. **Click the Add button.**

You now have members in a computer group. Click the Computer Accounts tab (a single square) in Workgroup Manager and notice the computer you added now has a computer account also, as shown in Figure 16-16.

Working with managed preferences

In Workgroup Manager, use the section under the Preferences icon to manage preferences for accounts connected to the Open Directory domain. The left side of the Preferences pane uses the same tabs (users, groups, computers, and computer groups) as the Accounts pane. The Preferences pane also lists the same accounts under each tab as the Accounts pane. Figure 16-17 shows Workgroup Manager with the Preferences icon on the toolbar selected and a computer group selected.

Note the icons on the right side of the Workgroup Manager window under the Overview tab, such as Applications, Classic, Dock, and so on. These icons represent preference manifests that have been preset in Workgroup Manager. Some of the preset preference icons don't apply to different types of accounts and therefore aren't displayed.

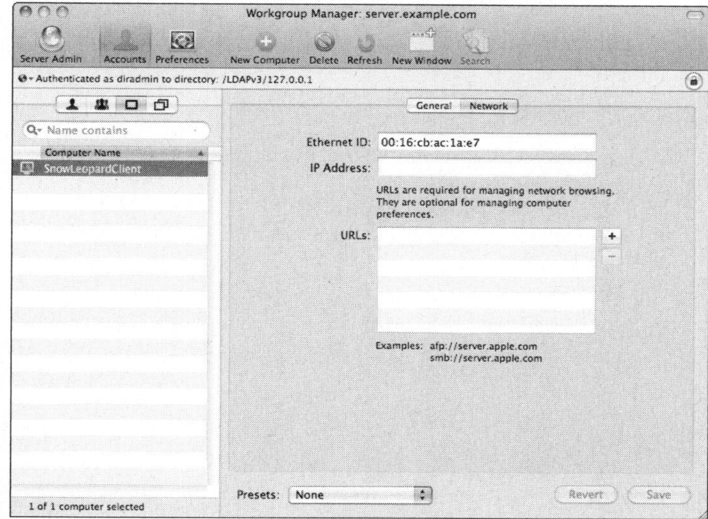

Figure 16-16: A computer account shown in Workgroup Manager.

Although the Overview tab has many commonly managed preferences, nearly any preference list in Mac OS X can be managed. Other preference manifests can be added in the Details tab.

For this example, you configure the list of applications that can be launched within a computer group by following these steps in Workgroup Manager:

1. **Click the Preferences icon in the toolbar and select the Computer Group tab (two overlapping squares) above the list of accounts.**
2. **Click the Applications icon under the Overview tab.**

3. **Select Always from the Manage options and then select the Restrict Which Applications Are Allowed to Launch check box to enforce which applications are allowed to launch.**
4. **Click the Add (+) button and select the applications that the users will be permitted to open; click the Add button in the dialog.**
5. **Click the Apply Now button to save your settings.**

   Figure 16-18 shows the result of these steps so far, a list of applications allowed to launch in the Managed Computers computer group.

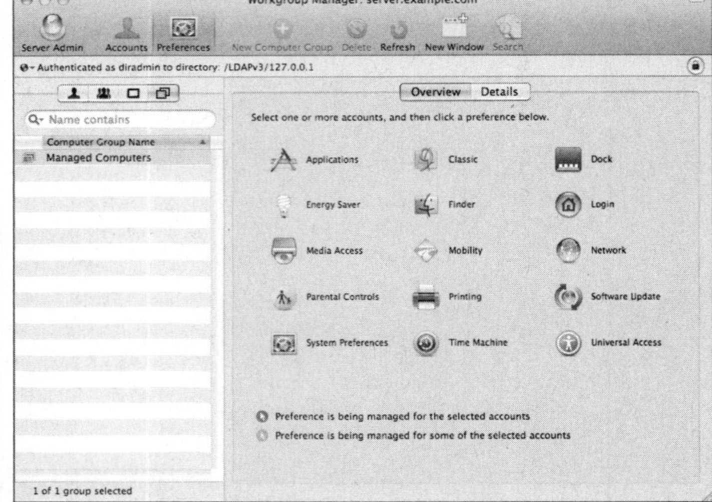

Figure 16-17: The Preferences screen for a computer group in Workgroup Manager.

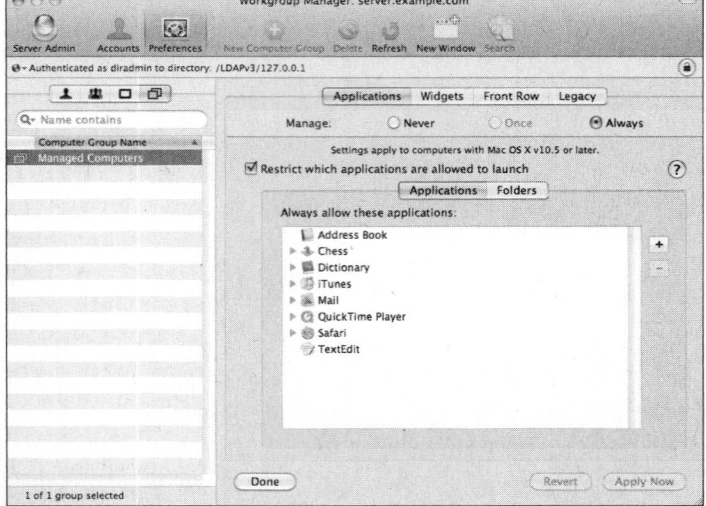

Figure 16-18: Managed preferences controlling the applications allowed to launch.

6. **Click the Done button to return to the Preferences Overview tab.**

You can also manage other preferences from the Overview tab. In Figure 16-19, the mouse pointer icon next to the icons for Applications, Dock, Finder, Media Access, and Network indicates that these items all have some managed preferences configured.

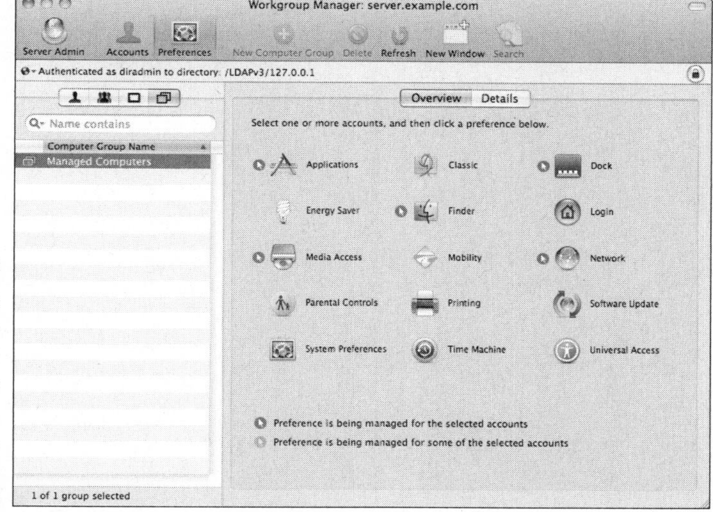

Figure 16-19: Multiple managed preferences shown in Workgroup Manager.

With the Details tab, you can view precise information about each preference manifest, as shown in Figure 16-20.

The Details tab allows you to edit the preference manifests by clicking an item in the list and then clicking the pencil icon below the list. A new pane opens to show the details of the preferences, as shown in Figure 16-21 for the Dock settings. This is also where you can find the option for the Often setting of a managed preference.

With the Details tab, you can import preferences from other applications or sources. Click the Add (+) button to add those preference files (in the `.plist` format) to Workgroup Manager.

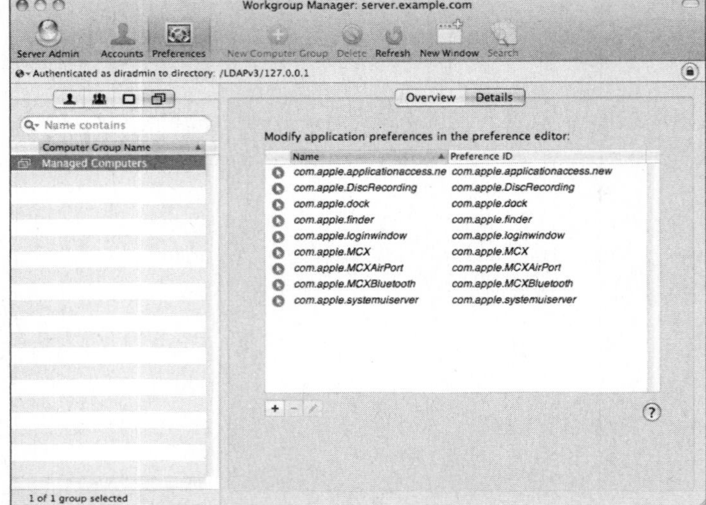

Figure 16-20: Specific details for each managed preference manifest.

com.apple.dock

New Key | Delete | Set Default | Delete Unmatched

Name	Type	Value
▾ Once	dictionary	7 items
autohide	boolean	false
largesize	real	128.000000
launchanim	boolean	true
magnification	boolean	false
mineffect	string	genie
orientation	string	bottom
tilesize	real	64.000000
▸ Often	dictionary	empty
▸ Always	dictionary	empty

Done | Revert | Apply Now

Figure 16-21: A preference manifest for Dock settings shown in Workgroup Manager.

You can also set managed preferences for user, group, or computer accounts from their respective tabs above the list of accounts.

Chapter 17

Creating Mobile Accounts for Notebooks

In This Chapter

- Firing up Workgroup Manager
- Exploring mobile account options for networked notebooks
- Configuring mobility settings
- Deploying mobile home folders
- Synching mobile clients

You've had enough sitting at your desk and it's time to get out of the office, but how do you take your data with you when you go home? What if you need to make a presentation at a client's office out of town? Do you drag your entire network infrastructure with you? Imagine the airline luggage fees.

In this chapter, you determine the best method for managing client computers that aren't tied down — most frequently these are notebook computers. Instead of having user home folders stored only on a server volume or only on the client computer, mobility settings offer a combination of these two choices. Snow Leopard Server lets you create mobile home folders for Mac, Windows, and Linux clients.

With mobile accounts, domain information such as mobile preferences and user account data, as well as user data, are all updated when the user connects to the network. Mobile accounts can also have a portable home folder synchronized between a server volume and the internal hard drive. I examine the options in this chapter, and you see how to create a mobile account and a portable home folder.

Later in this chapter, I describe how to create and manage mobile accounts and home folder synchronization in Workgroup Manager.

Connecting Workgroup Manager to a Shared Domain

As with several of the topics in this book, you need to know the basics of Workgroup Manager. Run Workgroup Manager from any network-connected system or directly on an Open Directory server. Follow these steps to launch and connect to the directory in Workgroup Manager:

1. **Launch the Workgroup Manager application from /Applications/Server/ on your client system, if you've installed Server Tools, or from the same location on the Open Directory server itself.**
2. **Choose Server⇨Connect.**
3. **Enter the IP address or hostname of the directory server in the Address field of the dialog that appears. Authenticate as the server's local administrator by typing in the Username and Password fields.**
4. **Click the Connect button.**
5. **Choose the shared directory domain from the pop-up menu just above the list of users in Workgroup Manager.**

   If this is strictly an Open Directory domain and you're working directly on the Open Directory server, choose /LDAPv3/127.0.0.1/. If you're working on a connected system, choose /LDAPv3/*your hostname or IP address*/. If you're using Active Directory, choose /Active Directory/*Your Domain*/ from the list. Other choices are possible depending on your directory configuration.
6. **Click the lock icon to the right of the Shared Directory pop-up menu and authenticate as the directory administrator that you created as part of the directory configuration.**

You're now ready to manage the users, groups, and computers in the directory domain. Workgroup Manager, logged in to an Open Directory master server and shared domain, with a user account selected, is shown in Figure 17-1.

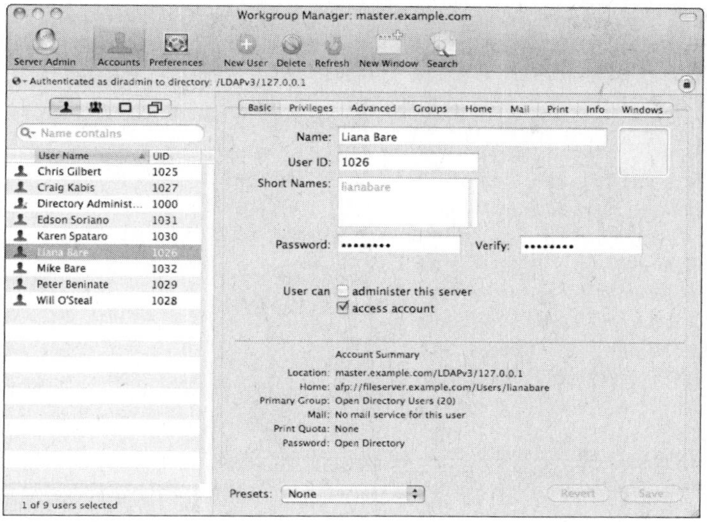

Figure 17-1: Workgroup Manager connected to an Open Directory master.

The Nightmare of Networked Notebooks

In previous chapters, you've been introduced to the managed client concept from the perspective of a desktop system, like an iMac, that never needs to change location. The difference for a notebook user is taking his notebook to another location, in or out of the office. What happens to the user's authentication information and data when he disconnects from the network? How can the user continue to log in to his notebook and access his documents and other data away from the network directory and file sharing? The answer is the mobile account.

Unlike other accounts, a mobile account caches the user's account credentials on the local hard drive. User data could be stored on the local hard drive or a network volume, but the local hard drive makes the most logical sense in this configuration.

To make it even better, you can configure a mobile account to have a portable home folder. Building on the mobile account, a user's home folder is synchronized between a server volume and the local drive. Synchronization occurs at login and at a predetermined periodic interval. The directory administrator configures the interval.

This choice gives a notebook user freedom of movement while maintaining her data on the server and local drive.

FileVault and Mac mobile home folders

For better security, Mac OS X home folders can also be encrypted with FileVault. *FileVault* uses disk images to encrypt the user's data. This technology is available to regular local home folders and is configured from the Security pane in System Preferences. FileVault is also a choice for portable home folders, configured with Workgroup Manager's mobility settings. I show you this option later in this chapter in the section, "Taking data on the road with portable home folders."

A downside to using FileVault is that it imposes some limitations on backups using Time Machine. For instance, Time Machine can't restore individual files from a FileVault-encrypted archive.

Warning: It's imperative to set a *master password* before enabling FileVault. The master password is used to recover an encrypted account if the user's password is lost. Without one, the user's data will be forever encrypted if he forgets his account password.

Here are also some other options for accounts and home folders that can be used for notebook clients:

- **External account:** Like a mobile account, but the user's account data can be stored on any volume connected to the client, including an external USB or FireWire hard drive, flash drive, or even an iPod. That volume can be removed and connected to another Mac OS X system. The user can log in with the account credentials stored on the external volume.
- **External account with portable home folder:** The combination of an external account and portable home folder, both stored on an external volume attached to the client.

  One of the most flexible choices, this option allows a user to synchronize a home folder to a portable drive and take it to another computer and have full access to his data. Also the most unsecured option because the portable drive can be easily lost or stolen.

Other users, besides notebook users, can benefit from external and mobile accounts and portable home folders. Regular network accounts can be used interchangeably with mobile accounts and portable home folders, with significantly less impact on network activity. Synchronizing users' home folders provides redundancy in the event of a hardware failure.

Creating portable home folders sets up a two-way mirror of files between the server and the local hard drive. Never combine regular network home folders with portable home folders: Data loss is a likely outcome. The portable home folder client tracks changes and performs the sync operation by comparing the files between the server and the local drive. If a file has previously changed on the server and the portable home folder process wasn't aware of the change, the local file will be overwritten back to the server.

Set a master password on each computer in the Security pane of System Preferences. You can also require a master password be set when a mobile account logs in to a managed computer, which you see in the section, "Taking data on the road with portable home folders," later in this chapter.

Planning and Deploying Mobile Accounts

Just as you've seen with other services in Mac OS X Server, planning ahead before you decide on deploying mobile accounts and portable home folders saves you from wasted time and energy.

Here's the basic planning and deployment process: First, decide the type of account you'll use to manage mobility settings. Then examine the options for mobile accounts and portable home folders that I describe in the preceding section. Configure directory and file-sharing services on your servers. Finalize connections by binding clients to the directory and log in to mobile accounts, creating portable home folders as necessary.

Simplifying mobile management with computer and group accounts

As we discuss in Chapters 5 and 6, accounts come in different types: user, group, computer (or machine), and computer groups. Managing mobility options is possible for any of the account types, or combinations thereof. But for simplicity, with multiple accounts needing mobility and portability settings, group and computer group accounts make the best choice.

Manage your notebook systems with computer groups. When users of multiple systems always need a particular setting, such as mobility, creating a group of those systems makes your job easier.

When managing desktop systems with mobile accounts and portable homes, unless you're managing only a few user accounts, also use groups and computer groups. You probably will separate your notebook and desktop systems into separate computer groups.

To create a computer group, you need one or more clients bound to a shared directory, as described in Chapter 6. After the clients are bound, use Workgroup Manager to create a computer group by following the directions in Chapter 16.

If you decide to manage settings based on a group of users instead of a group of computers, create a user group instead. To create a user group, follow the steps in Chapter 16 for creating a group account.

You can designate a group to be a member of another group. Adding groups to groups creates *nested groups*. This technique can save you time when managing large numbers of user accounts. It also facilitates the inheritance of permissions and managed settings, which we discuss in Chapters 8 and 16, respectively.

You can now manage a group or computer group by clicking Workgroup Manager's Preferences icon in the toolbar, which we describe in Chapter 16, and the mobility settings, which we examine through the rest of this chapter.

Configuring mobility settings

To get started with mobility, the user needs an account in a shared directory. Haven't created a directory yet? Check out Chapters 5 and 6.

Directory information, including the Lightweight Directory Access Protocol (LDAP) account and password data, is cached from the shared directory to the local system. By itself, a mobile account doesn't include any documents or data from the user's home folder.

When a mobile account is enabled, the user can log out and log in again without being attached to the network where the account data resides. After returning to the network and reconnecting to the directory, the local cached authentication data is resynchronized and any updates to the LDAP or password data are cached again on the local system. You can also have a mobile account expire if it goes unused.

Any standard Open Directory network account can become a mobile account. Mobility settings can be configured for the account itself, a group that the account is a member of, a computer where a user can log in, or a group of computers where users can log in.

If, as the directory administrator, you set mobility in more than one of these locations, rules of inheritance and precedence for client preferences take effect. Chapter 16 contains details on the inheritance and precedence of managed preferences in Mac OS X.

In these steps, you configure the mobility settings for a computer group. To set up the mobile account:

1. **Open Workgroup Manager and connect to the shared directory.**
2. **In Workgroup Manager, click the Accounts icon and then click the Computer Groups tab above the list of accounts.**

The Computer Groups tab is the icon represented by two overlapping squares, the fourth tab following the Users tab, Groups tab, and Computers tab.

If your planning leads you to manage individual user accounts, groups of users, or individual computers, select that account instead of the computer group in Workgroup Manager.

3. **Click the Preferences icon.**

   The right side of Workgroup Manager displays the icons for the various managed preferences.

   In Figure 17-2, note the small, dark gray circle enclosing a mouse pointer next to the Mobility icon. This indicates that the preferences are being managed for the selected account.

Figure 17-2: Managed preferences of a computer group in Workgroup Manager.

4. **Click the Mobility icon.**
5. **Select the Account Creation tab and then click the Creation sub-tab.**
6. **By default, Manage is set to Never; select Always.**

   Preferences can be managed never, once, or always in Workgroup Manager. Once isn't an available option for some mobility settings. Figure 17-3 shows the mobile Account Creation settings for a computer group.

7. **Select the Create Mobile Account When User Logs in to Network Account check box.**

   Selecting this option creates the mobile account on the local hard drive of a Mac OS X system.

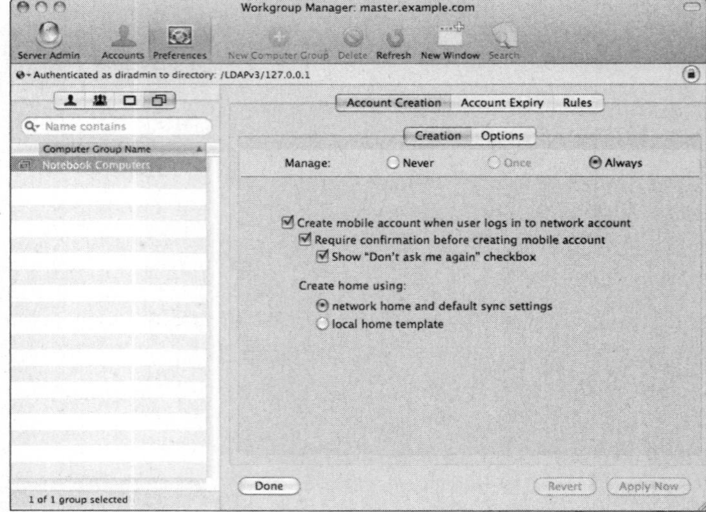

Figure 17-3: Mobile Account Creation settings in Workgroup Manager.

8. **(Optional) Deselect the Require Confirmation Before Creating Mobile Account check box to keep the user from having to confirm mobile account creation.**

   (Optional) Deselect the Show "Don't Ask Me Again" check box to prevent the user from having to confirm again when she logs in to a managed computer.

9. **(Optional) Choose how a new home folder is created by selecting Network Home and Default Sync Settings or Local Home Template.**

   The first option uses a network volume and creates either a network home or a portable home, depending on the sync settings in the Rules tab. The second choice uses the default home folder settings on the local hard drive.

10. **Click the Apply Now button to save the settings.**
11. **(Optional) Click the Options sub-tab under the Account Creation tab.**

    Here is where you have choices for creating a FileVault-encrypted home folder and where the users' home folders will be created. Click Always to manage these settings. Enable FileVault by selecting the Encrypt Contents with FileVault check box.

12. **Select either the Use Computer Master Password, If Available or the Require Computer Master Password check box.**

Select the second choice to require and verify a valid master password on the local system.

A master password is the critical failsafe for encrypted FileVault home folders. It provides the ability to restore access to an encrypted account if the user forgets his password.

The remaining choices in the Options tab set where the home folder is stored. By default, On Startup Volume is selected. The other choices are: At Path, with a field to enter the specific location in the file system where the home folder will be stored; and User Chooses, with a pop-up selection. The pop-up menu choices are Any Volume, Any Internal Volume, and Any External Volume. By choosing Any Volume or Any External Volume, the user can create an external account.

13. **After making any changes, click the Apply Now button to save your settings.**

Two more tabs are in the mobility settings after Account Creation. The second tab is Account Expiry. The settings in this tab control when mobile accounts will expire on the mobile computer, as shown in Figure 17-4 for a computer group. In other words, the cached account on the local hard drive will be deleted when it expires.

Your security policies may require accounts to be deleted if users don't connect periodically to the shared directory. But be careful with this setting. If an account goes unused for the period set by the expiry settings, the mobile account's home folder is deleted, and the user can't log in while away from the network.

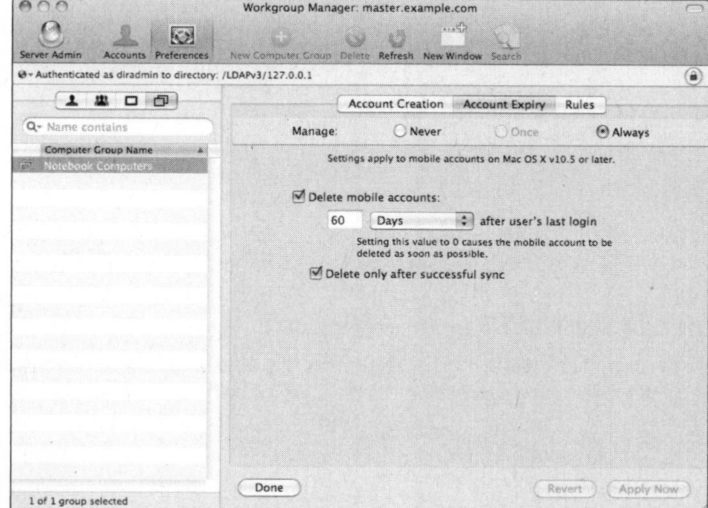

Figure 17-4: Account expiration settings in Workgroup Manager.

Select the Delete Mobile Accounts check box and set the timeframe for when the account will be deleted, to have a mobile account deleted after that timeframe. Select the Delete Only After Successful Sync check box if you want to be certain a mobile account is synchronized to the server before deletion occurs.

The third tab in mobility preferences is the Rules tab. Here's where you configure the settings for portable home folders, which I detail in the following section.

Taking data on the road with portable home folders

Of course the account itself isn't terribly useful without the user's data. Use compatible file-sharing services on the network to create a portable home folder. To do so, you need an auto-mount share point configured in the directory for user home folders so that it appears to the user without intervention by the user. An auto-mountable share point must have a network mount record in the directory domain.

Although synchronization of the user's home folder provides hardware redundancy — the user's account is easily synchronized with another system if a hard drive fails or another problem develops — synchronization isn't a replacement for a good backup strategy. Changes in files on the local system, files that are modified, deleted, or corrupted on the local system, are synchronized to the server's volume. Similarly, if a problem exists on the server, the file changes get synchronized back to the local hard drive.

Creating share points for use as mobile home folders

When you create home folders for your users, take care to select the correct file-sharing protocol. For Mac clients, the home folder must be shared with the AFP protocol. (Don't use SMB for a Mac home folder.) Home folders for Windows clients must use SMB. Linux clients can use SMB or NFS.

Use Server Admin to set up file sharing for network and portable home folders. You can find instructions for setting up share points in Chapter 9.

Configuring the mobile home folder

Your server should already be bound to the shared directory or configured as an Open Directory master or replica, as I describe in Chapter 6.

After the binding and the share point are ready, use Workgroup Manager to set the network home folder and enable portable home synchronization. Here's how:

1. **Open Workgroup Manager and connect to the shared directory.**
2. **In Workgroup Manager, click the Accounts icon and then click the Users tab above the list of accounts.**

   The Users tab is the icon represented by the single silhouetted figure, the leftmost tab.
3. **In the list of accounts under the tabs, click a user's name and then click the Home tab in the right side of the Server Admin window.**
4. **Click the share point you previously created for user home folders and then click the Save button.**

   You've set the location where the home folder will be stored on the network, as shown in Figure 17-5.

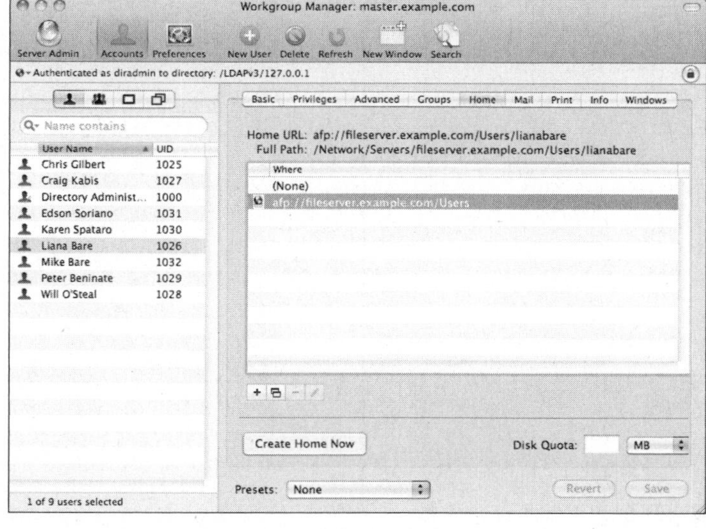

Figure 17-5: Setting a user's network home folder in Workgroup Manager.

5. **Select the Computer Groups tab and then click the name of a group you want to use.(See the section, "Simplifying mobile management with computer and group accounts," earlier in this chapter.)**
6. **Click the Preferences icon and then click the Mobility icon.**

   If you haven't yet, you need to set up account creation, as I outline in the section, "Configuring mobility settings," earlier in this chapter.

7. **Click the Rules tab.**

   Here's where you have a multitude of options for the portable home folders.

   The second sub-tab, Preferences Sync, controls synchronization of preference files from the user's home folder. You come back to this in just a minute.

8. **Click Home Sync sub-tab.**

9. **Select Once or Always to set Sync settings for each login or always, respectively, and then decide the intervals for sync by selecting one or more of the check boxes:**

   - *At Login:* Sync occurs when the user logs in to her account. The user sees a progress bar while the sync is in progress.
   - *At Logout:* Sync occurs when the user logs out of her account. The user sees the same progress bar.
   - *In the Background:* An automatic sync without any user notification.
   - *Manually:* Sync triggered by the user from the user's account in the Accounts pane of System Preferences or by selecting Sync Now from the Home Sync status menu when the user is logged in.

   Figure 17-6 shows the options for home folder synchronization.

Figure 17-6: Home folder synchronization settings in Workgroup Manager.

10. **(Optional) Set the list of sync locations.**

    Below the four options for when sync occurs are the locations that will sync. By default, this includes the user's home folder, indicated by the tilde (~) sign. Add additional locations to sync by clicking the plus (+) button and then typing the path in the new field. Select any location and click the minus (–) button to remove that sync path. Click the ellipses (. . .) button to open a new window and select a location in the file system to sync.

11. **(Optional) Set the list of locations that won't synchronize in the Skip Items that Match Any of the Following area.**

    By default, several locations in the user's home folder are skipped when sync occurs. Generally these locations are unnecessary because they contain inconsequential files. The same plus, minus, and ellipses buttons apply to this list.

12. **(Optional) Select the Merge with User's Settings check box to combine the synchronization settings a user can set in the Account pane of System Preferences.**

13. **Click the Preferences Sync sub-tab.**

    The settings in Preference Sync are similar to those in Home Sync but only affect preference files. This tab is configured in the same way as Home Sync in Steps 9–11 earlier.

14. **(Optional) Click the Options sub-tab.**

    To modify the background sync interval from its 20-minute default or change the default for the Home Sync status menu, select Once or Always. Then modify the background interval and, if desired, deselect the Show Status in Menu Bar check box. See Figure 17-7 to view the additional options available when using a computer group.

15. **Click the Apply Now button to save the settings.**

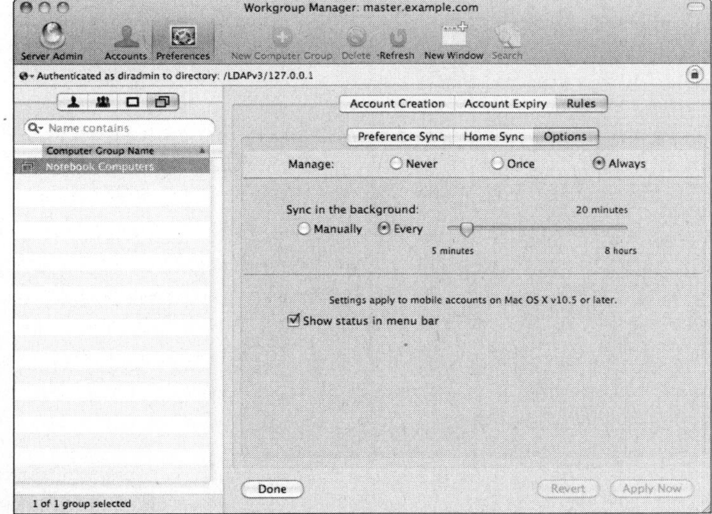

Figure 17-7: Additional options for home folder sync in Workgroup Manager.

Maintaining regular backups of the server volume and the local hard drive remains a critical part of your network deployment. Easier backup of just the server volume, if the portable home folders regularly and reliably sync to the server, is a side benefit of synchronizing home folders. An always-on backup system for laptops should still be a part of your backup strategy, especially for road warriors whose systems are more susceptible to a bad fall or the evildoers looking to steal a fancy Mac laptop.

Putting sync to work on the client

After the services have been configured and managed preferences set, the client needs to connect to the directory and file sharing, and a user will log in to his account. During login and logout, if sync has been enabled at this time, the user sees a window with a scrolling bar indicating the synchronization status. In Figure 17-8, you see an example of this window on a Mac. This window is also displayed if a user triggers a manual sync.

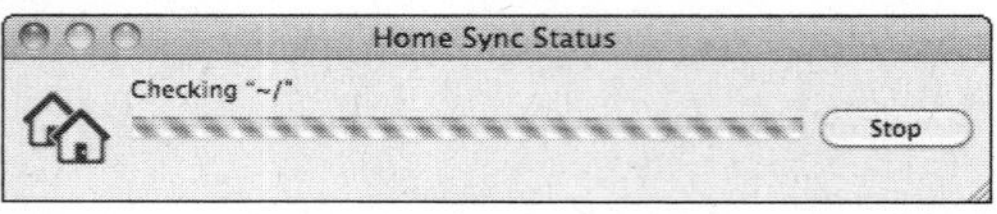

Figure 17-8: Home folder sync at login, logout, and during manual sync.

If you selected the options to have the user confirm the creation of the mobile account in the section, "Configuring mobility settings," earlier in this chapter, the user confirms the mobile account. From then on, the account is much the same as a local account. The following are two differences a user sees.

- **The addition of the Home Sync status menu (shown in Figure 17-9) is indicated by an icon depicting two overlapping houses, found to the left of the clock and other menu extras in the menu bar.**

  This menu displays the current status of the home synchronization with the network home folder server. The user sees the date and time of the last sync and can choose Sync Home Now to manually sync her home folder with the server.

  The two house icons in the menu bar icon alternate between the normal black outline and a gray version of each house when the background sync process is running.

- **In the Accounts pane of System Preferences, a mobile tag is added under the user's name in the list of accounts.** A mobile account in System Preferences is shown in Figure 17-10. The user also sees an additional button under the Password tab: Mobile Account Settings.

  Clicking this button displays choices for the background sync interval, the folders that are synced, and whether the Home Sync status menu is displayed. These settings, however, may be overridden by the managed preferences in the Mobility settings of Workgroup Manager.

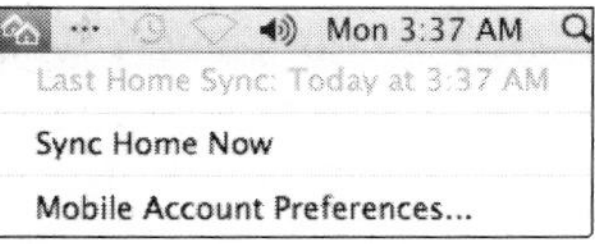

Figure 17-9: The Home Sync status menu for a portable home folder.

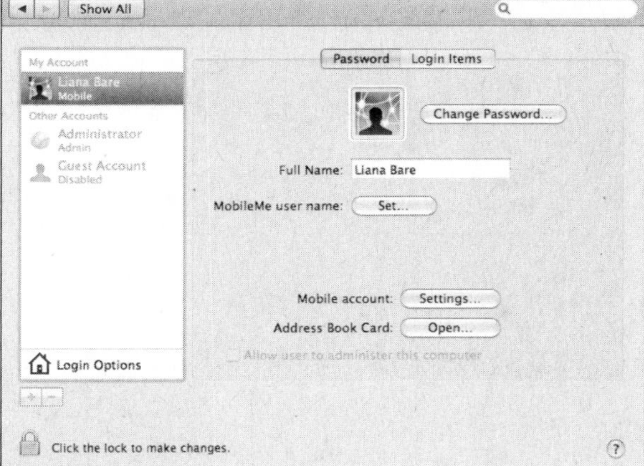

Figure 17-10: A mobile Mac user's account settings in System Preferences.

Chapter 18

Keeping Your Server Secure

In This Chapter

- Setting up firewalls
- Creating and using SSL certificates
- Setting up virtual private networks

One aspect of managing clients is using server security to keep clients from compromising the network. Snow Leopard Server comes with tools to prevent snooping, malware, and malicious attacks. In other chapters, I describe password encryption with authentication, Secure Sockets Layer (SSL) data encryption, the use of secure certificates, and spam and virus blockers for individual services including file sharing, e-mail, and the Web.

This chapter looks at overall issues, including using the firewall to guard access to the network and using and creating secure certificates for encryption. I end with configuring a virtual private network to give off-site users secure access to the local network. Server Preferences can do some of this: set firewalls, create and import certificates, and set up a virtual private network. I also discuss using Server Admin if you need to go deeper.

If you're using your server as an Internet gateway with network address translation (NAT), you can use the Gateway Setup Assistant to guide you through the configuration of your firewall and virtual private network, among other things, all at once. First, turn on NAT: in Server Admin, select your server, click Settings, and then click Services. Select the NAT check box and then click the Save button. Second, to get to the Assistant, click the triangle next to your server to expand the list of services. Select NAT, click Overview, and then click Gateway Setup Assistant.

Configuring the Firewall

A *firewall* blocks certain types of incoming traffic from the Internet, while allowing outgoing traffic to the Internet. Your job is to configure the firewall to allow incoming traffic in response to outgoing traffic from your users. For example, if your users try to access a Web site, you want traffic from Web servers to reach the users.

If your network already has a firewall on another server or in a security gateway appliance, you may not need to run Snow Leopard Server's firewall. You do need to run a firewall on your Mac server if it's acting as an Internet gateway, with the Mac in between the Internet connection and the local network. You also need to run a firewall on the server if your Internet connection goes directly into a wireless router and the router doesn't have a firewall built in or running on it. In this case, the server needs to be connected to the router via Ethernet.

A firewall blocks incoming traffic through software ports (settings identified by port numbers) and by port type: TCP (Transmission Control Protocol) and UDP (User Datagram Protocol). A port can be "open," to allow traffic to come through, or "closed," to block traffic. Each service has a standard port associated with it. For instance, the default port for IMAP e-mail is TCP port 143. When used with SSL encryption, the default IMAP port is TCP 993. Some services have a range of ports. Web service defaults to TCP 8080, but has a range of TCP 8000–8999 that you can use.

Apple has a large list of ports that Mac OS X Server uses here: `http://support.apple.com/kb/TS1629`. Server Admin Help also has a list of ports; search for *TCP and UDP port reference.*

In earlier chapters, I describe changing some of the default ports for e-mail, iCal, and other services. You can also set these ports all at once. I start with Server Preferences.

Setting firewalls with Server Preferences

The benefit to configuring the firewall with Server Preferences is that you don't need to know what the port numbers are for the common services. Just select the services that you want the firewall to allow, and Server Preferences sets the ports for you. For less common services, you need a port number.

1. **Click the Security icon and click the big switch to the On position.**
2. **Click the Add (+) button and choose a service from the Add Service pop-up menu (see Figure 18-1).**
3. **If the service you want isn't listed, choose Other, and then enter the service name and a port number.**
4. **Repeat Step 2 (and Step 3 if necessary) until you have the set of services you want the firewall to accept incoming connections for.**

   Figure 18-2 shows what Server Preferences looks like with some services configured.

Figure 18-1: Choose a server to allow through the firewall.

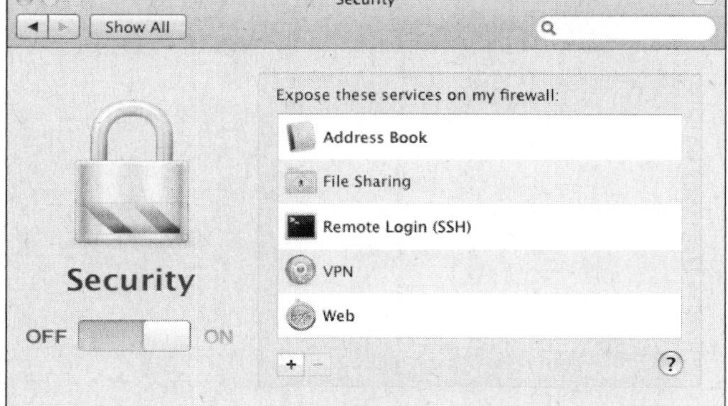

Figure 18-2: The firewall configured with several services in Server Preferences.

To remove a service from the list, select it and click the Delete (–) button.

Network routers and firewalls

If you're using a network router (such as a DSL or cable router) that provides the Internet connection, network address translation (NAT), and a firewall, you have two options for configuring the router. (You use the router's software, often accessed through a Web browser.) Your options are

- **Run the firewall on the server:** In this case, on your router, you have to make the server the router's default host. This is a setting you make on the router that tells it to send all incoming connect requests to the server.
- **Run the firewall on the router:** Here, you need to configure *port forwarding* (or *port mapping*) on the router. This means you set the router to forward traffic from the service port numbers to your server's IP address (shown in the Server Preferences Information pane).

Using an AirPort Extreme or Time Capsule firewall

If you have Apple's AirPort Extreme Base Station or Time Capsule wireless routers, the Server Preferences Security pane displays an additional button to let you choose the firewall in Snow Leopard Server or in these Apple devices. This additional button is either Switch to AirPort Management or Switch to Firewall Security.

Clicking the Switch to AirPort Management button sets the firewall to run on the device. Clicking the Switch to Firewall Security button designates Mac OS X Server as the firewall provider. When you're asked for a password, enter the password for the device, not the wireless network password.

By default, the firewall is turned on in AirPort Extreme and Time Capsule. To keep the firewall running on the device, you need to enable port mapping on the device with the AirPort Utility. To have the firewall run on the server, use AirPort Utility to enable a default host on the device.

After you make a change in the Security pane, Server Preferences may ask you to reset the AirPort Extreme Base Station or Time Capsule. Just be aware that doing this disrupts the DHCP (Dynamic Host Configuration Protocol) service and the Internet connection for a minute or two.

Configuring a firewall with Server Admin

Server Admin provides more fine-grained control over firewall settings than does Server Preferences. You can select services to allow through the firewall, as with Server Preferences. Server Admin not only offers more services but also lets you add your own services and ports, such as those used by third-party server software. Server Admin also enables you to create new rules for allowing or blocking ports.

When you first turn on and start the firewall, most ports for services are blocked. You have to set which ports to allow. The ports that are opened by default are those needed to allow you to log in and administer the Mac.

Enabling the firewall

Before you can configure the firewall, you have to enable the firewall service. You can do it in Server Preferences (as I describe earlier). In Server Admin, the procedure is the same as with other services:

1. **Open Server Admin and select the server in the left column.**
2. **Click the Settings icon in the toolbar and then click the Services tab.**
3. **Select the Firewall check box and then click the Save button.**

As with other services, you also need to start it to get it running:

1. **In Server Admin, click the triangle next to your server in the left column to expand the list of services.**
2. **Select Firewall from the list.**
3. **Click the Start Firewall button in the lower left.**

You could now stop the firewall by clicking the same button, which changes to Stop Firewall. With the firewall stopped, all incoming traffic is allowed.

Allowing services through the firewall and editing ports

Like Server Preferences, Server Admin lets you set which services you want to allow through the firewall by selecting them from a list. The list of services is much larger in Server Admin. If your service isn't in the list, you can add it to the list. You can also change the port number. To do this in Server Admin:

1. **Click the triangle next to your server in the left column to expand the list of services and select Firewall from the list.**
2. **Click the Settings icon in the toolbar and then click the Services tab.**

   Server Admin looks like Figure 18-3.

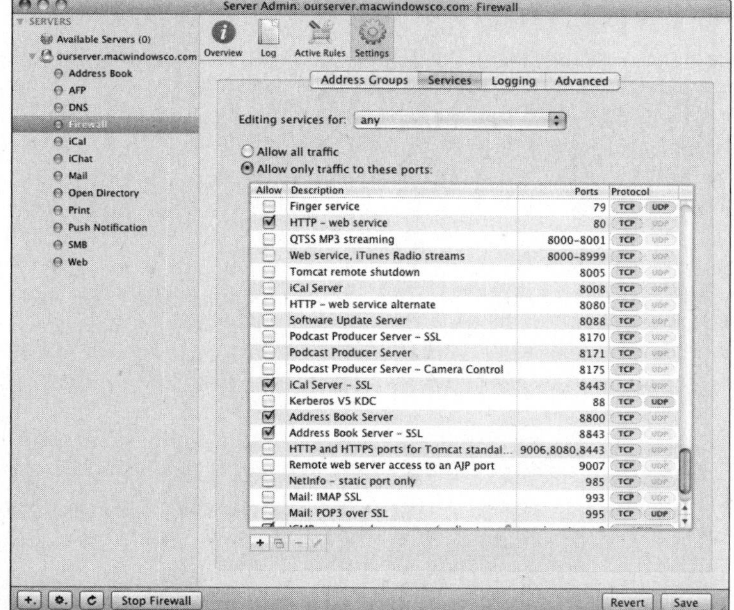

Figure 18-3: The Services tab of Firewall Settings in Server Admin.

3. **Select the services/ports that you wish to allow traffic on.**
4. **To change a port number, service name, or protocol, double-click the service you want to edit.**

   A dialog appears with fields for the service name and port number.
5. **From the Protocol dialog, choose TCP, UDP, or TCP and UDP and click OK.**

   The Port field can contain a range of ports (such as 8000–8999) or a list of port numbers separated by a comma (with no spaces).
6. **To add a new port, click the Add (+) button.**
7. **When the same dialog reappears, type a service name and a port number, and choose a protocol from the pop-up menu.**
8. **Click OK and then click the Save button.**

I've assumed in the preceding steps that Any was chosen in the Editing Services For pop-up menu. This means that the set of ports you selected is applied to all IP addresses that receive traffic. You can also choose an address group, which is a range of addresses that you apply settings to. Snow Leopard Server automatically creates two address groups covering the ranges of private IP addresses, the 10-net range (10.x.x.x) and the 192.168-net range (192.168.x.x). The next section describes creating your own address groups.

Creating address groups

An address group can be a single IP address, such as for a device or server, and it can also be a range of addresses designated by an address and subnet mask. An address group can have multiple entries. Here are two forms you can use to represent an address group (IP address with a subnet mask):

- **Netmask notation:** 192.168.0.0:255.255.255.0
- **CIDR notation:** 192.168.0.0/24

This Web page has a simple explanation of CIDR notation: `www.alexonlinux.com/what-is-cidr-notation`.

To create an address group for use with your firewall, do the following:

1. **In Server Admin, click the triangle next to your server in the left column to expand the list of services and then select Firewall.**
2. **Click the Settings icon and then click the Address Groups tab.**

   Server Admin looks like Figure 18-4, with the two default address groups and Any.

   The name of the address group is the text next to the triangle (such as 192.168-net). The addresses in a group appear below its name.

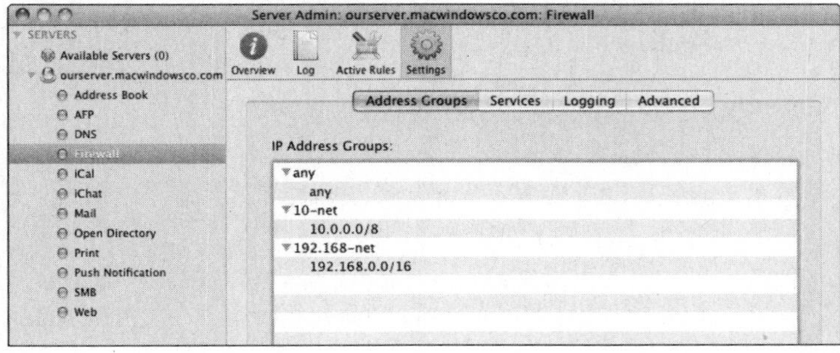

Figure 18-4: The Address Groups tab of Firewall Settings in Server Admin.

3. **Click the Add (+) button located under the IP Address Groups field.**
4. **In the new dialog, type a name for the address group, and then click the Add (+) button to the right of the Addresses in Group field.**
5. **Type an IP address or an IP address with a subnet mask in netmask or CIDR notation.**
6. **Keep using the Add (+) button to add as many IP addresses as you want a rule to affect.**
7. **Click the Delete (–) button to remove any IP addresses if you don't want the rule to apply.**
8. **Click OK in the dialog and then click the Save button.**

Playing by your own rules

If you want to get into deep firewall configuration territory, you can use the Advanced tab of Firewall Settings to create your own rules that describe what to do with incoming traffic. You can set a rule to allow or deny traffic, and you can define both the source and the destination of the traffic. You can apply this rule to standard services or services that you create. Here's how:

1. **In Server Admin, click the triangle next to your server in the left column to expand the list of services and then select Firewall.**
2. **Click the Settings icon in the toolbar and click the Advanced tab.**
3. **Click the Add (+) button or duplicate an existing rule by selecting it, clicking the Duplicate button, and double-clicking the rule.**

   The editing dialog, shown in Figure 18-5, appears.
4. **Select choices in the top third of the dialog:**
   - *Action pop-up menu:* You can choose Allow or Deny to define access through the firewall. A third option, Other, lets you type additional (more advanced) commands.
   - *Protocol pop-up menu:* Select TCP, UDP, or Other. Choose the latter to type another protocol in the field (such as ICMP, IGMP, IPENCAP, or ESP).

- *Service pop-up menu:* Choose 1 of over 100 services, including third-party software. You also have a choice for Other.
- *Log All Packets Matching This Rule check box:* A simple choice.

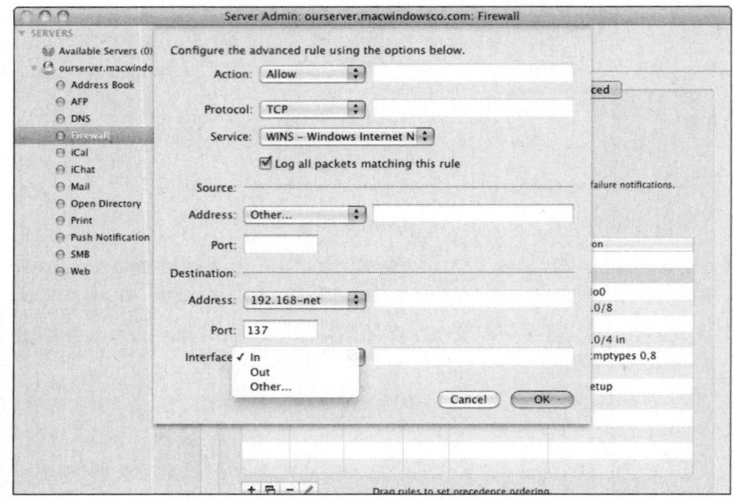

Figure 18-5: Create custom firewall rules in this dialog.

5. **Select the source of the traffic to be filtered.**

   The Address pop-up menu contains the address groups that are configured. Choose Other to type in a source IP address range you want to filter. (Use CIDR notation.) Type in a source port number if you're using a non-standard service port.

6. **Select the destination for the traffic to be filtered.**

   The Address pop-up menu contains configured address groups, including Any. Or choose Other to type a destination IP address range in CIDR notation. Enter a destination port number if you're using a non-standard service port.

7. **In the Interface pop-up menu, choose In to apply the rule to incoming traffic; choose Out to apply the rule to packets the server sends; or choose Other to type an interface name (such as en0, en1, or fw1).**

8. **Click OK.**

Be careful with creating and deploying your own firewall rules. You could inadvertently block traffic that your network needs to function properly.

Secure Certificates

A *Secure Sockets Layer (SSL) certificate* is a small file that enables the server to prove its identify to client computers and other networks as well as enables encrypted communications. A certificate contains your server's domain name and organization information; it also has a cryptographic key associated with it (a *public key*). You can use SSL certificates with Web, e-mail, iCal, and iChat services to encrypt data sent between clients and the server.

You can purchase an SSL certificate from a trusted certificate authority such as VeriSign (`www.verisign.com`), Thawte (`www.thawte.com`), and GlobalSign (`www.globalsign.com`). You can also create self-signed certificates on Snow Leopard Server. A self-signed certificate is created automatically when you install Snow Leopard Server. With self-signed certificates, the user's software asks whether the certificate should be trusted. With third-party certificates, the user's application accepts certificates without asking the user.

In previous chapters, I describe how to select an SSL certificate for use when configuring certain services. In this section, I describe how to create a new certificate and how to import a trusted certificate. You can perform these tasks with either Server Preferences or Server Admin. I also describe some of the other certificate-related tasks that you can do in Server Admin. I end this section describing signing certificates for others with Keychain Access.

SSL certificates in Server Preferences

With Server Preferences, you can select a certificate to use, create a self-signed certificate, and import a certificate. Just open Server Preferences, click the Information icon, and follow the directions in the following sections.

Using an SSL certificate

1. **In Server Preferences' Information pane, click the Edit button to the right of SSL Certificate.**
2. **Select the Use SSL Certificate check box (as shown in Figure 18-6).**
3. **Choose a certificate from the pop-up menu.**

   At least one certificate is listed, the self-signed certificate created by the server, named after the server.

If you don't see any certificates or want to create another, you can create a self-signed certificate.

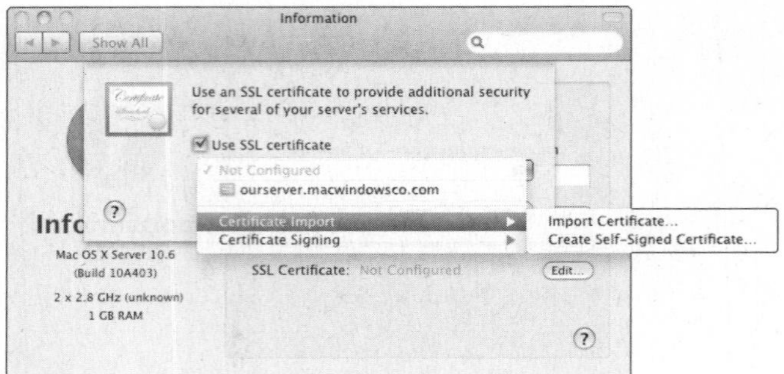

Figure 18-6: Selecting and creating secure certificates with Server Preferences.

Creating a self-signed certificate

1. **In the Information pane, click the Edit button to the right of SSL Certificate.**

   The dialog in Figure 18-6 appears.

2. **Select the Use SSL Certificate check box.**

3. **In the pop-up menu, choose Certificate Import⇨Create Self-Signed Certificate.**

   The Certificate Assistant opens.

4. **Type a fully qualified DNS name for the server and click Continue.**

   Don't change the other default settings: Identity Type = Self Signed Root; Certificate Type = SSL Server; Let Me Override Defaults is deselected.

Importing a certificate

To import a certificate, such as one purchased from a certificate authority or created by another server, do the following:

1. **Locate the files containing the certificate and the matching private key in the Finder and then position the folder's window in a place where you can get to it.**

2. **In the Information pane, click the Edit button to the right of SSL Certificate and select the Use SSL Certificate check box.**

3. **In the pop-up menu, choose Certificate Import⇨Import Certificate.**

   A new dialog slides down.

4. **Drag the certificate and private key files from the Finder to the dialog and then click the Import button.**

5. **Choose your imported certificate from the pop-up menu.**

SSL certificates in Server Admin

With Server Admin, you can add and delete certificates and renew a certificate with an updated or signed version. Server Admin also gives you access to the Certificate Assistant, which helps you create custom certificates.

Creating a self-signed certificate with Server Admin

To create a self-signed certificate in Server Admin, do the following:

1. **Select the server in the left column.**
2. **Click the Certificates button in the toolbar, and then click the Add (+) button and choose Create a Certificate Identity from the pop-up menu, as shown in Figure 18-7.**

   This launches the Certificate Assistant.
3. **Type a name for the certificate.**
4. **Leave the Let Me Override Defaults check box deselected and click the Continue button.**

   The Certificate Assistant creates the certificate (as Server Preferences does) and Certificate Assistant quits. You're finished.

   If you select the Let Me Override Defaults check box, a series of screens appear that let you edit or enter an e-mail address and contact info, Key size, algorithm (RSA is the default), and other parameters.

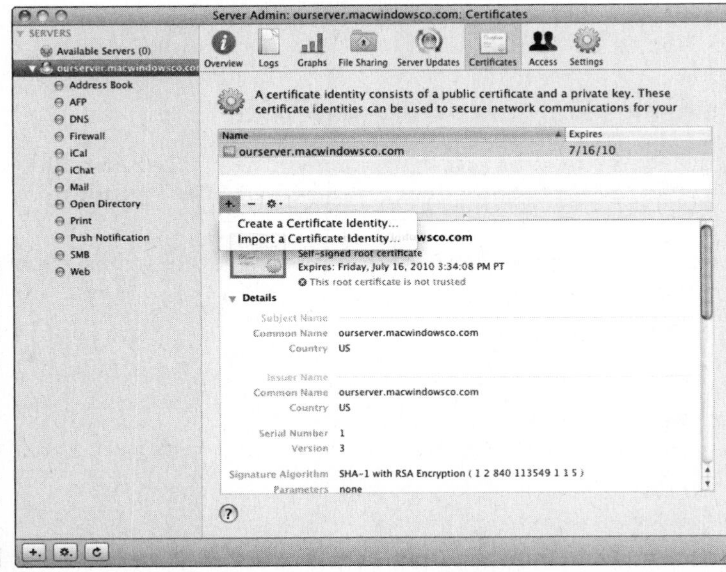

Figure 18-7: The Certificates pane showing the certificate created during server setup.

5. **Click the Learn More buttons on these screens for help regarding what the choices are.**

The certificate appears in the list in the Certificates pane of Server Admin; it also appears in pop-up menus in the Server Admin configuration windows of various services, including Web, e-mail, VPN, and others.

Creating a request to a certificate authority

You can use Server Admin to create a certificate signing request (CSR) to send to a certificate authority. The authority *signs,* or authorizes, a certificate you've created and supplies a public key. Certificate authorities require certain information, so you'll probably use the Let Me Override Defaults option when you create the certificate, as I describe in the preceding section. After the certificate is created, you can create a CSR file in Server Admin. Follow these steps:

1. **Select the server in the left column.**
2. **Click the Certificates button in the toolbar and then select the certificate that you've created to be signed.**
3. **Click the gear icon below the list of certificates and choose Generate Certificate Signing Request (CSR) from the pop-up menu.**

   A signing request is generated and displayed in a new dialog.
4. **Click the Save button.**

   A Save dialog asks you to pick a location on the hard drive.

You can send this file (which ends in `.csr`) to your certificate authority, which sends back a signed certificate. To use it, replace the certificate you used to generate the CSR, as I describe in the following section.

Renewing/replacing an existing certificate

Use the same procedure to renew an expired certificate or replace a self-signed certificate with a signed version. You must also replace certificates if you change the DNS name of the server or virtual hosts. Here's how:

1. **Launch Server Admin and select the server in the left column.**
2. **Click the Certificates icon in the toolbar and then select the certificate that you want to replace.**
3. **Click the gear icon below the list of certificates and choose Replace Certificate with Signed or Renewed Certificate in the pop-up menu.**
4. **Drag the certificate you received from the certificate authority to the dialog that slides down.**
5. **Click the Replace Certificate button.**

Becoming a certificate authority

You may want to act as a certificate authority, with the ability to sign certificates created elsewhere in the organization. Use the Keychain Assistant to create a certificate authority and to sign certificates.

To create a certificate authority, do the following:

1. **Launch Keychain Access (in /Applications/Utilities/).**
2. **In the Keychain Access menu, choose Certificate Assistant⇨Create a Certificate Authority.**

   The Certificate Assistant launches.
3. **Choose to create a Self Signed Root CA and then click through the screens, providing information as needed.**

   The process is much shorter if you choose not to override the defaults.

You can also use the Keychain Access to create a signed certificate for someone who's sent you a certificate signing request file. Here's how:

1. **Launch Keychain Access.**
2. **In the Keychain Access menu, choose Certificate Assistant⇨Create a Certificate for Someone Else as a Certificate Authority.**

   The Certificate Assistant launches.
3. **When asked, drag the CSR file you received from the Finder into Certificate Assistant.**
4. **Click through the screens, following the directions.**

At the end of the process, the Mail application launches and creates a new e-mail message with the new signed certificate file attached.

Virtual Private Networks

A *virtual private network (VPN)* is a secure encrypted connection to a local network from outside it, typically made over the Internet. Remote users connected through a VPN see the local network, including servers and printers, as if they're connected directly to it. You can also connect two remote local networks through a virtual private network. In Snow Leopard Server, you create virtual private network connections with Server Preferences or Server Admin, or both. This section looks at both.

Worth mentioning is that Gateway Setup Assistant may be your third choice for setting VPN service, if you're using the Mac server as an Internet gateway. Look at the first page of this chapter to find out how to open it.

VPN protocols: L2TP/IPSec and PPTP

Snow Leopard Server supports two alternative protocols for transporting encrypted data: *Layer Two Tunneling Protocol/Secure Internet Protocol* (*L2TP/IPSec,* or *L2TP over IPSec*) and *Point-to-Point Tunneling Protocol (PPTP).* You can use either or both. PPTP is a Microsoft technology that's long been used in Windows networks. If you have older clients, before Windows XP and before Mac OS X 10.3, you need to use PPTP. L2TP/IPSec is newer, with bits coming from Cisco and Microsoft. L2TP/IPSec is the preferred VPN protocol in Snow Leopard Server for various reasons, including the fact that it supports Kerberos authentication.

The shared secret

IPSec uses a *shared secret,* a password stored on the server and clients. The shared secret is *not* used for authentication or login, and it doesn't play a role in encryption. The shared secret is a token that's exchanged between computers to establish trust. If a client doesn't have the shared secret, it can't connect. Users don't type a shared secret — it's stored on the computers.

The shared secret must be at least 8 characters, but 12 or more is better, and can include letters, numbers, and punctuation but no spaces. The shared secret shouldn't be easy to remember; it should be a random string of characters.

You can use the Password Assistant in Server Preferences to generate a good shared secret. In Server Preferences, do the following:

1. **Click the Accounts icon (click Show All if it's not visible).**
2. **Select any user account and then click the Reset Password button.**
3. **Click the Key icon to bring up the Password Assistant.**
4. **In the Type pop-up menu, choose Random; in the length slider, choose 12 or more (this is the number of characters).**
5. **Write down the password generated.**
6. **Close the Password Assistant and then click Cancel in the New Password dialog.**

In Server Admin, you can use a certificate instead of a shared secret with IPSec VPN connections.

Getting your network ready for VPN

To access the local network from outside through a virtual private network, you may need to configure some other aspects of your network first:

- **DHCP IP address range:** When you configure VPN service, you set a range of IP addresses that are assigned to the remote VPN users. These are addresses on the server's network. This range must not contain static IP addresses used on the network and must not overlap ranges provided by a DHCP server, an Internet router, or an AirPort Base Station. Make sure these devices aren't assigning IP addresses from ranges that overlap with those that the VPN service is providing to remote users.

  The IP address that VPN service assigns to a remote computer for its VPN connection is *in addition* to the IP address that the remote computer is already using to connect to the Internet. The VPN IP address is released back to the server when the VPN session concludes.

- **Port forwarding:** If you have an Internet router, including a DSL or cable router, you need to set them up to use port forwarding (also known as port mapping), so as to forward traffic to your server's IP address.
- **Firewall VPN ports:** If you have a firewall running on the server or on a separate device, the administrator needs to open ports on the firewall to allow VPN traffic. These are TCP port 1723; UDP ports 500, 1701, and 4500; and IP protocol 50. For PPTP, use TCP port 1723.
- **Firewall ports for services:** If the only way you're allowing access from remote users is through an encrypted VPN connection, you don't have a reason to open the firewall ports for specific services — all the traffic goes through the VPN instead of the firewall. This means you could set the firewall to block those ports for increased security.

  You could also have a mixture: Keep open Web and e-mail ports on the firewall, but close file sharing and iCal to restrict those types of access to a VPN connection. If you have a firewall between your workgroup and the rest of your organization, you may also want to keep ports open for people in your organization who are outside the workgroup.

Setting VPN in Server Preferences

Server Preferences automates the configuration of a VPN service. Server Preferences allows you to easily do four things: turn VPN service on or off, set a VPN shared secret, edit the IP address range for VPN users, and export a VPN client configuration file for automating VPN setup of Mac OS X clients.

Turning on VPN service in Server Preferences enables L2TP/IPSec only. To enable PPTP, use Server Admin.

In Server Preferences, click the VPN icon to get to the VPN pane (see Figure 18-8). Unlike other services, the big switch isn't the first step in getting VPN running. You can't turn on the VPN service until you enter a shared secret:

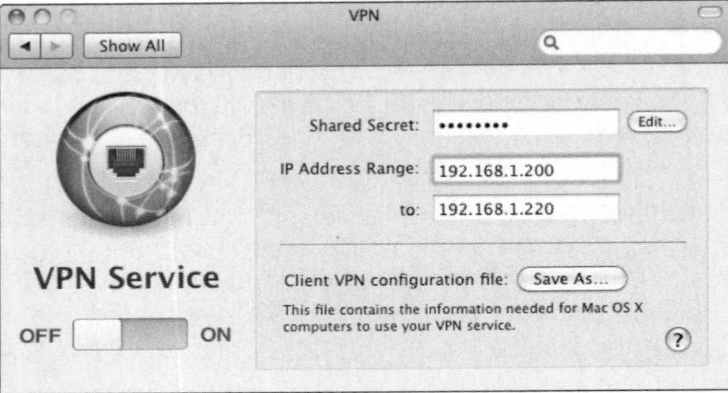

Figure 18-8: The VPN pane in Server Preferences.

1. **In the Server Preferences VPN pane, click the Edit button next to the Shared Secret field.**
2. **Select the Show Shared Secret check box to enable you to see what you're typing. Then type a password.**

   See the section, "The shared secret," earlier in this chapter.
3. **Click OK and then, in the Server Preferences VPN pane, look over the IP Address Range fields.**

   This is the range the server reserves for users connected through the VPN service. You may want to make the range larger to allow more simultaneous VPN users, or to avoid a conflict. (See the preceding section for more about the VPN IP address range and conflicts.) You can change the *first* address, which is the beginning of the range, or the *second* address, which is the end of the range, or both.
4. **Click the big switch to the On position.**

If you've previously configured a firewall, you may get a dialog telling you that your firewall has services that are *exposed*. If you click the Go to Security button, it takes you to the Server Preferences Security pane, where you can close firewall ports for services. If you select the Continue button, VPN service is activated with the firewall ports open. (See the preceding section to determine whether you need to close firewall ports for services.)

Setting VPN access with Server Admin

Server Admin offers advanced features, including a choice of authentication types, the ability to add PPTP, and the ability to use certificates instead of a shared secret. You can also limit VPN access to certain users.

Enabling VPN service

Before you configure VPN service with Server Admin, you have to turn it on. The easiest way is to go to Server Preferences and throw the big switch. You can also turn VPN service on in Server Admin:

1. **Open Server Admin and select the server in the left column.**
2. **Click the Settings icon in the toolbar and then click the Services tab.**
3. **Make sure the VPN check box is selected and click the Save button.**

Although you can now configure VPN service, it isn't running on the network. As with other services, you also need to start it to get it running:

1. **In Server Admin, click the triangle next to your server in the left column to expand the list of services and select VPN from the list.**
2. **Click the Start VPN button in the lower left.**

To start configuring, click the Settings icon in the toolbar. Server Admin looks like Figure 18-9, with the L2TP tab selected.

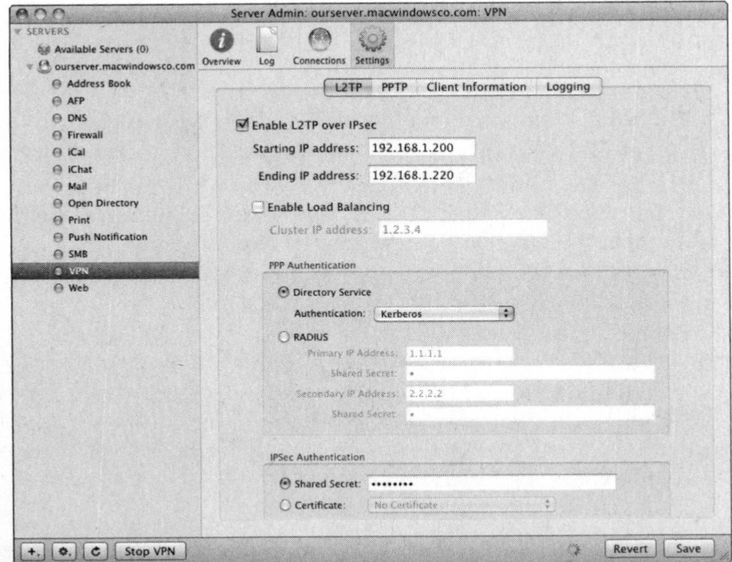

Figure 18-9: Server Admin's VPN Settings pane.

Configuring VPN Protocols

The L2TP tab, shown in Figure 18-9, is where you configure the L2TP/IPSec VPN service in Server Admin. This tab is similar to the PPTP tab, so I describe both here and point out differences.

Enabling protocols and setting the IP address range

At the top of both tabs is a check box to enable the protocol. When selected, the Starting IP Address and Ending IP Address fields are activated. This is the VPN IP address range, which I describe in the section, "Getting your network ready for VPN," earlier in this chapter. For L2TP/IPSec, this is the same setting as in Server Preferences (refer to Figure 18-8).

If you enable both L2TP and PPTP, use a separate, non-overlapping address range for each to avoid conflicts.

L2TP load balancing, PPTP 40-bit encryption

With L2TP, you can use *load balancing,* in which multiple servers share the VPN service duties. The server has no load balancing option for PPTP.

Instead, PPTP has an option called Allow 40-Bit Encryption Keys in Addition to 128-Bit. This setting isn't recommended, as 40-bit encryption is weak. It is better to ensure that all PPTP clients are 128-bit capable.

Selecting an authentication type

The PPP Authentication section is also the same for the L2TP and PPTP tabs. You can authenticate users with a directory server or with a RADIUS server. If you select the Directory Service option, you can choose Kerberos or Microsoft's MS-CHAP, which is the standard authentication scheme for Windows. If the Mac server is bound to a Kerberos authentication server, choose Kerberos. If not, choose MS-CHAP.

RADIUS (short for *Remote Authentication Dial in User Service*) is a service available in Snow Leopard Server that authorizes Open Directory users and groups to access Apple AirPort Base Stations on the network. RADIUS is a service that you turn on and start in Server Admin, like other services. If you use RADIUS to authenticate L2TP and PPTP connections, enter the IP address and shared secret for a primary and secondary RADIUS server. This is a different shared secret than the IPSec shared secret.

Setting IPSec authentication: Shared secret versus certificate

In addition to user authentication, IPSec adds an additional layer. You can choose to use a shared secret or a certificate. One difference is that shared secrets don't expire. The shared secret here is the same one you may have entered in Server Preferences.

The Client Information tab, routing definitions

The DNS server's IP address was likely stored in the Client Information tab when you enabled VPN services in Server Preferences or Server Admin. If not, you need to enter it.

The Client Information tab also enables you to set routing definitions, an advanced option that's worth mentioning. By default, all a user's network traffic is routed through the VPN connection. You can use network routing definitions to have only some of the traffic go through the VPN, while others (such as Web browsing) go through the remote users' normal Internet service provider (ISP). In this tab, you could specify a base IP address and a subnet mask to define a range of IP addresses that represent your local network. Then, only traffic targeted at those addresses could go through the VPN connection. Traffic targeted at other addresses, such as Web browsers, would go through the unencrypted ISP connection.

Limiting VPN access to certain users and groups

You can prevent certain users from accessing VPN services with access control lists (ACLs). Removing a user or group from an ACL for VPN prevents that user or group from connecting. Here's how:

1. **In Server Admin, select your server listed in the left column.**
2. **Click the Access icon in the toolbar and then click the Services tab.**
3. **Click the For Selected Services Below button and then select VPN.**
4. **Click the Allow Only Users and Groups below button, click the Add (+) button to bring up the Users & Groups window, and then drag users and groups to the list.**
5. **Click the Save button.**

Configuring VPN clients

The easiest way to set up Mac OS X clients for VPN is to use Server Preferences to create a VPN configuration file. In Server Preferences, click the VPN button and then click the Save As button. This creates and saves a file that you can distribute to Macs. On the Mac OS X client, open System Preferences, click the Network icon, and add a VPN interface. With the VPN interface selected, choose Import Configurations from the gear-icon pop-up menu and then select the VPN configuration file you created.

For Windows and Linux clients, you need to manually configure VPN configuration. You need the following information:

- **Account name:** This is the user account's short name on the Mac server.
- **User password:** This is the user's account password on the Mac server.

- **VPN server or host:** This is your server's DNS name or IP address.
- **VPN Type:** This is L2TP over IPSec or PPTP.
- **Shared secret:** This is visible in the VPN pane of Server Preferences (click the Edit button and the Show Shared Secret check box).
- **Firewall ports:** If users are running firewalls on their computers or on a remote network, that firewall must be configured to allow VPN traffic on TCP port 1723; UDP ports 500, 1701, and 4500; and on IP protocol 50. For PPTP, use TCP port 1723.

These Firewall port settings apply to Mac clients as well.

Part VI
The Part of Tens

"Fortunately at this grade level the Mac is very intuitive for them to use. Unfortunately, so is sailing mousepads across the classroom."

In this part . . .

Steve Jobs' keynote addresses (known as *Stevenotes*) at Macworld Expo and Apple's developers' conferences often ended with a simple statement: "There's just one more thing."

He'd then go on to make another product announcement, often something big. Things like the MacBook Pro, the iPod Touch, and the AirPort Base Station.

Well, here I am at the end of this book, and I have more to tell you. Nothing as big as the MacBook Pro, but I make up for it in quantity.

I have just 20 more things.

In Chapter 19, I present ten things you can add to Snow Leopard Server. These are mostly products from developers other than Apple, from free Dashboard widgets to enterprise-level servers that give add new capabilities.

Chapter 20 is my desperate attempt to get more articles into this book — ten more, to be exact. Here you find condensed how-to's for additional cool things to do with Snow Leopard Server, as well as some handy tips and some references to other information.

Chapter 19

Ten Things You Can Add to Snow Leopard Server

In This Chapter

- Performing network backups
- Understanding media assets and workflow
- Discovering widgets

Snow Leopard Server comes with so many different services and features for your users and your administrators that it's hard to imagine that you need to add anything extra. Although you may not *need* to run additional server software, you may desire to take advantage of some of the products that enhance Snow Leopard Server, or let you use it for some other purposes.

Antivirus for Your Server

Mac viruses and malware are fairly uncommon. Virus programmers tend to focus mostly on the several hundred million Windows PCs in the world. This doesn't let Mac OS X off the hook. You never know when a big Mac-focused virus wave will hit. Servers, in particular, are important computers to protect.

Intego's VirusBarrier Server ($300, `www.intego.com`) automatically checks files located on a Mac server and files that are launched from the server. VirusBarrier Server quarantines infected files it finds and sends an e-mail message to an administrator. It can also repair files that have been quarantined. As with all good virus packages, VirusBarrier Server automatically checks for and downloads updates of the latest virus definitions.

Snow Leopard Server's e-mail service already comes with well-respected open source antivirus software, ClamAV. But if you want another layer of protection, Intego makes another version, VirusBarrier Mail Gateway ($500), which automatically checks all e-mail messages.

One qualification, though. At press time, Intego guaranteed that it could identify all Mac-specific viruses, but not malware that infects Windows. This means Windows users could still infect other Windows clients via the server. I can't find any other virus protector for Mac OS X Server that checks for Windows viruses. Any developers out there want to take a crack at it?

Kerio MailServer

If you want an even more cross-platform groupware server with even more features, try adding Kerio MailServer to Snow Leopard Server. Kerio MailServer (`www.kerio.com`) is considered by some to be an alternative to Microsoft Exchange for small-to-mid-sized businesses, and it syncs with Active Directory and Open Directory. The big advantage over the built-in groupware of Snow Leopard Server is that Kerio MailServer supplies e-mail, calendar, contacts, notes, and tasks to just about any client: Outlook for Windows, Entourage, Apple Mail, iCal (including iCal on Mac OS X 10.4), and Address Book.

Like Snow Leopard Server's services, Kerio supports iPhone, but it also supports BlackBerry, Windows Mobile, Symbian, and Treo Palm. The remote console is cross-platform, too: You can manage Kerio MailServer from Windows, Linux, and Mac OS X. And, the server is also available for Windows and Linux.

Kerio MailServer has some expanded features, too. Although Snow Leopard Server lets users delegate calendars to other iCal users, Kerio MailServers let users delegate calendars to Outlook, Entourage, and iCal users. Another thing that Kerio has that Snow Leopard Server doesn't is integrated, automatic server backup.

Network Backup

With Time Machine, Snow Leopard Server does some great backup for all your clients — as long as they're running Mac OS X 10.5 or later. For backing up older Mac OS's or (gasp!) Windows or Linux clients and servers, you can add third-party software to Snow Leopard Server. Here are three that also come in versions for Windows:

- **EMC Retrospect Backup Server** (`www.retrospect.com`) is for small-to-medium-sized shops. Retrospect Server comes in several configurations, from a single server to multiple servers. Modules are used for your Mac and Windows clients (not Linux at publishing time). Retrospect is easy to use.
- **Tolis Group's BRU Server for Mac OS X** (`www.tolisgroup.com`) comes in packages from workgroup-to-enterprise levels. BRU Server can run concurrently with other services and includes error-recovery for restoring from damaged media.

- **Bakbone NetVault: Backup for Mac** (www.bakbone.com) is a full-blown enterprise-level backup system for big, complex networks. Bakbone NetVault: Backup for Mac supports Apple's Xsan and features modular scalability. Optimized for virtual machine backup. You can apply policy management tools to individuals and groups.

All these can back up to tape libraries.

Media Asset Management and Workflow

Asset managers take thousands of photo, image, video, and audio files sitting in a pile on your server and organize them. They keep track of the assets that are part of a workflow and what final projects they're used in. Asset managers tell you which version of a project is the current version, and they let you return to older versions. They also automate workflow, performing routine tasks, such as assembling pieces into a whole and converting files to different file formats. Lots of server-based asset manager products are available. The following list provides just a sampling of different types:

- **Adobe InDesign Server** (www.adobe.com/products/indesignserver) is aimed at automating InDesign-based print publishing, design, typography, and page layout. Because InDesign Server is highly customizable with an InDesign Markup Language, third parties sell pre-made workflow systems based on your type of publishing.
- **Canto Cumulus** (www.canto.com) was designed for photos and graphics, but now also handles audio and video. A sophisticated workflow product, you can send Cumulus an e-mail to place an attached file into a catalog. Cumulus tracks users' actions and lets you see what's being used. There's also a built-in photo editor.
- **Apple Final Cut Server** (www.apple.com/finalcutserver) is designed specifically for video and film professionals. Final Cut Server creates catalogs of clips, complete with still and video thumbnails; a clip can reside in multiple catalogs. You can browse or create custom searches that you can save. Final Cut Server automates production steps and runs scripts. The server comes with workflow templates with the names Television Station, Video Production, and Film Post-Production. The videos can be stored on removable FireWire drives and still remain in the catalog. Final Cut Server supports Mac and Windows clients.

General-Purpose Database Server

If you want to create a custom multi-user database with a graphics user interface, you have several choices. Here are two:

- **FileMaker Pro** (www.filemaker.com) can do invoicing, labeling, tracking inventory, or managing contacts with maps and video. For the user, you can create simple data entry forms or use sophisticated graphical interfaces. FileMaker is also a software development environment, so lots of pre-built FileMaker-based applications are available. You can also tie it into MySQL.
- **Panorama Enterprise Server** (www.provue.com) focuses on speed as a RAM-based database. Data fetchers are thousands of times faster than disk-based data retrieval. This server can also distribute the database to clients, automatically syncing changes with all users. This reduces the server load. And the software comes with powerful data analysis tools.

Apple Remote Desktop

Apple Remote Desktop (www.apple.com/remotedesktop) is a remote adminstration tool for Mac clients and servers. You can use this tool to manage any Mac with Mac OS X v10.3.9 or later, including Snow Leopard Server. You can use this tool to distribute, install, and upgrade software on hundreds of Macs at the same time.

You use Apple Remote Desktop to generate reports about what applications are being used, what versions of Mac OS X are installed, and who is logging into the computers. Apple Remote Desktop is also a remote control program that lets you see and control what's going on with any Mac from your Mac. You can use this feature to give tech support to a user or fix a problem remotely. You can also perform remote Spotlight searches on the other Macs. You can even copy any files you find to your Mac or delete them.

You have to set up each Mac that you're going to administer with Apple Remote Desktop. But you can partly automate that procedure with Apple Remote Desktop itself.

InterMapper, a Network Monitor

Dartware's InterMapper (www.intermapper.com) is a tool for your entire network; at its base, it provides maps of your network. You can create a map to show the location of servers, clients, switches, and routers. And InterMapper shows the existence of notebook computers on your maps. You can create schematic maps and maps superimposed on a building floor plan or on a map of a city or school district. InterMapper even interacts with Google Earth for long-distance mapping. Other maps get you back into a building.

But InterMapper is also a problem-solving tool: It can point out problems before they manifest themselves in downtime or slowdowns. You can check router utilization and traffic at various points on the network. InterMapper can perform tests that target an area or a device. A traffic analyzer can show you exactly who (or what) is generating a large amount of network traffic. InterMapper stores its data in an SQL database, which lets you generate various types of reports.

You can receive alerts by e-mail and other methods. You can use InterMapper from a Web browser or from an iPhone. InterMapper runs on Mac OS X, Windows, and several flavors of Linux and Unix.

TechTool Pro

If something goes wrong with your server hardware, MicroMat's TechTool Pro (`www.micromat.com`) is good to have on hand for its hardware checking, troubleshooting, and repair and data recovery functions. TechTool Pro can check your Mac's system memory, which, when it goes bad, can cause all sorts of mysterious problems; it also checks the memory on your graphics card. TechTool Pro scans disks for bad blocks and directory corruption, scans files for problems, and performs a number of other tests.

The tests are also useful to check before you have problems. You can run individual tests or run the entire suite. TechTool Pro can detect a potential problem with a piece of hardware and recommend a way to proceed. You can run tests while your server does its thing because the software doesn't require a lot of resources.

The eDrive feature creates a bootable drive partition with every TechTool Pro tool installed. You don't have to erase the drive to create this partition, which you can use when your Mac refuses to boot.

Then TechTool Pro can fix drive problems. The Volume Rebuild feature recreates disk directories, even on damaged drives, to bring a drive back to life or to improve performance with optimization. TechTool Pro includes several types of data recovery to pull important files off damaged drives; it can even recover deleted files.

iPhone Apps for Servers

Who needs a notebook when you have an iPhone? Well, I do, but you can still use some interesting iPhone apps for server administrators. You can buy the following (and more) at the App Store in iTunes or from your iPhone:

- **iStat** (`www.bjango.com/apps/istat`) from Bjango, monitors any number of Mac, Linux, or Unix servers running the free iStat Server. You can view graphs of network and processor utilization, and read data on memory, disk space, temperature, and fans. The ping and traceroute functions store a history of the ten most recently used hostnames or IP addresses. iStat's traceroute can also resolve hostnames.

- **Jaadu VNC (formerly Teleport)** (`www.jaaduvnc.com`) from Jugaari lets you view and control Mac, Windows, and Linux PCs, including Snow Leopard Server — just enable sharing on the computer. Jaadu VNC has great use of iPhone gestures and a smooth typing implementation. The zoom also works well. If your computer has multiple displays, Jaadu VNC can see them all.

Dashboard Widgets

Snow Leopard Server comes with some handy Dashboard widgets to give you a quick view of what's going on with your server. Here are a few more, all available from `www.apple.com/downloads/dashboard`, and they're all free. They're one-trick ponies that display something quickly:

- **iStat Pro** from iSlayer is a configurable widget that displays a bunch of hardware information, including memory, storage, battery, temperatures, fans, running processes, and more. Activity Monitor already provides some of this info, but iStat Pro throws in more. You have to run iStat Pro from the server or from a remote control program, such as Apple Desktop Remote or VNC.
- **IP Subnet Calculator** by Jeremy Williams calculates the network address and broadcast address when you type an IP address and subnet mask. This widget also tells you the number of hosts in a subnet, which is helpful when you're assigning IP addresses.
- **WhoisConnected** from Oxorr shows you which applications running on a Mac are connected to the network and what they are doing. This includes Web browser windows, file services, Software Update, and behind-the-scenes processes, such as Bonjour and the Apple Remote Desktop. This widget can be useful on your administrator Mac.
- **iServer from Leaping Bytes** displays a list of computers connected to the Mac via AFP file sharing, SSH terminal sessions, Apple Remote Desktop, iTunes, and iPhoto.

Chapter 20

Ten Cool Things That Didn't Make It into the Book

In This Chapter

- Working with round robin DNS
- Putting users' home folders on the server
- Working from the command line
- Changing server names
- Clustering your mail services
- Stopping Macs from losing Active Directory binding
- Uncovering Ruby on Rails and Server Admin
- Making the server auto-restart
- Getting help at Apple.com

One of the difficult things about writing this book was deciding which of Snow Leopard Server's many aspects didn't fit in the 400-plus pages. Some features are cool but obscure; others just don't fit in with the other topics. So, in this chapter, I want to squeeze in a few more useful bits, in no particular order. Some of these are simple things that anyone can use — others are pretty technical. But they're all pretty cool.

One Site, Multiple Macs with Round Robin DNS

Say you have a Mac mini serving a Web site, but the site is getting popular, and the mini can't handle the traffic. You could drop three or four grand on Mac Pro or Xserve. Or, you could add a few more Mac mini's to share the load of the single Web site.

You can do this by using the *round robin DNS* technique. Snow Leopard Server's DNS service allows you to set up a pool of IP addresses for a single domain name. Snow Leopard Server's DNS service (or any BIND-compliant DNS server) cycles these IP addresses when asked for the domain name. You can mirror the Web content on four Mac minis, each with a different IP address, but with the same domain name, say `www.abc.edu`. Then set up the DNS service with the four IP addresses for `www.abc.edu`. The first four users are each sent to a different Mac mini.

Don't confuse this with load balancing, a more complicated (and expensive) setup that takes into account the servers' loads and their processing power. Round robin DNS simply routes domain requests to the different servers. A good idea is to use a small TTL (time to live) number for the zone to mitigate local caching effects.

User Home Folders on the Server

To take file sharing to the ultimate, is to put your users' home folders on the server. On a Mac, the *home* folder is the directory that's named after the user. This folder contains all of a user's data, settings, bookmarks, and so forth. When you locate users' home folders on the server, they log in to a Mac and authenticate to the server. Users then can log in to different computers and still get the same access to their home folders. Server-based home folders can put a heavy burden on the server, however. For Mac clients, use the AFP or NFS protocol to share the folder. For Windows, use SMB. Create home folder share points in the /Users directory, with the users' short names, such as /Users/ronmckernan. Select the share point and click the Enable Automount check box. In the new dialog, select User Home Folders and Group Folders.

In Workgroup Manager, click the Accounts button, select the user, and then click the Home tab. In the list of share points, select the share point you just created and auto-mounted. (If you don't see it, click the Refresh icon in the toolbar.) Click the Create Home Now button. Finally, click the Save button.

A Disk Quota box is also on this page. You can type in a number in megabytes or gigabytes to limit the amount of space the user's home directory can take up on the server.

Snow Leopard from the Command Line

One of the things that I try to do in this book is spare you from typing commands. But the fact remains that just about everything you can do in this book — and much more — can be done with commands in a Unix shell, in Terminal, which you can find in /Applications/Utilities.

Apple offers a 300-page *Command-Line Administration* PDF reference here:

```
www.apple.com/server/macosx/resources/documentation.html
```

If you don't know your way around a Unix shell, this reference won't help you. But if you do, it's all there. Also check out *UNIX For Dummies,* 5th Edition (Wiley), by John R. Levine and Margaret Levine Young.

Changing the Server's Names: DNS, Computer, Local Host

When you first set up Snow Leopard Server, Server Assistant asks you for the server's DNS name (such as `ourserver.abc.edu`). This is the name that shows up in Server Admin's left column. But what happens if you type the wrong name or include a typo (such as `areserver.abc.edu`)? Server Admin doesn't let you change it and for good reason.

If you've set up other services, they'd stop working if the server's DNS name changed and you didn't readjust them. There could be unintended consequences as well. But, if you just installed Snow Leopard Server and typed the wrong DNS name, reinstalling the whole OS is burdensome. If you feel a little daring, there is a little command you can use in Terminal:

```
sudo scutil --set OldName NewName.domain.tld
```

For example, it might look like this:

```
sudo scutil --set areserver ourserver.abc.edu
```

The *DNS name* is also called the *Internet hostname,* or the *local hostname,* which is used only on the local network for services (such as printers) that use Bonjour to publicize themselves. This is not the same as the Mac *computer name* used to identify the server in the Finder of Mac users, on Windows clients, in Apple Remote Desktop, and in other places. You can also use this same command-line tool to change the local host and computer names:

```
sudo scutil --set LocalHostName newLocalHostName
sudo scutil --set ComputerName newComputerName
```

Clustering Mail Services

You can distribute the load of a mail server by creating a mail cluster. This is a group of mail servers sharing the mail data store with Apple's network-based storage solution, Xsan software (`www.apple.com/xsan/`), and the storage hardware Xsan requires. If one server fails, the others pick up the slack.

First, set up Xsan on the network. To create the cluster's first member, open Server Admin, select your server, and select Mail. Then click the Settings icon, click the Advanced tab, click the Clustering tab, and then click the Change button. A setup assistant appears to guide you through the procedure.

After a mail server is part of the cluster, when you make changes to its mail settings (POP, IMAP, SMTP, and others), these changes are made automatically to all the servers in the cluster.

Macs Losing Active Directory Binding

In Chapter 7, we talk about configuring Snow Leopard Server to connect Mac users to Microsoft Active Directory. But a problem often occurs where the Mac clients lose their binding to Active Directory, even when Mac OS X Server is configured correctly. Network logins just don't work anymore. A forced unbind sometimes can cause the problem.

One thing you can do works: You can delete a Kerberos file on the Mac client. In the Finder, open the Go menu and select Connect to Folder. Then type the following path:

```
/private/var/db/dslocal/nodes/Default/config/
```

After that folder opens, delete the following file: Kerberos:*YOURDOMAIN.NET*.plist. (This filename can use `.com`, `.org`, or whatever you have.) The file will be re-created the next time the client connects to Active Directory.

You can also do this from Terminal:

```
sudo -s
cd /var/db/dslocal/nodes/Default/config
ls -l Kerberos:*
```

This lists the realm for each Active Directory domain. You can then remove the relevant realms for the client Mac using this for each realm:

```
rm Kerberos\:AD.yourdomain.net
sudo killall DirectoryService
```

The `killall` command restarts Directory Service on the client. The Kerberos configuration files will be re-created the next time the client connects to Active Directory.

Ruby on Rails

If the preceding tip isn't geeky enough for you, try this one: Snow Leopard Server comes with built-in support for *Ruby on Rails* (`www.rubyonrails.org`), an open source language and framework for creating Web-based applications. Mac OS X Server comes with several Ruby on Rails component packages (called *gems* in Ruby-speak), one of which is the Mongrel Web server.

Apple has information about developing Ruby on Rails applications here:

```
http://developer.apple.com/tools/developonrailsleopard.html
```

Apple also has some information about deploying Ruby on Rails and the Mongrel Web server in the *Web Technologies Administration* PDF document, available here:

```
www.apple.com/server/macosx/resources/documentation.html
```

Groups of Servers in Server Admin

If you think about it, Server Admin looks a little like iTunes. You have a list of servers in a left column. Click one, and you see stuff on the right. The comparison is a stretch, but when you have a lot of Mac servers on the network, you can create the equivalent of iTunes playlists. You can even create the equivalent of smart playlists.

With Server Admin, the "playlist" is called a *group,* and the "songs" are *servers.* The group lives in the left column, and, when you expand it, displays the servers in that group. You can group servers by function, geography, or anything you like. As with iTunes playlists, servers can be in more than one server group. You even have the equivalent of smart playlists: smart groups.

To create a server group, click the Add (+) button at the bottom left of the window, select Add Group, and give the group a name. The group appears in the left column. Now you can drag servers into the new group.

To create a smart group, click the Add (+) button and select Add Smart Group. Give the smart group a name and then add the criteria that decides which servers are added to the smart group list. Click OK, and the group appears in the left column, with a list of servers that meet your criteria.

Set the Server to Auto-Restart

If you want your server to get back up and running after a power failure or a system freeze, you can tell Mac OS X Server to start up automatically. While logged on to the server Mac as an administrator, open *System* Preferences (not *Server* Preferences). Click the Energy Saver icon and then click the Options tab. Select the Restart Automatically After a Power Failure check box and/or the Restart Automatically If the Computer Freezes check box. For the latter setting, the power management hardware restarts five minutes after a kernel panic or a freeze.

Help at Apple.com

Apple has quite a bit of information about Mac OS X Server at its Web site. Unfortunately, finding what you want can take some time. Here's a list of several different ways you can enter Apple.com that might provide a quicker route to what you need regarding Mac OS X Server:

- **Recently updated tech support articles:** This page lists the newest and most recently modified troubleshooting and how-to articles. This is a good page to check a few days after Apple releases a software update.

  ```
  http://support.apple.com/kb/index?page=articles
  ```

- **Mac OS X Server support:** Here you'll find links to support pages for individual Mac OS X Server services, such as file sharing, iCal Server, and the rest. It also has links to popular how-to and troubleshooting articles, and to recent software updates related to Mac OS X Server.

  ```
  www.apple.com/support/macosxserver
  ```

- **Apple Discussions pages:** Here you can post a question or search the forum for an answer to a question that someone else may have asked. This first page lists forums for everything Apple, but a Server Product category has areas on Mac OS X Server, Xserve, and other IT topics. To post a question, log in with an Apple ID, such as your iTunes account.

  ```
  http://discussions.apple.com
  ```

Index

Symbols and Numerics

• A •

• B •

• C •

• D •

• F •

• G •

• H •

• I •

• J •

• K •

• L •

• M •

• N •

• O •

• P •

• S •

• T •

• W •